Cambridge studies in medieval life and thought

Edited by WALTER ULLMANN, LITT.D., F.B.A.
Professor of Medieval History in the
University of Cambridge

Third series, vol. 8

THE JUST WAR IN THE
MIDDLE AGES

CAMBRIDGE STUDIES IN
MEDIEVAL LIFE AND THOUGHT

THIRD SERIES

THE JUST WAR
IN THE
MIDDLE AGES

FREDERICK H. RUSSELL

Assistant Professor of History
Rutgers University

CAMBRIDGE UNIVERSITY PRESS

CAMBRIDGE

LONDON · NEW YORK · MELBOURNE

Published by the Syndics of the Cambridge University Press
The Pitt Building, Trumpington Street, Cambridge CB2 1RP
Bentley House, 200 Euston Road, London NW1 2DB
32 East 57th Street, New York, NY 10022, USA
296 Beaconsfield Parade, Middle Park, Melbourne 3206, Australia

Library of Congress catalogue card number: 74–25655

ISBN 0 521 20690 1 hard covers
ISBN 0 521 29276 X paperback

First published 1975
First paperback edition 1977
Reprinted 1979

First printed in Great Britain by
Western Printing Services Ltd, Bristol
Reprinted in Great Britain at the
University Press, Cambridge

CONTENTS

v

PARENTIBUS MEIS
cum homagio filiali

PREFACE

This book has been put together in many forms at different times and places, although the bulk of it was originally a dissertation at The Johns Hopkins University. In spite of many treatments of just war theories, the full chronological evolution has not been treated, a deficiency this book attempts to remedy. When I began work on the topic, I barely comprehended its scope. I was motivated by a desire to provide a careful analysis in depth of both the just war and its uncomfortable ally, the crusade, from their first emergence in ancient Greece and Israel. The just war presents a seamless web of premises and assumptions that forms an important part of the intellectual and political history of western civilisation.

Manifold problems of research and interpretation presented themselves from the very beginning. The texts are terse, and the Latin language is highly inflected, such that much was said in a minimum of words. The discussion in English is necessarily lengthier. Close attention must be paid to the interstices of arguments couched as commentaries on authoritative texts. The basic requirements for a just war, a just cause, legitimate authority and a righteous intention say at once too much and too little, for they obscure crucial nuances and divergences of opinion as well as the chronological changes. The evolution of the theories proceeded under the influence of changing intellectual and political conditions by the progressive drawing of conclusions logically implicit in the bald statement of the requirement. The just war theories developed within the confines of biblical exegesis and broader legal and theological schemes; they were not viewed in isolation. To render the evolution clearly I have had to violate the scholastics' order of presentation for a more discrete analysis. Since several distinct problems were often discussed in the same passage, I have had to adopt a sort of tunnel vision in order to avoid consideration of much interesting but tangential material. Thus

the imagery of the swords and the full depth of the crusading movement and its papal legislation have of necessity not received much
attention. For reasons of time and space I have been unable to treat
the just war theories advanced in the fourteenth and fifteenth centuries that form a separate but complementary study. Once achieved,
this study would bridge the gap between the medieval tradition and
that of early modern Europe for which the documents have been
made available by the Carnegie Endowment for International Peace.

Another problem of broad interpretation of the just war theories is
the standpoint of those who have written on the just war. Whether
concerned with historical judgments of the Middle Ages, modern
international law, or modern pacifism, many observers have distorted the medieval just war to fit within their own schemes. As an
attempt at objectivity about a subject inevitably open to bias, I have
sought to explain the just war theories as they appeared to medieval
thinkers, *wie es eigentlich gewesen ist*.

Important developments were often first broached in works
available only in manuscript, at times making research very painstaking. Unable to render critical editions of the passages, I have produced the reading that made the best sense from the one or several
manuscripts available, and tried to avoid too much reliance on
passages whose attribution is in doubt. Quotations of the sources
have been kept to a minimum due to the high cost of printing. I have
probably overlooked many important manuscripts and only hope I
have distorted neither the manuscript tradition nor the basic outlines
of the theories. For the errors that remain, I beg the indulgence of
the reader.

The basic research for this book was made possible by the financial
support of a Fulbright Fellowship to Paris administered by the
Commission Franco-américaine d'Echanges Universitaires et Cul-
turels. The kind assistance of Mr Patrick Carroll and M. Antoine
Prost of the Commission is greatly appreciated. I was able to con-
tinue the manuscript research with a National Endowment for the
Humanities Summer Stipend for Younger Humanists. In this country
I was aided by research grants from The Johns Hopkins University
and the Research Council of Rutgers University. To all these agencies
I express my deep gratitude.

Many libraries and their staffs on both sides of the Atlantic supplied me with often rare printed and manuscript sources and periodicals, also supplying interesting and always congenial conditions of study, even under conditions of crisis. The basic manuscript studies were undertaken in Paris at the Bibliothèque Nationale and at the Institut de Recherche et d'Histoire des Textes of the Centre Nationale de Recherche Scientifique, with especial thanks to Mme J. Rambaud-Buhot of the former and Mlle E. Brayer of the latter institution. Elsewhere in Paris I made use of the library at the Sorbonne, and in England I worked in the British Museum and at the Cambridge University Library. On these shores the staffs of the following university libraries went out of their way to assist me: The Johns Hopkins University; the Catholic University of America; Yale University and the Institute of Medieval Canon Law formerly located there; the Alexander, Dana and Newark Law libraries of Rutgers University (with especial thanks to Messrs Gilbert Cohen, James Doele, James Merritt and Morris Sherman); Seton Hall University; Drew University; College of Saint Elizabeth; Haverford College; Duns Scotus College; Princeton University; Princeton Theological Seminary; University of Pennsylvania; and Saint Michael's College of the University of Toronto. The public libraries of New York City and Newark, New Jersey, were also most helpful.

It is indeed a pleasure in this century of international conflict to acknowledge my gratitude to an international body of scholars concerned with medieval society in all its facets. At Johns Hopkins my ideas were shaped by the helpful criticism of Professors Richard Goldthwaite, Frederic C. Lane and Robert W. Tucker and of my fellow graduate students Dr Theodore Evergates, Mr Walter Pakter and Mrs Gabrielle Spiegel. In both his written works and his personal advice Professor Stephan Kuttner has left me and many others in his debt. In France Professors Bernard Guenée and Jacques LeGoff of the University of Paris and in Germany Professor Alfons Becker and his student Herr Ernst-Dieter Hehl at the University of Mainz offered many helpful insights and suggestions. Professors James Alexander of the University of Georgia, Richard Kay of the University of Kansas, Edward Peters of the University of Pennsylvania and Robert Somerville of Columbia University supplied me with a friendly barrage of pertinent questions. At Rutgers ongoing challenges have come from Professors Robert Kann, Irwin Merker, James Muldoon and Paul Rosenfeld, with Professor Leo Troy and Norman L. Cantor giving me aid. I wish also to acknowledge the comments offered by members of the Johns Hopkins seminar, the Columbia University Seminar in the History of Legal and Political Thought and the participants in the Fourth International Congress of Medieval Canon Law held at the Pontifical Institute of Mediaeval Studies in Toronto in 1972.

Since he was a visiting professor at Johns Hopkins in 1965 Professor Walter Ullmann has been an inspiration and a wise advisor. My greatest debt is owed to Professor John W. Baldwin of Johns Hopkins, who initially suggested the topic, then as dissertation director guided its development, and finally encouraged its completion in its present form. This mass of good advice only underscores my own personal responsibility for the sins of commission and omission that remain.

Lastly, my wife Emily, who bore the brunt of my irascibility and frustrations occasioned by the just war, served as subeditor, typist and charitable critic. Without her logistical and moral support this book could not have been brought to completion.

Mount Tabor, New Jersey
1974   F.H.R.

ABBREVIATIONS

Accursius, *Glossa Ordinaria* Accursius, *Glossa Ordinaria*, to *Corpus Iuris Civilis*. Source: the standard medieval edition of the *Corpus Iuris Civilis*. Lyons, 1612; and other editions of the early modern period.

B.N. Lat. Manuscripts from Paris, Bibliothèque Nationale, Fonds Latin.

C. Causa in Pars Secunda of the Decretum Gratiani. Source: *Corpus Iuris Canonici*. ed. A. Friedberg. Volume I. Leipzig, 1879.

Cod. *Codex Iustinianus*. Source: *Corpus Iuris Civilis*. ed. P. Krueger. Volume II. Berlin, 1877.

Comp. I. *Compilatio Prima* of the *Quinque Compilationes Antiquae*. Source: *Quinque Compilationes Antiquae*. ed. A. Friedberg. Leipzig, 1882.

C.S.E.L. *Corpus Scriptorum Ecclesiasticorum Latinorum*. Vienna, 1872–.

d. dictum Gratiani.

D. Distinctio in Pars Prima of the Decretum Gratiani. Source: *Corpus Iuris Canonici*. ed. A. Friedberg. Volume I. Leipzig, 1879.

De penit. De penitencia of Quaestio III, Causa XXXIII of Pars Secunda of the Decretum Gratiani. Source: *Corpus Iuris Canonici*. ed. A. Friedberg. Volume I. Leipzig, 1879.

Dig. *Digesta Iustiniani*. Source: *Corpus Iuris Civilis*. ed. T. Mommsen and P. Krueger. Volume I. Berlin, 1872.

Inst. *Institutiones Iustiniani*. Source: *Corpus Iuris Civilis*. ed. P. Krueger. Volume I. Berlin, 1872.

Mazar. Manuscripts from Paris, Bibliothèque Mazarine.

M.G.H. *Monumenta Germaniae Historica*.

P.L. *Patrologia Latina*. ed. J. P. Migne, 221 vols. Paris, 1844–65.

pr. principium.

Sext *Liber Sextus Decretalium Bonifacii VIII*. Source: *Corpus Iuris Canonici*. ed. A. Friedberg. Volume II. Leipzig, 1881.

S.T. Thomas Aquinas, *Summa Theologiae*
    Abbreviations:
        1–2 – Pars Prima Secundae.
        2–2 – Pars Secunda Secundae.
        q. – Quaestio.
        a. – Articulus.

v. *sub verbo*.

X. *Decretales Gregorii IX*. Source: *Corpus Iuris Canonici*. ed. A. Friedberg. Volume II. Leipzig, 1881.

INTRODUCTION

Since the dawn of history warfare has been one of man's most distinctive activities; the course of history has often been radically changed by the outcome of a single battle. Attempts have been made to encourage, to restrain and to eliminate wars, and attitudes towards it have ranged from the conviction that human effort reaches its apogee in an apocalyptic struggle to the categorical rejection of all forms of violence. More concretely, war has been seen as a primary expression of political activity and for western man warfare has served as 'the cradle of the nation.'[1] Many forms of human endeavor have been seen as wars, such as the Christian's war of the spirit against the flesh, and the wars politicians declare on social ills. Rather than providing a general survey of medieval attitudes towards peace, conflict and warfare, this study concentrates upon those theories of the just war elaborated by scholars of the high Middle Ages.

Theories of the just war arose out of the need to justify warfare on juridical, moral and especially religious grounds. Indeed, religious foundations motivated many 'just' wars, and religion has often served the political purposes of a war.[2] Anthropologically, religion and politics are 'twin companions' that often aid each other in their respective evolutions.[3] This study explores some of the complex relationships between religion and politics in the high Middle Ages, during which two broad historical movements developed side by side. Christian morality and doctrine were refined according to the needs and mental attitudes of the time, and Europe was seeking new bases of political organisation to fill the vacuum created by the disappearance of Roman imperial authority.

[1] Cf. J. Wellhausen, *Israelitische und jüdische Geschichte*, p. 26, quoted in G. von Rad, *Der heilige Krieg im alten Israel* (Zurich, 1951) p. 14.

[2] A. Nussbaum, 'Just War – A Legal Concept?', *Michigan Law Review*, XLII (1943), 478.

[3] Ihering, *Geist des römischen Rechts*, I, 256, quoted in C. Philippson, *The International Law and Customs of Ancient Greece and Rome* (2 vols., London, 1911), I, 44.

In Christian thought two types of war have been seen as permissible, the holy war and the just war. The holy war is fought for the goals or ideals of the faith and is waged by divine authority or on the authority of some religious leader. When the latter is an ecclesiastical official, the holy war becomes a crusade. The crusading ideal is historically bound up with a theocratic view of society, while the just war is usually fought on public authority for more mundane goals such as defense of territory, persons and rights. Content with the achievement of more concrete political objectives, the just war stops short of countenancing the utter destruction of the adversaries and tends to limit the incidence of violence by codes of right conduct, of non-combatant immunity and by other humanitarian restraints lacking in the holy war. In the holy war Christian participation is a positive duty, while in just wars participation is licit but restricted.

In the Middle Ages the distinctions between holy war, crusade and just war were difficult to draw in theory and were glossed over by those concerned to justify a particular war. In the heat of combat and controversy belligerents forsook the more restrained just war for the holy war. At the moment a just war was deemed necessary, it easily became a holy war that pursued the supreme goals of the belligerents.[4] The concept of a crusade encompassed both religious motivations for bellicosity and juridical institutions designed to punish those who offended the Christian religion. Hence the crusade became a strange hybrid of holy war and just war marked by an increasingly explicit chain of command. The holy war and the crusade will here be considered only as a part of the general medieval debate of the right to war rather than as an independent phenomenon.

While historical studies on theories of warfare are not lacking, the few detailed studies of medieval theories have often considered warfare from the vantage point of broader historical, political or religious movements. Early in this century Alfred Vanderpol, concerned with the need to eliminate war, surveyed the scholastic doctrines.[5] Consisting largely of isolated extracts, his work did not provide extensive analysis or correlation with the historical context whence the theories sprang. In 1935 Robert Regout published a more systematic survey,

---

[4] For a modern parallel, cf. J. Maritain, 'Considérations françaises sur les choses d'Espagne,' in A. Mendizabal, *Aux origines d'une tragédie: la politique espagnole de 1923 à 1936* (Paris, 1937) p. 38, n. 1.

[5] A. Vanderpol, *La doctrine scolastique du droit de guerre* (Paris, 1919).

but his analysis was scanty and he only considered the more salient portions of the works of major thinkers.[6] More recently Roland H. Bainton published an excellent general survey, but his discussion of the Middle Ages is less exhaustive than it is for other periods.[7] In analysing the theoretical foundations and historical development of the medieval just war the present study attempts to fill this lacuna.

After an introductory section on just war theories in antiquity, the foundations of the medieval just war in the writings of Augustine and its shaping in the early Middle Ages are briefly considered, with emphasis placed on those elements of the theories that were to figure strongly in the debates of medieval scholastics. The rest of the work is devoted to those thinkers who wrote within the confines of the specific disciplines of Roman or civil law, canon law and theology. The scope of the work does not permit full treatment of the publicistic literature or of the place of the just war in the evolution of separate national legal systems. According to Bainton, for a just war theory to mature there must be three preconditions: national consolidation, monarchical government, and a system of military defense.[8] Since all three were present in some form during the high Middle Ages, a history of just war theories forms a commentary on the evolution of these institutions.

In Hellenic Greece warfare was considered a normal form of conflict between different peoples, although hostilities between Greek city-states were not properly considered as wars by such observers as Plato.[9] It was Aristotle who coined the term 'just war,' applying it to wars waged by Hellenes against non-Hellenes whom

[6] R. Regout, *La doctrine de la guerre juste de Saint Augustin à nos jours, d'après les théologiens et les canonistes catholiques* (Paris, 1935). Other works on selected topics include: G. Hubrecht, 'La "juste guerre" dans le Décret de Gratien,' *Studia Gratiana*, III (1955), 161–77; and 'La juste guerre dans la doctrine chrétienne dès origines au milieu du xvie siècle,' *Recueils de la Société Jean Bodin pour l'histoire comparative des institutions*, XV (1961), 107–23; H. Pissard, *La guerre sainte en pays chrétien* (Paris, 1912); M. Villey, *La croisade: essai sur la formation d'une théorie juridique* (Caen, 1942); M. D. Chenu, 'L'évolution de la théologie de la guerre,' *La parole de Dieu* (2 vols., Paris, 1964); B. de Solages, 'La genèse et l'orientation de la théologie de la guerre juste,' *Bulletin de littérature ecclésiastique*, II (1940), 61–80; J. A. Brundage, *Medieval Canon Law and the Crusader* (Madison, Milwaukee and London, 1969); L. B. Walters, Jr, 'Five Classic Just War Theories: A Study in the Thought of Thomas Aquinas, Vitoria, Suarez, Gentili and Grotius' (Dissertation, Yale University, 1971); M. H. Keen, *The Laws of War in the Late Middle Ages* (London and Toronto, 1965).

[7] R. H. Bainton, *Christian Attitudes toward War and Peace* (Nashville, Tennessee, 1960).

[8] *Ibid.*, p. 45.

[9] Plato, *Republic*, 469c, 470bc, 471ab; *Laws*, I, 628. Cf. Herodotus, *History*, VII, 9, 2; Bainton, *Christian Attitudes*, pp. 37–9.

he considered barbarians. War was a natural form of acquisition, and since some men by their virtue, equated with justice, deserved to extend their rule over less worthy men, wars by which they enslaved others were naturally just. Men should only resort to war to prevent their own enslavement, that is, in self-defense, or to obtain an empire for the benefit of the governed or to enslave those non-Hellenes deserving of slavery. In Aristotelian terms warfare was thus not an end in itself but a means to such higher goals as peace, glory and strength.[10] When defense of a city was justified, any means of defense was licit, and wars were usually won by superiority of numbers, strength of allies and skillful leadership. Soldiers were a distinct community formed to secure victory, and so their courage, justice and nobility in the face of death were most laudable.[11] Yet when any city-state made war an end rather than a means it was destined to fall.[12] Aristotle's just war furthered the moral ends of peace and justice. His notion of justice in war was more moral and abstract than juridical in application, hence it was not subject to demonstration in a court of law. While justice was necessary lest bare might prevail over virtue, Aristotle and the Greek philosophers were unable to provide a way of distinguishing a just war from a merely successful one.[13] Yet his view of warfare when combined with Christian social doctrine by Thomas Aquinas exerted a powerful influence on the medieval theories.

Rome's fundamental contribution to the just war was the development of the concept of just causes. The legal foundation of the Roman just war was the analysis of contractual obligation. The etymology of *pax* stems from *pangere*, to make a pact or contract wherein the rights and duties of both parties were specified.[14] Breach of contract in private law justified a civil suit by the injured party to recover his *damna* and *iniuriae*, his damages and injuries. Similarly, in relations

[10] Aristotle, *Politics*, I, 7, 1255a, 3–1255b, 3; 1255b, 37–40; I, 9, 1256b, 23–26; VII, 14, 1333a, 30, 35; 1333b, 37–1334a, 3, 15; *De Rhetorica ad Alexanderum*, 2, 1425a, 10–16; *Nicomachean Ethics*, X, 7, 1177b, 9–11.

[11] *Politics*, VII, 2, 1331a, 14–19; *De Rhetorica ad Alexanderum*, 2, 1425a, 19–23; 38, 1447a, 2–7; *Nicomachean Ethics*, III, 6, 1115a, 29–32; III, 8, 1116b, 7; III, 9, 1117b, 14; VIII, 9, 1160a; *De Rhetorica*, I, 9, 1366b.

[12] *Politics*, VII, 14, 1334a, 7–8.

[13] Nussbaum, 'Just War,' 453. Cf. Philippson, *International Law*, II, 236f., 269, 350; *Oxford Classical Dictionary* (Oxford, 1961), v. *War, rules of*, p. 958.

[14] Philippson, *ibid.*, I, 376; Th. Mommsen, *Droit public romain*, trans. P. Girard (7 vols., Paris, 1889–96), VI², 213; J. Imbert, 'Pax Romana,' *Recueils Bodin*, XIV (1961), 308.

between states the injured city-state enjoyed rights to seek compensation and redress, acting both as judge and party in its own cause. Hence every just war had to be occasioned by the prior guilt of the offending party. Every city-state with juridical autonomy was responsible for redeeming injuries done to foreigners by its citizens, and when it defaulted on this responsibility, the other city-state had the right to punish it by war. Denial of justice became the primary cause of a just war seen as an extraordinary legal process. The Romans made war more civilised through the mitigating and regularising effects of a positive law that echoed the *ius gentium*.[15]

From this vantage point Cicero explored more specific examples of just causes. No war was just unless it was declared and waged to recover lost goods (*rebus repetitis*).[16] Included in the category of goods was anything for which satisfaction was demanded, whether real property or incorporeal rights.[17] Consequently warfare was not a willful exercise of violence but a just and pious endeavor occasioned by a delict or injustice of the enemy.[18] A war waged without cause was not really war but *latrocinium* or piracy, and the *causa belli* was a necessary precondition for a *justum bellum*.[19] The good city-state only went to war for its honor or its safety. Cicero broadened the scope of just causes to include punishment (*ultio*) of the enemy for the latter's misdeeds and repulsion of enemy attack.[20] By judicious use of just wars in defending its allies Rome had extended its sway over the whole world. Wars were also justified on the broad grounds of defense of territory, citizens, or even a city-state's independent existence.[21] The prior guilt of the offending party rendered its cause automatically unjust and justified the Roman title to defense. The

---

[15] E. Seckel, *Über Krieg und Recht in Rom* (Berlin, 1915), pp. 9f.; A. Heuss, 'Die völkerrechtlichen Grundlagen der römischen Aussenpolitik in republikanischer Zeit,' *Klio*, Beiheft XXXI (1933), 23–5; Philippson, *International Law*, II, 200, 233, 337.

[16] Cicero, *De Officiis*, I, 11, 36: 'Nullum bellum esse iustum nisi quod aut rebus repetitis geratur aut denunciatum ante sit et interdictum.'

[17] Cf. Nussbaum, 'Just War,' p. 454.

[18] Heuss, 'Die völkerrechtliche Grundlagen', pp. 19–21.

[19] *Livy*, History, I, 32, 6; XXXVIII, 19, 38–45.

[20] Cicero, *De Republica*, II, 23, 35: 'Illa iniusta bella sunt, quae sunt sine causa suscepta. Nam extra ulciscendi aut propulsandorum hostium causam bellum geri nullum potest...Nullum bellum iustum habetur nisi denunciatum, nisi indictum, nisi repetitis rebus.' *Ibid.*, III, 23, 34: 'Nullum bellum suscipi a civitate optima nisi aut pro fide aut pro salute.'

[21] *Ibid.*, II, 23, 35: 'Noster autem populus sociis defendis terrarum iam omnium potitus est.' Cf. *ibid.*, III, 18, 28.

Roman just war best described by Cicero contained the juridical concept of war guilt.

True to their legal view of the just war the Romans required not only the prior guilt of an enemy but a formal and authoritative declaration of war. In the Republic the first step towards this was the *repetitio rerum*, a broad and formal demand to a foreign power for redress of injuries suffered by Rome or its citizens. If satisfaction was not forthcoming within thirty-three days, the *fetiales* or fetial priests would issue the formal declaration of war upon authorisation by the Senate and people.[22] Rome was assumed to have a legitimate and necessary cause for war if the civil action of *repetitio rerum* was of no avail, or if goods seized from Roman citizens were not returned or injuries to Rome were not rectified.[23] By this procedure the just war had a religious as well as a formal aspect, for by adhering to the *ius fetiale* the Romans hoped the gods would aid them in battle. Waged in accordance with express or indirect divine commands, the war was not only a *bellum justum* but also a *bellum pium*, a dutiful war. Both divine and human law demanded warfare after auguries had indicated divine propitiation for the undertaking.[24] With the coming of the Empire and its concentration of authority the *princeps* or Emperor alone decided matters of war and peace. The formal declaration and the fetial priest slipped into oblivion, since Rome now was seldom overtly aggressive and always denied such a charge.[25] The emphasis on authoritative declaration was designed to prevent illicit Roman wars, and by the time Christian writers came to discuss the just war the Emperor possessed the sole authority to declare and wage it.

As an extraordinary legal procedure the Roman just war had to be waged justly, in theory at least. For Cicero, wars should be won by virtue and courage rather than by base, infamous or treacherous means.[26] Faith and honor should be maintained even with Rome's enemies, and an oath sworn even under enemy compulsion had to

[22] A. Berger, 'Encyclopedic Dictionary of Roman Law,' *Transactions of the American Philosophical Society*, XLIII[2] (1953), v. *bellum*, 372; v. *repetitio rerum*, 675; v. *Lex de bello indicendo* 550; v. *indicere bellum*, 449; v. *denuntiare bellum*, 431; v. *indictio belli*, 499; v. *fetiales*, 470; v. *Ius fetiale*, 528; v. *Senatus*, 695.

[23] Mommsen, *Droit public romain*, VI[1], 390f.

[24] Nussbaum, 'Just War,' 454; Philippson, *International Law*, II, 180, 193.

[25] Mommsen, *Droit public romain*, III, 113; V, 242; VI[1], 394.

[26] Cicero, *De Officiis*, III, 22, 86–7.

be observed on pain of committing sacrilege.[27] Once victory was in sight, mercy should be shown to enemies unless they had acted cruelly and barbarously, and when besieging cities only those guilty of resisting Rome were to be punished, while the inoffensive majority was to be spared.[28] Naturally Cicero realised that cruelty and injustice could result from legalistic formalism and chicanery,[29] yet his principles of right conduct of warfare were employed by later Christian writers.

On the other hand the Roman just war entailed legal consequences favorable to the Romans, for the declaration of war abrogated any obligation to respect the enemy's rights. As total war the Roman just war countenanced capture of civilians, devastation of land and plundering of cities. Booty and territory became the property of the government, although booty was sometimes sold for the common profit of the soldiers.[30] One of Rome's best means of acquiring territory, the *occupatio bellica*, transferred sovereignty over captured territory to Rome at the successful conclusion of a just war.[31] Captured soldiers and civilians could be enslaved rather than killed. The etymology of *servi*, slaves, was considered to depend upon *servare*, to save the lives of prisoners.[32] These often drastic legal consequences of the Roman just war passed almost intact into medieval opinions.

With the coming of Rome's empire came also the stoic universalism and its notion of a world brotherhood governed in orderly fashion by the *ius gentium*. Yet beneath this veneer Rome's just war primarily benefited Rome to the detriment of other peoples. Nowhere was this situation more clearly expressed than in the Roman attitude toward those peoples with whom Rome had no legal relations, the barbarians who were excluded from all legal protection. In the Twelve Tables *hostis* was synonymous with *peregrinus* or stranger.[33] Ulpian defined as *hostes* those against whom

---

[27] *Ibid.*, I, 13, 29–40; III, 29, 107–8.

[28] *Ibid.*, I, 11, 35; I, 24, 82.

[29] E.g. *ibid.*, I, 10, 33. For this formalism and the degeneration of moral scrupulousness in the imperial period, cf. Philippson, *International Law*, I, 412; II, 223, 287; Heuss, 'Die völkerrechtlichen Grundlagen,' 24.

[30] Seckel, *Krieg und Recht*, p. 15; Berger, 'Encyclopedic Dictionary,' v. *occupatio rerum hostilium*, 696; v. *praeda*, 641.

[31] Philippson, *International Law*, II, 243.

[32] Berger, 'Encyclopedic Dictionary,' v. *deditio*, 427; v. *servus*, 704.

[33] *Ibid.*, v. *barbari*, 371; v. *hostis*, 489.

Rome had publicly declared war or who had declared war on the Roman people. Other enemies he termed *latrunculi* and *praedones*, robbers and brigands who, not enjoying rights accorded to public enemies, were beyond the pale of Roman law.[34] Cicero exemplified Roman suspicion of foreigners when he maintained that an oath to give ransom to a pirate need not be fulfilled since the pirate was not a *legitimus hostis* but a common enemy of mankind lacking in all honor.[35] The protection of the rules of war was not extended to pirates and sometimes not to barbarians.[36] While Ulpian was willing to consider Germans and Parthians as *hostes*, other, less sophisticated Romans tended to view all those peoples outside the Mediterranean city-state culture as barbarians with no legal standing. The lumping together in Roman minds of the two dissimilar legal categories of brigands and barbarians served as a model for later Christian hostility to pagans, infidels, rebels, and heretics.[37]

At its maturity the Roman just war served so to glorify those soldiers who died fighting for the Roman *patria*.[38] Not only legal, moral and meritorious, the Roman just war fostered the growth of an administrative *ius militare*. Thus Frontinus in the first century A.D. and Vegetius in the fourth compiled manuals of military strategy and tactics that were employed even in Thomas Aquinas' benediction of the Christian just war.[39]

A different sort of legal relationship existed in the Old Testament between the ancient Hebrews, distinguished from other tribes by their Covenant with Jahweh and by circumcision. As God's Chosen People the Hebrews were obliged to worship Him alone, and in return He granted them His favor and protection. Exodus, Numbers, Deuteronomy, Joshua and Judges record the vicissitudes of the

[34] Ulpian expanded this definition from that of Pomponius; both were enshrined in Justinian's *Digest*, 49, 15, 24; 50, 16, 118 and 234. In general, see J. Gaudemet, 'L'étranger au bas empire,' *Recueils Bodin*, IX (1958), 207-35.

[35] Cicero, *De Officiis*, III, 29, 107-8.

[36] *Oxford Classical Dictionary*, v. *War, rules of*, p. 958.

[37] E.g. canon 27 of the Third Lateran Council of 1179; cf. below, ch. 5, nn. 98, 175, 193, 207, and ch. 6, nn. 78-87.

[38] Inst. I, 25, pr. For the subsequent history of this idea, cf. E. Kantorowicz, *The King's Two Bodies. A Study in Mediaeval Political Theology* (Princeton, 1957), pp. 232-72.

[39] Frontinus, *Strategematicon* (ed. A. Dederich, Leipzig, 1855); Vegetius, *Epitoma Rei Militaris* (ed. C. Lang, Leipzig, 1869). Cf. Aquinas, S.T. 2-2, q. 40, art. 1, ad 4; art. 3, resp. For Vincent of Beauvais' extensive use of Vegetius and Frontinus, see his *Speculum Doctrinale* XI, *passim*.

Hebrews' faith in Jahweh and of their hard-won establishment in Israel. It is often difficult to distinguish a holy war for the faith and a just war to conquer promised territories, for the holy war was the cradle of the nation. God commanded the waging of wars under the direction of religious leaders rather than kings. As His direct representatives leaders were bound to cooperate with Jahweh, the Lord of war by Whose aid the Hebrews prevailed against His enemies.[40] Since Israel was an agent of divine power in the world, God allowed the Canaanites, worshippers of Baal, to remain in power for a while in order that Israel maintain its fighting trim, but eventually the Israelites mercilessly destroyed Baal and the Canaanites.[41]

The Israelite code of warfare, contained in Deuteronomy 20, showed the harshness brought to bear on struggles with other peoples. Enemy cities within Israel were to be destroyed and those without could be incorporated as tributaries upon their surrender. Refusal to submit to the Israelites entailed the killing of all males and the Israelite enjoyment of women, children, cattle and goods.[42] God commanded Joshua to wage war against the people of Ai by means of ambushes. Successful in this, Joshua reduced the city to rubble and killed a reported twelve thousand men and women.[43] The final Old Testament war was the Maccabees' revolt in the name of Jahweh against the Seleucids and their Hellenising Jewish allies. Refraining from fighting on the Sabbath, many of the Maccabees were consequently butchered, and henceforth the leaders decided that while attacks were still prohibited on the Sabbath, they could licitly defend themselves with force on that day.[44]

The holy war could be extended to purposes other than the conquest and destruction of enemy tribes. During the incident of the Golden Calf (Exodus 32: 26–8) Moses bid those 'on the Lord's side' to join him. The sons of Levi gathered around as Moses related a command from Jahweh that every man should kill his brothers, friends and neighbors, and then rushed out and killed about three thousand men. This perplexing passage could be interpreted as an

---

[40] E.g. Exodus 15: 3–5, 15; Numbers 10: 35; Judges 7: 2–25. Cf. Bainton, *Christian Attitudes*, pp. 44f., C. Erdmann, *Die Entstehung des Kreuzzugsgedankens* (Stuttgart, 1935), p. 1.
[41] Judges 3: 1–2; II Kings 10: 28; Deuteronomy 7: 1–2; 13: 15–16; Numbers 21: 2.
[42] Cf. also Numbers 31.
[43] Joshua 8.
[44] I Maccabees 2: 38–41.

indication of a divine intention that a select group of men could enforce divine law on others to the point of massacre.[45] The Hebrew holy war could serve not only the needs of internal discipline but as a struggle of apocalyptic proportions. Ezekiel prophesied the coming of Gog of Magog as a pestilence on the face of Israel, whereby Gog would be met by the fury of Jahweh and the Israelites. After mass slaughter and Gog's final destruction a Redeemer would save God's people. Ezekiel's enigmatic prophecy extended the ideal of the holy war to the whole universe.[46] To patristic and medieval writers the Old Testament served as an exemplary tapestry of divinely-sanctioned aggressive holy wars unrestrained by any feelings of mercy or guilt.

The New Testament is as barren of references to wars as the Old Testament is replete, hence New Testament teachings on warfare and related matters could lead to equivocal conclusions. On one hand Jesus used a whip of cords to cleanse the temple of shameful business-men, but it is not clear whether the whip itself or Jesus' wrath was the effective force,[47] and He stated that He came not to bring peace but the sword.[48] An interpretation favoring holy warfare could be deduced from these passages, but other passages more clearly favored the exercise of Roman power. The classic if difficult passage concerns divided loyalties, in which Jesus advised followers to 'render unto Caesar the things that are Caesar's,'[49] and Paul appeared to preach submission to governmental authority that, as a divine institution, punished sin and encouraged right conduct.[50] Luke, the Roman publican, could envision the cooperation of Rome and Christianity for all men,[51] and John the Baptist did not rebuke for their pro-fession the soldiers who sought his advice but cautioned them to do violence to no one, to refrain from false accusations and to be content with their wages.[52]

On the other hand certain passages appeared to prohibit Christian participation in war. In His Sermon on the Mount Christ counseled His followers not to resist evil but to turn the other cheek to blows. Christians should love their enemies and not judge one another.[53]

[45] M. Walzer, 'Exodus 32 and the Theory of the Holy War: the History of a Citation,' *Harvard Theological Review*, LXI (1968), 2–4.
[46] Ezekiel 38–9.
[47] John 2: 15. For this section Bainton, *Christian Attitudes*, pp. 53–65, is used extensively.
[48] Matthew 10: 34.   [49] Mark 12: 17.   [50] Romans 13: 1–4.
[51] Luke 2: 1; 22: 24–8.   [52] Luke 3: 14.
[53] Matthew 5: 39, 41; 7: 1; cf. Luke 6: 27–9; Romans 14: 13.

Peter was commanded to sheath his sword, for those who lived by the sword also perished by it.[54] Self-defense appeared illicit, for Christ advised His followers to give place to wrath and to leave vengeance for their injuries to God.[55]

The New Testament in neither approving nor condemning warfare expressly only provided general principles of human conduct rather than specific precepts, and so subsequent Christian writers were forced to accommodate Evangelical precepts to the Hebrew and Roman examples of holy and just wars. The response of the early Church was at best equivocal. Before Constantine's conversion churchmen tended to condemn warfare in general and Roman wars in particular. On New Testament grounds they concluded that wars violated Christian charity and that Roman wars only resulted in violence and bloodshed. Even while employing military metaphors to describe proper Christian conduct, many Christians rejected worldly military service in favor of the *militia Christi*, a pacific expression of their struggle against evil.[56] The example of Old Testament wars however constituted a vexation, for if God really prohibited war and killing, how could He have authorised so many wars? Eagerly pressed by Gnostics and Manicheans, Origen answered that the Old Testament wars had been necessary for Jewish kingdoms, but since wars were no longer permitted, God allowed the kingdoms to disintegrate.[57] More effectively, Origen considered the Old Testament as an allegory of the New, consequently Christians should study the historical books of the Old Testament with the understanding that these wars should be understood as spiritual wars against the devil. They functioned as *exempla* for moral edification rather than as guides for making decisions. Here Origen's treatment

---

[54] Matthew 26: 52.

[55] Romans 12: 19. Gratian cited these examples as scriptural warrants for the contention that military service was sinful: C. 23, pr.

[56] Cf. Bainton, *Christian Attitudes*, pp. 67–81. See also his earlier 'The Early Church and War,' *Harvard Theological Review*, XXXIX (1946), 189–213. The sectarian question of whether the early Church was pacifistic has been treated by: A. Harnack, *Militia Christi: die christliche Religion und der Soldatenstand in den ersten drei Jahrhunderten* (Tübingen, 1905); C. J. Cadoux, *The Early Christian Attitude to War* (London, 1919); E. A. Ryan, 'The Rejection of Military Service by the Early Christians,' *Theological Studies*, XIII (1952), 1–32; S. Windass and J. Newman, 'The Early Christian Attitude to War,' *Irish Theological Quarterly*, XXIX (1962), 235–47; S. Windass, *Christianity versus Violence: A Social and Historical Study of War and Christianity* (London, 1964), ch. 1.

[57] Origen, *Contra Celsum*, VII, 26; Tertullian, *Adversus Marcionem*, IV, 16; both cited from Bainton, *Christian Attitudes*, p. 82.

provided the twelfth-century canonist Gratian with his point of departure for a consideration of Christian military service.[58] If men must fight, they should respect the rules of the just war, but the Christian's social role was fulfilled in his prayers for the conditions of men.[59]

Upon Constantine's settlement Christian attitudes entered a new and less hesitant phase. The Emperor's benefactions to the Church and the peace he achieved exerted a subtle but powerful pressure on Christian theologians to accommodate Christian citizenship to Roman wars. The gradual evolution in attitude was signaled by Eusebius of Caesarea, Constantine's bishop and advisor, who identified the Roman Empire with the divine peace-keeping mission. After all, since Augustus and Christ had been contemporaries, one Empire and the religion of one God were congruent divine institutions.[60] Eusebius distinguished two levels of Christian vocation. The laity was to shoulder the burdens of citizenship and wage just wars, while on a higher level the clergy was to remain aloof from society in total dedication to God.[61] The consequences of this attitude were twofold: one group of Christians was exempted from military service by both Christian opinion and Roman practice, setting the stage for similar medieval exemptions of clerics from military service; and participation by Christian laymen in Roman wars was now whole-heartedly approved.[62] St John Chrysostom in the east and St Jerome in the west saw in the *Pax Romana* maintained by a few professional soldiers the fulfillment of the pacific prophecies of Isaiah and the New Testament.[63]

The fuller development of a Christian just war theory was furthered in the writings of Ambrose, a new kind of Christian. Trained in imperial administration and the former prefect in Milan, Ambrose brought a Roman political orientation to his ministry. For him Augustus had prepared the way for Christianity by pacifying the

[58] Origen, *Homilia in Jesu Nave*, xv, 1; *Patrologia Graeca*, 12, p. 897. Cf. C. 23 q. 1 c. 1.
[59] Bainton, *Christian Attitudes*, pp. 82–4.
[60] *Ibid.*, pp. 86f. Cf. B. Paradisi, 'La paix au ive et ve siècles', *Recueils Bodin*, xiv (1961), 339.
[61] Bainton, *ibid.*, p. 84.
[62] *Ibid.*, p. 88. *Codex Theodosiani*, ed. Th. Mommsen and P. Meyer (Berlin, 1905), 16, 2, 2, 6, 9, 10, 11, 15, 16, 21, 24, 36. Seckel, *Krieg und Recht*, p. 39, observes the development of the *Berufsoldat* in the Empire.
[63] St John Chrysostom, *Expositio in Psalm. 45, 3*; *Patrologia Graeca*, 55, p. 207. Jerome, *Commentarium in Michaeum*, I, 4; P.L. 25, pp. 1187f.

strife-torn Romans.[64] The courage of soldiers who defended the Empire against barbarians and Roman citizens from thieves was full of justice, and Ambrose prayed for the success of imperial armies.[65]

As a result of its liberation by Constantine, the Church had to face the new and greater dangers posed by the various heresies. For the older antagonism between Empire and Christianity was substituted the new and more explosive division between heresy and orthodoxy. Ambrose was instrumental in fostering imperial repression of heretics. After his meeting with the Emperor Gratian in 379, all heresies opposed to divine and imperial laws were ordered out of existence. By the Edict of Thessalonica in 381, destined to become the imperial constitution *Cunctos populos*, orthodox Christianity became the official religion of the Empire. Subsequent legislation obliged the imperial government to defend orthodoxy, Church and clerics against heretics. According to the imperial policy of persecution, heretics were subjected to all sorts of civil disabilities and in some cases were liable to capital punishment.[66] Subsequent legislation rendered heresy a public crime assimilated to the *crimen laesae maiestatis*, or treason.[67] In short, to be a heretic was to be a traitor to Rome, and Ambrose served as the quasi-official apologist for this eventual conclusion.

The dangers posed by heresy were all the more dangerous because the barbarians attacking Rome on many fronts tended also to be heretics. To the Roman animosity toward the barbarian was added the element of religious animosity between believer and unbeliever, thus rendering the internal and external threats to the *Pax Romana* more politically explosive. To point the way out of this crisis Ambrose about 378 wrote the *De Fide Christiana* for the Emperor Gratian, who was at the time attempting to consolidate Roman authority on the Danube after the defeat of the Arian Valens by the

---

[64] Ambrose, *Enarratio in Psalm. 45*, 21; P.L. 14, pp. 1198f. Cf. F. H. Dudden, *Life and Times of Saint Ambrose* (2 vols., Oxford, 1935), II, 538.

[65] Ambrose, *De Officiis Ministrorum*, I, 27, 129; P.L. 16, p. 66: 'Fortitudo, quae in bello tuetur a barbaris patriam, vel domi defendit infirmos, vel a latronibus socios, plena sit iustitiae.' (Cf. C. 23 q. 3 c. 5.) *De Fide Christiana*, II, 16, 143; P.L. 16, p. 614.

[66] *Codex Theodosiani*, 16, 1, 2. (Cf. Cod. 1, 1.) For other relevant imperial legislation, see ibid., 16, 5, 5, 7, 9, 11, 12, 14. On these edicts, see W. K. Boyd, *The Ecclesiastical Edicts of the Theodosian Code* (New York, 1902), pp. 33f., 43f.; C. N. Cochrane, *Christianity and Classical Culture* (rev. ed., New York, 1957), pp. 327f., 333.

[67] *Codex Theodosiani*, 16, 5, 40, paras. 1, 5, Cf. Cod. 1, 5, 4.

Visigoths. Ambrose assured Gratian of victory, for it had been fore-told in the prophecies of Ezekiel and confirmed by Gratian's faith. Ambrose even identified Gog, the wicked enemy of Ezekiel's prophecies, with the contemporary Goths, who were thereby des-tined to destruction. Yet on the other hand the Roman defeat at Adrianople had been divinely sent as punishment for the sins of the Arian Valens. As in the Old Testament God now sent wars as punish-ment for sinners. Arian heretics in the imperial government were obviously incapable of defending the Empire from cruel and heretical neighbors; by contrast the Italians were steadfast con-fessors of the faith whom God would defend and avenge through the orthodox Gratian. Christians engaged in combat against an alien faith should have the aid of an orthodox Emperor. Divine indigna-tion against heresy was the fundamental cause of the hostile inroads into the Empire, for breach of faith and lack of Roman virtue paved the way for breaches of the imperial frontiers.[68]

Even if Rome had a hand in her own misfortunes, for Ambrose the barbarians still functioned as the primary villains. By not submitting the judgment of their crimes to the Emperors, the barbarians set themselves up as enemies of Rome deserving of punishment. Ambrose instinctively regarded all barbarians as enemies (*hostes*) of the Roman people.[69] Wherever heresy, or *perfidia* as Ambrose legalistically termed it, broke out, attacks on the Empire would soon follow. Thus in Ambrose's mind catholic orthodoxy stood or fell with the *Pax Romana*. *Fides Romana* and *fides catholica* were coexten-sive and mutually interdependent. Should the amalgam of those two qualities disintegrate, the world would come to an end.[70] In response Ambrose desired a sort of perpetual holy war motivated by the bellicose virtues of Joshua and the Maccabees who had fought for God and their rights.[71]

The Ambrosian combination of Roman and Christian morality showed him to be a Christian Cicero, for even his comments on the Roman just war were supported with references to Old Testament wars. Thus courage alone did not justify fighting, for the cause had

---

[68] Ambrose, *De Fide Christiana*, II, 16, 136–43; P.L. 16, pp. 611–14.
[69] Ambrose, *Expositio in Psalm. 118, Sermo 20*, 24; P.L. 15, pp. 1568f. Cf. *De Officiis*, I, 29, 141; P.L. 16, pp. 69f. and Dudden, *Ambrose*, II, 538.
[70] Ambrose, *Expositio in Lucam*, XI, 10; P.L. 15, pp. 1898f.
[71] Ambrose, *De Officiis*, I, 40, 195–8; P.L. 16, pp. 87–90.

to be just. David's wars, for example, were just because David always consulted with God prior to the opening of hostilities.[72] Yet participation in warfare was now foreign to the duties of the clergy, unlike the formerly proper bellicose activities of Joshua, Jerobaal, Samson and David.[73] On the other hand Ambrose as a good Roman insisted that honesty should prevail over utility in deciding for or against war. Fidelity, loyalty and respect for the enemy's rights must be maintained in wartime.[74] The less flattering side of Roman practice was also mirrored in Ambrose's writings, for he allowed usury, usually prohibited to Christians, to be exacted from enemies in a just war. His link between warfare and usury, two morally suspect activities, confirmed that any viable means of punishing an unjust enemy was licit. Ambrose even approved the tactic of giving wine to barbarians so that in their inebriation they might be more easily vanquished.[75] Conquering powers have often resorted to similar measures, and Ambrose's opinions indicate the intensity of his conviction that heretical barbarians deserved whatever forms of hostility the Roman Christians could levy against them.

Still, his intolerance of contemporary barbarians contrasted markedly with the earlier Roman notions of right conduct in a just war. His diffuse analysis was, however, a potent compound that would exert a formative influence over medieval theory and practice. Yet it remained an unstable amalgam of examples of Old Testament wars and Roman morality serving as a clumsy weapon against barbarians and heretics. Blessed with a succession of orthodox and forceful emperors, Ambrose did not feel obliged to examine the authority required for a just and holy Romano–Christian war. Still lacking was a systematic grounding of the just war on both Old and New Testament moral principles. For Christianity and the just war to survive the collapse of Roman imperial authority they had to be made independent of the connection with Rome, a task to which Augustine at great length addressed himself.

---

[72] *Ibid.*, I, 35, 176; P.L. 16, p. 80.

[73] *Ibid.*, I, 35, 175; P.L. 16, p. 80; cf. the similar opinion that Gratian attributed to Ambrose, C. 23 q. 8 c. 3.

[74] *Ibid.*, I, 29, 139–40; II, 7, 33; III, 8, 54–6; III, 10, 67–9; P.L. 16, pp. 68f., 119, 170, 173f.

[75] Ambrose, *De Tobia*, 15, 51; P.L. 14, pp. 816f. Cf. Deuteronomy 23: 20 and C. 14 q. 4 c. 12. For the medieval treatment of this passage, see J. W. Baldwin, *Masters Princes and Merchants. The Social Views of Peter the Chanter and his Circle* (2 vols., Princeton, 1970), I, 279f.; II, 196. Ambrose, *De Helia et Ieiunio*. 15, 54; C.S.E.L. 32², p. 444.

Chapter 1

ST AUGUSTINE AND THE JUST WAR
IN THE EARLY MIDDLE AGES

The die for the medieval just war was cast by St Augustine, who combined Roman and Judaeo–Christian elements in a mode of thought that was to influence opinion throughout the Middle Ages and beyond. The just war served as Augustine's means of reconciling the evangelical precepts of patience and the pacifistic tendencies of the early Church with Roman legal notions.[1] Central to his attitude was the conviction that war was both a consequence of sin and a remedy for it. The real evils in war were not war itself but the love of violence and cruelty, greed and the *libido dominandi* or lust for rule that so often accompanied it.[2] Although the sin originated in man's wounded will rather than in his actions, when man's evil volition led him to sinful acts, war provided a rough punishment. Inspired by the Old Testament Augustine argued that by divine judgment wars punished peoples for sins and crimes, even those unrelated to the war. Even wicked men could serve God's providence by punishing the sins of other peoples. Every war had peace as its goal, hence war was an instrument of peace and should only be waged to secure peace of some sort.[3]

Frequent reference to the Old and New Testaments provided

[1] The development of Augustine's attitudes toward warfare is too complex and too closely related to his own experience to receive adequate treatment here. A recent excellent biography is P. R. L. Brown, *Augustine of Hippo* (London, Berkeley and Los Angeles, 1967); cf. also the same author's *Religion and Society in the Age of Saint Augustine* (New York and London, 1972). Among the copious bibliography of works dealing with Augustine's thought on war, the following may be cited: Regout, *La guerre juste*, pp. 38–44; H. Deane, *The Political and Social Ideas of St Augustine* (New York, 1963), ch. 5; Windass, *Christianity versus Violence*, ch. 2.

[2] Augustine, *Contra Faustum Manichaeum*, XXII, 74; C.S.E.L. 25, p. 672: 'Nocendi cupiditas, ulciscendi crudelitas, inpacatus atque inplacabilis animus, feritas rebellandi, libido dominandi et si qua similia, haec sunt, quae in bellis iure culpantur.' Cf. C. 23 q. 1 c. 4.

[3] *De Civitate Dei*, XIX, 12, 1; XIX, 13, 1–2; XIX, 15; P.L. 41, pp. 637f., 641, 643. *Ennaratio in Psalm. 73*, 78; P.L. 36, pp. 934f.; *Contra Faustum*, XXII, 75; C.S.E.L. 25, pp. 467f. *Epist. 139*, 6; C.S.E.L. 57, p. 135: 'Pacem habere debet voluntas, bellum necessitas, ut liberet deus a necessitate et conservet in pace. non enim pax queritur, ut bellum excitetur, sed bellum geritur, ut pax adquiratur, esto ergo etiam bellando pacificus, ut eos, quos expugnas, ad pacis utilitatem vincendo perducas.' (Cf. C. 23, q. 1 c. 3.)

Augustine with a means of defeating the doctrinaire pacifism of the Manichean heresy and also with guidance to contemporary Christians who still harbored suspicion of war and military service. Augustine saw in Moses' wars a just and righteous retribution, and compared the punishment of unwilling souls to that dealt a child by a loving father. The just warrior restrained sinners from evil, thus acting against their will but in their own best interest.[4] Recognising that the legitimacy of warfare had to be grounded in evangelical precepts, Augustine sought support in one of the touchstones of his thought, the notion of charity. Punishment of evil-doers that prevented them from doing further wrong when administered without being moved by revenge or taking pleasure in suffering was an act of love. The precept 'resist not evil' (Matt. 5: 39) did not prohibit wars, for the real danger in soldiering was not military service itself but the malice that so often accompanied it, and the command to 'turn the other cheek' (Luke 6: 29) referred to the inward disposition of the heart rather than to the outward deed. Patience and benevolence did not always conflict with the inflicting of physical punishment, for when Moses put sinners to death he was motivated not by cruelty but by love. Hatred was to be overcome by a love for one's enemies that did not preclude a benevolent severity.[5] By this distinction between the inward disposition of the heart and outward acts, to be accepted without serious question in the Middle Ages, Augustine claimed to reconcile war and the New Testament. Since according to the 'inwardness' of his ethics the intention rather than the hostile act was normative, any hostile act was justified provided it was motivated by charity. The spirituality of the Sermon on the Mount that had induced earlier Christians to renounce war now justified it. To treat evangelical precepts in this way was to revalue them politically such that warfare now became necessary rather than inherently sinful.[6]

---

[4] *Contra Faustum*, XXII, 74, 78; C.S.E.L. 25, pp. 672, 678. *Epist. 138*, 2, 14; C.S.E.L. 44, p. 141. Cf. J. Mausbach, *Die Ethik des heiligen Augustinus* (2 vols., Freiburg im B., 1909), I, 313.

[5] *Sermo 302*, 15; P.L. 38, p. 1391: 'Non enim beneficere prohibet militia, sed malitia.' *De Sermone Domini in Monte*, I, 19, 59; I, 20, 63; P.L. 34, pp. 1260-2. *Contra Faustum*, XXII, 76, 79; C.S.E.L. 25, pp. 674, 680. (Cf. C. 23 q. 1 c. 2; C. 23 q. 4 c. 44.) *Epist. 47*, 5; C.S.E.L. 34², p. 135. (Cf. C. 23 q. 5 c. 8.) *Epist. 138*, 2, 13–15; C.S.E.L. 44, pp. 138, 140–2. (Cf. C. 23 q. 1 c. 2.) *Epist.* 189, 4; C.S.E.L. 57, pp. 133f.

[6] Cf. Windass, *Christianity versus Violence*, pp. 24f., 27–9. Windass (p. 82) concludes that for just war theories to be compatible with the New Testament, the scriptural commands must be 'put in brackets,' such that the literal meaning of the Sermon on the Mount is shorn of its applicability.

Love for one's neighbor could legitimate his death, and not to resist evil became an attitude compatible with outward belligerence toward him. The new *miles Christi* now fought other men as well as sin and the devil.

Augustine's intellectual revaluation denied the use of physical violence to private persons. A private Christian could not kill an attacker in self-defense, for that would entail hatred and loss of love. In such cases Augustine bore witness to the pacifistic tendencies of the early Church. Only rulers and officials acting in the line of duty were able to kill without giving vent to hatred and other sinful passions.[7] Private pacifism was thus joined to a justification of public warfare that underscored the later medieval emphasis on the legitimate authority necessary to wage just wars.

Having provided a Christian justification of warfare, Augustine turned to define the just war itself. In commenting on Joshua he formulated the first new definition of the just war since Cicero, one that became the single most important statement of the later medieval theories: 'iusta bella ulciscuntur iniurias,' just wars avenge injuries. War was justified when a people or a city neglected either to punish wrongs done by its members or to restore what it had unjustly seized.[8] On its surface this definition appears merely to echo Cicero, but interpretations of it could lead in diverse directions. At stake were the proper causes and scope of the just war; the two poles within which wandered the medieval just war were a narrow or Ciceronian view and a broader view more attuned to the theocratic complexion of medieval political thought. The narrow view, Cicero's *rebus repetitis*, required a clear violation of the pre-existing rights of the injured and therefore just party. The resulting just war was limited in its aims to securing redress of grievances and compensation for losses

---

[7] *Contra Faustum,* XXII, 70; C.S.E.L. 25, p. 667. *De Libero Arbitrio,* I, 5, 12, 34; C.S.E.L. 74, p. 12. Cf. *Epist.* 47, 5; above, n. 5. For fuller discussion of Augustine's thoughts on violence see R. Hartigan, 'Saint Augustine on War and Killing: The Problem of the Innocent,' *Journal of the History of Ideas,* XXVII (1966), 196f. Hartigan (p. 201) claims that for Augustine, as long as a Christian kills without rancor and on public authority, he does not violate the law of charity but rather obeys it in wreaking retributive justice, itself an aspect of charity. Augustine considered private violence the most degrading form of action: P. R. L. Brown, 'Saint Augustine,' *Trends in Medieval Political Thought,* p. 14.

[8] *Quaestiones in Heptateuchum,* VI, 10; C.S.E.L. 28², p. 428: 'Iusta autem bella ea definiri solent quae ulciscuntur iniurias, si qua gens vel civitas quae bello petenda est, vel vindicare neglexerit quod a suis inprobe factum est, vel reddere quod per iniurias ablatum est.' Cf. C. 23 q. 2 c. 2. For Cicero's definitions, see above, introduction, nn. 16, 20.

occasioned by the crimes of the offending party to the persons, property (*res*) or rights (*iura*) of the aggrieved party. The goal of this just war was a simple return to the *status quo ante bellum* and rejected the pursuit of a new and improved position of rights and property by the just party. Such a war was analogous to the pursuit of compensatory damages in private law.[9]

In the broader interpretation, Augustine's just war could be seen as a penal sanction analogous to the awarding of punitive damages in private law. The just war was thus total and unlimited in its licit use of violence, for it not only avenged the violation of existing legal rights but also avenged the moral order injured by the sins of the guilty party regardless of injuries done to the just party acting as a defender of that order. As sins as well as crimes, seen in the context of a broadened concept of justice whereby not only illegal but immoral or sacrilegious acts were punishable, the transgressions were both a crime against the law and a sin against righteousness. Augustine's notion of justice included respect for divine rights, and so he contrasted heavenly and earthly forms of justice by exploiting the ambivalent meaning of *ius*. Whereas *ius* for the Romans stood for a body of law recognised as valid by those whom it affected, Augustine employed *ius* in the sense of righteousness, thus equating *ius* with *iustitia* and *iustitia* with *vera iustitia*. Where there was no righteousness, there was no true justice.[10] Righteousness demanded that God also must be rendered His due; without this man lost his self-control and his justice in dealing with other men. Seen in this light any violation of God's laws, and, by easy extension, any violation of Christian doctrine, could be seen as an injustice warranting unlimited violent punishment.[11] Further, the subjective *culpa* or guilt of the enemy merited punishment of the enemy population without regard to the distinction between soldiers and civilians. Motivated by a

---

[9] Cf. Walzer, 'Exodus 32,' 5, n. 7; H. Black, *Black's Law Dictionary* (4th ed., St Paul, Minn., 1951), v. *damages*, pp. 466–9.

[10] *De Civitate Dei*, XIX, 21; P.L. 40, pp. 648f. For the problems and consequences of Augustine's distinction between justice and true justice, see Deane, *St Augustine*, pp. 83, 98f. 119–21; J. Adams, *The 'Populus' in Jerome and Augustine. A Study in the Patristic Sense of Community* (New Haven and London, 1971) esp. ch. 2 and Appendix A.

[11] Hartigan ('Saint Augustine on War and Killing,' 199) argues that in Augustine's definition an intimate connection between the juridical and moral orders exists, such that a delict or crime is also a sin.

righteous wrath, the just warriors could kill with impunity even those who were morally innocent. Objective determination of personal guilt was not only unnecessary but irrelevant.[12] The offense need not be directly committed against the just party. While in the heat of conflict and controversy the distinction between the two interpretations perhaps broke down, it remained valid at least in theory. Augustine's emphasis on *ulciscuntur iniurias* at the expense of Cicero's *res repetitis* when coupled with his analysis of *iustitia* paved the way for later justifications of holy wars and crusades that punished all manner of wickedness and vice. In context Augustine's definition espoused an expanded concept of war guilt.

While Augustine did not elucidate the consequences of his definition, in discussing God's command to Joshua to make war on the people of Ai, he declared that any war waged on divine command was a just war. Earlier Christian writers had avoided confronting the question of whether God ever ordained wars Himself, but here Augustine saw God as the author of the war and Joshua as His minister of justice. The war was just *sine dubitatione*, for it had been occasioned by an offense against God by the people of Ai, and so as His executors the Israelites acted without sinful *libido* and were absolved of any responsibility for the war.[13] Augustine appeared to choose the theocratic interpretation here, and it was no accident that in his definition he referred to divinely ordained wars as a sort of *deus ex machina* that served as an all-too-easy way to justify warfare. Since God's wars were automatically just, a divinely-inspired just war could be linked to the Pauline derivation of ruling authority from God with the result that wars to defend righteousness could be waged by rulers even without an express divine command. The *bellum Deo auctore*, however indirect was the divine authorisation, also opened the way further to the development of holy wars and

---

[12] Hartigan (*ibid.*, 201, 203) strongly criticises Augustine's views as inconsistent with his theology of sin and guilt, and considers Augustine negligent in not providing for assessment of individual moral guilt.

[13] *Quaestiones in Heptateuchum*, VI, 10; C.S.E.L. 28², pp. 428f.: 'Quod deus iubet loquens ad Iesum, ut constituat sibi retrorsus insidias, id est insidiantes bellatores ad insidiandum hostibus. . . . sed etiam hoc genus belli sine dubitatione iustum est, quod deus imperat, apud quem non est iniquitas et novit quid cuique fieri debeat. in quo bello ductor exercitus vel ipse populus non tam auctor belli quam minister iudicandus est.' Cf. Joshua 8 and C. 23 q. 2 c. 2. Elsewhere Augustine argued that wise men only waged just wars when these were made necessary by the iniquity of the enemy: *De Civitate Dei*, XIX, 7; P.L. 41, p. 634.

crusades within the just war.[14] Nowhere is Augustine's defeat of early Christian pacifism clearer than in his treatment of wars endowed with a divine purpose.

Augustine's just war did not attempt to distinguish between offensive and defensive warfare. Defense of the *patria*, its citizens and property was a just cause for war,[15] as was the refusal of the Amorites to grant the Israelites the right of innocent passage (Numbers 21: 21–5). Since the refusal contradicted the equitable conventions of human society, by which Augustine probably meant the *ius gentium*, God had caused the Israelites to wage war against the Amorites and thereby punished them by appropriating their lands for the Israelites.[16] Although this war might be considered an aggressive one, Augustine treated it rather as a war legitimated by divine command. While a war of conquest was unjust, the concept of *ulcisci iniurias* rather than defense was the necessary point of departure for every *ius ad bellum*. Augustine did come close to recognising that both belligerents could have some measure of justice in their respective causes. The problem turned on which belligerent had a juster cause. When victory went to this party, the peace was desirable and the victory was to be congratulated. It was worse when the injurious party prevailed over the juster party.[17] While the notion of just causes on both sides may be defensible morally, it is juridically inoperable, for both belligerents can harm their enemy out of proportion to their share of justice, and a legal determination of where justice lay would have to be found for one or the other.[18] Perhaps partly for this reason medieval legists allowed this tentative facet of Augustine's thought to slumber in obscurity.

Inspired by the Roman just war Augustine required that the just

14 Cf. Windass, *Christianity versus Violence*, pp. 32–4.

15 E.g. *De Civitate Dei*, III, 10; P.L. 41, p. 85.

16 *Quaestiones in Heptateuchum*, IV, 44; C.S.E.L. 28², pp. 352f.: 'Hic certe Israhel possedit civitates Amorrhaeorum quas bello superavit, quia non eas anathemavit; nam si anathemasset, possidere illi non liceret hic inde ad usus suos aliquid praedae usurparet. notandum est sane quemadmodum iusta bella gerebantur. innoxius enim transitus negabatur, qui iure humanae societatis aequissimo patere debebat. sed iam ut deus sua promissa compleret, adiuvit hic Israhelitas, quibus Amorrhaeorum terram dare oportebat.' Cf. Numbers 21: 21–5; C. 23 q. 2 c. 3.

17 *De Civitate Dei*, XV, 4; P.L. 41, pp. 440–1: 'Quando autem vincunt qui causa iustiore pugnabant, quis dubitet gratulandum esse, et provenisse optabilem pacem?' Cf. *ibid.*, IV, 15; P.L. 41, p. 124.

18 If the analysis here is valid, then Bainton's interpretation (*Christian Attitudes*, p. 99) that the just war was just only on one side is in need of modification.

war be waged on legitimate authority. Either God or the ruler, be he king or prince, had the unequivocal responsibility to decide whether recourse to war was necessary and to authorise a just war. Soldiers alone were the proper officials for waging war.[19] Implicit here is the prohibition on killing not only by clerics but also by any private Christian. The question of obedience arose when a soldier did not agree with his prince that the war had a just cause. Since obedience of subjects to kings was a general human convention, in doubtful cases Augustine advised the soldier as a servant of civic peace to obey even a sacrilegious king and to fight even an unjust war unless the prince ordered deeds that clearly contravened divine precepts.[20] The Christian soldier even obeyed the military commands of an infidel Emperor such as Julian.[21] When an official killed on order he was not guilty of murder, and if he refused an order to kill he was guilty of treason.[22] Never was Augustine more Roman, for to allow disobedience to an unjust command would give free vent to the individual passions he so ardently condemned. Rather than incur this risk Augustine absolved the individual soldier of moral responsibility for his official actions.

Whenever Augustine discussed authority and obedience he naturally turned to the highest authority, God Himself. In the Old Testament account of the war with the Amorites, the Israelites themselves were depicted as defeating their foes, but in Augustine's account it was God who effected the defeat in order to fulfill His promises to His Chosen People.[23] Indeed, God's authority and aid justified a war that otherwise would have been an illicit usurpation of Amorite territory. In the *City of God* Augustine enumerated instances in which divine authority made exceptions to its own prohibition on killing. Some men waged war in obedience to a direct divine command while others acting in conformity with God's

---

19 *Contra Faustum*, XXII, 74–5; C.S.E.L. 25, pp. 672f. Cf. C. 23 q. 1 c. 4. *Quaestiones in Hepta-teuchum*, VI, 10; C.S.E.L. 28², p. 428: 'Hinc admonemus non iniuste fieri ab his qui iustum bellum gerunt, ut nihil homo iustus praecipue cogitare debeat in his rebus, nisi ut iustum bellum suscipiat, cui bellare fas est; non enim omnibus fas est.' Cf. C. 23 q. 2 c. 2.

20 *Confessiones*, III, 8, 15; C.S.E.L. 33, p. 57.

21 *Enarr. in Psalm. 124*, 7; P.L. 37, p. 1654. Cf. C. 11 q. 3 cc. 94, 98.

22 *De Civitate Dei*, I, 21, 26; P.L. 41, pp. 35, 39. Cf. C. 23 q. 5 c. 13.

23 Above, n. 16. This observation supports Brown's conclusion that Augustine made a deliberate study of the Old Testament to show that in His sovereignty God alone controlled the outcome of policies and the conscious intentions of the protagonists: 'Saint Augustine,' p. 4 n. 11.

ordinance put wicked men to death. In either case their obedience rendered them innocent of transgressing the Sixth Commandment.[24] Divine sanction of the right to punish wickedness was Augustine's strongest justification of the right to wage war. Here again he resorted to the *deus ex machina* of divinely-inspired Old Testament wars to bolster his argument, a strategy he employed even in considering the proper means of waging a just war. Since God had ordered Joshua to lay ambushes for the people of Ai, similar ambushes, ruses and strategems that otherwise were prohibited could be employed.[25] While this opinion provoked sympathetic response in the Middle Ages, it appeared to conflict with Augustine's more Ciceronian notion that *fides* or fidelity once promised to an enemy must be observed.[26] In sum, Augustine's just war like the rest of his thought was permeated with divine activity. In rendering the just war capable of furthering divine purposes, Augustine made of the just war a much more comprehensive doctrine than it had been with Cicero and the Romans.

Evidence of this expansion of the just war can best be seen in Augustine's complex doctrine of religious persecution. Since wickedness included the sin of improper belief, Augustine saw a divine purpose in such persecution. While he never explicitly discussed the just war in this context, his justification of persecution shared certain common attitudes with it. Augustine viewed all forms of religious belief other than orthodoxy as a common threat to the faith, and he eventually concluded, against the backdrop of imperial repression of heretics in which he had a hand, that the ecclesiastical hierarchy had the right and the duty to seek imperial coercion of heretics *qua* heretics.[27] The Donatists of North Africa raised two problems for Augustine. First, by their heretical ideas and preaching they cut themselves off from the Church and endangered the faith of the orthodox. When persecuted they claimed martyrdom, thereby attracting many zealots to their cause. Second, Donatist clerics and Circumcellion brigands attacked orthodox Christians and churches.

---

[24] *De Civitate Dei*, I, 21; P.L. 41, p. 35. Cf. C. 23 q. 5 c. 9.
[25] Above, n. 13.
[26] *Epist. 189*, 6; C.S.E.L. 57, p. 135. Cf. C. 23 q. 1 c. 3.
[27] Cf. Deane, *St Augustine*, ch. 6; Walzer, 'Exodus 32,' 5–8; P. R. L. Brown, 'St Augustine's Attitude to Religious Coercion,' *Journal of Roman Studies*, LIV (1964), 107–16; *Augustine*, esp. ch. 21; W. H. C. Frend, *The Donatist Church* (Oxford, 1952); Cochrane, *Christianity and Classical Culture*, pp. 326–36. Cf. above, introduction, n. 66.

In this harsh atmosphere Augustine pronounced his strongest condemnations on Circumcellion violence, and he did not always distinguish the heresy itself from the violence of its partisans.

As with the just war Augustine developed his position on persecution by references to both Testaments. The moral status of persecution was determined by its end. For example, both Pharaoh and Moses persecuted the Israelites, but the former was unrighteously motivated by *libido dominandi*, while the latter was moved by love in administering beneficial discipline. Hence the Church in urging persecution of heretics acted benevolently in expelling evil and was motivated by a desire to heal rather than by hatred. While both good and bad persecutors performed the same acts, true to his distinction between inward disposition and outward acts, Augustine saw punishment of heretics as a form of charity.[28] Christ's scourging of the temple and His persecution of Saul further justified ecclesiastical attempts to return heretics to orthodoxy. In the parable of the Great Supper (Luke 14: 16–24) Augustine interpreted the phrase 'compelle intrare' to refer to heretics and schismatics who were 'compelled to come in' to the orthodox Church. Once inside by compulsion, these gradually would give their assent to its teachings. Here Augustine explicitly forbade the use of violence, a fact often neglected because of his use of military metaphors and euphemisms for violence.[29] Since Peter had attempted to defend Christ with the sword, orthodox Christians could rightfully fight to defend the Church. Christ's injunction to 'resist not evil' did not preclude legitimate authorities from violently expelling impious and unjust men whose maintenance of power injured God.[30] In effecting coercion of heresy the Church even imitated God Himself.[31]

With its great influence the clergy was able to compel men to the good,[32] yet it was unable directly to employ violence in defense of

[28] *Epist. 93*, 2, 6 and 8; C.S.E.L. 34², pp. 450–2. (Cf. Walzer, 'Exodus 32,' 6; C. 23 q. 4 c. 37.) *Contra Epist. Parmeniani*, III, 1, 3; III, 5, 26; C.S.E.L. 51, pp. 100–4; 132–4. *Epist. 173*, 2; C.S.E.L. 44, p. 641. (Cf. C. 23 q. 4 c. 54.)

[29] *Contra Gaudentium*, I, 25, 28; C.S.E.L. 51, p. 227; *Sermo 112*, 7, 8; P.L. 38, pp. 647f.

[30] *Contra litteras Petiliani*, II, 19, 43; II, 80, 178; II, 88, 195; C.S.E.L. 52, pp. 44, 110, 120f. Augustine distorted the Gospel account to fit his own polemical purpose, for Christ had actually rebuked Peter for drawing his sword. *Epist. 185*, 22–3; C.S.E.L. 57, p. 21. Cf. C. 23 q. 4 c. 43.

[31] *Epist. 185*, 23; C.S.E.L. 57, p. 22. Cf. C. 23 q. 6 c. 1.

[32] *Contra Gaudentium*, I, 25, 28; C.S.E.L. 51, p. 227; *Sermo 112*, 7, 8; P.L. 38, pp. 647f.

the Church and the faith and so it must seek the aid of legitimate public authority. Augustine counseled orthodox clergy and ordinary African Christians to seek protection against violence from the emperors, who though they had formerly persecuted Christians now served the Lord by chastising heretics.[33] By this doctrine of imperial aid in religious persecution Augustine cast the mold for the medieval hierarchy's frequent appeals for the aid of secular authorities against its enemies. Medieval legists eagerly employed both Roman law and Augustine's doctrine of religious persecution as hammer and anvil to forge their justifications of wars and crusades. Recourse to public means of coercion had as purposes the protection of the orthodox and the conversion of the heretics themselves.

In reality Augustine's doctrines of the just war and the punishment of heresy were not so much coherent positions as clusters of ideas grouped around the central theme of sin and its punishment, for the terminology of *ulcisci iniurias* could serve a host of purposes. His tendency to shift imperceptibly from the legal to the moral order would later endow the just war with the purpose of punishing sinners of any stripe. To restrain this possibility Augustine himself limited execution of persecution to Roman officials, but his theory of punishment of sin and heresy would have been more coherent had he more strictly limited its purposes.[34] Similarly, by encouraging killing in defense of the fragile goods of this world, the just war served as a necessary and terrible evil, albeit the lesser of two evils.[35] It has been claimed that Augustine's just war merely restored particular and concrete rights that had been violated.[36] At face value this is what Augustine meant, but when viewed in the context of his attitudes as well as of his specific prescriptions, as it was in the Middle Ages, his just war also defended the whole moral order. His criteria of cause, intention, authority and obedience were all modeled on the Old Testament wars. For him, the Old Testament was a double

---

[33] *Epist. 87*, 8; C.S.E.L. 34², p. 404; *Epist. 185*, 7, 28; C.S.E.L. 57, pp. 26f. (Cf. C. 23 q. 3, cc. 2, 3.) *Epist. 93*, 3, 9–10; C.S.E.L. 34², pp. 453f. *De cathechizandis rudibus*, I, 27, 53; P.L. 40, p. 346.

[34] Cf. Hartigan, 'Saint Augustine on War and Killing,' 203f.; Deane, *St Augustine*, pp. 215–20, 223; Walzer, 'Exodus 32,' 7f. The latter two authors criticise Augustine's doctrine of persecution for its inconsistency with his general political assumptions and for its influence on later thought.

[35] J. Figgis, *The Political Aspects of the 'City of God'* (London, 1921), p. 65.

[36] Regout, *La guerre juste*, p. 44; Bainton, *Christian Attitudes*, p. 95.

image, serving both as a record of man's relationship to God now abrogated by Christ and as a body of precedents to guide future courses of action.[37] The New Testament doctrines of love and purity of motive were thus accommodated to the savagery of the Old, and the pacific witness was defeated. Since God as well as the emperor could order a just war, God's officials on earth could authorise a just war in defense not only of the moral order but in defense of the rights of the Church hierarchy.[38]

While this extension of the purposes of the just war was only accomplished in the Middle Ages, Augustine took the Roman just war that had atrophied under excessive formalism and imperial legislation and revived it on the moral level while managing to retain its essential Roman legal features. His ambiguous legacy, worked out with great inner turmoil in a specific historical situation and bearing the quirks of its author, guided the actions of early medieval men, resurfaced in Gratian's canon law and achieved systematisation in the Thomistic doctrine of the just war as one waged by a legitimate authority acting with just cause and righteous intention.

Already in the fifth century Augustine's influence inspired a number of spurious works, including the letter *Gravi de pugna* that assured Christians apprehensive over the outcome of a war that God was on their side and would grant victory in a just battle. Divine aid and favor were thus necessary to achieve victory, although Augustine himself had only claimed that Providence governed the outcome of wars without necessarily granting victory to the just party. The assumption of *Gravi de pugna* nevertheless reinforced the Germanic legal practice of the ordeal, whereby justice was proved by the result. Common opinion thereafter required that wars must serve religious ends in order to be justified, and conversely viewed successful wars as indications of divine favor.[39] One of the homilies of

---

[37] Brown, 'St. Augustine's Attitude to Religious Coercion,' p. 114.

[38] Brown, 'St. Augustine,' p. 16; cf. H. X. Arquillière, *L'augustinisme politique* (Paris, 1934), pp. 3f.

[39] Pseudo-Augustine, *Epist. 13*; P.L. 33, p. 1098: 'Gravi de pugna conqueris: dubites nolo, utile tibi tuisque dabo consilium: arripe manibus arma, oratio aures pulset Auctoris; quia quando pugnatur, Deus apertis caelis prospectat, et partem quam inspicit iustam, ibi dat palmam.' Cf. Gregory of Tours, *Historia Francorum*, VII, 32; M. G. H. *Scriptores Rerum Merovingicarum*, ed. W. Arndt (Hanover, 1885), I, 312f.; K. G. Cram, *Iudicium Belli. Zum Rechtscharakter des Krieges im deutschen Mittelalter* (Muenster and Cologne, 1955), pp. 8–15,

Maximus of Turin, also attributed to Augustine, condemned military service performed to acquire booty, and recommended the payment of wages to forestall fighting out of greed.[40]

The genuine Augustinian opinions in all their complexity were neglected, and even his formula for the just war disappeared from view. In its stead Isidore of Seville (d. 636) contrasted in more purely Roman fashion a just war waged upon formal declaration to recover lost goods or to repel and punish enemies with the unjust war waged out of madness and without legitimate cause.[41] Spoils belonging to the victors were to be divided according to the merits of the participants.[42] Although Isidore's jejune approach was outmoded even in Cicero's day and also failed to reflect the impact of Christianity and barbarian practice, it nevertheless served as the conduit through which the Roman just war was transmitted to the high Middle Ages.

With the collapse of Roman authority in the west, early medieval observers tailored ancient thought on warfare to their own necessities. Restraint of extra-legal violence was more important than the proper definition of the just war. Since most thinkers were ecclesiastics, early medieval thought betrayed a clerical bias that both encouraged religiously-motivated wars and cast suspicion on the morality of most acts of violence. In center stage were the careers of a pope, Gregory the Great, and an emperor, Charlemagne, that served as *exempla* for both debate and emulation.

Gregory's position was pivotal. Torn by strife between heretical Lombards and the vestiges of Roman authority, Italy looked to the pope as the last barrier against anarchy. Like an Old Testament patriarch, Gregory responded by seizing the military initiative. He organised the defense of threatened cities, gave copious counsel on

---

94. Only with the revival of jurisprudence in the twelfth century was the conviction of *Gravi de pugna* eclipsed.

40 Maximus of Turin, *Homilia 114*; P.L. 57, pp. 517–19. Cf. C. 23 q. 1 c. 5. Augustine's own similar but less forceful statement is in *Epist. 138*, 2, 15, cited above, n. 5. Cf. C. 23 q. 1 c. 2. Gratian's use of both passages fixed the condemnation of fighting for booty within the medieval theories.

41 Isidore of Seville, *Etymologiarum sive Originum Libri XX*, XVIII, 1, 2–4, ed. W. M. Lindsay (2 vols., Oxford, 1911), II (not paginated): 'Iustum bellum est quod ex praedicto geritur de rebus repetitis aut propulsandorum hostium causa. Iniustum bellum est quod de furore, non de legitima ratione initur...Nam extra ulciscendi aut propulsandorum hostium causa bellum geri iustum nullum potest.' Cf. C. 23 q. 2 c. 1. For the varying medieval emphasis on a formal declaration, see Cram, *Iudicium Belli*, pp. 187–91.

42 Isidore, *loc. cit.*, XVIII, 1, 8; XVIII, 2, 1 and 8.

tactical maneuvers, and even concluded truces, all the while linking the cause of God, St Peter and the papacy to specific military arrangements.[43] As a cleric lacking legitimate political authority, Gregory betrayed qualms about his own direct role, and so he urged the remaining imperial officials to act as *bellatores Domini* in suppressing Donatists and other enemies of the Church. Unlike Augustine, he explicitly considered the coercion of heretics as proper wars.[44] Gregory's life and works made difficult later attempts to distinguish between wars and persecution and between ecclesiastical and secular spheres of authority. Like the pseudo-Augustinian *Gravi de pugna*, Gregory was convinced that rulers could count on divine aid in performing military tasks at the behest of the clergy, while he insisted that their refusal to do so rendered them liable to horrible divine punishment inflicted by ferocious enemies.[45] The program of repression of barbarians and heretics adumbrated by Ambrose and Augustine had now found a papal executor.

Charlemagne eagerly adopted Gregory's program as his own, as is shown by the status accorded to a tract that counseled the just king to drive out impious men and to defend the Church and kingdom against all adversaries.[46] Papal prayers for success aided Charlemagne's wars against pagans and infidels, and in accepting the duty to defend the Church, he was assured of victory over all barbarian nations.[47] Charlemagne's far-reaching imperial program of religious, moral and political authority was celebrated by his court scholars, who linked the expansion of Christianity and the interests of the

[43] Gregory I, *Registrum Epistolarum*, II, 34; M.G.H. *Epistolae*, ed. P. Ewald and M. Hartmann (2 vols., Berlin, 1891–9), I, 130f. *Reg.* II, 7; I, 106; *Reg.* II, 32–3; I, 129; *Reg.* V, 36; I, 319. Cf. F. H. Dudden, *Gregory the Great* (2 vols., London, 1905), I, 15f., II, 9–13, and C. 23 q. I c. 7; C. 23 q. 8 cc. 17–18.

[44] *Reg.* I, 72–3; I, 92f.; *Reg.* IV, 7, 26, 32; I, 239, 261, 267; *Reg.* V, 6; I, 287. Cf. C. 23 q. 4 cc. 48–9; C. 23 q. 6 c. 4; C. 23 q. 8 c. 20. *Liber Moralium*, XXXI, 6, 8; P.L. 76, p. 576. Cf. Dudden, *Gregory*, II, 239.

[45] *Reg.* VIII, 4; II, 7. Dudden, *ibid.*, II, 42, 238f. Cf. Erdmann, *Kreuzzugsgedanke*, p. 8. Erdmann sees Augustine as justifying a *Ketzerkrieg* to purge the Church of heretics and Gregory as propounding a *Missionskrieg* to extend the Christian faith to new territories.

[46] Pseudo-Cyprian, *De XII Abusivis Saeculi*, 9; *Texte und Untersuchungen zur Geschichte der altchristlichen Literatur*, XXXIV¹, ed. S. Hellmann (Leipzig, 1909), 51f. For the influence of this tract on Carolingian thought, see W. Ullmann, *The Carolingian Renaissance and the Idea of Kingship* (London, 1969), pp. 51, n. 1, 117, 122; E. Peters, *The Shadow King*. '*Rex Inutilis' in Medieval Law and Literature, 751–1327* (New Haven, 1970), pp. 63, 70.

[47] M.G.H. *Epistolae Karolini Aevi*, IV, no. 92, 137f.; Thegan, *Vita Hludowici Imperatoris*, 5; M.G.H. *Scriptores*, II, ed. G. Pertz (Hanover, 1828), 591f. For other examples, see Ullmann, *ibid.*, pp. 126, 171, 177. Cf. L. Wallach, *Alcuin and Charlemagne* (Ithaca, 1959), pp. 14, 19f.

clergy to Charlemagne's various wars. The papal requests for aid legitimated Charlemagne's Italian campaigns against the Lombards, and the Saxons' refusal to submit to Christianity justified their conquest and forced conversion.[48] Wars were not seen as public, Roman, just, or holy, but rather as justified by Charlemagne's authority and ecclesiastical purposes. This lack of precise delimitation of various sorts of wars was characteristic of the Carolingian unitary conception of society, for as the new people of God the Franks admitted no separation of function between Church, clergy, laity, kingdom and Empire. Hence even clergymen, contrary to the ancient prohibitions, were now obliged to participate in the military campaigns of the Christian Emperor.[49]

After Charlemagne's death the Empire was beset with external invasion and internal strife. In response, the Frankish episcopate came to see itself as a separate estate that was constantly subjected to violence at the hands of the feuding heirs of Charlemagne. Later Carolingian writers bent their efforts to a defense of themselves and their churches that resuscitated the Carolingian *deus ex machina*, the holy war of expansion and conversion. Writing around the middle of the ninth century, men like Hincmar of Rheims, Hrabanus Maurus and Sedulius Scotus resorted to the Augustinian *bellum Deo auctore* and the assurance of *Gravi de pugna* to encourage wars to defend the Empire and the faith. The Old Testament wars prefigured the Church's perpetual *bellum iustissimum* against the manifold enemies of its unity. Such just, necessary and divinely-aided warfare strengthened Christian resolve to execute divine vengeance and to seek a higher spiritual peace rather than to remain content with a temporal peace that rendered men timid and lax.[50]

---

[48] E.g. Alcuin, *Epist.* 6, 7, 25; M.G.H. *Epistolae*, IV, 31f., 66; Einhard, *Vie de Charlemagne*, 6, 7, ed. L. Halphen (Paris, 1923), pp. 18–24. Alcuin had qualms about the harshness of Charlemagne's policies, but the court scholars were capable of whitewashing his massacres: Alcuin, *Epist.* 110–11, 113, 211; *Epistolae*, IV, 157, 160, 164, 352; cf. H. Fichtenau, *The Carolingian Empire*, trans. P. Munz (Oxford, 1957), pp. 21f.

[49] Cf. Fichtenau, *ibid.*, p. 93; Ullmann, *Carolingian Renaissance*, pp. 17, 21. For the problem of participation in warfare by higher clerics, see now F. Prinz, *Klerus und Krieg* (Stuttgart, 1971).

[50] Hincmar of Rheims, *De Regis Persona et Regio Ministerio*, 2, 7–12; P.L. 125, pp. 835, 840–3. Cf. above, nn. 39, 46. Hrabanus Maurus, *De Universo*, XX, 1; P.L. 111, p. 534; *Epist.* XV, 3; M.G.H. *Epistolae*, V, ed. E. Dümmler (Berlin, 1899), 408; *Commentarium in Paralipomena*, IV, 13; P.L. 109, p. 486; *Appendix ad Expositionem in Librum Iudith*, 10; P.L. 109, p. 622. Hrabanus was among those ecclesiastics who showed a renewed interest in Vegetius' *Epitoma Rei Militaris*: Prinz, *Klerus und Krieg*, pp. 111f. Sedulius Scotus, *Liber de Rectoribus*

While these writers merely reasserted by now traditional ideals, the goal of the Carolingian holy war had been revalued from aggression to defense. Thus Agobard of Lyons contrasted Charlemagne's foreign wars with the present unjust internal discord. The clergy should pray for the subjection of barbarians to the Empire and for an end to the barbarisation of the Empire's own subjects.[51] More pointedly, Hincmar of Rheims lamented that while Christians had in earlier times suffered from pagan attacks, now contrary to divine and human law the Church was suffering at the hands of Christian kings who were supposed to be its guardians, and then he predictably favored a new campaign against pagans. Here Hincmar seemed to equate the Church with its upper clergy and their property, for he argued that ecclesiastical property should be immune from royal interference on pain of perdition.[52] The strife of secular officials was illegal, unjust and deserving of excommunication, and the harassment of bishops was without rational cause since their tasks included the preaching of peace and wars against the vices, but excluded participation in wars of earthly kings.[53] Hincmar thus contradicted the earlier ecclesiastical involvement in Carolingian wars, but nevertheless his solution to internal violence was the holy war, justified as before by the clergy but now to be waged without its active participation.

The endemic violence likewise influenced ecclesiastical attitudes toward military service in general. Agobard recalled the early Church when he advised *milites Christi* to bear witness to their faith not by killing but by dying, and Hrabanus Maurus considered them as true Israelites able to protect the Church and combat evil without material weapons.[54] Agobard went so far as to dispute the assumption that

Christianis, 13, 16–17; *Quellen und Untersuchungen zur lateinischen Philologie des Mittelalters*, I¹ (ed. S. Hellmann, Munich, 1909), 60, 74f., 77f.

[51] Agobard of Lyons, *Liber Apologeticum. Liber pro Filiis et contra Iudith Uxorem Ludovici Pii*, I, 3–4; M.G.H. *Scriptores*, xv¹ (ed. G. Waitz), 275f.

[52] Hincmar, *Epistola Synodi Carisiacensis ad Hludowicum Regem Germaniae Directa*, 5–7, 15; M.G.H. *Leges*, section II, tome 2, ed. A. Boretius and V. Krause (Hanover, 1897), 430–2, 438. For Hincmar's view of the royal duty to defend and protect Church property, see Ullmann, *Carolingian Renaissance*, p. 123.

[53] Hincmar, *Epistola Synodi Carisiacensis*, 13, 15; M.G.H. *Leges*, II, 437, 440. For other examples of ecclesiastical protests, cf. *Collectio Sangallensis*, 30, 42; M.G.H. *Leges*, ed. K. Zeumer (Hanover, 1886), 415, 425.

[54] Agobard, *Adversus Legem Gundobadi*, 3; M.G.H. *Epistolae*, v, 161. Hrabanus Maurus, *Commentarium in Librum Iudicum*, I, 13; P.L. 108, p. 1141. Cf. Sedulius Scotus, *Liber*, 15, 70.

divine judgment was revealed by the outcome of battle, and Sedulius Scotus qualified his approval of warfare when he contrasted the good prince who sought peace even for his enemies and only went to war for a necessary and just cause with the wicked prince who continued to fight after refusing an offer of peace.[55] These equivocal, incomplete and often inconsistent opinions indicated a hollowness of conviction about Carolingian warfare and its providential role. The tensions between Old and New Testaments were dimly perceived but these writers were unable to reconcile them because in their proud lack of originality they were unable to arrive at a clear distinction between sacred and profane activities. Hence their Christian soldiers drew upon a mixed arsenal of spiritual and material weapons in wars against a motley assemblage of enemies. With the Empire now split into warring camps of orthodox Christians, the just war was bound to atrophy at the hands of a now querelous and frightened clergy.

Clerical disenchantment with lay violence was also translated into a systematic suspicion of warfare and killing expressed in the penitential literature. Early in the ninth century Halitgar of Cambrai levied a penance on anyone who killed in a public military expedition or who killed out of hostility or covetousness.[56] According to the *Poenitentiale Pseudo-Theodori* of about 835, a penance was imposed for homicide committed in a public war or on orders of one's lord, who in turn incurred a ten-year penance.[57] The *Poenitentiale Arundel*, written at the end of the turbulent ninth century, imposed a penance of a full year for homicide in a royal battle and a penance of two years in a war of doubtful justice waged by a prince rather than a king. Even if a war was clearly just, a one-year penance was still necessary.[58] Hrabanus Maurus concluded that penances should be levied for homicides committed in wars between Carolingian kings because God probably considered them culpable. Hrabanus himself was convinced that such homicides were motivated by avarice or the

---

[55] Agobard, *Liber contra Iudicium Dei*, 5; P.L. 104, p. 254; *Sententiae, ibid.*, p. 263. Sedulius Scotus, *Liber*, 17, 77f.

[56] Halitgar of Cambrai, *Liber Poenitentialis*, tit. *De homicidio*, P.L. 105, p. 702. Cf. H. Schmitz, *Die Bussbücher und die Bussdisciplin der Kirche* (2 vols., Mainz, 1883, Düsseldorf, 1898), I, 46; H. Wasserschleben, *Die Bussordnungen der abendländischen Kirche* (Halle, 1851), p. 81.

[57] *Poenitentiale Pseudo-Theodori*, VI, 14; in Wasserschleben, *ibid.*, pp. 587f. Cf. *ibid.*, 154, 173, 225, 478; Schmitz, *Bussbücher*, I, 555, 559.

[58] *Poenitentiale Arundel*, 11; in Schmitz, *Bussbücher*, I, 441.

desire to curry the favor of temporal lords in contempt of the precepts of the eternal Lord.[59] There was a great difference between someone who sought to destroy Christian peace and one who desired to defend equity against iniquity with earthly weapons.[60] Hrabanus looked to both Testaments in a vain search for specific guidance, but in the end he was forced to draw upon his own observation and experience.

The penitential literature betrayed the suspicion that almost all wars of contemporary princes were tainted with sin that required penance, and yet this suspicion did not amount to a unified and frontal attack upon warfare itself. After all, Hincmar felt that those who died faithfully in war merited prayers, offerings and masses.[61] Indeed, the mechanical nature of most penitentials did not so much deny the possibility of just warfare as it exemplified the 'outwardness' of Carolingian ethical attitudes that, quite in contrast to Augustine, placed more emphasis on actions than on intentions.[62] For this reason Carolingian attitudes toward warfare could harbor without reconciliation an enthusiastic support for the holy war and a deep suspicion of killing even in a just war. Unable to distinguish between holy wars and just wars, both the enthusiasm and the suspicion survived the Carolingian era to enrich the high medieval debates.[63]

The writings of contemporary popes exhibited similar ambivalence toward the legitimacy of warfare and the proper role of the clergy. On one hand Leo IV, himself active in combatting Saracen raids along the Italian coast, in 853 urged the Frankish army to combat the enemies of their faith and region. He also expressed the hope that whosoever died while fighting enemies of the faith and the Christian *patria* would merit eternal life.[64] In 876 John VIII more

---

[59] Hrabanus Maurus, *Liber Poenitentium*, 15; P.L. 112, pp. 1411f.

[60] *Ibid.*, pp. 1412f.; *Poenitentiale*, 4; P.L. 110, pp. 471f. Cf. Erdmann, *Kreuzzugsgedanke*, p. 14.

[61] Hincmar, *De Regis Persona*, 15; P.L. 125, p. 844.

[62] Fichtenau, *Carolingian Empire*, p. 172.

[63] The suspicion of all killing in warfare continued to nip at the heels of the just war theories. For the imposition of penances on warriors in the tenth and eleventh centuries, see below, n. 73, H. E. J. Cowdrey, 'Bishop Ermenfrid of Sion and the Penitential Ordinance following the Battle of Hastings,' *Journal of Ecclesiastical History*, xx (1969), 225–42; and R. Southern, *Western Society and the Church in the Middle Ages* (Baltimore, 1970), pp. 40, 226. For the survival of the suspicion in the high Middle Ages, see below, ch. 3, n. 17 and ch. 6, n. 7.

[64] Leo IV, *Epist. 28*, 1; M.G.H. *Epistolae*, v, ed. A. de Hirsch-Gereuth (Berlin, 1899), 601.

directly implored Charles the Bald and his bishops for aid against Saracen pirates, and expressed the fear that without such aid the Christian religion and the imperial glory would soon be reduced to ruins.[65] Beset by internal strife, Charles was unable to honor the papal request, so John, understanding the situation, then forbade the counts and bishops of Louis the German's kingdom to invade that of Charles. In his opinion, those who fought the Church were doomed while those who died in its defense were crowned by their nobly-shed blood. Later John went so far as to promise indulgences to those who died defending the Church and salvation to those who fell in wars against infidels and pagans.[66] The Saracen threat was probably not as serious as John pictured it, and was based more on their violence than their infidelity. Like Hincmar, John condemned all wars between Christians, perhaps because his major enemies were local Roman Christians who eventually had him murdered.[67] Yet his momentary expedient took on an afterlife in the crusades.

A quite different attitude toward non-believers was advanced by Nicholas I, who reserved the judgment of non-Christians to God alone and would prohibit their conversion by force, and yet he also forbade penitents to use weapons except against pagans.[68] To clerics who were by their office sufficiently fortified by the privileges of Peter he denied the right to use instruments of coercion.[69] The waging of war, occasioned by diabolical frauds, gave vent to cupidity, wrath and jealousy. If necessity did not justify a war, it should not be waged during Lent or at any other time, and yet Nicholas allowed wars in defense of property, *patria* or paternal rights to be waged whenever necessary and whenever the means of defense were available, lest man by his inactivity tempt God to wreak

Cf. C. 23 q. 5 c. 46; C. 23 q. 8 c. 9. For the context and importance of Leo's remarks, cf. Brundage, *Canon Law and the Crusader*, p. 22; Villey, *La croisade*, pp. 28f.; Erdmann, *Kreuzzugsgedanke*, pp. 23f.

[65] John VIII, *Epist. 22, Epist. 36*; M.G.H. *Epistolae*, ed. E. Caspar (Berlin, 1928), 20f., 36. Cf. Ullmann, *Carolingian Renaissance*, p. 123.

[66] *Epist. 150*, 126; *Epistolae passim Collectae*, no. 8; M.G.H. *Epistolae*, VII, 325. Cf. Brundage, *Canon Law and the Crusader*, pp. 22f.

[67] F. E. Engreen, 'Pope John the Eighth and the Arabs,' *Speculum*, XX (1945), 319, 325, 329.

[68] Nicholas I, *Responsa ad Consulta Bulgarorum*, 41 and 102; M.G.H. *Epistolae*, VI, ed. E. Perels (Berlin, 1925), 582f., 599. *Epist. 139*; *ibid.*, 659.

[69] *Epist. 60*; *ibid.*, 371. Elsewhere Nicholas condemned as incompatible with their spiritual duties the bishops' involvement even in mounting watch for pirates: *Epist. 38*; *ibid.*, 309f. Cf. Prinz, *Klerus und Krieg*, pp. 22f. and C. 23 q. 8 c. 19.

vengeance Himself.[70] Safely within the *militia Christi* tradition, Nicholas strongly restricted the right to war, but his grudging tolerance of defensive wars was understandable in a violent age when few clerical observers cared to deny the right of self-defense to a man or kingdom.

After the chaos of the tenth century, the order and authority that waxed anew in the eleventh encouraged ecclesiastics to seek new ways of limiting the violence of the lay nobility and of harnessing it to clerical purposes. The peace movement, the Investiture Contest and the crusades all contributed to a more precise justification of war that found its way into nascent canonical jurisprudence.

Since the petty violence was often directed against churches and clerics, local churchmen joined forces with peasants and merchants in peace associations. Promulgated in synods and councils, the Truce of God limited the use of violence to certain time periods, while the Peace of God declared certain occupational classes, such as clerics, to be immune from all violence. The peace movement was not necessarily pacifistic, for it was directed against violence rather than war itself, and sometimes waged a feud against transgressors of its statutes.[71]

A more frontal attack upon the usual wars of lay nobles was launched during the Investiture Contest by Hildebrand, who as Pope Gregory VII held kings responsible for the deaths incurred in their wars for earthly power, wars that led men to perdition.[72] In the Roman synod of 1078 Gregory declared that knights could scarcely pursue their profession without sin, and excluded them from penance unless they put aside their weapons. Implicitly denying any legitimate purpose to purely secular warfare, Gregory then added that knights undergoing penance could nevertheless fight to defend justice on the advice of their bishops.[73] Kings and soldiers were useful

---

[70] *Responsa*, 46; *ibid.*, 585. The scriptural antecedents of this passage are Deuteronomy 6: 16 and Joshua 6: 1–20. For the importance of this letter, see Erdmann, *Kreuzzugsgedanke*, p. 16. Canonists and theologians would use this passage to support their view that wars could be waged even during Lent when necessary: C. 23 q. 8 c. 15.

[71] Recent study of the peace movement has been summarised in H. E. J. Cowdrey, 'The Peace and the Truce of God in the Eleventh Century,' *Past and Present*, no. 46 (1970), 42–67.

[72] Gregory VII, *Registrum*, VIII, 21; M.G.H. *Epistolae Selectae*, II, ed. E. Caspar (Berlin, 1920–3), 559. Cf. K. Leyser, 'The Polemics of the Papal Revolution,' *Trends in Medieval Political Thought*, pp. 57f.

[73] *Reg.* VI, 5b, c. 6; *Epist. Selectae*, 404. Cf. the manual *De Vera et Falsa Penitencia*, 15, 30; P.L. 40, p. 1125; W. Ullmann, *The Growth of Papal Government in the Middle Ages* (3rd–

to Christian society when on papal command they waged a *bellum Christi* against heretics and other enemies of God and the Roman Church.[74] Even bishops were bound by oath to aid the papacy with troops when so ordered.[75] In effect Gregory was attempting to emancipate the papacy from dependence on the secular ruler for military aid, for he entered into a military alliance with the Normans in southern Italy and urged his Saxon allies to wage a *iustum bellum* against Henry IV, whom he considered not only as an enemy of the papacy and Christianity itself but also as linked to the barbarians of former times.[76] The papal role as Gregory envisaged it included leading an army of fifty thousand men who had answered his summons to defend the faith by a campaign to liberate the Holy Land.[77] Completing the program of the first Gregory, Gregory VII thus accomplished a radical transformation of the meaning of *militia Christi* from that of spiritual conflicts and monkish asceticism to the literal meaning of knightly bellicosity now obedient to papal purposes and initiative.[78] This pivotal transformation made possible the shaping of the crusading movement by Urban II.

As a French Cluniac monk Urban II had observed the operation of the peace movement, and as pope he capitalised upon Gregory's spiritualisation of warfare which in the wars against Henry IV had turned Europe against itself in a kind of internal crusade. Seeking ways to lessen the incidence of violence within European Christian society, Urban in 1093 promulgated the Truce of God at the Council of Troia, and in his famous speech to the Council of Clermont in 1095 he exhorted knights to desist from their wicked combats against

4th ed., London, 1970), p. 376; Villey, *La croisade*, p. 38. Wrenched out of context, this Gregorian passage took on a different cast: De penit., dist. 5 c. 6; Peter the Lombard, *Sententiarum*, IV, 16, 3. Cf. below, ch. 3, n. 17; ch. 6, n. 7.

[74] *Reg.* I, 46; II, 49; IX, 3–4; *Epist. Selectae*, 70, 190, 576, 578. Cf. Ullmann, *Papal Government*, pp. 289 n. 1, 303f.

[75] Cf. *Reg.* VI, 17a; *Epist. Selectae*, 428f. Probably because it violated the tradition of clerical non-combatance, and in spite of Gregory's attack on custom, this part of the episcopal oath never was widely used: Ullmann, *Papal Government*, p. 296; Erdmann, *Kreuzzugsgedanke*, p. 196.

[76] Lambert of Hersfeld, cited in Villey, *La croisade*, p. 37.

[77] Reg. I, 49; II, 31; *Epist. Selectae*, 75, 166f. Cf. Ullmann, *Papal Government*, pp. 306f.; Leyser, 'Polemics,' pp. 54f., 58.

[78] Erdmann, *Kreuzzugsgedanke*, pp. 186f., 314; I. Robinson, 'Gregory VII and the Soldiers of Christ,' *History*, LVIII (1973), 169–92. For the support marshaled for this innovation by such Gregorians as Manegold of Lautenbach and Gerhoh of Reichersberg, see Erdmann, *ibid.*, 216f.; Villey, *La croisade*, pp. 30f.; P. Classen, *Gerhoch von Reichersberg* (Wiesbaden, 1960), pp. 46, 102, 129, 132, 147, 419.

Christians and to fight the righteous war against the infidel. As incentive he promised the spiritual reward of heaven and the temporal rewards of peace, prosperity and plunder. In effect he preached a papal war waged by knights against infidels in the Holy Land.[79] Since order at home was necessary for the success of the venture, violence was both suppressed by granting crusaders immunity from violence according to the Peace of God, and redirected against the distant infidel. It was not so much the Augustinian just war as it was the fanaticism of the crusade distantly sired by Augustine's anti-Donatist writings that finally triumphed over the pacifism of the early Church. Now the Christian soldier was a warrior whose battles against the enemies of the faith were both ordered and glorified by the papacy.[80]

The most explosive synthesis of Gregorianism and the crusading ideal was found in the writings of St Bernard of Clairvaux, who attributed possession and direction of the sword of material coercion to the pope and limited the role of secular authorities solely to its exercise.[81] Unlike the more radical Gregorians, however, Bernard championed a cooperation of secular and ecclesiastical authority, for he called upon the Emperor to fulfill his duties as defender of the Church by combatting schism and heresy, and obliged bishops to participate in their king's expeditions.[82] Bernard's apologia for the

---

[79] *Concilium Trojanum*; P.L. 151, p. 748; Mansi, *Sacrorum Conciliorum Nova et Amplissima Collectio*, xx, 789; *The Councils of Urban II*, I, *Decreta Claromontensia*, ed. R. Somerville (Amsterdam, 1972), 74. Recently H. E. J. Cowdrey has focused on the events and attitudes that laid the groundwork for Urban's explosive synthesis of the holy war, pilgrimage and peace movement traditions: 'Pope Urban II's Preaching of the First Crusade,' *History*, LV (1970), 177–88; 'Cluny and the First Crusade,' *Revue Bénédictine*, LXXXIII (1973), 285–311; and 'Peace and Truce of God,' esp. 57, 62. Mr Cowdrey has kindly allowed me to see a draft of his forthcoming article, 'The Genesis of the Crusades,' which pursues at greater length the background of the crusades that is sketched here.

[80] Cf. H. Hoffmann, *Gottesfriede und Treuga Dei*, M.G.H.*Schriften* xx (1964), p. 223; Erdmann, *Kreuzzugsgedankens*, pp. 223, 308; Windass, *Christianity versus Violence*, pp. 43, 49.

[81] Bernard of Clairvaux, *De Consideratione*, IV, 3, 7; *Opera Omnia*, III (Rome, 1963), 454. The diversity of interpretations surrounding the passage need not concern us here, for it is clear at least that Bernard intended that the pope direct the use of the sword. Cf. *Epist. 256*, 1; P.L. 182, pp. 463f.; Pissard, *La guerre sainte*, p. 22; Ullmann, *Papal Government*, pp. 431f.

[82] *Epist. 139*, 1; P.L. 183, pp. 293f.; *Epist. 244*, 4; P.L. 182, pp. 301f. The phrase 'accingere gladio tuo super femur tuum' is based on Exodus 32: 27, the narration of the 'holy war' of the Levites. Cf. also *In Canticorum Sermo 66*, 12, 14; P.L. 183, pp. 1101f. Cf. *De Moribus et Officio Episcoporum*, VIII, 31; P.L. 182, pp. 829f.; Pissard, *ibid.*, pp. 19f.; Ullmann, *Papal Government*, p. 432; S. Chodorow, *Christian Political Theory and Church Politics in the Mid-Twelfth Century. The Ecclesiology of Gratian's Decretum* (Berkeley and Los Angeles, 1972), pp. 58f., 228.

Templars contrasted the evil of purely secular military service with the glory of warfare waged in defense of God and His Church. Locating the justice of warfare in its intention and exuding the confidence of *Gravi de pugna*, Bernard assumed that a righteous cause necessarily produced a favorable result, while the pursuit of unrighteous intentions rendered a warrior not only ineffective in battle but also a murderer doomed to eternal damnation. Living in communal poverty, fraternal love, chastity and virtue, the 'new' knights of Christ (*equites Christi*) by contrast committed not homicide but 'malicide.' Among their numbers were former criminals who now as true Israelites avenged their Savior without quarter. Europe's loss of its violent elements was the Holy Land's gain of faithful defenders who incarnated the ideal qualities of both monks and warriors.[83] Never was the connection between the peace movement and the crusade made clearer, nor was the glorification of Christian militarism more intoxicatingly expressed. The *deus ex machina* of the crusades enabled Bernard to achieve a mystical amalgam in which pacifism and religious bellicosity, clergy and laity, lost their separate forces and identities.

While clerics themselves were not permitted to fight wars, save for Bernard's knight-monks, the guiding role of the ecclesiastical hierarchy was reinforced by churchmen who, less given to flights of imagination than Bernard, turned their efforts to the Christianisation of chivalry within the elastic confines of canon law. Around 1085 the Gregorian Anselm of Lucca published a *Collectio Canonum* that assembled texts, drawn mainly from Augustine and Gregory I, to support ecclesiastical rights to direct the *ius gladii* and *vis armata* against heretics, excommunicates, enemies of peace and infidels.[84] Anselm's collection served as an effective montage of texts justifying

---

[83] *Liber ad Milites Templi de Laude Novae Militiae*, I, 2, II, 3, III, 4–6, IV, 7–8, V, 10, XIII, 31; *Opera Omnia*, III, 215–21, 223, 239. Cf. P. Alphandéry and A. Dupront, *La chrétienté et l'idée de croisade* (2 vols., Paris, 1954–9), I, 158f. Bernard's influence on the crusading idea has recently been discussed in E. O. Blake, 'The Formation of the "Crusade Idea",' *Journal of Ecclesiastical History*, XXI (1970), 27–9. Cf. Peter the Venerable's comparison of the crusades to the Old Testament wars, whereby crusaders became the 'exercitus Dei viventis'; *The Letters of Peter the Venerable*, 130, 162, ed. G. Constable (2 vols., Cambridge, Mass., 1967), I, 327f., 395.

[84] E.g. *Collectio Canonum*, XII, 53–4, 68–72 (= Cod. I, I, 2; I, 5, 2–5); XIII, 5, 6, 8, 14–16, 28–9. Cf. A. Stickler, 'Il potere coattivo materiale della Chiesa nella Riforma Gregoriana secondo Anselmo di Lucca,' *Studi Gregoriani*, II (1947), 235–85, especially the table of canons

coercion against any and all enemies of the Church. More moderate and comprehensive were the early twelfth-century collections of Ivo of Chartres that included all manner of texts dealing with warfare without attempting to reconcile the many contradictions. For example, Ivo balanced a text that levied an ecclesiastical ban on deserters with Hrabanus Maurus' imposition of penance even for killing in a just war.[85] Many extracts concerned the Gregorians' doctrine of ecclesiastical coercion,[86] and Ivo included the pseudo-Augustinian *Gravi de pugna*.[87]

These various eleventh- and twelfth-century developments, couched in a luxury of military metaphors, represented the papacy's declaration of independence from the Empire and from secular princes in general. With the traditional roles reversed, the ecclesiastical hierarchy possessed and utilised its own authority to punish its manifold enemies. The most significant contribution of this period was the synthesis of the crusade out of the holy war and the just war. Before Augustine, the holy war had been almost any war waged on religious grounds by men who were convinced that God Himself approved, as with the Levites' action in Exodus 32. Under Augustinian influence the Carolingian holy war had been the prerogative of legitimate secular authority often acting with clerical prodding. Now the crusade had become a specifically medieval juridical institution unrelated to more usual notions of public welfare and defense of the *patria*. This holy war of the medieval Church was also a just war, in view of the religious foundations of Augustine's just war. As an instrument of unity it encompassed religious virtue, organisation and discipline. Now directly authorised by the pope rather than God, the crusade as an expression of the ecclesiastical *ius gladii* was the Church's ultimate just war, sharing with other just wars the requirements of authority, necessity, just cause, right

between 248 and 249, 264, 266, 279f. Cf. Anselm's *Liber contra Wibertum*; M.G.H. *Libelli de Lite*, I, 522–7; Erdmann, *Kreuzzugsgedanke*, pp. 225, 228f.

[85] Ivo, *Decretum*, x, 122: 'qui arma proiciunt in praelio.' (The text is a radical transformation of canon 3 of the council of Arles that read 'qui arma proiciunt in pace': Erdmann, *Kreuzzugsgedanke*, pp. 247f.). *Decretum*, x, 152.

[86] E.g. Ivo, *Decretum*, x, 59, 90, 95, 99. Many canons of the *Decretum* were also included in Ivo's *Panormia*. The texts are in P.L. 161.

[87] *Decretum*, x, 109; *Panormia*, vIII, 43. Cf. above, n. 39. Had the confidence of this letter been incorporated into Gratian's analysis of war, the shape of the high medieval theories may well have been quite different.

intention and defense of the *patria*.[88] As a peculiarly medieval hybrid, the crusade would have a long and varied future.

Freed from the yoke of the Roman Empire, the Church now expanded its territorial influence and its discipline by ever more frequent military engagements, all the while guarding as a kind of counterpoint a deep suspicion of military service and warfare not firmly under its control. In this atmosphere the lack of original analysis of the just war itself enabled the construction of a just war built on the strength of traditional and accepted notions as is witnessed by the calls for a holy war or crusade as a way to internal peace, appeals that were voiced by Churchmen otherwise as diverse as Agobard of Lyons and Urban II. The notion of defense comprised defense both of individual churches, their clerics and property, and defense of the Church seen as the universal *patria*. Wars and crusades were legitimate instruments for realising the ideal of justice which in Gregorian terms was viewed as righteousness.[89] From this flowed the common and confident assertion that God automatically granted victory to righteous warriors. This Christianisation of warfare encouraged neglect of just wars waged for purely secular goals, and yet Gratian's synthesis of both ancient and medieval concepts of just warfare eventually passed into the arsenal of secular rulers who desired to maintain internal peace and build a strong military defense.

[88] Walzer, 'Exodus 32,' 7f. Since Walzer does not recognise the juridical nature of the crusades, his interpretation of Exodus 32 does not apply to them. A similar lack of distinction between holy war, crusade and just war detracts from the otherwise excellent study of Pissard, *La guerre sainte*. Cf. Erdmann, *Kreuzzugsgedanke*, p. 1; A. Dupront, 'Le mythe de croisade. Etude de sociologie religieuse' (6 vols., Thèse, Lettres, Université de Paris, 1956), I, 22, 107; VI^2, 45; Villey, *La croisade*, pp. 262, 273, 275f.; Stickler, 'Il potere coattivo materiale,' 264, 279f.; Regout, *La guerre juste*, p. 49.

[89] Erdmann, *Kreuzzugsgedanke*, pp. 6–9, 26; Ullmann, *Papal Government*, pp. 307f. For the notion of defense of *patria* applied to Christian society at large, see Kantorowicz, *King's Two Bodies*, pp. 232–49.

Chapter 2

THE MEDIEVAL ROMANISTS'
ANALYSIS OF WAR

The practice of Roman law never completely died out after the barbarian migrations of the early Middle Ages. In Italy, southern France and Visigothic Spain kings promulgated and attempted to enforce law codes based on Roman law, and the Carolingians continued the tradition of Roman law legislation, especially in their Italian territories. While Roman law was taught in the Italian schools that survived, the science of Roman jurisprudence did not undergo further significant development until the late eleventh century, when semi-autonomous city-states began to exercise jurisdiction over their own affairs. Under the leadership of a certain Irnerius, Bologna became the center of a revival of Roman jurisprudence in the twelfth century. The Romanists or civil lawyers were confronted with the need to gloss and comment upon the fundamental texts contained in Justinian's *Corpus Iuris Civilis*, especially those in the *Codex*, the *Digesta* of legal opinions, and the *Institutiones*. The modest task of the Glossators was to explicate Justinian's compilations with an eye to contemporary practice. Most prominent among their efforts was the *Glossa Ordinaria* or ordinary gloss completed by Accursius around 1250. Later Romanists who commented upon this gloss and sought to apply Roman law more precisely to contemporary practice came to be known as post-Glossators or Commentators.[1]

---

[1] Among the copious secondary literature on the survival and revival of Roman jurisprudence the following works may be cited: P. Vinogradoff, *Roman Law in Medieval Europe*, 2nd ed. (Oxford, 1929; rep. with a bibliographical foreword by P. Stein, Cambridge, 1967); E. Meynial, 'Roman Law,' *The Legacy of the Middle Ages*, ed. C. Crump and E. F. Jacob (Oxford, 1926), pp. 363–99; C. Calisse, *A History of Italian Law*, trans. L. Register (Boston, 1928); H. Kantorowicz, *Studies in the Glossators of the Roman Law* (Cambridge, 1938); H. J. Wolff, *Roman Law: An Historical Introduction* (Norman, Oklahoma, 1950), pp. 162–206; H. F. Jolowicz, *Historical Introduction to the Study of Roman Law* (3rd ed., Cambridge, 1972); F. Calasso, *Medio Evo del diritto* (Milan, 1954); M. Cappelletti, J. H. Merryman and J. M. Perillo, *The Italian Legal System: An Introduction* (Stanford, 1967), pp. 1–29. Two comprehensive treatments are F. Savigny, *Geschichte des römischen Rechts im Mittelalter* (2nd ed., 7 vols., Heidelberg, 1834–51) and M. Conrat, *Geschichte der Quellen und Literatur des römischen Rechts im früheren Mittelalter* (Leipzig, 1891; rep. Aalen, 1963). Helpful basic

On the one hand the task of the Romanists was made easier because they were not directly faced with the necessity to accommodate Christian doctrine to Roman law. Since they did not have to reconcile Old and New Testaments, their glosses did not deal with the internal tensions of Christian ethics that confronted canonists and theologians. Their discussions of war focused rather on the Roman law notions of self-defense, restraint of private and illicit violence, the conditions justifying recourse to war and the legal consequences of war. On the other hand they were forced to incorporate within the scope of their debates the contemporary feudal customs and the legislation of the Holy Roman Empire that differed significantly from the received Roman law. Justinian's corpus itself did not explicitly invoke the Roman conception of the just war, consequently the Romanists were not forced to advance any original theories of the just war, but rather attempted to tailor, consolidate and refine concepts handed down to them in view of the changing conditions of the high Middle Ages. Yet canon lawyers of this period were conversant with the Roman law, and some, like Innocent IV and Hostiensis, were themselves experts in Roman law who drew heavily on their knowledge of it when they elaborated theories of the just war. In this way such Roman law concepts as immediacy and moderation found their way into the canonistic analysis of war.[2]

THE RIGHT OF SELF-DEFENSE

The fundamental Roman law notion of self-defense against violence was the maxim, 'vim vi defendere omnes leges omniaque iura permittunt.'[3] All laws and statutes permitted the use of violence in defense against an aggressor. The classic example of this right was killing with impunity a thief who was attempting to steal during the night. In daytime the thief could be killed with impunity only when

---

information is supplied by S. Sass, 'Research in Roman Law; A guide to the Sources and their English Translations,' *Law Library Journal*, LVI (1963), 210–33; 'Medieval Roman Law; A Guide to the Sources and Literature,' *ibid.*, LVIII (1965), 134–59. The series *Ius Romanum Medii Aevi* (Milan, 1961–) and the *Bulletino dell'Istituto di diritto romano* contain more recent scholarship.

[2] On the relations between Roman and canon law in the high Middle Ages, see especially P. Legendre, *La pénétration du droit romain dans le droit canonique classique de Gratien à Innocent IV (1140–1254)* (Paris, 1964).

[3] Dig. 9.2.45.4. Cf. S. Kuttner, *Kanonistische Schuldlehre von Gratian bis auf die Dekretalen Gregors IX (Studi e Testi*, 64; Vatican City, 1935), pp. 334–9.

he was armed.[4] In the common opinion of the Glossators as expressed by Azo, the right of self-defense was derived both from the relationships established by nature among men and by the *ius gentium*.[5] Yet the exercise of this right was restricted, for under certain conditions violence used in self-defense was deemed culpable, and the right was also restrained when recourse to judicial authority was possible. Indeed, as Accursius said, the purpose of law was to enable men to resist violence.[6]

The ancient Roman law had developed two concepts that narrowed the conditions in which use of violence was licit, *incontinenti* and *moderamen inculpatae tutelae*. *Incontinenti* referred to the immediate repulsion of a violent attack on one's person, which Ulpian considered legal.[7] By contrast, repulsion of violence *ex intervallo*, after a delay, was considered culpable. *Moderamen inculpatae tutelae* or 'moderation of blameless protection' referred to the observance of reasonable limits when violently defending oneself or one's property. The temperance of an intended victim's actions rendered them blameless.[8] According to the Code, a person could legally defend his rightful possessions against violent attack when he observed the moderation proper to the circumstances.[9] These two concepts were evolved to confine the resort to private violence to purely defensive measures and to prevent vengeance and protracted violence.[10]

The medieval Romanists usually invoked these two concepts together when they discussed self-defense.[11] They expressed some doubt about the length of time during which the victim was considered to repel the attack *incontinenti*. Placentinus limited this period to the same day as the attack because that was sufficient time for the

[4] Berger, 'Encyclopedic Dictionary,' v. *vim vi repellere licet*, 765. Cf. Cod. 3.27.1 and Dig. 9.2.4.

[5] Gaines Post, *Studies in Medieval Legal Thought* (Princeton, 1964), p. 541, n. 115, cites an unpublished gloss of Irnerius to Dig. 1.1.5, v. *ex hoc iure gentium*; MS. Royal 11, C. III, fol. 1. He further (*ibid.*, p. 543, n. 123) cites Azo, *Summa Institutionum*, to Inst. 1.2.

[6] Accursius, *Glossa Ordinaria*, to Inst. 1.1.2, v. *utuntur*.

[7] E.g. Dig. 43.16.3.9. Cf. Berger, 'Encyclopedic Dictionary,' v. *continens*, 413.

[8] Berger, *ibid.*, v. *moderatio*, 585; v. *inculpanter*, 498.

[9] Cod. 8.4.1.

[10] E.g. Dig. 9.2.45.4.

[11] Rogerius, *Summa Codicis*, to Cod. 8.4; in A. Gaudenzi, *Bibliotheca Iuridica Medii Aevi* (3 vols., Bologna, 1892–1914), I, pp. 144b–145a. The *Summa Trecensis*, perhaps also written by Rogerius, expanded on the analysis in the *Summa Codicis: Summa Trecensis*, to Cod. 8.4.6, ed. H. Fitting (Berlin, 1894), p. 267.

victim to summon aid. To delay longer than a day constituted not the repulsion of an injury but vengeance.[12] In Azo's view, repulsion of violence *incontinenti* could take place as long as the victim persisted at efforts in his own defense and did not turn to other matters, even if this should take a year.[13] The principle that repulsion was *incontinenti* so long as the victim did not turn his attention to other affairs became common opinion by its incorporation into the *Glossa Ordinaria* of Accursius.[14]

The concept of moderation, inherently difficult to apply to violence, provoked attempts to give it more theoretical precision. For Azo and Accursius, moderation was determined by two criteria. If the attack was carried out without weapons, then the defense must be effected without weapons. Conversely an armed attack or the use of weapons to induce terror rendered moderate and legitimate an armed defense of person and property. Both moderation and *incontinenti* required that violence be used for simple defense and not for vengeance.[15] With their understanding of *incontinenti* and moderation the Romanists were unanimous in holding that the right to repel violence by violence did not extend so far as to permit vendettas or indiscriminate attacks on personal enemies.

These limitations on the exercise of the right to self-defense were, however, of doubtful efficacy in restraining violence, since determination that a victim was guilty of reacting after an interval, or with excessive violence, or out of vengeance, was difficult to prove and would usually be made after the violence had ceased. Recognising these difficulties, the Romanists sought to bring disputes into court at the outset rather than to have them resolved by violence. Azo considered violent self-defense less admissible when there was a possibility of judicial intervention in the conflict,[16] and even condemned the violent recovery of one's own territory when it was

---

[12] Placentinus, *Summa Codicis*, to Cod. 8.4 (Mainz, 1536), p. 374; text compared with B.N. Lat. 4539, fols. 91vb–92ra and B.N. Lat. 4441, fols. 83vb–84ra.

[13] Azo, *Summa Codicis*, to Cod. 8.4 (Lyons, 1564), fol. 215va; *Lectura in Codicem*, to Cod. 8.4.1 (Paris, 1611), p. 615.

[14] Accursius, *Glossa Ordinaria*, to Inst. 4.15.6, v. *is ab eo*; to Dig. 43.16.3.9, v. *continenti*. Odofredus, *Lectura Codicis*, to Cod. 8.4.1 (Lyon, 1552), fol. 140va.

[15] Azo, *Summa Codicis*, to Cod. 8.4, fol. 215va–vb; *Lectura in Codicem*, to Cod. 8.4, p. 615. Accursius, *Glossa Ordinaria*, to Cod. 3.27.1, vv. *ultionem, resistendi*; ibid., to Cod. 8.4.1, v. *moderatione*; ibid., to Dig. 9.2.45, v. *ulciscendo*.

[16] Azo, *Summa Codicis*, to Cod. 8.4, fol. 215vb.

effected without judicial authority.[17] When the rightful lord of a property violently expelled its present possessor without judicial authority, he lost the ownership of his own property through his illegal violence.[18] Odofredus advised anyone who had suffered a violent attack not to assert his rights on his own authority but rather to seek remedies in a court of law.[19] His preference for legal remedies was based on his emphasis of recourse to authority for the settlement of disputes.[20] For him the enforcement of laws was an unarmed form of military service, and only in serious cases where the unarmed legal militia of lawyers had failed should military aid be employed.[21] While the Romanists did not deny the victim of a violent attack all right to use violence, they did deny the attacker any right to defend himself, and held him responsible for all crimes committed during the incident by either party.[22] Furthermore, anyone who came into possession of property through violence was bound to make restitution for it.[23]

The problem of self-defense did not provoke sharp debate by the Romanists, perhaps because they did not discuss self-defense in relation to war. For them self-defense justified violence and killing only to prevent being robbed or murdered, but they condemned all other uses of violence by private persons and sought to settle private conflicts in the law courts. In the medieval context of warring families and city-states, where few public authorities were capable of keeping the peace, the canonists would attempt to remedy the deficiencies of the Romanists' analysis.

THE LAWS OF WAR

Since in Roman law the right of self-defense pertained only to

---

[17] Azo, *Lectura in Codicem*, to Cod. 8.4.6, v. *rescripto*, p. 616.

[18] Azo, *Summa Codicis*, to Cod. 8.4, fol. 216va. The passage is a close paraphrase of Cod. 8.4.7.

[19] Odofredus, *Lectura Codicis*, to Cod. 9.12.7, fol. 196va–vb.

[20] *Ibid.*, to Cod. 9.39, fol. 209ra. The passage concerns the bringing of recalcitrant brigands to justice.

[21] *Ibid.*, to Cod. 2.1, fol. 82ra; *ibid.*, to Cod. 1.46, fol. 52rb; *ibid.*, to Cod. 1.46.1. In the last passage Odofredus referred to the enforcement of civil laws by the *podestà* of an Italian commune. The *podestà* should derive his authority from the emperor, and employ literate lawyers rather than illiterate soldiers wherever possible.

[22] E.g. Azo, *Summa Codicis*, to. Cod. 9.12, fol. 239ra. For Innocent IV's expansion of this opinion, see below, ch. 5, nn. 59, 136.

[23] E.g. Placentinus, *Summa Codicis*, to Cod. 8.4, p. 374; text compared with B.N. Lat. 4539, fo. 92ra–rb and B.N. Lat. 4441, fol. 84ra–rb. Azo, *Summa Codicis*, to Cod. 8.4, fol. 216va. Odofredus, *Lectura Codicis* to Cod. 8.4.5, fol. 141rb; *ibid.*, to Cod. 8.4.8, fols.143vb–144ra

private persons, the Romanists needed to place public war and its justification within the general framework of laws. The task had largely been accomplished in the Institutes and Digest of Justinian, where the laws pertaining to war were treated as part of the *ius gentium*.[24] Roman law saw wars as a means to repel injuries,[25] while Azo and Accursius justified war waged by the Roman people to repel violence.[26] Accursius used the term *bellum licitum* when describing the Roman war, and further considered any way occasioned by a prior injury to be licit according to the *ius gentium*.[27] In their formal framework of the laws of war the Romanists added no new elements to the treatment found in Justinian's compilation, and remained safely within the just war tradition common to Cicero, Augustine and the medieval canonists.

With its emphasis on unitary imperial authority, ancient Roman law provided no means for determining the locus of authority for waging war when public authority was divided. The medieval mixture of public and private rights to render justice confronted the Romanists with the necessity to adapt Roman law to contemporary political realities, but few of them during the twelfth and thirteenth centuries grappled at length with these problems as they related to war. In the Roman Empire a *ius militare* had been developed to regulate the rights and duties of soldiers. Much of the Romanists' treatment of military law had little direct relevance to the Middle Ages, but their comments on military discipline tended to limit the right to wage war to proper authorities. Thus Rogerius prohibited anyone under penalty of treason from outfitting an army to wage war without the express order of a prince.[28] In the twelfth century only the first nine books of the Code were available to the Glossators, but when the last three books became known around 1200, a short

---

[24] Cf. Dig. 1.1.3; 1.1.5; Inst. 1.2.2.

[25] Post, *Studies*, p. 541, n. 115: above, n. 5. Placentinus, *Summa Institutionum*, to Inst. 1.2 (Lyons, 1536), pp. 5–6; text compared with B.N. Lat. 4539, fol. 113ra and B.N. Lat. 4441, fol. 1vb.

[26] Azo, *Summa Institutionum*, to Inst. 1.2 (Lyons, 1564), fol. 280ra. Accursius, *Glossa Ordinaria*, to Inst. 1.2.2, v. *bella*.

[27] *Ibid.*, to Dig. 1.1.5, v. *bella*: 'Ergo ius gentium iniquum est, cum iniquum inducat, sed dic, quod dicit de bello licito, ut indicto a populo Romano vel imperatore....Item dicit de bello indicto ad iniuriam propulsandum, quod licet....Non autem de alio, ne inde iniuriae nascatur occasio.' Cf. *ibid.*, to Dig. 41.1.5.7, v. *fiunt*. The same elements of authority and avenging of injuries were found in Gratian: C. 23 q. 2 d. p. c. 2.

[28] Rogerius, *Summa Codicis*, to Cod. 9.7; in Gaudenzi, *Bibliotheca*, I, fol. 163a.

title provided the Glossators with a clear prohibition on the use of weapons without princely authorisation.[29] On the strength of this, Azo argued that the prince alone, meaning the Emperor, possessed the authority to wreak vengeance on the enemies of the Empire. He conceded that the prince could delegate this authority, but he considered all persons who used weapons without authority as guilty of treason. In an oblique comment on his own time, Azo observed that lack of princely control over the use of weapons endangered peace and gave rise to acts of malice.[30] Odofredus stated explicitly the conclusion implicit in earlier Romanists' analysis that only the Emperor could legally wage war.[31]

The Romanists' limitation of the authority to wage war to the Emperor, while consonant with Roman law, did not bear directly on the division of authority that characterised feudalism. Under what conditions was a vassal obliged to fight in his lord's war, and when could he escape this obligation? Did the military activities of a feudal lord enjoy the status of a just war, or were they cases of private and therefore illicit violence? How could the quasi-private feudal war or *guerra* and the judicial duel or *pugna* be distinguished from the just war of the prince armed with full public authority? After all, the Romanists otherwise had taken great pains to distinguish private violence from war and to provide analyses of legal remedies such as compositions or treaties of peace to regulate such violence. By way of solution the Romanists commented on the *Libri Feudorum*, a compilation of feudal customs, primarily Lombard ones, that was drafted for the Emperor Frederick I around 1170 and which came to be included in the *Corpus Iuris Civilis*.[32] According to these customs, the count or ruler of an area was obliged to proceed judicially to end any *guerra* between two of his subordinate *ministeriales*, since their

---

[29] Cod. 11.47: 'Ut armorum usus inscio principe interdictus sit.'

[30] Azo, *Summa Codicis*, to Cod. 11.47, fol. 272ra. Accursius, *Glossa Ordinaria*, to Cod. 11.47. 1, v. *movendorum*.

[31] Odofredus, *Lectura Codicis*, to Cod. 11.47, fol. 56va: 'Dicit quod nullus poterit movere guerram et arma portare sine licentia imperatoris. hoc dicit et sic videtur alias licitum bellum.'

[32] For the Romanists' treatment of feudal customs in general, see H. Kantorowicz, 'De pugna. La letteratura langobardistica sul duello giudiziano,' *Studi in onore di Enrico Besta*, II (Milan, 1937–9), 1–25; rep. in *Rechtshistorische Studien*, ed. H. Coing and G. Immel (Karlsruhe, 1970), pp. 255–71. Cf. Kantorowicz, *Studies*, p. 195. E. M. Meijers, *Etudes d'histoire du droit*, III, ed. R. Feenstra and H. F. W. D. Fischer (Leyden, 1959), 261–70.

lack of authority prevented them from waging a real war.[33] More significantly, Hugolinus and the *Glossa Ordinaria* observed that feudal custom obliged a vassal to aid his lord in the latter's *guerra* even when the vassal doubted its justice, and also to defend his lord even when the latter went on the offensive, unless the lord was under ecclesiastical excommunication or royal ban.[34] The logic of feudal overlordship also required a vassal to aid his lord against himself, on pain of losing his fief, when his lord made war on him, while conversely the lord's unjust war on his vassal deprived him of his proprietary right over the vassal's fief.[35] Similarly, a vassal was bound to aid his lord even against his own brother or son, an obligation that was also incumbent on the lord as part of the feudal nexus of reciprocal rights and duties. Default by either party was a felony that entailed loss of the fief for the vassal and loss of proprietary right to the fief for the lord.[36]

Writing around 1250, Odofredus discussed the problems of feudal obedience in greater detail. A vassal was bound to fight under his lord in a *guerra* unless the war was patently unjust or when obedience to his lord involved him in sin or perjury. In case the war was unjust but nevertheless a public war or was waged in self-defense, Odofredus left the decision of whether to fight to the vassal himself, whose failure to participate did not render him liable to lose his fief. When the vassal merely had doubts about the justice of the war, Odofredus agreed that he was obliged to participate.[37] Here Odofredus raised as many problems as he attempted to solve. It was clear that a vassal was not bound to aid his lord in a palpably unjust war, but neither was he forbidden to do so. Moreover, by contending that a war could be unjust yet public and defensive, Odofredus further confused

---

[33] *Libri Feudorum*, 2.27.8.

[34] Hugolinus, *Summa super Usibus Feudorum*, IIII; in Gaudenzi, *Bibliotheca*, II, 189b; Accursius, *Glossa Ordinaria*, to *Libri Feudorum* 2.7, v. *iuste aliquem offendere*.

[35] Accursius, *Glossa Ordinaria*, to *Libri Feudorum* 2.28.1, v. *contra omnes*.

[36] *Ibid.*, to *Libri Feudorum* 2.28.1, v. *fratrem*.

[37] Odofredus, *Summa in Usus Feudorum*, c. 21 (Alcalá, 1584), fols. 70v–71v: '...quod si dominus habet guerram, debet vassallus eum iuvare. Sed quid si dominus habet guerram iniustam? Respon. si vassallus scit, quod iusta est, planum est. Si vero scit quod iniusta, quia publicum est tunc ad defendum, si vult, potest; sed non tenetur, si non vult, per hoc non perdit feudum. Si vero dubitat sit iusta, vel non, tunc indistincte debet eum adiuvare...Sed videtur quod postquam scit vassallus quod habet guerram iniustam, sine distinctione non teneatur eum adiuvare...nec vassallus tenetur adiuvare dominum, ne incidat in peccatum vel periurium.'

the issue, since a defensive war was generally if not explicitly considered to be just, and an unjust defensive war was perhaps even self-contradictory. Odofredus may have intended to approve the lord's right to wage war and to compel the obedience of his vassals, but his attempt was vitiated by allowing the vassal a measure of independent judgment about the justice of the war. In effect Odofredus took two contradictory positions both grounded in Roman law: first, no obligations could force the vassal to participate in sinful or illicit activities; and second, a vassal's dutiful obedience to his lord overrode his own opinion of the justice of the war. Somewhat more satisfactory solutions would have to be devised by the canonists.[38]

Thus far the Romanists in proceeding on the two distinct levels of the Roman just war and the *guerrae* of feudal lords and vassals had not confronted the wars waged by rulers at least *de facto* independent of the Holy (Roman) Empire. Johannes Bazianus did view military expeditions as justified by reasons of public utility, but his opinion did not specify the sort of prince that could wage war on his own authority.[39] Reflecting the Romanists' imperial bias, the *Glossa Ordinaria* reserved a vassal's primary loyalty to the person of the Emperor, since the vassal's obligation to him had been prior in time.[40] Still, no way had been devised to include the wars of kings within the framework of the just war. While Azo and Accursius may have countenanced the exercise of legitimate authority independent or partly independent of the Emperor, they did not explicitly accord to kings or other magistrates the right to wage their own just wars.[41] When Odofredus inquired whether a vassal could aid his lord against the vassal's own *patria* his treatment was more satisfactory, for he concluded that the vassal's loyalty to his own *patria* overrode fidelity to his lord, such that a vassal could even kill his own father with impunity. By reference to a pertinent canon law text Odofredus

[38] The first principle was based on Inst. 3.26.7; Dig. 17.1.6.3; Dig. 17.1.22.6. The second principle depended on obedience owed by soldiers, according to the *ius militare*, to an authoritative imperial command: Cod. 12.35; Dig. 49.16. For the canonistic treatments, see below, ch. 5, pp. 138ff.

[39] Johannes Bazianus, *Libellus de Ordine Iudiciorum*; in Gaudenzi, *Bibliotheca*, II, 220. Cf. Post, *Studies*, p. 275.

[40] Accursius, *Glossa Ordinaria*, to *Libri Feudorum* 2.28.1, v. *dominum antiquiorem*.

[41] Cf. M. Gilmore, *Argument from Roman Law in Political Thought, 1200–1600* (Cambridge, Mass., 1941), pp. 17–44; J. W. Perrin, 'Legatus, the Lawyers, and the Terminology of Power in Roman Law,' *Studia Gratiana*, XI (1967), 461–89; idem, 'Azo, Roman Law, and Sovereign European States,' *ibid.*, XV (1972), 97, 101.

held that just wars were those waged under any conditions for defense of the *patria*.[42] Although Odofredus did not specify the sort of political unit that he considered a *patria*, his opinion was the most extreme Romanistic justification of defensive war waged for the *patria*, and showed his awareness of the strength of contemporary monarchies and city-states.

For war to be recognised as such in ancient Roman law, the opponents had to be considered specifically as enemies, since not all acts of violence were committed by public enemies of the Roman Empire. The legal notion of *hostes* was therefore fundamental to the Romanists' analysis of war. Enemies or *hostes* were defined in the Digest as those against whom the Roman people had publicly declared war, or who had declared war on the Roman people. The definition emphasised the legal position of the enemies rather than their violent and unjust actions. Those persons who committed hostile acts against Roman citizens but were not declared enemies were termed robbers (*latrunculi*) or brigands (*praedones*).[43] Accursius attempted to distinguish between a full state of war with publicly-declared *hostes* and hostilities with peoples having no legal relations with Rome. The war against *hostes* he termed *bellum*, while other forms of hostility he termed *guerra*. The situations differed legally, for in a *guerra* there was no right of *postliminium*.[44] In effect Accursius distinguished several levels of legal relationships between peoples. He recalled the Roman just war when he stated that a *bellum* only commenced with a formal declaration of hostility regardless of prior acts of violence. In contrast to the ancient Roman law, however, he held that the Roman people had the right to declare a full legal *bellum* on their rebellious subjects, although he did not explain his contention.[45] His treatment was probably a veiled reference to the wars waged between Christian princes within Europe, especially within the empire.

In effect the Romanists described three sorts of wars, the just war

[42] Odofredus, *Summa in Usus Feudorum*, c. 24, fols. 75v–77r. Odofredus based his assertion that war could be waged at all times in defense of the *patria* on a canon from Gratian: C. 23 q. 8 c. 15. Cf. Post, *Studies*, p. 444, n. 38.

[43] Dig. 49.15.24; Dig. 50.16.118; Dig. 50.16.234. Cf. Berger, 'Encyclopedic Dictionary,' v. *hostis*, 489.

[44] Accursius, *Glossa Ordinaria*, to Dig. 49.15.5.2, v. *hospitium*; *ibid.*, to Dig. 49.15.24, v. *hostes*. For the concept of *postliminium*, see below, n. 54.

[45] Accursius, *Glossa Ordinaria*, to Dig. 4.5.5, v. *hostes*; *ibid.*, to Dig. 49.15.24, v. *decrevit*.

of Roman law and the Empire, the feudal *guerra* that could be just or unjust without really enjoying the legal status of the Roman just war, and, more hesitantly, the just wars waged in defense of the *patria* by kings and other magistrates. The Romanists' commentaries on feudal military obligations were on the whole neither exhaustive nor comprehensive. The Empire and the Roman notion of *patria* loomed larger in their thought than reciprocal feudal rights and duties. Yet they did provide a legacy for the later Commentators, canon lawyers and apologists for the rising national states. Primarily secular in attitude, they tended to leave to the canonists the vexing problems of proper relations between pope, emperor and kings. Yet before the end of the thirteenth century many civilians, often in the employ of kings, began forcefully to appropriate defense of the *patria* for the service of independent monarchies. Thus Bracton in England, Andrew of Isernia in Naples and Jean de Blanot, Jacques de Révigny and Pierre de Belleperche in France all argued with varying degrees of precision that a vassal's first obligation was not to his immediate overlord but to his king, who as guardian of public utility was charged with the defense of the *patria*, crown and realm. Rather than the universal Empire, the limited territorial kingdom now became the *communis patria* that commanded the primary allegiance of all its feudal and non-feudal subjects.[46] On the more practical level, an anonymous French cleric in mid-century recorded a count's command that his vassals join the king's necessary battle against England.[47] In spite of their earlier hesitations, civil lawyers in the late thirteenth century came to employ the just war as a tool of statecraft in the arsenal of kingdoms that, *de jure* or *de facto*, operated outside the jurisdiction of the Holy (Roman) Empire.

The Romanists not only buttressed the just war as a legal procedure endowed with specific obligations, but they also maintained the ancient Roman hostility toward barbarians, pagans and heretics. In their view the concept of *hostes* was linked closely to that of *barbari*.[48] Drawing upon the Code, they prohibited the sale or distribution of

---

[46] Citations in Post, *Studies*, pp. 341–3, 445–8, 473–81; Kantorowicz, *King's Two Bodies*, pp. 247f. For Beaumanoir's opinions see below, conclusion, nn. 1–3.

[47] 'Curialis,' no. 202; in L. Wahrmund, ed., *Quellen zur Geschichte des römisch-kanonischen Processes im Mittelalter*, I (3) (Innsbruck and Heidelberg, 1905), 60.

[48] E.g. Azo, *Lectura in Codicem*, to Cod. 8.50.5, v. *a barbaris*, p. 667. Accursius, *Glossa Ordinaria*, to Cod. 8.50.20. For the concept of *barbari* as *hostes*, see above, introduction, nn. 33–4, 69.

weapons to barbarian enemies, lest these become more formidable to the Roman people.[49] The late Roman Empire had bequeathed to the Middle Ages the legal theory and practice of religious persecution, although Justinian's Code had sought to restrain Christian harassment of Jews and pagans.[50] Placentinus repeated the civil disabilities of the Justinian Code that pertained to heretics.[51] Azo went one step further in considering pagans subject to the penalties established for heretics, and mentioned the Saracens as contemporary examples of infidelity and idolatry, although he did repeat the cautions of the Justinian text.[52] He assimilated together all those who deviated from orthodoxy, such as heretics, Jews, pagans, and infidels, and held them liable to punishment on account of their beliefs rather than for any acts of rapine, while Accursius compared the crime of heresy to the crime of treason.[53] Although the penalties for religious deviation were not expressly connected with the Romanist analysis of war, by the assimilation of pagans and heretics to *hostes* they became part of the Romanists' stress on imperial enforcement of religious orthodoxy that the canonists invoked as justification for the crusades. That the Romanists themselves were silent on that specifically medieval war, the crusade, indicates their recognition that the crusade as the war of the papacy lay outside the scope of their analysis.

THE LEGAL CONSEQUENCES OF WAR

In ancient Roman law war created legal conditions that were regulated by the specifically Roman concept of *postliminium*, which placed limitations on personal rights and procedures for the transfer

---

[49] *Summa Trecensis*, to Cod. 4.41, p. 115. Placentinus, *Summa Codicis*, to Cod. 4.41, p. 175; text compared with B.N. Lat. 4539, fol. 47ra and B.N. Lat. 4441, fol. 48ra.

[50] Cod. 1.11.6.

[51] Placentinus, *Summa Codicis*, to Cod. 1.5, p. 11; text compared with B.N. Lat. 4539, fol. 6ra and B.N. Lat. 4441, fol. 19ra–rb.

[52] Azo, *Summa Codicis*, to Cod. 1.11, fol. 7rb-va. Yet in another passage Azo denied to pagans the benefit of the interdict *unde vi* on the foundation of the same law in the Code: *Lectura in Codicem*, to Cod. 8.4.7, v. *vel apud homines quoslibet*, p. 617.

[53] Accursius, *Glossa Ordinaria*, to Cod. 1.5.4, v. *subire*. The Romanistic assimilation of religious persecution to the right of war was evidently made explicit later by Vivianus, for according to Accursius, *ibid.*, to Dig. 4.5.5: 'Si interdictum fuit alicui aqua et igni, capite minuitur...Imperator fuit in exercitu contra Saracenos et hostes populi Romani. deseruit aliquis imperatorem vel magistratus militum forte, et transtulit se ad hostes. sine dubio ille capite minuitur...Vivian.'

of property. In the law of Justinian, perhaps the most decisive consequence of war was on the person of someone captured by a legally declared enemy. The captive became the slave of his captor, his legal rights such as the right to make a will were suspended, and his marriage was dissolved. However, in the event that a Roman citizen returned from captivity, he regained his full legal rights. The captive who returned had to take possession of his things anew. Upon their recovery goods captured in war again became the property of their former possessor. Someone who was captured or kidnapped by brigands (*latrones*) was not legally a captive, since brigands were not legally considered *hostes*. In this event the captive retained his prior legal status while in captivity, but since he was not captured in the course of a *bellum*, he did not receive the rights of *postliminium* upon his eventual return from captivity.[54]

The Romanists generally repeated the conclusions of the Justinianean compilation on these matters without much discussion, but Placentinus commented that prisoners of war who escaped from their captors or who were liberated by enemies of their captors did not become captives again, but rather merited reception, protection, and the rights of *postliminium*.[55] According to contemporary Italian practice described by Accursius, a citizen of one city did not become a slave when captured by men from another city, for these legally were not enemies but merely bandits. A citizen thus captured retained his free personal status and ability to make a will.[56] Accursius refused to accord the legal status of war to the violent quarrels between citizens of different cities, since these quarrels lacked *publica licentia*.[57] For Odofredus, the concept of *postliminium* applied not to Roman territory but to Christian territory and people. A Christian who strayed beyond the frontiers of Christian territory came under the jurisdiction of non-Christians, whom Odofredus considered as enemies even without a declared state of war. Such a Christian was eligible for *postliminium* upon his return within Christian borders.[58]

---

[54] Berger, 'Encyclopedic Dictionary,' v. *captivitas*, pp. 380f.; *ibid*., v. *postliminium*, p. 639; *ibid*., v. *redemptus ab hoste*, p. 670. Cf. Cod. 8.50; Dig. 49.15.

[55] Placentinus, *Summa Codicis*, to Cod. 8.50 (= 8.54 in Placentinus's text), p. 414; text compared with B.N. Lat. 4539, fol. 101va and B.N. Lat. 4441, fol. 93va.

[56] Accursius, *Glossa Ordinaria*, to Dig. 28.1.13.

[57] *Ibid*., to Dig. 49.15.24, v. *vel praedones*.

[58] Odofredus, *Lectura Codicis*, to Cod. 8.40, fol. 175vb.

Here Odofredus exemplified the attitude, common to many Romanists, as well as to other Christians, that instinctively regarded all non-Christians as *ipso facto* enemies. Legally indistinguishable in this sense, Romans and Christians were joined together in persistent hostility, if not outright war, against non-Christians, while sanguinary battles between Christians were denied the legal status of war, with all its attendant consequences.

A legal consequence of war far more immediately significant for the Middle Ages was that property seized during hostilities immediately became the possession of the captor. According to Roman public law enemy land was occupied at the conclusion of a victorious war. Occupation of immovable property always led to its acquisition by the Roman people, not the individual soldier. Similarly, *praeda*, booty or movable property, became the property of Rome when it was seized by common military action, but when it was seized by the actions of an individual soldier it became his property.[59] The Romanists repeated Justinian's treatment without much comment and were content to stress the legal status of war or hostilities in determining whether transfer of property was to be effected. Thus Accursius limited himself to the laconic observation that property could be gained or lost only in a licit war.[60]

The Romanists' primary concern was to define the legal conditions of belligerency, and so they expounded more a doctrine of *licitum bellum* or licit war than theories of the just war. Their main accomplishments were illustrations of the legal differences between states of war and peace, and an insistence that no hostile encounter could enjoy the status of war without the sanction of public authority. Hence they were more able than earlier medieval writers to distinguish war from other forms of violence. Still, when compared with the wealth of canonistic commentaries on the just war, the Romanists' analysis exhibited several shortcomings. While they were naturally concerned with the justice of warfare, their comments followed the conventional lines of the Justinianean corpus. Their just war theories therefore failed adequately to integrate ancient Roman law and contemporary jurisdictional conflicts. Since they did not link the private right of self-defense to public warfare, they had difficulties

---

[59] Berger, 'Encyclopedic Dictionary,' v. *occupatio rerum hostilium*, 606; *ibid.*, v. *praeda*, 641.
[60] Accursius, *Glossa Ordinaria*, to Dig. 41.2.1. v. *bello*.

in constructing theoretical limitations on participation in the often illicit clashes of the feudal nobility. Until the middle of the thirteenth century they remained captive of the Roman law restriction of the right to declare and wage public wars to the Emperor, and so their formal theory of war underwent little evolution and provoked few sharp controversies.

Even taking into account their self-imposed limitations of focus, the civilians' opinions seem disproportionately meagre when compared with those of the canonists. This apparent dearth of debate remains puzzling, although it may be partly explained by the Romanists' primary interest in expounding classical Roman legal procedures more usual and normal than warfare. Moreover, in the present state of scholarship the works of few twelfth- and thirteenth-century civilians are available in printed editions and even fewer in critical editions. The editions that do exist are difficult of access and surrounded with controversies as to authorship and accuracy.[61] What can be said with certainty is that the civilians of the twelfth and thirteenth centuries performed the great service of giving canonists a solid education in the Roman just war. By the late thirteenth century the canonists' theories had so matured as to be capable of a reciprocal enrichment of Romanistic jurisprudence that helped to produce Bartolus, Baldus, and the other great civilians of the late Middle Ages.

[61] Recent reprints of early modern editions have somewhat alleviated these problems, but an inestimable amount of material remains in manuscripts. The appearance of a *Repertorium der Zivilistik* now in preparation by Dr Peter Weimar and others will enable scholars more fully to assess the wealth of Romanistic material from the twelfth to the fifteenth centuries.

Chapter 3

THE JUST WAR IN GRATIAN'S DECRETUM

The city of Bologna that witnessed the revival of Roman law studies was moreover the birthplace of the medieval science of canon law. Around 1140 the Camaldolese monk Gratian completed a massive compilation of canon law in the shape of a textbook known as the *Concordia Discordantium Canonum* or, more frequently, the Decretum. The appearance of the Decretum marked a watershed in the history of canon law, for it climaxed the development of early medieval canon law collections and inaugurated the period of systematic canonical jurisprudence. The earlier collections, such as the Dionysio-Hadriana and pseudo-Isidorian decretals of the Carolingian era, the collections of Burchard of Worms and Anselm of Lucca in the eleventh century, and the *Decretum* and *Panormia* of Ivo of Chartres in the early twelfth, had transmitted ecclesiastical legislation and patristic opinion in rather haphazard and spasmodic fashion. Drawing upon these works, Gratian imposed upon their contents a systematic organisation. This compilation was almost immediately accepted as authoritative in the nascent canon law schools of Western Europe. For the rest of the twelfth century canon lawyers used the Decretum as a point of departure for their own elaborations of canon law problems, and even in the thirteenth century, when papal legislative activity was producing authoritative pronouncements or decretals, canon lawyers often mined Gratian for basic positions. Theologians, moreover, not so well endowed with a basic textbook of practical ethics within their own discipline, also used the Decretum as the point of departure for their observations and speculations. For both canonists and theologians then, Master Gratian's definitive compilation posed the basic problems to be resolved, defined the boundaries of debate, and provided a framework within which broader solutions could be worked out. Gratian's accomplishment lay not so much in the originality of his treatment as in his conscientious montage of texts bearing on problems of Christian morality and Church discipline.

References to war and military service or *militia* are scattered throughout the Decretum. In Distinctio I Gratian cited Isidore of Seville's opinion, derived from Roman law, that repulsion of violence by violence was justified by natural law, and that wars were regulated by the *ius gentium*.[1] The locus classicus of texts concerning warfare was the lengthy Causa 23. The influence of St Augustine suffused the entire Causa; it would be difficult to fault Gratian for the comprehensiveness of his selection of Augustinian texts. His more immediate sources included the canonical collection of Anselm of Lucca, from whom he took texts bearing on the persecution of heretics, and that of Ivo of Chartres, from whom he took many texts pertaining to war itself. Yet under his close scrutiny and with his fidelity to Augustine, the simple confidence of the pseudo-Augustinian letter *Gravi de pugna* disappeared from consideration.[2] Defense against attack, judicial punishment of wicked men, and the Church's role in warfare were however considered in somewhat diffuse and overlapping fashion. Since war was embedded in the Causa alongside tangential issues, Gratian's thought on war must be carefully extricated from these other issues. Only then can the extent of his contribution be determined. The task is made more difficult because much of what Gratian seemed to be saying about war was said by often indirect analogy. For example, the casus with which Gratian prefaced the Causa concerned a hypothetical but plausible situation: certain bishops had fallen into heresy together with the people committed to their care. Furthermore, these bishops were coercing orthodox Christians to accept their heresy. In response the pope had ordered the orthodox bishops of the region, who also held civil jurisdiction from the Emperor, to defend the orthodox from the heretics and to compel the heretics to return to orthodoxy. In compliance with the papal mandate the bishops had assembled an army and had combated the heretics in open battles and by ambushes. Some of the heretics were killed, some despoiled of their property, while others were returned to the unity of the faith through the correcting influence of incarceration.[3] At first this situation may appear far-fetched and contrived, but, given the spread of religious

---

[1] D. 1 c. 7; D. 1 c. 9. Cf. Dig. 1.1.3 and 5; Inst. 1.2.2.
[2] Cf. above, ch. 1, nn. 39, 50, 87.
[3] C. 23, pr.

dissent and the expansion of the frontiers of Christianity in the twelfth century, it was not too far removed from contemporary events. Moreover, it succinctly incorporated most of the issues raised in the Causa. Not only was the context for the discussion of the just war established, but the way was also opened for wide-ranging discussion of physical coercion. This Causa has attracted the attention of scholars of diverse orientations.[4] Here the analysis will proceed topically rather than by precisely following the order of Gratian's exposition. Thus the justification of war and killing logically takes first place, followed by the formulation of the just war, the problems of authority and conduct, and the legitimate roles of Church and clergymen in warfare.

THE JUSTIFICATION OF CORPORAL PUNISHMENT

At the outset of his Causa Gratian had to confront the New Testament passages that appeared to prohibit all recourse to physical force by Christians. How could the Christian perform military service in the face of precepts such as 'Turn the other cheek' (Matt. 5: 29) and 'Give place to wrath' (Rom. 12: 19)? These same pacific precepts had so troubled Augustine that he had developed the doctrine by which love of a sinner became the motive for his punishment.[5] The position Augustine had worked out with great intellectual diligence and emotional turmoil, Gratian arrived at by means of a skillful if less painful dialectic. Showing his awareness of the fundamental threat posed by these precepts to a Christian doctrine of the just war, Gratian entitled the first quaestio 'Is military service a sin?' In his preface to the quaestio Gratian asserted that the purposes of military service were to repel injuries and to inflict punishment. He then marshaled a selection of passages from both Old and New Testaments that enjoined Christians to exercise patience and compliance in the face of adversity and deference to divine authority in the judgment and punishment of other men. Since these evangelical 'precepts of patience' were incompatible with the purposes of

[4] Among these treatments are Regout, *La guerre juste*, pp. 61–6; Hubrecht, 'La juste guerre'; C. Horoy, *Droit international et droit de gens public d'après le Decretum de Gratien* (Paris, 1887); A. Stickler, 'De Ecclesiastica Potestate Coactiva Materialis apud Magistrum Gratianum,' *Salesianum*, VI (1942), 2–23; 96–119; idem, 'Magistri Gratiani Sententia de Potestate Ecclesiae in Statum,' *Apollinaris*, XXI (1948), 36–111; Chodorow, *Christian Political Theory*, pp. 228–46.

[5] Above, ch. 1, n. 5.

military service, he concluded, dialectically to be sure, that military service appeared sinful.[6]

Gratian's first canon, taken from Origen, cautioned Christians not to emulate the wars narrated in the Old Testament, for these wars merely prefigured the spiritual wars fought by Christians against spiritual enemies such as the devil.[7] After this canon Gratian interjected his dictum that, as the soul was more important than the body, so the precepts of patience applied more to the inward disposition of a person than to his external acts,[8] and supported this contention with a composite passage from Augustine counselling the maintenance of the precepts of patience in the inward disposition (*preparatio cordis*). The passage then justified punishment of an evil-doer as an act of benevolence, performed in his own best interest even though against his will. Wars waged with a benevolent disposition were useful in separating the sinner from his sin. Evangelical precepts did not prohibit all wars, for had this been the case John the Baptist would have advised the Roman soldiers to lay down their arms. Instead he only advised them to be content with their wages.[9] Gratian ended the quaestio by affirming that all military service was not sinful and that the precepts of patience referred to a person's inward attitude.[10] The entire quaestio hewed to the Augustinian outlook without deviation or addition.

Elsewhere in Causa 23 Gratian and his texts supported the conflation of the inward disposition and the necessity to punish a sinner in his own best interest. Thus mutilation of pirates and thieves prevented them from further wickedness.[11] In quaestio 4, dealing broadly with the problem of vengeance and punishment (*vindicta*), Gratian stated that the precept to love one's enemy did not go so far as to permit sinning with impunity.[12] While mercy should be accorded to all men, it did not obviate the necessity to punish sinners.[13] In quaestio 5, concerned with capital punishment, he re-

---

[6] C. 23 q. 1, pr. Cf. Matt. 5: 39, 41; Romans 12: 19; Matt. 26: 52; Deuteronomy 32: 35; Matt. 7: 1; Matt. 13: 30; Romans 14: 4.
[7] C. 23 q. 1 c. 1. Gratian wrongly attributed this canon to Gregory I.
[8] C. 23 q. 1 d. p. c. 1.
[9] C. 23 q. 1 c. 2. Cf. Luke 3: 14 and C. 5 q. 5 cc. 2, 3.
[10] C. 23 q. 1 d. p. c. 7. Cf. 23 q. 1 c. 5.
[11] C. 23 q. 3 c. 6.
[12] C. 23 q. 4 d. p. c. 32.
[13] C. 23 q. 4 cc. 25, 35, 44.

affirmed the consonance of the precepts of patience with judicially sanctioned capital punishment,[14] and punishment of a criminal freed him from his sin.[15] Indeed those who punished wicked men were not guilty of cruelty but were rather ministers of God and avengers of His wrath.[16]

In contrast to his position that military service was not inherently sinful, Gratian did include several passages that at least cast suspicion upon such activity. Canon 47 of quaestio 4 of Causa 23 was taken from a letter of Urban II that enjoined penance for killers of excommunicates. Yet Urban praised their zeal in upholding the Church, exculpated them of the charge of homicide, and enjoined penance only because such killing was likely to occasion excesses born of human fragility. Elsewhere in the Decretum knights were prohibited from returning to military service after undergoing penance unless they did so with episcopal permission in defending justice or in fighting against pagans.[17] Still, while these passages did cast some doubt about the moral status of fighting, in Gratian's treatment they hardly amounted to a frontal attack on the legitimacy of military service. Since knights should always fight in defense of

[14] C. 23 q. 5 cc. 13, 16, 18, 30, 41.

[15] C. 23 q. 5 c. 17.

[16] C. 23 q. 5 cc. 27–9. Cf. C. 23 q. 8 cc. 13, 14. In other parts of the Decretum Gratian restated his position that Christian morality not only required the maintenance of pacific, charitable and merciful attitudes, but also that these attitudes themselves often legitimated recourse to force, violence and corporal punishment: e.g. D. 45 c. 11, d. p. c. 13; C. 11 q. 3 c. 70.

[17] C. 33 q. 2 cc. 8, 15; De penit. dist. 5 cc. 3, 4, 8. A passage taken from Gregory VII could be used to condemn military service: De penit. dist. 5 c. 6: 'Ideoque miles, vel negotiator, vel alicui offitio deditus, quod sine peccato exerceri non possit…deponat [miles], ulteriusque non ferat, nisi consilio religiosorum episcoporum pro defendenda iusticia.' This obviously did not prohibit all military service: cf. above, ch. 1, n. 73. The *De penitencia* was not originally a part of the Decretum but was added later in the twelfth century, probably by persons other than Gratian: G. LeBras, Ch. Lefebvre, J. Rambaud, *L'âge classique, 1140–1378. Sources et théorie du droit* (*Histoire du droit et des institutions de l'église en Occident*, vii), (Paris 1965), pp. 82–90. The later addition of this canon to the Decretum, as well as its content, probably accounts for its relative neglect by later canonists. By contrast, the passage was included in Peter the Lombard's Sentences, 4, 16, 3, thereby bringing it to the theologians' attention: below, ch. 6, n. 7. But even the theologians did not interpret it as a condemnation of all military service, but only as a criticism of illicit military service. For earlier suspicions of military service, see above, ch. 1, nn. 55–60. The development of the just war theories after Gratian partly explain why these suspicions went out of fashion. These passages withered on the vine because they were vestiges of the older concepts of penance, and occasioned restatement rather than development. Cf. Rufinus, *Summa Decretorum* (ed. H. Singer, Paderborn, 1902, rep. Aalen, 1963), to C. 33 q. 2 c. 8, v. *armis nunquam cingere*, p. 499; *ibid.*, to De penit. dist. 5, p. 503; *Glossa Ordinaria*, to C. 33 q. 8 c. 8, v. *numquam cingere*; *ibid.*, to De penit. dist. 5 cc. 3, 4, 6, 8.

justice, rather than injustice, and since fighting against pagans had usually been considered meritorious, in Gratian's opinion episcopal permission to fight for worthwhile causes should probably not be hard to obtain. Gratian did not bring these passages to bear on his discussion of military service; as a result of that discussion they became in succeeding generations mere archaic survivals of medieval suspicions, serving henceforth as reminders of the abuses, rather than the uses of armed force.

It is clear that Gratian himself found military service free of any inherent and inescapable moral stigma. With Augustine pointing the way Gratian betrayed no hesitation in asserting that physical punishment of sin, even punishment by war, was consonant with the evangelical precepts of patience. To transform Christian charity into a motivation for waging war was, after all, Augustine's intellectual accomplishment, however we might esteem its moral or psychological validity. Gratian made this Augustinian transformation into the cornerstone of his own and therefore the medieval jurisprudential analysis of warfare. This interpretation of the precepts of patience became the hinge upon which turned his entire subsequent analysis of war and punishment. Gratian's wholesale acceptance of Augustine's doctrine so convinced succeeding canonists and theologians that on this issue they were stimulated not to vigorous debate but to endless, unoriginal and tedious repetition of the assertion that love and patience did not prohibit warfare and killing. Having proved to his own satisfaction that military service was not an unqualified evil, Gratian turned to consider the legitimate purposes and conditions of warfare, the positive virtues of military service, and also the moral perils and abuses associated with warfare.

THE FORMULATION OF THE JUST WAR

The attitudes that must be maintained in performance of military service naturally carried over to the waging of war itself. Thus the pacific inward disposition and love for one's enemy, far from imposing an absolute rule over external actions, encouraged vigorous prosecution of war. Citing Augustinian texts taken from Ivo of Chartres, in quaestio 1 Gratian detailed the legitimate purposes of warfare. Peace was the desirable condition, while resort to war must only be in case of necessity. Military prowess, itself a gift of God, and warfare were instrumentalities of peace; for this reason warriors must be pacific even in warfare, for their goal is to return their enemy by conquest to a state of peace. Once victory was achieved, mercy should be shown to the enemy captives.[18] Thus wars are only licit when they are necessary to return to a peaceful situation. Good men go to war against violent attackers,[19] and wage wars of pacification (*bella pacata*) to coerce the wicked and sustain the good.[20]

Throughout quaestio 1 Gratian dispersed exhortations to military virtues and condemnation of wartime vices. The famous sermon of John the Baptist (Luke 3: 14) advising the Roman soldiers to 'do violence to no man, neither accuse any falsely; and be content with your wages' argued that Christian discipline did not fault all wars but only those in which soldiers sought more than their legitimate and necessary wages for their services. By contrast wars motivated by cupidity and fought with desire for booty and private gain were naturally condemned.[21] The highest praise of a soldier was his obedience to the utility of commonweal and to the commands of a prince or legitimate authority.[22] Conversely, actions were condemned that stemmed from a litany of inward vices, including lust for doing harm, cruelty of punishment, implacable and unsatisfied vehemence, savagery and lust for domination.[23] Further examples of similar citations here would commit the prolixity that Gratian and his successors themselves evidenced without adding further insight. Gratian's manifold quotations of these pompous exhortations however bespeak his recognition that the bellicose vices were very much a part of the life style of the medieval knight. Gratian was neither the first nor the last ecclesiastical writer to lament these traits. Against the well-known greed, rapacity, and ferocity of the knightly class of his time Gratian opposed the patristic portrait of the Christian soldier, thereby striking at the core of knightly practice.

To justify warfare and the motives of waging it according to Christian principles was, however, only a general preparation for Gratian's central task: to describe what made a particular war just. If

---

[18] C. 23 q. 1 c. 3. Cf. C. 23 q. 8 c. 15. [19] C. 23 q. 1 c. 4.

[20] C. 23 q. 1 c. 6. The passage, attributed to Augustine, is of uncertain provenance; Gratian probably found it in Ivo of Chartres' *Decretum*, x, 105. Still, the style and content bespeak Augustine.

[21] C. 23 q. 1 c. 2 para. 5; C. 23 q. 1 cc. 4–6. [22] C. 23 q. 1 cc. 4, 5, 7.

[23] C. 23 q. 1 c. 4.

all wars were waged in pursuit of peace, then, lacking further qualification, all wars must be deemed just. It was even possible for a soldier
to fight virtuously in a war manifestly unjust in its origin. Obviously
aiming to forestall these conclusions, Gratian devoted the second
quaestio of Causa 23 to definitions or formulae of wars that not only
were waged to attain peace but also could be considered fully just
according to Christian standards of morality. This quaestio was
destined to become the single most important point of departure for
the canonists' analyses of war. The first canon, inspired by Cicero
and taken from Isidore of Seville by way of Ivo of Chartres, defined
the just war as one waged by an edict either to recover lost goods
(*res*) or to repel an enemy attack.[24] That a just war repels an enemy
attack was and has remained fundamental to all such formulations.
Elsewhere Gratian cited similar passages that justified war as a means
of defense of self, associates, the Church, the *patria*, or the commonwealth.[25] In the same first canon Gratian added another Isidorian
passage that defined a judge as one who pronounced judgment
according to law and justice.[26] The importance of Gratian's confla-

---

[24] C. 23 q. 2 c. 1: 'Iustum est bellum, quod ex edicto geritur de rebus repetendis, aut propulsandorum hominum causa.' In the course of its transmission this statement not surprisingly underwent several textual variants. Cicero's *repetitis rebus* (*De Republica*, III, 23,
35) was repeated by Isidore (*Etymologiarum*, XVIII, 1, 2) and Ivo (*Decretum*, X, 116; *Panormia*,
VIII, 54); Cicero's *propulsandorum hostium* was likewise unchanged until Gratian's *propulsandorum hominum*. Cicero's *causa ulciscendi aut propulsandorum hostium* and his definition
of unjust wars as those undertaken *sine causa*, and Isidore's addition *non de legitima ratione*
were not included in Ivo's collections. This meant that Gratian neither invoked explicitly
the notion of just cause, nor conveyed the definition of an unjust war.

More significant perhaps were Cicero's *bellum denuntiatum* and *bellum indictum* that became Isidore's *bellum gerere ex praedicto* and was continued by Ivo. Gratian modified the
phrase to *bellum gerere ex edicto*, but the sixteenth-century correctors of the Decretum
restored *ex praedicto*. Cf. Horoy, *Droit international*, p. 125; Regout, *La guerre juste*, p. 63,
n. 1; Hubrecht, 'La juste guerre,' pp. 169f. The issue at stake here is whether a just war
must be preceded by a formal announcement as it was in ancient Roman practice, or
whether it must be waged on an authoritative edict. The Romans assumed that war was
waged on authority, and so placed emphasis on the formal declaration (*praedictum*). In the
Middle Ages, when the locus of authority was more difficult to locate, it was necessary to
make clear that a war was indeed authorised by a legitimate official. Conversely, the for-
mality of the declaration was not seen as so important. Gratian here merely strengthened
the requirement of authority by substituting *edictum* for *praedictum*. The edict that set the
war in motion would usually be made known to friend and foe alike. The common
meaning here is that war must be declared publicly by legitimate authority. In the Middle
Ages, *bellum indicere* and *bellum gerere* came to refer not only to the declaration but also the
waging of war, and Gratian's formula is consonant with this practice: cf. Cram, *Iudicium
Belli*, pp. 187–91.

[25] E.g. C. 23 q. 3 c. 5; C. 23 q. 1 c. 7; C. 23 q. 4 c. 48; C. 23 q. 8 c. 15.

[26] C. 23 q. 2 c. 1.

tion of war and justice is that it emphasised the similarity between a judicial process and the just war. Both recourses to force were means of correcting an injust situation: the one an ordinary procedure; the other an extraordinary measure warranted by extreme circumstances. Since in either case recourse to armed violence in pursuit of justice was the prerogative of constituted authority, the initiative rested with officials rather than private individuals. A private war was *eo ipso* unjust.[27] Implicit in the passage is the recognition that the party waging a just war was acting as judge in his own cause.

The second canon of the quaestio contains Augustine's crucial definition of the just war as that which avenged injuries. As examples of these injuries Augustine had mentioned the neglect by an authority to punish its own subjects for crimes committed against the injured party and the refusal to restore goods unjustly seized.[28] In effect these two examples functioned as different species of the generic title of injustice. Isidore's use of *aut* in the first canon and Augustine's use of *vel...vel* here appear to confirm this.[29] Logically if not chronologically,

[27] Cf. Regout, *La guerre juste*, p. 65; Hubrecht, 'La juste guerre,' pp. 169f.; idem, 'La juste guerre dans la doctrine chrétienne,' p. 114; Horoy, *Droit international*, p. 124; Cram, *Iudicium Belli*, pp. 15, 180; Baldwin, *Masters Princes and Merchants*, 1, 206.

[28] C. 23 q. 2 c. 2: 'Iusta autem bella solent diffiniri, que ulciscuntur iniurias, sic gens et civitas, petenda est, que vel vindicare neglexerit quod a suis inprobe factum est, vel reddere quod per iniurias ablatum est.' For the original passage, see above, ch. 1, n. 8; cf. Regout, *La guerre juste*, p. 63, n. 2. From the notes in Friedberg's edition it appears that Gratian may have taken the passage directly from Augustine, improbable as that might seem. I have been unable to discover citations of this passage during the early Middle Ages. To Gratian, then, should go the credit for introducing Augustine's crucial definition into medieval discussions of the just war, at least until possible intermediary citations have been discovered.

[29] Cf. Regout, *La guerre juste*, p. 63, nn. 2, 3. The precise interpretation of *aut* and *vel* is often difficult in significant texts. Both can be used as disjunctive conjunctions, but indicate varying degrees of contrast, *aut* expressing the stronger opposition and *vel* sometimes taking the coordinate meaning 'and': C. T. Lewis and C. Short, *A Latin Dictionary* (Oxford, 1879), pp. 210, 1963. Isidore's sense in canon 1 is obviously that either the recovery of lost goods or the repulsion of attack constitutes a just cause for war. Similarly, in canon 2 Augustine means that either neglect to punish subjects or refusal to restore lost goods constitutes a sufficient instance of an injury to be avenged. In both cases the conjunctions indicate disjunction rather than a coordinate and continuous train of thought. This is necessary to understand, for if *aut* and *vel* were continuous, then the requirements in both clauses would have to be met for the wars to be just. Obviously it was not preferable to suffer both types of injuries before being entitled to wage a just war. Conversely, Gratian's own redefinition of the just war (n. 30 below) illustrates *vel* used as a coordinate conjunction meaning 'and,' for Gratian could not have meant that a just war was one waged either by edict or to avenge injuries without contradicting Isidore, Augustine and common sense. Furthermore, *vel quo iniuriae ulciscuntur* is a purpose clause that explains the reason for the edict. For the interpretation of other texts where this problem arises, see W. Ullmann, *Principles of*

Augustine's definition merely enlarged upon Isidore's *de rebus repetendis*. The enemy in a just war committed three types of injustices: he had either launched an attack, or refused to punish his own subjects for their misdeeds, or stolen property and refused to return it. Correspondingly these were three causes for a just war: to repel the invasion; to recover property; and to avenge prior injuries. Realising the need for consolidation of these elements to avoid confusion, Gratian proposed a hybrid definition: 'A just war is waged by an authoritative edict to avenge injuries.'[30]

Immediately following his own definition Gratian provided another example of a just cause for war with an Augustinian passage concerning the war between the Israelites and the Amorites. The latter had denied the Israelites the right of free passage across their territory, for which reason the Israelites waged a victorious just war. Augustine termed this a just war because the Israelites had been denied a right accorded to them by human society in general.[31] Although neither Augustine nor Gratian explicitly linked this right to the *ius gentium* Gratian's positioning of this canon strongly suggests that he considered denial of passage an injury to be avenged, since it was a denial of a legal right. Modern notions of state sovereignty of course attribute no legal status to the 'right of innocent passage,' through foreign territory.

Gratian's achievement in this quaestio was to make the first attempt after Isidore to define the characteristics of the just war. He made this much clear: no war could be considered just unless commenced by an authoritative edict; and, even with proper authority, a just war must fulfill the second requirement that it be waged to right a legal wrong or injury. Still, Gratian's attempt at definition is deficient; both medieval and modern writers could take him to task for not going far enough. He did not arrive at a neat and comprehensive formula that fastened the just war theory to specific institutions. By what means should a just war be waged? What, specifically, were just causes? Gratian never actually invoked the terms 'justa

---

Government and Politics in the Middle Ages (London, 1961), p. 165; idem, *Individual and Society in the Middle Ages* (Baltimore, 1966), p. 71, n. 21; and Chodorow, *Christian Political Theory*, pp. 99–101.

[30] C. 23 q. 2 d. p. c. 2: 'Cum ergo iustum bellum sit, quod ex edicto geritur, vel quod iniuriae ulciscuntur.'

[31] C. 23 q. 2 c. 3.

causa' and 'recta intentio,' nor did he mention explicitly the just cause of defending one's person, associates, property, rights or *patria* against hostile attack. Just what authorities could declare a just war? What were the legal conditions and consequences? Were there limitations on the violence that could licitly be employed? How did the just war relate to other legitimate types of armed violence? What bearing did military virtues and vices have on the justice of a war? Gratian of course realised that his treatment here was a partial one. In other parts of Causa 23 he endeavored to flesh out the skeleton of his formulation in quaestio 2, and both succeeding canonists and theologians performed a similar task of amplification. In a sense the rest of the present work is a contribution to the history of that task.

More specifically, a close assessment of Gratian's formulation of the just war must consider his use of key terms, especially those contained in the phrase 'just wars punish injuries' ('iusta bella ulciscuntur iniurias'). An *iniuria* was the infringement of a legal right, but what sort of right? Gratian's use of *iniuria* could theoretically apply to transgression of statutory laws, natural law, the *ius gentium*, biblical commands or even church canons. But in quaestio 2 Gratian used *iniuria* in conjunction with such legal concepts as *res repetere*, *petenda*, *disceptare iure* and *delictum*, which suggests that he viewed the just war as a quasi-legal procedure employed by competent judicial authority in defense of legal rights of human justice. Gratian here did not envision the just war as a means of defending scriptural or doctrinal positions or ecclesiastical discipline, although other parts of Causa 23 came close to doing so. His citation of *res repetere* also could be considered as avenging injuries, where *res* meant any kind of movable or immovable property. If *iniuria* did not present problems of interpretation in quaestio 2, it did in quaestio 3, where Gratian introduced patristic texts that praised repulsion of injuries done to one's *socii*, allies or associates. Thus Ambrose lauded that fortitude that in war protected the *patria* from barbarians and at home defended the weak or one's associates from brigands.[32] Those who were capable of repelling injuries to associates but did not do so were thereby as guilty as the actual culprits.[33] Gratian's dictum agreed by

---

[32] C. 23 q. 3 c. 5.
[33] C. 23 q. 3 c. 7; cf. C. 23 q. 3 cc. 8, 11; C. 23 q. 8 c. 12.

asserting that injuries done to associates must be repelled by recourse to arms, that the wicked should be rendered unable to perform further misdeeds and the good be able to uphold the Church.[34] The problem with this seemingly conventional train of thought is this: if repelling injuries done to one's associates is licit, then is intervention by a third party in a conflict also licit? After all, the right of intervention has remained a thorny issue of international law and politics. Could someone not party to a dispute intervene, militarily, and would his intervention constitute a just war? Since the third party would have no jurisdiction over the disputants, the criterion of legitimate authority could not be met and the intervention would therefore be unjust. Gratian probably had no clear idea of this possibility, and while it may seem that posing this question of Gratian unfairly brings modern concepts to bear on the Decretum, the sense of Gratian's discussion is that the Church had the right and the duty to intervene in public affairs to defend itself, orthodox Christians, and the poor and helpless, and furthermore, the Church had the right to invoke the aid of legitimate authority in its intervention. The question can, however, be conveniently solved, at least for quaestio 3, by close study of the meaning of *socii*. The term here is used not for allies subject to another prince but in the sense of family, friends, neighbors, fellow citizens and persons over whom the defender had legitimate authority. The quaestio therefore did not grant police power or the right of intervention to a third party lacking authority over the 'associates.' While quaestio 3 therefore did justify the repulsion of injuries even by warfare, it neither linked this repulsion explicitly to the just war nor even concerned wars between independent powers. The focus is on internal law and order rather than any nascent concept of international law. One must look elsewhere in Causa 23 and in subsequent commentaries to find suggestions of the right of intervention.[35]

A more immediately crucial problem is the meaning of *ulciscuntur* in this context. The root of the term is *ultio*, meaning variously repulsion, vengeance, and punishment. Thus the phrase *ulciscuntur iniurias* perpetuated the ambiguities inherent in Augustine's treat-

[34] C. 23 q. 3 d. p. c. 10.
[35] The discussion here slightly modifies these earlier analyses of the quaestio: Horoy, *Droit international*, pp. 123, 139–45; Regout, *La guerre juste*, pp. 65f.; Hubrecht, 'La juste guerre.' p. 171. For Gratian's treatment of the Church's right to intervene, see below, pp. 72ff.

ment, for it could entail merciless and unrestrained revenge for a trivial injury, restrained defense against hostile attack, recovery of stolen goods, or even the punishment of evil-doers.[36] Quaestio 2 provided little elaboration on the meaning of *ulciscuntur*. Elsewhere Gratian made clear that punishment or *ultio* did not justify unrestrained vengeance or needless cruelty. Certain attitudes associated with war, such as the desire to harm, the lust for domination, and the cruelty of punishment were to be reprehended, but not war itself.[37] And in discussing use of arms in repelling injuries done to associates Gratian cited two Augustinian passages that condemned the retributive and vengeful punishment of the 'eye for an eye' tradition as unjust and vicious justice, and prohibited punishment of enemies of the Church out of motives of revenge rather than from the laudable desire to protect the Church.[38] Persons who avenged their own injuries could not be ordained as clerics.[39] A passage from Leo IV used *ultio* in the sense of protection: the pope was *ultor sui gregis* bound to defend and aid his flock rather than to act as an avenger.[40] The term *vindicta*, similar in meaning to *ultio*, was examined in quaestio 4, devoted to the uses and abuses of vengeance. The lengthy and diffuse quaestio mentioned war only a few times, but its general tenor was that *vindicta* was licit when justified and inflicted according to proper motives such as love of justice, but not by love of inflicting punishment.[41] Gratian's selection of texts did not contain an explicit elaboration of the concepts of *ultio* and *vindicta* in this regard. He only posed this problem of interpretation and left its solution to his successors.

By invoking loaded terms such as *iniuria*, *ultio* and *vindicta* in his

---

[36] Regout (*La juste guerre*, pp. 63–5) concludes that defense and recuperation of goods are envisaged as redressing injustices, merely as the execution of an authoritative decree, and do not have the force of a penal sanction or judicial punishment. But it seems that if defense and recuperation are invoked to restore a situation to justice by force of arms, these titles to a just war envisage more than mere redress of injuries, and force employed in execution of an extraordinary legal judgment does indeed constitute a penal sanction of unlimited extent. The theoretical problem is similar to the distinction between compensatory and punitive damages; cf. above, ch. 1, n. 9.

[37] C. 23 q. 1 c. 4.

[38] C. 23 q. 3 cc. 1–2.

[39] D. 46 c. 8.

[40] C. 23 q. 8 c. 8.

[41] E.g. C. 23 q. 4 d. p. c. 54. Cf. C. 23 q. 3 c. 1; C. 23 q. 5 c. 16. For other examples, among many, of the use of *ultio* and *vindicta*, see C. 23 q. 4 cc. 26–8, d. p. c. 30. Cf. Horoy, *Droit international*, p. 150; Chodorow, *Christian Political Theory*, pp. 233f.

discussion of war and related matters, Gratian involved himself and his successors in a delicate balancing act. On the one hand he had to maintain the requirements of the just war formula, while on the other he had to exclude passionate and unrestrained violence from attaining status within the just war formula. To ensure this he linked, albeit without helpful clarity, the moral imperatives governing the motivations of the belligerents analysed in quaestio 1 and elsewhere to the legal grounds for waging a just war posited in quaestio 2. In other words, by this linkage of subjective and objective criteria he sought to require that a just war would be waged by soldiers who exhibited the virtues but not the vices associated with warfare. And yet he realised that reliance on the virtues of the Christian soldier was only a fragile means of ensuring that a war was justified in its origin and conduct. Recourse to a doctrine of legitimate authority was necessary to prevent *iniuria*, *ultio* and *vindicta* from transforming the just war into indiscriminate slaughter.

AUTHORITY, OBEDIENCE AND CONDUCT

The most crucial issue in any just war theory is the locus of authority capable of waging war. In the Augustinian tradition within which Gratian operated, the emphasis on authority was a logical and indeed necessary concomitant of the pacific and charitable inward disposition. For unlike the private person involved in a dispute who might be motivated by cruelty, revenge or hatred, public officials were assumed capable of maintaining the proper attitudes. While few today would be willing to go along with the notion that public officials by virtue of their office are rendered incapable of passionate and willful actions, Augustine's notion and its foundations were necessary to the medieval analysis of war and were destined to have a long history. As a result, Gratian followed Augustine in emphasising legitimate authority as an objective legal criterion to complement and reinforce the more subjective and less judiciable moral criterion of the inward attitude.

Gratian's major concern was to limit the execution of justice to officials acting on legitimate authority. Only in this way could he prevent *ultio*, *vindicta*, and the avenging of injuries from degenerating into unrestrained vengeance and brutality. The texts in quaestio 2, in asserting that a just war must be waged on authority, set in motion the whole sequence of legal consequences and moral cautions attendant upon the just war. Only legitimate authorities and soldiers under their command were capable of undertaking a just war.[42] Wars should only be undertaken on the command of God or some legitimate *imperium*.[43] Even bishops, since they lacked authority in this matter, were forbidden to avenge injuries done to them.[44] Licit use of the sword was restricted to those acting on legitimate superior authority. Those who used the sword without authority fell under the condemnation of Christ's 'they that take the sword shall perish with the sword' (Matt. 26: 52). A soldier or other minister who killed a man in war or put a culprit to death was not held guilty of murder. In these passages, Gratian clearly distinguished between men who killed on command and with proper attitude and murderers who as private persons killed on their own authority.[45] There are, however, several passages that could be interpreted as justifying killing without any express command of superior authority. Thus men did act as avengers of divine wrath and ministers of God when they killed evil-doers,[46] and slayers of excommunicated persons were not guilty of murder.[47] These passages, however, simply do not expressly confront the issue of authority but are devoted to expressing the principle that wicked men deserve to be put to death as punishment for their misdeeds. In other passages soon to be discussed Gratian attempted to delimit the authority requisite for punishment of those who transgressed moral laws and Church doctrine.

The notion concomitant with the assertion of authority was the duty of obedience on the part of soldiers in the ranks. The just man in military service could justly wage war at the command of the prince, even if the prince were a sacrilegious person, so long as his orders did not contravene divine precepts. In case of doubt concerning the consonance of military commands with divine precepts, the soldier was to render the accustomed obedience. Obedience to evil commands, or even in a war motivated by greed, rendered the warrior innocent of any blame, while the prince's iniquity was upon his head alone.[48] For example, Christian soldiers had obeyed the military

---

[42] C. 23 q. 2 c. 2.   [43] C. 23 q. 1 c. 4.   [44] C. 23 q. 4 c. 27.

[45] C. 23 q. 4 c. 36; C. 23 q. 5 cc. 8, 9, para. 4, 13, 14, 40, 41, d. p. c. 48; C. 23 q. 8 cc. 14, 33. Cf. Brundage, *Medieval Canon Law*, p. 20.

[46] C. 23 q. 5 cc. 27–9 (Jerome).   [47] C. 23 q. 5 c. 47 (Urban II).

[48] C. 23 q. 1 c. 4; C. 23 q. 5 c. 25. Indirectly, Gratian's citation of Fulbert of Chartres' famous

commands of Julian the Apostate, but they rightly refused to obey his orders to persecute Christians.[49] The tenor of Gratian's analysis was to remove warfare from the sphere of private, individual and non-authoritative initiative. His view did not take into account the complex moral and legal dilemmas surrounding obedience in warfare that occupied the attention of his successors.

If authority, obedience and a just cause were present, the problems remained of how to conduct a just war and what consequences followed upon a just war. Gratian's treatment here was sketchy at best. He did cite Augustine's opinion that fidelity or good faith must be maintained when it had been promised to an enemy.[50] Conversely, if faith had not been promised and the war was just, it could be waged by such means as ruses, ambushes and strategems.[51] A more crucial point was the necessity of continuing bellicose operations without cease. In Gratian's time prelates were attempting to enforce the Truce of God. Implicitly opposing this institution, Gratian held that when war was necessary to defend self, ancestral laws or the *patria*, it could be waged at all times, even during Lent, lest men tempt God to intervene because they did not do what they could in their own just defense. This opinion was but an application of Augustine's premise that wars were waged only out of necessity to secure peace, and not voluntarily.[52] Consonant with the Peace of God movement, Gratian did however exempt pilgrims, clerics, monks, women and the unarmed poor from violence, on pain of excommunication and anathema. This is as close as he came to upholding some kind of non-combatant immunity.[53] Another contemporary ecclesiastical movement to reduce the level of violence was the condemnation of weapons judged too deadly to be used against Christians that was levied by the second Lateran Council

statement of the reciprocal duties of lord and vassal within the feudal contract also counseled obedience of a vassal to his lord's commands, although war was not specifically mentioned: C. 22 q. 5 c. 18.

[49] C. 11 q. 3 cc. 94, 98 (Augustine: cf. above, ch. 1, n. 21). On several occasions, however, Gratian cited texts that prohibited knights from fulfilling oaths and obligations that required the commission of illegal or immoral acts or obedience to excommunicated or deposed rulers, but these texts did not mention warfare explicitly: C. 15 q. 6 cc. 2–5; C. 22 q. 4 cc. 1, 5, 6, 8, 12, 13, 18, 19.

[50] C. 23 q. 1 c. 3. Cf. Cicero, *De Republica*, III, 29, 107–8.

[51] C. 23 q. 2 c. 2.

[52] C. 23 q. 8 c. 15. Cf. C. 23 q. 1 c. 3. For the Truce of God, see above, ch. 1, n. 71.

[53] C. 24 q. 3 cc. 22–5. Cf. C. 17 q. 4 c. 29.

(*c.* 29). While Gratian did include some of this council's canons in the Decretum, he left this measure out. Speculation as to why canonistic compilers left certain canons out or omitted portions of canons is often sheer guesswork, intriguing as that may be. Here however Gratian's position suggests the reason for the omission: if a war was necessary and just, then all possible means to victory must be employed including the use of more effective weapons. And if the war was unnecessary, then it should not take place at all, much less during Lent or with deadly weapons. Later compilers included the 1139 prohibition in *Compilatio Prima* and the Gregorian decretals, but most canonistic commentaries remained faithful to Gratian on this score.[54]

Once a just war had been won, what were the legitimate fruits of victory, and who should enjoy them? In one passage bearing on these questions Gratian cited an Ambrosian passage that attributed the spoils gained in war to the king or prince, who should in turn distribute a portion of these to his soldiers according to the efforts they had expended.[55] This is perhaps an oblique statement that to the victor go the spoils. In an age of widespread pillaging and conquest this is all Gratian had to say on these issues, and he did not link them to the just war. His interest lay more in reconciling just war with received doctrine than in its contemporary application. After accepting Gratian's outline of the just war, subsequent commentators naturally turned their attention to its practical consequences.

A serious difficulty with Gratian's analysis was the lack of precision in identifying those institutions that possessed the requisite authority to wage a just war. Gratian's references could cover a host of authorities, from the Emperor or king down to the most lowly vassal, or at least they did not absolutely exclude any of these. Lacking at his time was a clearly understood concept of public authority that could render viable the distinctions between public and private initiative and superior and inferior jurisdiction. This imprecision continued to plague medieval discussions of the just war, and called forth some of the most profound analysis of medieval political observers.

[54] Cf. Comp. I, 5. 19. 1; X, 5. 15. 1. For canonistic commentaries on this problem, see below, ch. 5, nn. 81–6.
[55] C. 23 q. 5 c. 25.

THE ROLE OF CHURCH AND CHURCHMEN IN WARFARE

In the medieval context a most important facet of the problem of authority was the legitimate role of the Church in war and violence. Having lived through the later stages of the Investiture Contest, possibly as an attentive witness, Gratian realised the necessity of considering the relationships between the Church and lay rulers and the chain of command between the Church hierarchy, lay officials and ordinary Christians. If the Church had the duty to uphold the Christian faithful and their doctrine, then how were the enemies of the Church and the faithful to be treated? In short, could the Church undertake wars and crusades, and could clergymen take part in wars of lay lords?

Even a war waged with ecclesiastical involvement of some sort, in order to be just, naturally had to meet the broad and basic criteria of proper authority and just cause. In an oblique way Gratian treated this problem in passages scattered through the first seven quaestiones of Causa 23 before arriving at a fuller treatment in quaestio 8. Proper understanding of Gratian's thought here is difficult because he neither discussed these wars separately from the wars and police actions of secular rulers nor satisfactorily analysed the various elements of a Church-related just war.

To enlarge the scope of the just war, Gratian invoked the ultimate authority, God Himself. On this point he most clearly showed his conflation of legal and moral categories. In the Augustinian passages of quaestio 2 God was portrayed as the most indisputably legitimate authority whose wars were just without doubt. The Israelites who fought His wars were His special ministers and therefore were innocent of transgressing the Sixth Commandment not to kill. Thus God ordered the Israelites to lay ambushes so as to capture the city of Ai (Joshua 8),[56] and, in a passage ostensibly concerned with the right of innocent passage, Augustine considered the Israelite conquest of the Amorites (Numbers 21: 21-5) a just war because it was waged on divine command.[57] For Gratian a divine command was a

---

[56] C. 23 q. 2 c. 2.

[57] C. 23 q. 2 c. 3. The passage did not explicitly invoke God as the author of the war, but the original Augustinian passage had also justified the war as a response to a divine command: cf. above, ch. 1, n. 16. Gratian merely took the extract from Ivo of Chartres. At any rate, after canon 2 reference to divine commands would have been redundant. For other

sufficient justification for war, a special case of the general requirement that a just war be waged by authoritative edict. It was of course
self-evident that God's cause would be just. The consequence of this
linkage of just war and divine authority for Church-related wars
cannot be overestimated, for by it Gratian covertly extended divine
authority to ecclesiastical authority. This extension meant that
Christians, as God's latter-day Chosen People directed on earth by
the Church hierarchy, could legitimately wage war against its visible
enemies; moreover, it transferred the still-inchoate notion of the just
cause to the realm of defense of the faith against its enemies. Thus the
just war became a licit and even laudable form of Christian aggression, and military service became not merely tolerable but even
pleasing to God.

Still, Gratian had not yet made explicit his extension of divine
authority to the Church. The problem confronting him, as it had the
early Church, was how to interpret the examples of the Old Testament wars in a Christian moral context. In quaestio I Gratian had
cited Origen's homily to the effect that Old Testament wars did not
sanction Christian religious wars, and had overcome this objection
by reference to Augustinian analysis of the precepts of patience.[58]
Lest Origen stand in contradiction, and to make clear that these wars
indeed served as examples to be followed by Christians, Gratian
brought passages to bear that justified resort to violence for Christian
moral purposes. A pseudo-Augustinian passage stated that wars
served peace when they coerced evil-doers and sustained the
righteous;[59] they punished the wicked and raised up good and
pious men.[60] Men who obeyed divine commandments in killing
evil-doers were avenging hands of God and the instruments of his
wrath.[61] Those who were contemptuous of divine mandates should
be coerced by severe vengeance lest the evil spread.[62] Such measures
were not motivated by a lust for inflicting punishment (*ultio*) but
rather by the judge's love of justice that sought to render justice to
the unjust.[63] Punishment of the wicked, however, was an affair for
the authorities, and a bishop or pope could not avenge injuries done

---

examples of divine commands to kill and wage war, see C. 23 q. I c. 4; C. 23 q. 5 c. 9
para. 4.

[58] C. 23 q. I cc. 1, d. p. c. 1, 2.   [59] C. 23 q. I c. 6.   [60] C. 23 q. 5 c. 23.

[61] C. 23 q. 5 cc. 27, 29.   [62] C. 23 q. 3 c. 9.

[63] C. 23 q. 3 cc. I, d. p. c. I.

to himself but only those done to the Church.[64] By the examples of Moses and Christ, the Church justly punished the wicked and thereby placated God. Wars coerced enemies of the Church and the Christian religion, and victory was assured by the merits of the faith.[65] The fundamental distinction was between the just and laudable persecution of the wicked, and the culpable persecution of the good by the wicked.[66] According to Augustine, the Church in its efforts to compel the wicked to the good was imitating none less than God Himself.[67]

Granted that the Church had the authority to become involved in war, in what ways should this authority be expressed, and who should respond to a divine commandment to wage war passed through the intermediary of the Church? Following Augustine, Gratian was unwilling to entrust the sword of divine wrath to anyone lacking authority. Augustine had seen Roman imperial authority as a means for carrying out religious persecution, albeit at the behest of the Church. Yet Augustine's doctrine of war against heretics had not been entirely coherent, and he had viewed warfare as only one means among many for returning heretics to the orthodox fold.[68] The early Middle Ages had assigned to temporal rulers the duty of defending orthodoxy and persecuting heresy. During the Investiture Contest papal proponents had urged a more active role on the Church, whereby it would undertake the physical correction of those who resisted the execution of ecclesiastical discipline as well as the requirements of orthodoxy.[69] According to Gratian's choice of texts the Church was indeed to play a more active role, not only initiating but also directing persecution of those guilty of sin or religious heterodoxy, including heretics and infidels. Furthermore, these persecutions were to be initiated and supervised by the Church. In effect Gratian elaborated a justification of religious persecution that was later employed to justify crusades against infidels, heretics, and those who contemptuously disputed the exercise of papal authority. Now the

---

64 C. 23 q. 4 cc. 26–8, d. p. c. 30; D. 46 c. 8. Cf. Horoy, *Droit international*, p. 150; Chodorow, *Christian Political Theory*, pp. 233f.

65 C. 23 q. 4 cc. 43–5, 47–9.

66 C. 23 q. 4 d. p. c. 49, cc. 50–4.

67 C. 23 q. 6 c. 1; cf. above, ch. 1, n. 31.

68 Cf. above, ch. 1, nn. 27–34 and Pissard, *La guerre sainte*, p. 2.

69 For a brief overview of this evolution, see most recently Chodorow, *Christian Political Theory*, pp. 223–7.

Church could licitly wage war on God's behalf but without His explicit intervention. The Church thus had a moral mandate to wage war on its own behalf. In this sense Causa 23 was a summation of the doctrines developed by papal proponents in the course of the Investiture Contest.

Heretics occupied the attention of Gratian's sanctions more than any other types of enemies. While their persecution was just and proper, heretics themselves could not legitimately persecute orthodox Christians.[70] The Church had the right to coerce heretics to return to orthodoxy even against their will.[71] In quaestio 4 Gratian quoted a number of passages to justify the physical coercion of heretics and all evil-doers in general at the behest of the Church,[72] and in quaestio 5 Gratian used several texts to show religious persecution as a justification for war. Canon 43, a passage from Pelagius I written about 560, concerned the Venetians and Ligurians who were harassing the papacy. At one point they were termed schismatics, without the mention of heresy, but the rubric for the passage in Gratian's text levelled the charge of heresy. Canon 46 was Leo IV's exhortation to the Frankish army that promised them the kingdom of Heaven should they die in war. The rubric was again more specific: those who died in battle against the infidels merited eternal salvation. In canon 47, a more contemporary passage from Urban II, the text and the rubric were in complete accord: those who killed excommunicates on behalf of the Church were not considered murderers.[73] And in quaestio 7 Gratian held that heretics who merely by their heresy lacked the fundamental spirit of justice, could have no just claim in any matter, and therefore could not even legally possess property. Catholics were justified in confiscating the property of heretics.[74]

Although Gratian did not always mention wars in these contexts,

---

[70] C. 23 q. 3 c. 4.

[71] C. 23 q. 4 cc. 38–40; Cf. 23 q. 5 cc. 43–4.

[72] E.g. passages from Augustine: C. 23 q. 4 cc. 38–43; and from Gregory the Great: C. 23 q. 4 cc. 47–9.

[73] C. 23 q. 5 c. 46: (rubric) 'In certamine, quod contra infideles geritur, quisquis moritur, celeste regnum meretur.' C. 23 q. 5 c. 47: (rubric) 'Non sunt homicidae, que adversus excommunicatos zelo matris ecclesiae armantur.' C. 23 q. 5 c. 46 and C. 23 q. 8 c. 9 were fragments from Leo IV's exhortations to the Franks to combat the infidels: see above, ch. 1, n. 64. For the doctrinal evolution in the manuscript tradition of the Decretum, see Hubrecht, 'La juste guerre,' 173, n. 70, citing information supplied by Mme Rambaud.

[74] C. 23 q. 7 c. 4, d. p. c. 4.

warfare often involved confiscation on a large scale, and the hypothetical case that initiated Causa 23 concerned wars in which the
property of heretics was confiscated. In Gratian's treatment, then, just
warfare and persecution of heretics were conflated. Similarly,
enemies of the Church, the powerful rich, murderers, sacrilegious
persons, schismatics, infidels, excommunicated persons all merited
physical punishment inflicted by lay officials at the behest of the
Church.[75] Gratian drew the great bulk of these passages from those
works of Augustine and Gregory the Great that dealt with the
defense of the Church against its visible enemies and employed terms
of sweeping, even exaggerated, moral condemnations. It is clear that
anyone seen as a threat to the Church on earth merited physical
punishment even by war. The waging of these wars was a positive
moral duty, and no limits were set on the extent of violence that
could be employed.

The selection of texts in the first 7 quaestiones had constituted a
digest of traditional opinion on the Church's indirect authority over
warfare. As part of the exercise of their ordinary duties lay officials
were to punish criminals of all sorts, while in matters concerning the
Church, ecclesiastical authorities had the right to seek military aid
from lay rulers, when spiritual censures had proved ineffective.[76] In
effect the Church had the right to order persecution but was not to
become directly involved in its execution; in other words, it
possessed the *ius coactivae potestatis* but not the *executio iuris*.[77] As it
stood this analysis was deficient because it did not take into account
the involvement of contemporary ecclesiastics in warfare. After all,
the papacy was claiming and exercising an increasing control over
secular rulers that often resulted in violence, as in the military engagements of the Investiture Contest, and had on its own authority called
the crusades into existence. Popes were, moreover, involved in
authorising the use of force to punish those who attacked churches
and clerics, and bishops who had secular as well as spiritual authority
often sent contingents of troops to their overlord's battles, and often

---

[75] E.g. C. 23 q. 5 cc. 8, 18, 23, 32, 40, 41, 43, 44. Cf. Chodorow, *Christian Political Theory*,
pp. 225f.
[76] E.g. C. 23 q. 1 c. 2 para. 4; C. 23 q. 3 cc. 2, 3, 10; C. 23 q. 4 c. 41; C. 23 q. 5 c. 39 (and
the texts cited in n. 75 above); C. 23 q. 8 c. 10. The 'socii' of quaestio 3 could be taken to
mean orthodox Christians: Horoy, *Droit international*, p. 143.
[77] Chodorow, *Christian Political Theory*, p. 225.

accompanied their temporal overlords on campaign. Simple clerics were known to participate actively in war and violence.[78] But in Gratian's analysis of war thus far, soldiers acting on legitimate lay authority were the only persons for whom the *métier* of arms was licit. Realising the inadequacy of his treatment, Gratian devoted quaestio 8 expressly to the use of physical force by clerics. The dialectical statement that prefaced the quaestio contended that any cleric whatsoever was prohibited from taking up arms simply because Christ had forbidden Peter to use his material sword in defense of his Master (Matt. 26: 52). The right for clerics to use the corporal sword had been abrogated by Christ's example of patience. Henceforward clerics were only permitted to use the spiritual sword of the word of God. Gratian concluded with the well-known requirement of bearing the sword only on legitimate authority and the assertion that the prohibition on self-defense referred especially to prelates.[79] If this contention were allowed to stand unqualified, then all clerics would be forbidden to engage in political activities, a prohibition that would fly in the face of contemporary practice.

The most general rule was a canon of the eleventh council of Toledo (A.D. 675) that prohibited priests from participating in any proceedings (*iudicia*) involving bloodshed.[80] Canons from other councils added further prohibitions: prayers and offerings were not to be made for a cleric dying in war,[81] and clerics who voluntarily bore arms should be degraded and retired to monasteries, for they could not serve both God and secular society.[82] According to a spurious canon attributed to Ambrose, the proper weapons for clerics were

---

[78] In 1138 King David of Scotland, seeking to profit from the disorder of Stephen's reign, invaded northern England. Stephen's lieutenant in the north, the archbishop of York, called a council that decided to muster the Yorkshire levies. Each contingent of the shire levy was commanded by its parish priest: J. Beeler, *Warfare in Feudal Europe, 730–1200* (Ithaca, New York, 1971), pp. 107f. This nicely illustrates the dilemma Gratian faced in reconciling clerical status and contemporary practice. If the present interpretation is correct, then Gratian would have considered the archbishop's activity licit, but would have condemned that of the parish clergy. For other examples of clerical participation in warfare within Europe, see Brundage, *Canon Law and the Crusader*, pp. 28f., Baldwin, *Masters Princes and Merchants*, I, 205f., Prinz, *Klerus und Krieg*, chs. 3–6.

[79] C. 23 q. 8, pr. For a close analysis of this quaestio, see Chodorow, *Christian Political Theory*, pp. 239–43.

[80] C. 23 q. 8 c. 30: 'His a quibus Domini sacramenta tractanda sunt, iudicium sanguinis non licet.' The sense is that no cleric could pass a judgment that expressly sentenced someone to suffer loss of blood.

[81] C. 23 q. 8 c. 4.   [82] C. 23 q. 8 cc. 5–6.

prayers and tears.[83] Consistent with his earlier position that the Church should exercise religious persecution, Gratian qualified these rules with his own opinion: while clerics could not themselves bear arms, they could legitimately exhort (*hortari*) others to defend the oppressed and attack the enemies of God.[84] What followed was a number of examples, taken from the Carolingian period, of papal efforts in defense against infidels and enemies of the Church. Leo IV, who in about 852 had called a force together to defend Rome against Saracen pirates, also saw himself as avenger and defender of his flock.[85] Pope Adrian I had exhorted Charlemagne to wage war against the Lombards.[86] After quotations of two similar passages dealing with Gregory the Great's activities, Gratian concluded that priests themselves had the authority to persuade proper officials and to order anyone else to bear arms in service of the Church.[87] Having made this statement, Gratian adduced authorities that proceeded to cast doubts and raise complications about his dictum. Nicholas I prohibited bishops even from performing the auxiliary duty of watching out for pirates, lest they become involved in secular affairs,[88] and Gregory the Great, even while strenuously directing military operations against the Lombards, in fear of God refused to become directly responsible for the death of any one of them, lest the Lombards lose all their leaders.[89] While one may excuse Gregory's confidence in the might of his own forces, these two canons immediately raised several serious questions. If accepted as normative without qualification,

---

[83] C. 23 q. 8 c. 3. This canon and the two previous ones are *paleae* found in no mss. before the thirteenth century. Evidently they were added to reinforce the prohibition on direct clerical participation in warfare that, in spite of Gratian, had not been carefully observed: Hubrecht, 'La juste guerre,' 174, n. 43bis, citing a note from Mme Rambaud.

[84] C. 23 q. 8 d. p. c. 6: 'Sacerdotes propria manu arma arripere non debent; sed alios ad arripiendum ad oppressorum defensionem, atque ad inimicorum Dei oppugnationem eis licet hortari.' Cf. D. 36, c. 3.

[85] C. 23 q. 8 cc. 7–8. Pope Alexander II had urged the expulsion of Saracens who persecuted Christians: C. 23 q. 8 c. 11.

[86] C. 23 q. 8 c. 10.

[87] C. 23 q. 8 cc. 17–18. Cf. above, ch. 1, n. 43. C. 23 q. 8 d. p. c. 18: 'Sacerdotes, etsi propria manu arma arripere non debeant, tamen vel his, quibus huiusmodi offitia conmissa sunt, persuadere, vel quibuslibet, ut ea arripiant, sua auctoritate valeant inperare.' Cf. Chodorow, *Christian Political Theory*, p. 240. One can assume here that Gratian's use of 'priests' did not mean that he accorded to all priests the right to order lay officials to take up arms, for that would have diluted the focus of authority beyond reasonable limits, but this looseness of terminology required efforts at greater precision.

[88] C. 23 q. 8 c. 19. Cf. I Timothy 2: 4 and above, ch. 1, n. 69.

[89] C. 23 q. 8 c. 20. Cf. above, ch. 1, n. 44.

Gratian's earlier approval of ecclesiastical involvement was now contradicted. Bishops must then refrain from all secular activities whether or not these might result, however indirectly, in death.

This conclusion was obviously too radical for Gratian's temperament, and so in his next dicta he attempted to answer the objections posed by Nicholas and Gregory. How, he asked, could the actions of Gregory I and Leo IV be normative in the face of the prohibitions levied by Gregory himself and Nicholas I? As a practical solution to the dilemma Gratian distinguished those bishops who, rejecting temporal income, lived solely on tithes and offerings (*levitica portio*) from other bishops who enjoyed income from the temporal possession of their sees. Bishops of the latter type, in effect those with regalia or secular authority, were bound to fulfill obligations occasioned by their secular position.[90] The problem then became how these obligations could be met without violating the canonical prohibitions. At this point Gratian's argument broke down, for he could only repeat the duty of prelates to render service owed. He must have recalled the *casus* that focused the entire Causa, where the bishops held regalia from the Emperor and therefore had the right to authorise war as well as the duty to aid their temporal overlord. In later dicta Gratian tried again to explain away the objections. He concluded that bishops holding regalia or temporal power should accompany the military expeditions of their overlords, provided they had obtained papal consent.[91] The failure of the Frankish bishops to secure this consent, rather than any inherent impropriety in looking out for pirates, seems to be Gratian's interpretation of the reason for Nicholas's condemnation in canon 19. Even armed with this consent, however, regalian bishops should not actually participate in battle but rather should restrict themselves to prayers for the host.[92] Gratian had thus, at least to his own satisfaction, overcome the objections. By his distinction between regalian and non-regalian

---

[90] C. 23 q. 8 d. p. c. 20. Cf. Chodorow, *Christian Political Theory*, pp. 242f. Gratian employed several passages from diverse sources to expand upon his distinction: C. 23 q. 8 cc. 21–5. Yet none of these explicitly dealt with ecclesiastical participation in warfare, and canon 25 is a palea. On the general problem of the regalia, see J. Gaudemet, 'Regale, droit de,' *Dictionnaire de droit canonique*, VII, 493–532; on Gratian's dilemma in particular, see R. L. Benson, *The Bishop-Elect. A Study in Medieval Ecclesiastical Office* (Princeton, 1968), pp. 53–5.

[91] C. 23 q. 8 d. p. c. 25, cc. 26–8.

[92] C. 23 q. 8 d. p. c. 27.

bishops Gratian limited the application of the Pauline prohibition on clerical participation in secular affairs contained in canon 19 only to those bishops who lived independently of secular affairs. Bishops with regalia could of course perform the secular business pertaining to their sees. Yet his solution was not entirely satisfactory, for it did not meet Nicholas's objection head on, and did not come to grips with episcopal involvement in activities that resulted in death.

In his final dictum of the quaestio Gratian attempted to encapsulate his analysis in a neat formula. The example of Gregory the Great authorised prelates to demand (*postulare*) that emperors and other princes defend the faithful, and that of Leo IV enabled prelates firmly to exhort (*adhortari*) anyone whomsoever (*quoslibet*) to defend themselves against the adversaries of the faith and furthermore to summon (*citare*) everyone to keep the force of the infidels at a distance. Gratian then repeated that no bishop had the right, either by his own or imperial authority, to command the shedding of blood.[93]

This dictum was both Gratian's most important opinion and also the most difficult to interpret. He seemed to be claiming that prelates had two kinds of authority to initiate the waging of wars. There was, first, the traditional indirect authority, justified by Gregory, to demand that secular rulers render military defense to the faithful. Second, Gratian asserted that prelates could directly summon any Christian to defend the Church and the faithful against infidels and other adversaries of the Church, this latter case justified by the actions Leo IV took in an age when the Church could not depend on the cooperation of secular officials and deputised ordinary Christians for the occasion. Embedded in this dictum is the claim that the Church itself had the authority directly to wage war. Since neither Gregory I nor Leo IV held regalia from any lay lord, their authority to command the use of the sword must have been spiritual rather than secular. Realising the importance of this departure from tradition, Gratian immediately appended the prohibition on clerical shedding of blood, lest zealous prelates be tempted to participate personally in the hostilities. The verbs used in Gratian's earlier dicta provide further proof that Gratian intended to accord the right of

---

[93] C. 23 q. 8 d. p. c. 28: 'Licet ergo prelatis ecclesiae exemplo B. Gregorii ab inperatoribus vel quibuslibet ducibus defensionem fidelibus postulare. Licet etiam cum B. Leone quoslibet ad sui defensionem contra adversarios sanctae fidei viriliter adhortari, atque ad vim infidelium procul arcendam quosque citare.' Cf. C. 23 q. 8 d. p. c. 18.

direct initiative to the Church. All these expressions taken together prove that Gratian accorded to the Church the authority to issue commands binding on lay rulers and ordinary Christians alike, even though the verbs do convey varying degrees of intensity. Gratian's treatment here was a further elaboration of the program adumbrated by Gregory VII.[94]

Gratian's final position seems to be that bishops with regalia could initiate wars on their temporal authority and could actively participate in their overlord's campaigns provided they neither ordered killings nor participated personally in violence. However, such bishops presumably should refuse to fulfill their regalian obligations when the pope disapproved. On their own spiritual authority prelates, especially the pope, could also command the waging of a particular war for ecclesiastical purposes. These prelates might order lay officials or even ordinary Christians to take up arms in defense of the Church. In the latter case it appears, although Gratian did not explicitly so state, that bishops even without regalia could order laymen to act as direct agents of ecclesiastical authority. Gratian thus accorded to churchmen both temporal and spiritual authority over warfare.

The essential outlines of Gratian's treatment in quaestio 8 do however seem somewhat out of focus. Evidently, Gratian could not refer to the imagery of the two swords.[95] The sole instance of the sword was the passage in the beginning of the quaestio which concluded that clerics should not directly invoke the material sword of physical coercion. A further difficulty for the development of the Church's role in just wars was Gratian's refusal to denominate military actions expressly as wars. A consideration of the reasons for Gratian's non-employment of these terms leads to suggestions about what Gratian was trying to accomplish in the quaestio, and how well he accomplished his task. Throughout the quaestio he was involved in a delicate and convoluted balancing act, whereby the demands of canon law had to be reconciled with contemporary practice. It was

---

[94] Chodorow, *Christian Political Theory*, pp. 240–3, closely considers these dicta and arrives at the similar conclusion that the use of verbs of varying intensity indicates a looseness of terminology rather than a retreat from Gratian's strong position that the Church could wage wars on its own authority. It would seem that this looseness is an expression of Gratian's dilemma.

[95] Cf. Hubrecht, 'La juste guerre,' 176.

imperative that Gratian maintain the prohibition on clerical shedding of blood, and this was his most difficult obstacle. To maintain the absolute prohibition would revolutionise practice if enforced. The well-known case of Bishop Odo of Bayeux, who padded his mace so as not to cause external bleeding indicates the resistance Gratian would have faced. To prevent such cases of fulfilling the letter rather than the spirit of the prohibition, Gratian sought refuge in the by now conventional distinction between possession of a right and exercise of that right, and so churchmen could issue commands necessarily resulting in bloodshed, but if they did not expressly order bloodshed, they fulfilled the law as Gratian interpreted it. To us moderns Gratian's distinction between direct and indirect clerical involvement in bloodshed may seem inescapably unsatisfactory, but the logic of his position on ecclesiastical initiative in persecuting enemies made such reasoning imperative. Gratian's solution to Gregory the Great's refusal to order the deaths of Lombards in canon 20 was to prohibit even clerical mention of war and killing in their commands to lay-men, as well as maintaining the prohibition on direct clerical participation in full force.

Yet licit use of force obviously implied the right to kill. When in earlier quaestiones of the Causa Gratian recognised this implication, it caused him no trouble since he was referring primarily to lay authority, but in quaestio 8 he found it necessary to distinguish more precisely between authority and execution. Another aspect of his difficulty here is the relevance of his distinction between bishops with secular authority and duties and those who lived independently of them. Gratian had too much respect for legitimate temporal authority to undermine it by voiding the duties of clerical vassals. Coupled with the obligations of lay and ecclesiastical rulers to defend the Church, this respect overrode the objections of Gratian's authors. He then had to make a compromise whereby bishops with regalia could fulfill their duties to temporal overlords as long as they observed ecclesiastical discipline and the prohibition on direct participation in battle. Authority was preserved while execution was restricted. Gratian might have preferred that all bishops renounce their secular duties, but less perfect contemporary practice dictated his concession, and he refused to condemn bishops with regalia. What the distinction gained in relevance it lost in theoretical clarity. The chain of command between ecclesiastical and temporal rulers would remain complex so long as the distinction between the secular and the spiritual activities of the Church hierarchy was not clearly understood or observed.

Explanations of why Gratian blunted the force of his assertions must be speculative, but it is at least plausible to suggest that, since the older theory of indirect ecclesiastical involvement in the authorisation of war and violence coexisted with the newer claim of direct authorisation devised by papal proponents of the previous half-century, Gratian wished to tune down the Church's direct role in the use of force while safeguarding both the theoretical justification of that role and the traditional view of indirect power.[96] Of course, at the time Gratian was writing, the First Crusade was already a matter of record and another, this time abortive, crusade was about to commence. The papacy moreover was becoming increasingly involved in the use of force within Europe, both to maintain its temporal authority in Europe and to defend orthodoxy. Events would soon render Gratian's equivocal treatment insufficient as a guide for coherent action.

It is curious to observe in this connection that Gratian nowhere discussed *ex professo* the juristic problems of the crusades. True, he did mention examples of papal activity against the various enemies of the Church and promises of salvation for those who died in defense of Christians,[97] but he did not elaborate upon the crusade as an ecclesiastical institution. His task as he saw it was to develop principles that justified wars waged for religious purposes, but his treatment dealt with the prior holy war tradition rather than forging ahead in the construction of a theory which eventually concluded that crusades were just wars authorised solely by the papacy.[98]

In sum, Gratian's treatment in quaestio 8 justified ecclesiastical authority over certain types of warfare, while prohibiting direct clerical participation. The types of clerics whose duties included the

---

[96] Cf. Chodorow, *Christian Political Theory*, pp. 245f.

[97] E.g. C. 23 q. 5 c. 46; C. 23 q. 8 cc. 7, 9–11. Cf. Brundage, *Canon Law and the Crusader*, pp. 21–9, 36–9. Brundage (p. 22) observes that Leo IV's letter (C. 23 q. 5 c. 46; C. 23 q. 8 c. 9) was not a declaration of doctrine nor a remission of sin or its penalty, but rather a hortatory expression of hope. Had Gratian desired to launch a full discussion of the crusades, he certainly would have included canon 10 of I Lateran, *Eis qui Hierosolymam*.

[98] Cf. above, ch. 1, nn. 88–9; below, ch. 5, pp. 195ff.; Villey, *La croisade*, pp. 9–14, 21–40, 273–9; Brundage, *Canon Law and the Crusader*, pp. 39, 191f.

authorisation of war did not receive a definitive formulation. Further refinements of the juristic foundations of ecclesiastical wars were later constructed on the principles contained in the Decretum. Gratian's contribution was to safeguard both the prohibitions on clerical participation and the right of the Church to act, and to establish the proper use of ecclesiastical status while condemning its abuses.

Gratian's contributions to the development of just war theories lay primarily in his skillful combination of texts that had previously been merely listed by compilers such as Ivo of Chartres, and by the direction he gave to these texts by his dicta. In his treatment war emerges as a hostile situation that cannot be conducted with a hostile attitude. Yet how war was to be defined as a specific instance of violence remained unclear. What Gratian did was to advance a legal definition of the just war and to suggest the conditions under which it should be waged. Fundamentally, his notion of the just war had two requirements: authority and the presence of an injury to be avenged. Since injuries were defined in the broad and unspecific terms of the conflict between good and evil, moral categories impinged upon legal ones, and spiritual concerns upon temporal ones. To maintain coherence in this situation Gratian felt it necessary to orient his whole discussion toward the requirement of authority. In this he would have many successors. He drew heavily upon the Fathers for his justification of war and punishment according to Christian principles, and while the Fathers provided Gratian with potent exegetical arguments, his extensive use of them rendered his treatment more speculative than palpably applicable to the contemporary situation. In effect Gratian's just war functioned on two levels. First, there was the just war waged for the secular motives of avenging injuries and repelling enemy attacks, which Gratian derived ultimately from the Romans through Augustine and Isidore. The second level, derived from the Fathers and also from the early medieval ecclesiastics, concerned the holy war waged to avenge injuries done to Christianity or the Church by heretics, excommunicates, and infidels. With this combination Gratian provided materials for the future growth of international law, but he did not attempt to formulate that law. For example, on the basis of his texts he could not attempt the problematical distinction between offensive wars later to be considered unjust, and defensive wars that were assumed to be just. Subsequent canonists and theologians far surpassed the Decretum in precision and explanation, indeed they were compelled to do so by the lacunae in the Decretum and the force of events. A documentary survey written in any age rarely yields definitive conclusions, and the Decretum was no exception. Yet even his vaguer texts offered themselves to the contributions of subsequent jurists. To Master Gratian we owe the introduction of the concept of the just war into modern international jurisprudence. For centuries Gratian reigned as the foremost *auctor* in the jurisprudential speculation about war.

Chapter 4

THE JUST WAR ACCORDING TO
THE DECRETISTS

The influence of the Decretum was so great that very soon after its appearance a new school of canon lawyers appeared at Bologna. Well-versed in theology and Roman law as well as canon law, they sought to apply the rules of Christian conduct, which had been handed down through the ages, to contemporary realities. Since their method was to comment upon or 'gloss' the Decretum, they naturally came to be called Decretists. Their fame at the nascent university of Bologna stimulated the development of other schools of canon law in such places as Paris, Oxford and Cologne. The period between 1140 and about 1190 was the heyday of the Decretists when their opinions influenced the thoughts and actions of prelates at all levels, from provincial bishops to popes. After that period the Decretists yielded place to their canonistic successors, the Decretalists, who turned their attention to the new canon laws contained in decretal collections.[1]

Immediately recognising the importance of Gratian's Causa 23, the Decretists received his Augustinian treatment of the Christian theology of war and violence with more repetition than further elaboration, and turned to consider new formulations of the just war, further precisions on the requirements of its causes and authority, and devoted much of their attention to the role of the Church in warfare. The first major Decretist, Rufinus, writing about 1157, observed that the lengthy treatment of Causa 23 contained many assertions that, while valid regarding warfare, did not apply to other aspects of canon law, and so he asked for the indulgence of his

[1] The distinction between Decretists and Decretalists is not always easy to draw, since after 1190 many canonists commented both on the Decretum and on the decretals. Somewhat arbitrarily, I here consider as Decretists those who wrote before 1190 and those who did not make extensive use of the new decretals. For a brief survey of canon lawyers in the twelfth and thirteenth centuries, see Benson, *Bishop-Elect*, pp. 10–20. The standard guide to the commentaries is S. Kuttner, *Repertorium der Kanonistik* (*Studi e Testi*, 71) (Vatican City, 1937).

readers that he be allowed to omit the usual dialectical method of procedure in his commentary on this Causa.[2] By this somewhat cryptic statement Rufinus tacitly recognised that warfare was a subject set apart from more standard problems of canonical juris-prudence, and signalled to others the problematical status of warfare within canon law.

THE FORMULATION OF THE JUST WAR

In his *Summa Decretorum* Rufinus was the first to propose a formula for the just war that attempted to consolidate Gratian's treatment. According to him, a war was just on three grounds: on account of the one who proclaimed the war; of the one who fought it; and of the one who should be repelled by it. Whoever commanded or per-mitted the war should have *ordinaria potestas* or sufficient authority. The warrior, a person for whom the profession of soldiering was proper, must act with worthy zeal, and the adversary must deserve the war that was waged against him. Just presumptions of his guilt were sufficient to justify the war. Should any one of these three grounds be lacking, the war was unjust without further question.[3] Rufinus' definition was schematic rather than descriptive of specific institutions; for example, his use of *ordinaria potestas* made no direct reference to a particular institution. He likewise neglected to mention a specific just cause, relying merely on the judgment of the authority as to the presumed grounds for the war, and he did not employ terms such as prince, soldier, enemy and defense that were used in other formulations. Yet Rufinus did stress the requirement of authority by

---

[2] Rufinus, *Summa*, to C. 23 q. 1, pp. 403f.

[3] *Ibid.*, to C. 23 q. 2 c. 1, p. 405: 'Iustum bellum dicitur propter indicentem, propter belli-gerantem, et propter eum, qui bello pulsatur. Propter indicentem: ut ille, qui vi bellum indicit vel permittit, huius rei indulgende ordinariam habeat potestatem; propter bel-ligerantem: ut ille, qui bellum gerit, et bono zelo hoc faciat et talis persona sit, quam bellare non dedeceat; propter eum, qui bello fatigatur; ut scil. mereatur bello lacerari, vel, si non meretur, iustis tamen presumptionibus mereri putetur. Ubi aliquod horum trium defuerit, absolute iustum bellum esse non potest.' Johannes Faventinus repeated this formula verbatim: *Summa*, to C. 23 q. 2, B.N. Lat. 14606, fol. 121va. It was followed closely in the *Summa*: '*Omnis qui iuste iudicat*,' to C. 23 q. 2, Rouen, Bibl. Municipale 743 (E. 74), fol. 103vb and Luxembourg, Bibl. 144, fol. 330vb. Cf. *Summa*: '*Tractaturus Magister*,' to C. 23 q. 1, pr., B.N. Lat. 15994, fol. 69rb. After further reworking this formulation re-emerged as Aquinas' better-known authority, just cause and righteous intention: S.T. 2–2, q. 40 art. 1 resp. In a non-canonistic treatise, Rufinus reasserted the Augustinian just war that punished those who disturbed peace and order: *De Bono Pacis*, 2, 14; P.L. 150, pp. 1620f. Cf. Y. Congar, 'Maître Rufin et son *De bono pacis*,' *Revue des sciences philosophiques et théologiques*, IV (1957), 428–44.

referring to presumptions of guilt, underlining thereby the assumption that a just war was a procedure for legal redress of grievances that was invoked by the aggrieved authority when more normal procedures were of no avail. It is further evident that such an authority was both judge and party in his own cause.

The anonymous *Summa Parisiensis* of the French School, composed around 1160, amplified Rufinus' definition in holding that a just war must be waged only on princely order against public enemies, or for the recovery of property seized by force. Conversely, a war waged without these circumstances was unjust.[4] The *Summa Parisiensis* appears to contain the first explicit indication that the prince, whoever he might be, was the proper authority for waging war. Two Decretists introduced into debate the explicit requirement of the just cause. Around 1180 Sicard of Cremona devised a diagram to illustrate the relationships between the two major components of his formula, person and cause. The person directing the war must hold the *potestas principis*; the belligerents must be suitable to their occupation; and the person against whom the war was waged must deserve to be attacked, that is he must be an enemy. The cause must be just, such as inflicting deserved punishment, or protection of self, *patria*, faith or peace. Unjust causes included cruelty, cupidity, or ambition. In sum, a just war was waged either by a prince or on his edict, by suitable persons, against those who merited punishment for the sake of justice. This just war could be waged openly or by ruses.[5] Sicard's formula contained nothing really new except his explicit use of *causa*, and under that he somewhat clumsily subsumed what Gratian had considered as attitudes consonant with waging a just war. But the formula itself was an original attempt to organise the diverse strands of Gratian's treatment. The likewise anonymous *Summa: 'Elegantius in Iure Divino' (Summa Coloniensis)* of the Rhenish school proposed four criteria: the just cause; the quality of the belligerent; the directing authority; and the suitability of the time and place of the war. According to human law only princes had those public powers to wage war and on them devolved the counsel and precept necessary to wage just wars.[6] This formula is noteworthy in that it made a just

[4] *Summa Parisiensis*, to C. 23 q. 2, ed. T. P. McLaughlin (Toronto, 1952), p. 211.
[5] Sicard of Cremona, *Summa*, to C. 23 q. 1, pr., B.N. Lat. 14996, fol. 102v.
[6] *Summa: 'Elegantius in Iure Divino,'* to C. 23 q. 2, B.N. Lat. 14997, fol. 141r.

cause necessary and justified princely authority over war by reference to human law without invoking divine or ecclesiastical laws.

At the climax of the period Huguccio, the most brilliant of the Decretists, provided several concise formulae. According to one of them a war was just only if declared by legitimate authority against persons who could legitimately be attacked, and only when both adversaries regarded it to be just.[7] Huguccio neglected the objective cause of the war and concentrated on the authority and the subjective assessment of the war's justice by both parties. His formula assumed that even the guilty party would somehow realise that he deserved to become the target of the war. Further consideration of this formula will be deferred until later. The other definition advanced by Huguccio was more terse: 'A just war is waged by the just edict of a prince.'[8] Probably the most concise definition offered by any canonist, it was too concise to be sufficient or very useful, but it did lay emphasis on both the justice and the authority of the edict.

Some members of the Bolognese School took a different tack in analysing the components of the just war formulae. Stephen of Tournai led the way by claiming that a single war might either be just on both sides, or just on only one side, or even unjust on both sides. Perhaps with the scheme of Rufinus in mind, he explained that a war could be justly waged by someone who started the war and yet be unjust on the part of the person against whom the war was waged. Conversely a war might be unjustly waged against someone who justly deserved punishment by war. To exemplify his train of thought Stephen cited the Old Testament wars of Absalon against his father David and of Nebuchadnezzar against Jerusalem (II Samuel 11: 5-18; II Kings 25). David deserved punishment because of his adultery and homicide, and Jerusalem merited punishment for the

---

[7] Huguccio, *Summa*, to C. 23 q. 2, pr., B.N. Lat. 15397, fol. 47rb: 'ut si iustum sit, tria sunt necessaria, auctoritas eius qui habet potestatem indicendi bellum et quod indicatur eis quibus licet eis arma movere et quod iustum putetur, tam ab illo qui indicit quam ab illis quibus indicitur.' Precise understanding of Huguccio's positions on the just war and crusades is difficult, since his comments on C. 23 end at q. 4 c. 33: Kuttner, *Repertorium*, pp. 155–60. Here I have tried for the best reading of three Paris MSS. (B.N. Lat. 3892, 15396, 15397) that does not depend too heavily on the doubtful portions of the difficult B.N. Lat. 15397. Definitive estimations of Huguccio's thought await the appearance of a critical edition of the *Summa* now in preparation under the direction of Fr A. Stickler.

[8] *Ibid.*, C. 14 q. 4 c. 12, v. *ubi est ius belli*, B.N. Lat. 15397, fol. 5rb: 'Iustum bellum est quod geritur ex edicto principis iusto.'

sins of its people. Yet both Absalon and Nebuchadnezzar acted not from a love of justice but out of malice. Stephen illustrated the converse instance of a war justly waged against a people undeserving of such affliction with the rather contrived example of a war initiated because false witnesses proved that someone was an enemy of justice, who thereby had to become a fugitive or suffer persecution. Stephen may have had in mind Rufinus' just war waged on just presumptions of an enemy's guilt, or a war between a lord and his vassal, where a foe of the vassal had given false evidence to the lord. A war might also be adjudged just when orthodox princes defended the Church against its persecutors, just as the Israelites had waged war against the Philistines (I Samuel 4: 14–31; II Samuel 5). Here Stephen evidently considered the Israelites to have a just cause against the Philistines who merited punishment for their prior attack on the Israelites. Lastly, a war could be unjust on both sides as in the war between Saul and David, where Saul was moved solely by envy, and David was undeserving of such persecution (I Samuel 19: 23–6). A quite different example of a just war was Joshua's siege of the city of Ai. (The same incident in Joshua 8 was the point of departure for Augustine's definition of the just war cited in Causa 23 quaestio 2). This was a just war because it was waged by a legitimate king for the purposes of punishment and recovery of lost goods, and ambushes were licit because they were sanctioned by God.[9]

The author of the *Summa: 'Quoniam Status Ecclesiarum'* essentially

---

[9] Stephen of Tournai, *Summa Decretorum*, to C. 23 q. 2, B.N. Lat. 14609, fol. 65vb: 'Sic distinguendum est bellum aliquando iustum est merito pacientis, iniustum autem ratione inferentis. Aliquando iustum ratione inferentis, iniustum autem merito pacientis. Aliquando iustum ex utraque parte. Bellum iustum ex merito pacientis sed non ex ratione inferentis, sicut bellum absalon contra patrem suum david, et nabugodonosor contra iherusalem. Nam et david merebatur persecutionem pati propter adulterium et homicidium que fecerat; iherusalem propter peccata populi destrui meruerat, sed nec absalon neque nabugodonosor propter iusticiam immo propter maliciam id faciebat bellum. Iustum ex ratione inferentis non ex merito pacientis, quando aliquis falsis testibus probatus est inimicus iusticie et iniuste quantum ad se vel fugatur vel persecutionem patitur a iudice. Iuste autem quantum ad iudicem, ex utraque parte iustum est bellum quando et a fidelibus principibus ecclesiam defendentibus et contra persecutores ipsius ecclesie movetur. Quale gerebant filii israel contra philisteos. Iniustum ex utraque parte quale erat bellum quod movebat saul, quantum saul sola invidia id agebat et david persecutionem ab eo pati non meruerat. Iustum usque edicto principis de rebus ablatis dominus legitur in libro iosue ex precepto domini posuit insidias post civitatem urbis hayi...Probatur ergo hic actoritate [sic] iosue quod non peccat quis sive aperte sive in insidiis pugnat, dummodo iuste pugnet. Ulciscuntur si habent potestatem gladii vel licencia a principe plectanda punienda vel petenda a rege ad puniendum.'

reproduced Stephen's analysis,[10] and the *Summa: 'Cum in Tres Partes,'* a contemporary work of the Anglo-Norman School also followed Stephen with some minor variation, and went on to add another element that bore directly on Gratian's *ulciscuntur iniurias.* The author paraphrased the statement in the preface to the Decretum that the repulsion of violence by violence was justified by natural law. This statement would not be significant except that here it was incorporated into the formula of the just war. The author gave as an example the war waged by the Israelites against the Amorites (Numbers 21: 21–4), where the latter had denied the right of innocent passage. Anyone who had jurisdiction could wage a just war against offenders who had either been convicted in a prior court judgment or who had freely confessed their crime.[11] Unfortunately the passage did not clearly link the war with the Amorites to a more general statement, nor did it explain whether the jurisdiction was over the guilty party or not. For those who might so wish, there was embedded in the passage a suggestion of the right of intervention of a third party. In effect the author made no distinction between wars, rebellion, armed intervention and the administration of justice over those within one's proper sphere of jurisdictions. The passage illustrates both the difficulties in defining proper jurisdiction faced by the Decretists and the quasi-legal character of the just war.

The influence of Stephen of Tournai's approach extended also to other members of the Bolognese School. For one, Johannes Faventinus applied Rufinus' formula to these Old Testament wars, although without much elaboration, for he assumed examples of the various cases were well known.[12] More importantly, and in addition to a definition already mentioned,[13] Huguccio attempted to clarify Stephen's analysis of various elements that made wars just or unjust. He denied that one war could be justly waged by both belligerents, for if one justly attacked, the other unjustly defended himself. Conversely, if one party justly defended himself, then the attacker was acting unjustly. This is fine logic, but hardly susceptible of implementation, especially if the guilty party should remain tenaciously

---

[10] *Summa: 'Quoniam Status Ecclesiarum,'* to C. 23 q. 2, B.N. Lat. 16538, fol. 56rb; *Summa: 'Omnis qui iuste iudicat,'* to C. 23 q. 2, Rouen, Bibl. Municipale 743 (E. 74), fol. 103vb.

[11] *Summa: 'Cum in Tres Partes,'* to C. 23 q. 2, B.N. Lat. 16540, fol. 62r.

[12] Johannes Faventinus, *Summa,* to C. 23 q. 2, B.N. Lat. 14606, fol. 121va.

[13] Above, n. 7.

convinced of the justice of his own position. Tacitly acknowledging this difficulty, Huguccio immediately shifted the focus of the discussion to that of authority rather than the justice of one party or the other. War was justly waged on superior authority against enemies of the Empire or the Church. Wars against heretics were justified by both human and divine law.[14]

The issues posed by Stephen of Tournai and his successors are difficult to penetrate. At least it is clear that the claim that a war can be just on both sides had nothing in common with the modern views that see each belligerent as having a partial claim to justice.[15] With the one exception posed by Stephen of Tournai of a war waged on false premises taken in good faith, the Decretists insisted that one side had a monopoly of justice in a just war. If one side fought justly, then the other side *eo ipso* fought unjustly. There was no partial claim to justice in the overall dispute. When the Decretists held that the war was just on the part of the person under attack, they meant not that he was justified in defending himself, but rather that the attack upon him was justified and his defense was unjustified. The theological basis for this view was the notion of divine punishment for sin through human agency. Augustine had expressed a similar position when he observed that a people could be punished in war for sins committed in another connection although they were innocent of any wrongdoing in the events that occasioned the war.[16]

The Decretists' approach thus provided no clear formula for grappling with the problem of twelfth-century warfare. Its thrust was exegetical, theological and moral rather than legal or canonical, and that it was attempted at all is another example of the tropism toward the Old Testament of those Christian writers who viewed warfare through Augustinian lenses. It also indicates that canonical jurisprudence was not yet operating under a clearly understood distinction between moral theology and canon law. The examples

[14] Huguccio, *Summa*, to D. 1 c. 9, B.N. Lat. 15396, fol. 4ra and B.N. Lat. 3892, fol. 3rb: 'Quid si sit iustum bellum ex utraque parte? Respondeo non potest iustum nisi tantum ex altera parte. Si enim iste impugnat iuste, adversarius iniuste defendit, et si ille iuste defendit, iste iniuste impugnat. Ergo interveniente auctoritate maioris iuste purgatur [= pugnatur] contra hostes, sive imperii, sive ecclesie. Sed contra hereticos et tunc non solum de iure humano sed de iure divino.'

[15] On the problems of the more modern position that a war can be just on both sides, see Nussbaum, 'Just War,' 464, 478.

[16] *De Civitate Dei*, XIX, 15; P.L. 41, p. 643.

used in this approach were applicable alike to public warfare, rebellion, police action, intra-familial bloodshed (that could cover petty feudal warfare and family vendettas) and invasion. As discussed here wars had no necessary political overtones or judicial consequences. The line of Stephen of Tournai, if pursued, could serve as a moral justification of just about any war. The emphasis was not on attack and defense but on the punishment of sin and crime. Huguccio, easily the best legal mind among the Decretists, was the only one to acknowledge under this approach that wars and their antecedent conditions were not judiciable according to purely human laws. It was just at this point that he shifted his focus to authority and deftly brought the Old Testament wars up to date by referring to wars waged against enemies of the Empire and the Church. His definitions thus provided an umbrella under which all the various elements of the just war could find some shelter, and climaxed the Decretists' attempts to formulate the concept of the just war. Now just wars were more clearly seen as judicial proceedings, whether they were waged for secular or religious purposes.

Gratian had discussed religious persecution and religiously-motivated wars somewhat separately from the just war. During the Decretist period religious motivations began to figure in the very formulations of the just war even before Huguccio. After the *Summa: 'Elegantius in Iure Divino'* had enumerated four criteria for a just war that reserved to princes and human laws the jurisdiction over warfare,[17] the author then shifted his emphasis to include the biblical approach discussed above. He then referred to Nathan's prophecy to David (II Samuel 12: 10) that the sword would not depart from David's house, suggesting thereby that David and similar evil-doers would be punished for their misdeeds by divine providence. The author then mentioned a war unjustly suffered by someone who, accused by false witnesses, was unjustly convicted of being an enemy of the Emperor (*hostis imperii*) rather than a foe of justice (*inimicus iusticie*) as in the other summae. Even if he was later justly convicted on the same charge by truthful witnesses, he still was unjustly punished in the war.[18] While the exact meaning of this passage is

---

[17] Above, n. 6.
[18] *Summa: 'Elegantius in Iure Divino,'* to C. 23 q. 2, B.N. Lat. 14997, fol. 141r. Cf. above, nn. 9-10.

obscure, the passage indicates a groping effort to find a means of determining justice in war in a situation more contemporary than the wars of the Israelites. The author continued by asserting that a war could be just on both sides, as when defenders of the Church waged wars against persecutors of the Church, and then applied this general assertion to the Crusades against the Saracens. With this point of departure the author launched into a discussion of the reconciliation of the evangelical precepts of patience with the fact of war. If the Church of his day were to imitate evangelical patience and perfection, this would be no less than to submit to pagans, to empty predestination of its meaning, and to destroy the Lord's promise to be with the Church until the final consummation of the world! Just as the Maccabees revolted on the Sabbath rather than allow their religion to be overrun, so now the Church could find no other way to check the injuries done by the pagans. Violence must be repelled by violence, even in defense of the Christian religion. For the sake of the divine persons, the Church must allow suffering, pillaging and killing. It did not thereby transgress the precepts of patience but rather supported judicial severity and vigor. In support of his position the author cited a passage from Gratian that justified war against attacking Saracens. Every war by Saracens against Christians was unjust, as were all the wars waged against the Israelites and the war of Saul against David.[19]

It would be difficult to envisage a stronger exegetical justification of the crusades against the Moslems, but to construct his argument the author had to neglect both the frequent guilt of the Israelites portrayed in the Old Testament and by other exegetes, and the Augustinian attribution of the precepts of patience to the inward

---

[19] *Ibid.*, fol. 141v: 'Iustum pro utraque parte bellum est cum defensores ecclesie contra persecutores eius moventur, ut cum orientales nostri contra sarracenos arma ferunt. Nam si hodierni temporis ecclesia perfectionem evangelicam et patientiam imitata martirum paganis colla submitteret, evacuaretur predestinatio, et excideret promissio quam dominus eam contra ventus et sidera usque consummationem seculi permansuram repromisit. Quo ergo spiritu machabei sabbatis rebellare magis quam omnes introire elegerunt eodem nunc ecclesia paganorum iniuriam alia via conpescere non possit. Vim vi repellere decrevit. Qua in re divinarum vicem personarum ecclesia sustinet vim patientis et iudicis. Ideoque si predatur, si cedit, si occidit, non est patientie vel precepti transgressio sed iudiciorum vigor et iudicialis severitas...Iniustum utrunque bellum contra Christianos paganorum et in veteri lege contra populum dei nationum et saul contra david.' Cf. *ibid.*, to C. 23 q. 8 c. 11, v. *Dispar*, Bamberg, Can. 39, fol. 129v; cited in P. Herde, 'Christians and Saracens at the Time of the Crusades,' *Studia Gratiana*, XII (1967), 367, n. 31. For Gratian's view of the Saracens, see above, ch. 3, n. 85.

disposition that he could have found in Gratian. In his analysis the author first proposed a simple formula for waging just wars, but after consideration of Old Testament examples proceeded to justify the crusades in such a way as to dispense with the evangelical counsels of perfection in order to support all forms of violence employed by the Church against the Saracens. The tendency of the Decretists to seek support in the Old Testament was made more complete, for here the justice of the Church's cause was explicitly assimilated to the just causes of the ancient Israelites. The *Summa: 'Omnis qui iuste iudicat'* (*Summa Lipsiensis*) of the Anglo–Norman School reached similar conclusions in considering just the wars of Catholics against heretics and enemies of the Church, this time because of the Natural Law right to repulse enemies.[20] And Huguccio, it will be remembered, considered wars waged on superior authority against enemies of Church and Empire to be justified by laws both divine and human.[21]

The Decretists accomplished a painstaking consolidation of elements of the just war theory that had been dispersed in Gratian's fragmented treatment. Hereafter it was possible to express a theory of the just war in a more coherent formula. Huguccio especially improved upon Gratian in recognising the need for a more concrete authoritative mechanism, and others emphasised the need for a precise understanding of the just cause. They strengthened their positions by including a discussion of unjust wars. The growing problem of heresy and the existence of the Crusades were now woven into the very fabric of the just war as they had not been in Gratian. Yet the threads had not all been tied up, and dangled before the Decretists to spur them on to further discussion. Among these threads were specific causes and authorities that legitimised wars.

THE CAUSES OF THE JUST WAR

The Decretists' discussions of the just cause for war turned upon their analysis of defense against violence and injustice. Since Gratian had

---

[20] *Summa: 'Omnis qui iuste iudicat,'* to C. 23 q. 2, Rouen, Bibl. Municipale 743 (E. 74), fol. 103vb and Luxembourg, Bibl. 144, fol. 330vb: 'Unde manifeste apparet quod bellum quandoque est iniustum…quandoque iustum ratione utriusque, ut bellum catholicarum contra hereticos et hostes ecclesie. Iustum ergo propulsandorum hostium causa, quia hostes repellere de iure naturali est licitum.'

[21] Above, n. 14.

seldom employed the terms *defensio* and *tuitio* in his formulations, the task for the Decretists was twofold: to explain and justify defensive measures using the different laws adduced by Gratian; and to relate defense to warfare. Gratian had cited texts from Isidore that justified repelling violence by violence according to natural law (D. 1 c. 7) and considered wars as justified by the *ius gentium* (D. 1 c. 9). The Roman law notion of defense was contained in the phrases 'ut vim atque iniuriam propulsemus de iure gentium sit' (Dig. 1.1.3) and, from the *Lex Aquilia*, 'vim vi defendere omnes leges omniaque iura permittunt' (Dig. 9.2.45.4). More specifically the repulsion of force was considered a right according to natural law while repulsion of injuries came under the *ius gentium*. The medieval Romanists tended to view the *ius gentium* as a species of the natural law applicable only to humans, so there was little effective distinction in theory between repelling violence and repelling injuries. The medieval Romanists had also incorporated the notions of *incontinenti* or immediate repulsion and *moderamen inculpate tutele* or moderation of blameless defense into their analysis of licit defensive actions.[22] They were followed on this score by the Decretists, most of whom granted a similarly restricted right of self-defense against violence to every person according to both natural law and the *ius gentium*.[23]

The task was made more difficult for the Decretists because a clear

---

[22] Cf. above, ch. 2, pp. 41–4 and Post, *Studies*, p. 548.

[23] For the Decretist analysis of self-defense, especially in case of necessity, see Kuttner, *Schuldlehre*, pp. 334–55, 367 and Post, *Studies*, p. 527. The principal debate was between the view that self-defense was a right so fundamental that it belonged to private individuals, and the opposing Augustinian view that self-defense by private persons contradicted the evangelical precepts of patience and love for one's fellow man. Simon of Bisignano upheld the former position when he asserted that someone could even strike a cleric if he did so *incontinenti: Summa*, to D. 1 c. 7, B.N. Lat. 3934A, fol. 56rb. The *Summa*: '*Omnis qui iuste iudicat*' dispensed with the apostolic injunction, 'non vos vindicantes,' when it held that repulsion of violence was licit until the day of judgment: to C. 23 q. 1, pr, Rouen, Bibl. Municipale 743 (E. 74), fol. 103rb and Luxembourg, Bibl. 144, fol. 330ra. On the other hand, Huguccio was almost alone in holding that violent resistance against attack when waged by a private person was a mortal sin unless performed on judicial authority, no matter how impeccably justified was such resistance in natural law: *Summa*, to D. 1 c. 7, v. *violentie*, B.N. Lat. 15396, fol. 3vb and B.N. Lat. 3892, fol. 3ra: 'Michi videtur quod mortaliter peccet qui repercutit ferientem se, iuste vel iniuste, sive statim sive post, sive pro se sive pro alio, nisi faceret hoc auctoritate iudicis. Si vero aliter evadere non potest nisi repercutiat, potius debet mortem incurrere et quelibet mala tollerare quam malo consentire.' Cf. *Summa*: '*Inperatorie Maiestati*,' to D. 1 c. 7, Munich, Staatsbibl., Cod. Lat. Mon. 16084, fol. 2vb. Huguccio's position is a survival of Augustine's view that denied to the private individual the right to violent defense on the grounds that it entailed a loss of love: above, ch. 1, n. 7.

distinction was lacking between repulsion of violence in general and repulsion of injuries by warfare in particular. At the core of the issue as they saw it was Gratian's canon (D. 46 c. 8) that prohibited the avenging (*ultio*) of one's injuries by oneself. This seemingly contradicted the right to repel injuries that according to the *Lex Aquilia* belonged to everyone, and perhaps explains why the Decretists in their formulations of the just war avoided using the term as much as possible. Their solution, as it gradually evolved, first distinguished between violence and injury, unlike the Romanists, and then distinguished between avenging one's injuries without judicial license and repelling injuries with the sanction of legitimate authority. The former action was condemned because the person wronged was likely to avenge himself out of motives of hatred, lust for vengeance, and loss of love. In effect the right to repel injuries contained in the *Lex Aquilia* was limited to those possessing authority. Like Gratian, the Decretists were forced to emphasise authority in an effort to prevent unrestrained private violence. Thus Rufinus, the *Summa Parisiensis*, and Huguccio represented the common opinion in holding that those who avenged their own injuries were guilty of sin unless acting on judicial authority. Even though a judge was less than a perfect man, he still had the right to prosecute injuries that ordinary Christians seeking perfection were denied. Huguccio then invoked the principle that no one had the right to act as judge in his cause.[24] It remained to be seen whether this principle would be applied to the just war itself.

In the Decretistic analysis the right to repel violence with violence legitimated recourse to a just war according to the principles of the *ius gentium*,[25] and so the *ius gentium* applied only to just wars rather than to all instances of warfare.[26] The *Summa Parisiensis* enlarged Gratian's definition of a just war so that a city armed with a just cause

---

[24] Rufinus, *Summa*, to D. 46 c. 8, v. *iniuriarum suarum ultores*, p. 109; repeated by Johannes Faventinus, *Summa*, to D. 46, c. 8, B.N. Lat. 14606, fol. 23rb. *Summa Parisiensis*, to D. 46 c. 8, p. 41. Huguccio, *Summa*, to D. 46 c. 8, B.N. Lat. 15396, fol. 49vb: '. . .vel ultores, ex intervallo vel ultores sua auctoritate, cum non habeant potestatem. Sed si habent, videtur licere. . .Sed non si agatur in forma iuditii, quia nemo debet esse iudex in propria causa.'

[25] E.g. Paucapalea, *Summa*, to D. 1 c. 7 (*Die Summa des Paucapalea*, ed. J. F. von Schulte, Giessen, 1890), p. 6; *ibid.*, to D. 1 c. 9, v. *bella*, p. 6.

[26] E.g. *Summa*: '*Tractaturus Magister*,' to D. 1 c. 9, v. *bella*, B.N. Lat. 15994, fol. 3ra; Johannes Faventinus, *Summa*, to D. 1 c. 9, B.N. Lat. 14606, fol. 2va. The *Summa*: '*Omnis qui iuste iudicat*' added the theme of the just war waged against enemies of the Church: to D. 1 c. 9, Rouen, Bibl. Municipale 743 (E. 74), fol. 2va.

for war could licitly attack, occupy and then fortify another city. A military action against highwaymen and pirates was also licit and could be considered a war, which the author tacitly assumed to be just.²⁷ That defense against violence was a just cause for war was finally confirmed by the assertion that soldiers were ordered to protect against external enemies.²⁸ Rufinus argued that the prohibition on avenging one's own injuries did not apply when someone was faced with the necessity to defend himself in the thick of the fray (*continuata rixa*). He nevertheless prohibited the recommencement of hostilities after a period of time without the intervention of judicial authority.²⁹ Similarly, the *Summa: 'Tractaturus Magister'* distinguished between the repulsion of violence (*vis*) that was proper according to natural law if performed without hesitation (*incontinenti*), and the repulsion of an injury which was a purely human condition not applicable to other animals. As such, injury, unlike violence, could be repulsed by a war waged after an interval of time.³⁰ Sicard of Cremona, on the other hand, recognised no distinction between *vis* and *iniuria*. For him the crucial distinction was that between public and private violence used to repel injuries. He justified the use of unarmed private violence to repel injuries to self or associates, provided it was inflicted with moderation in the face of flagrant wrongdoing. After a period of time since the commission of the injury repulsion was licit only when effected on judicial authority, and Sicard advised observance of the precepts of patience lest the defender render himself guilty of avenging his own injuries. Violence without the sanction of public authority could, however, be employed by everyone except clerics, and even they could licitly fight to defend the faith (*pro fide tuenda*).³¹

The Decretists were in general agreement that the necessity of defense justified the recourse to armed violence,³² but it was Huguccio who sharpened the notion of the just cause for war. For

---

²⁷ *Summa Parisiensis*, to D. 1 c. 9, p. 2; *ibid.*, to C. 23 q. 2, p. 212.
²⁸ *Ibid.*, to C. 23 q. 1 c. 5, p. 211.
²⁹ Rufinus, *Summa*, to D. 1 c. 7, p. 9.
³⁰ *Summa: 'Tractaturus Magister,'* to D. 1 c. 7, B.N. Lat. 15994, fol. 2vb–3ra.
³¹ Sicard of Cremona, *Summa*, to C. 23 q. 3, B.N. Lat. 14996, fol. 103r.
³² E.g. Simon of Bisignano, *Summa*, to C. 23 q. 1 c. 3, B.N. Lat. 3934A, fol. 87va; *Summa: 'Inperatorie Maiestati,'* to D. 50, Munich, Staatsbibl., Cod. Lat. Mon. 16084, fol. 7rb; *Summa: 'Omnis qui iuste iudicat,'* to C. 23 q. 1 c. 3, Rouen, Bibl. Municipale 743 (E. 74), fol. 103va.

him a war was unjust if it was waged with direct clerical participation, or if the enemy did not deserve the affliction of war, or if it was a war of attack (*ad impugnandum*).[33] Huguccio here attempted to prohibit thoroughly aggressive wars, and he also explicitly considered defense of the *patria* a just cause. Men were not to be sparing in their attempts lest they tempt God by not contributing to their own defense.[34] A city, unlike a private person, could justly defend itself without transgressing the apostolic mandate *non vos vindicantes* (Romans 12: 19). Furthermore, a city unjustly attacked by another city could licitly defend itself on its own authority.[35] Denial of the right of free passage was also a just cause for war,[36] as was the besieging of heretics in case of necessity and for the sake of peace.[37] The Emperor could justly make war on his rebellious subjects, such as the Neapolitans, and also for the recovery of lost property and for other similar causes.[38] Huguccio followed the Romanists in defining *hostes* as those upon whom the Emperor had declared a just war,[39] and his analysis approached the Romanists' conception of war as an instrument of imperial authority employed to defend the *patria*, but unlike the Romanists and as an adaptation to the contemporary problems of the Emperor in Italy he included rebels in the category of *hostes*. With the exception of Huguccio the Decretists added little to the notion of defense as a just cause for war although they did come closer to linking defense to the just war. In their broadened view of the causes leading to a just war they expressly proposed

---

[33] Huguccio, *Summa*, to C. 23 q. 2 c. 1, B.N. Lat. 15397, fol. 47rb.

[34] *Ibid.*, to C. 23 q. 8 c. 15, v. *patrie*, B.N. Lat. 15397, fol. 52ra; *ibid.*, to C. 23 q. 3 d. p. c. 1, B.N. Lat. 15397, fol. 47va. For other Decretist opinions, see Post, *Studies*, pp. 436f.

[35] *Ibid.*, to C. 23 q. 8 c. 15, v. *patrie*, B.N. Lat. 15397, fol. 52ra; *ibid.*, to C. 23 q. 3 d. p. c. 1, B.N. Lat. 15397, fol. 47va.

[36] *Ibid.*, to C. 23 q. 8 c. 15, v. *si nulla necessitas*, B.N. Lat. 15397, fol. 52ra: '...per hoc videtur quod licet alicui se sua auctoritate defendere et pro sua defensione pugnare. Sed nonne scriptum est 'non vos vindicantes' etc.? Loquitur ergo quando una civitas movet iniuste bellum contra aliam. Tunc illa auctoritate sui iudicis potest se defendendo pugnare. Si enim se non defenderet, videtur temptare deum, quod non debet quis dum habeat quid facere possit.' Rolando Bandinelli (below, n. 40) considered the denial of the right of free passage as a just cause for war according to natural law, whereas Gratian had come close to ascribing that right to the *ius gentium*: C. 23 q. 2 c. 3.

[37] *Ibid.*, to C. 23, pr., B.N. Lat. 15397, fol. 46vb.

[38] *Ibid.*, to C. 23 q. 8 c. 15, v. *paternarum legum*, B.N. Lat. 15397, fol. 52ra: 'puta quando subiecti sunt et secundum leges nostras vivere nolunt. Sed sibi alias faciunt, nos impugnare videntur, ergo Napoli nolint recipere leges imperatorum, iuste potest imperator pugnare contra eos.'

[39] *Ibid.*, to C. 14 q. 4 c. 12, B.N. Lat. 15397, fol. 5rb.

defense of the *patria*, but they usually did not specify the political unit to be defended, although the *Summa Parisiensis* and Huguccio accorded to city-states the right to defend their *patria* by war. How this fit in with Huguccio's defense of imperial authority and how the defense of the *patria* was to be conducted remained to be seen. Still lacking was an effective distinction between war and the exercise of internal jurisdiction.

AUTHORITY AND OBEDIENCE

The Decretists were unanimous in requiring that a just war required initiation by a legitimate authority, but the crucial question turned on what rulers possessed this authority. The increasing discussion of this issue commenced with Rufinus' use of *ordinaria potestas* and Sicard of Cremona's *potestas principis*. Rolando Bandinelli, later to become Pope Alexander III, referred to superior jurisdiction as the legitimate authority for war. Exemplifying the hesitation of the early Decretists in distinguishing violence from war proper, he argued that war could be waged without legitimate authority to repel violence, since it was justified by natural law. Likewise he considered the right of free passage a part of the natural law, whereas Gratian and some other Decretists came closer to ascribing that right to the *ius gentium*. Denial of this right was a just cause for war even without the interposition of authority, as was the war of the Israelites against the Amorites. Here Rolando conveniently overlooked the divine authorisation for that war.[40] Sicard of Cremona similarly considered the right of laymen to repel injuries done to self or associates as justified by all laws, but only allowed such repulsion after an interval of time when it was ordered by public authority. In effect, this made the injured party a special agent of authority, unlike the ordinary office of soldier. While these statements perhaps raised the spectre of vigilante violence, Sicard obviously did not envision this consequence, for he clearly adhered to the requirement that a just war could only be waged on authority.[41]

Another way to distinguish repulsion of violence or injury from war itself was to specify the adversary. Following the Romanists,

---

[40] Rolando Bandinelli, *Summa*, to C. 23 q. 2 (*Die Summa Magistri Rolandi*, ed. F. Thaner, Innsbruck, 1874), p. 88.
[41] Above, nn. 5, 31.

Paucapalea, Rufinus and Huguccio distinguished *hostes* or publicly declared enemies of the Roman people against whom just wars were to be waged, from others who resorted to violence without public declaration. Violence could be employed against these rebels and brigands, but it was not really a war.[42] For Rufinus the just war required legitimate authorities possessed of a just cause, such as the repulsion of injuries.[43] While he used the term 'principes' without further delimitation, he nevertheless required princes to have received their authority from the emperor. They should also be suitable to their brutal office, and for this reason clerics were excluded from warfare because they could not properly fulfill the functions of the more turbulent laymen (*strenuus laicus*).[44] The *Summa: 'Elegantius in Iure Divino'* required imperial authorisation for making war.[45] Such strictures on requisite authority, if applied, would have rendered most of the wars in Western Europe, at least those outside of the empire, automatically unjust. At one point even Huguccio toyed with restricting the right to declare war to the Roman Emperor alone, but on consultation with Gratian (C. 23 q. 1 c. 4) he soon modified his position to include all legitimate princes.[46] If one of the prince's subjects injured another subject, the dispute should be referred to the prince for settlement rather than allowing the subjects to go to war, but could one city wage a just war against another? Obviously Huguccio had the wars between the Italian city-states in mind. In his opinion cities had no power to wage just wars unless armed with princely authority, as some Italian cities were. But he observed that the question was a difficult one, which indeed it

---

[42] Paucapalea, *Summa*, to D. 1 c. 10, p. 6; Rufinus, *Summa*, to D. 1 c. 10, p. 11. Huguccio, in repeating this definition, extended it to include rebels; above, nn. 38–9. The source is Dig. 50.16.118.

[43] Rufinus, *Summa*, to C. 23 q. 1, p. 404; Johannes Faventinus, *Summa*, to C. 23 q. 1, pr., B.N. Lat. 14606, fol. 121ra.

[44] Rufinus, *Summa*, to C. 23 q. 1 c. 4, p. 404.

[45] *Summa: 'Elegantius in Iure Divino,'* to C. 23 q. 2 c. 2, v. *cui bellare fas est*, B.N. Lat. 14997, fol.-141r.

[46] Huguccio, *Summa*, to C. 23 q. 2 c. 1, B.N. Lat. 15397, fol. 47rb: '*Iustum* esse dico, hic queritur, quid sit ille qui bellum posset indicere? Respondeo cum Iohannes [sic] imperator romanus possit concedere leges et edita. videtur quod solus possit bellum indicere. Sed superius danda est quod auctoritas penes principes est [C. 23 q. 1 c. 4]. Unde videtur quod quilibet princeps hoc possit.' Lacking further indication, 'Johannes' could refer either to Johannes Bazianus or Johannes Faventinus. I favor the former, because he was learned in Roman as well as canon law, perhaps the first *doctor utriusque iuris*, and adhered to the *ius strictum* school of the Romanist Bulgarus.

was.[47] In effect Huguccio shared the common opinion of the Decretists that princes were princes because they had the right to declare war. That the reasoning here was circular did not seem to bother him but rather reinforced the close connection between princely office and the authority to declare war. In discussing the repulsion of violence Huguccio expressed more precisely and juridically than his colleagues the conviction that a prince forcibly ejected from his own land could use weapons to regain his proper territory,[48] although he shrank back from terming this action a just war. Prudently, in view of the shifting complexity of twelfth-century politics, the Decretists did not take the final step of naming just what sorts of officials could be considered princes. Their approach remained functional and theoretical rather than specific.

Another dimension of the problem of authority was introduced in the *Summa: 'Cum in Tres Partes,'* which posed the principle that any violent change of possession must be accompanied by a judicial sentence in order to be valid. Inspired by Roman law, the author argued that in a war that was halted and then recommenced, if the true lord dispossessed someone who had taken forcible possession, then the property should be restored to its violent possessor (*predo*) by a judicial sentence.[49] Even the true lord could not dispense with this requirement, for if he waged the war at his own convenience, that is, when he had assembled sufficient forces to expel the possessor, he was guilty of repelling violence after a delay rather than *incontinenti*. As a result he had to relinquish legal possession of the property to its violent possessor, for in transgressing the law he had denied himself its protection. This passage indicates also that the distinction between *hostes* and *predones* or brigands and between war and *vim vi repellere* were not universally recognised by the Decretists. It is further possible to see mirrored here, at least in abstract legal

---

[47] *Ibid.,* to C. 23 q. 2 c. 1, B.N. Lat. 15397, fol. 47rb: 'Si duo sint in potestate principis, et alter̄alteri inferat iniuriam, referenda est ad principem questio, nec debet alter alteri indicere? Idem dico de duabus civitatibus. Sed sequens capitulum contradicere videtur, ad hoc enim vigor in edio [sic] constitutus est. Si ergo civitas insurgat in civitatem, non habet potestatem bellandi, nec iusta gerit bellum. Sed debet renuntiare principi et ita purgare [sic] eius auctoritate. Difficilis quid est hec questio.'

[48] *Ibid.,* to D. 1 c. 7, v. *violentie,* B.N. Lat. 15396, fol. 3vb and B.N. Lat. 3892, fol. 3ra: 'Si, quis princeps vi expelleretur de terra sua, servato cum moderamine inculpate tutele scilicet ut si armis facta sit, armis liceat repelli.'

[49] *Summa: 'Cum in Tres Partes,'* to C. 3 q. 1, B.N. Lat. 16540, fol. 10r.

principles, the conflict between public jurisdiction and private right and also the concept of disseizin that characterised petty feudal politics. In another context this summa and its close relative the *Summa: 'Quoniam Status Ecclesiarum'* required judicial authority for the performance of military service, and granted only to public powers possessed of the *ius gladii* the right to punish illicit violence and petty wars.[50] The related *Summa: 'Tractaturus Magister'* simply confirmed the necessity of legitimate power in waging war, while admitting that *repellere vim vi incontinenti* was licit without such authority,[51] and the *Summa Parisiensis* considered military action against robbers and pirates as a war.[52] With certain hesitations then, the Decretists arrived at a position that made prior authority necessary for any violent action save the immediate repulsion of violence as it was being inflicted. The *Summa: 'Cum in Tres Partes'* in its more concrete insistence on legal authority pointed the way of the future that would strive without cease to limit the petty violence of the feudal nobility, but it placed no similar restrictions on the violence that accompanied wars between full-fledged authorities. Still, these attempts to delimit the locus of authority indicate that the Decretists became increasingly aware that only officials with higher jurisdiction could wage just wars.

The Decretists' position on the suitability of those who actually fought consisted of three requirements: the soldier must be a layman; he must be acting on authority and with proper motives; and except in special circumstances he must be obedient to his commanders.[53] Rufinus' formula for the just war had established the first two requirements and the other Decretists were content to follow his lead without much elaboration. For example, Huguccio's soldier was a layman acting with good intentions in obedience to the authority of

---

[50] *Summa: 'Quoniam Status Ecclesiarum,'* to C. 23 q. 1 and to C. 23 q. 5, B.N. Lat. 16538, fols. 56rb and 58ra; *Summa: 'Cum in Tres Partes,'* to C. 23 q. 1 and to C. 23 q. 5, B.N. Lat. 16540, fols. 62r and 64r. Johannes Faventinus of the Bolognese school expressed a similar opinion: *Summa,* to C. 23 q. 2 c. 2, v. *que ulciscuntur* and to C. 23 q. 5, B.N. Lat. 14606, fols. 121vb and 123va.

[51] *Summa: 'Tractaturus Magister,'* to C. 23 q. 1 c. 4, v. *in eo ordine,* to C. 23 q. 2 c. 2, v. *ex edicto,* and to C. 23 q. 4 d. p. c. 15, v. *hanc vicissitudinem tollens,* B.N. Lat. 15994, fols. 68rb, 69rb and 72vb.

[52] *Summa Parisiensis,* to C. 23 q. 2, p. 212.

[53] E.g. Rufinus, Sicard of Cremona, Huguccio, *Summa: 'Quoniam Status Ecclesiarum'* and *Summa Parisiensis*: above, nn. 3, 31, 37, 44, 50 and below, n. 56.

the Emperor or some other superior authority,[54] and for Johannes Faventinus the soldiers of the Empire, fighting not for spoils but rather for the peace and increase of the Church and commonwealth, could still despoil public enemies.[55] Most treatises merely repeated Gratian's justification of obedience, for example the *Summa Parisiensis* was content to argue that the prince's orders were to be obeyed unless they clearly contradicted divine law.[56] The *Summa: 'Inperatorie Maiestati'* (*Summa Monacensis*) of the French School, however, made obedience conditional on the justice of the cause, hence if with just cause a soldier carried out an especially grisly command he was not guilty of any wrongdoing and was even still eligible for promotion to higher clerical orders, but when the cause was unjust he was culpable.[57] That a soldier must obey any command that did not contradict divine precepts evoked little comment, but the Decretists were stimulated to deny obedience to the command of a prince who for some reason was not considered qualified to issue binding orders. The *Summa: 'Inperatorie Maiestati'* refused to allow Christians who had formerly fought for an infidel prince to be promoted to higher clerical orders.[58] A more generally applicable opinion was that of Simon of Bisignano, who prohibited subjects from obeying the commands of heretical, schismatic, or excommunicated lords.[59] Huguccio more precisely forbade vassals of an excommunicated lord to perform those obligations stipulated in the feudal contract, including joining the lord's army, going to war with him, and defending him.[60] This position was potentially of crucial importance for the extension of ecclesiastical doctrine and disci-

---

[54] Huguccio, *Summa*, to C. 23, pr., B.N. Lat. 15397, fol. 46rb.

[55] Johannes Faventinus, *Summa*, to C. 23 q. 1 c. 5, B.N. Lat. 14606, fol. 121va.

[56] *Summa Parisiensis*, to C. 23 q. 1, pp. 210f. For Simon of Bisignano and the *Summa: 'Omnis qui iuste iudicat,'* see below, n. 59.

[57] *Summa: 'Inperatorie Maiestati,'* to D. 50, Munich, Staatsbibl. Cod. Lat. Mon. 16084, fol. 8ra.

[58] *Ibid.*

[59] Simon of Bisignano, *Summa*, to C. 11 q. 3 c. 93 and to C. 23 q. 8 c. 28, v. *religiosis imperatoribus*, B.N. Lat. 3934A, fols. 73rb and 88va; *Summa: 'Omnis qui iuste iudicat,'* to C. 23 q. 4, Rouen, Bibl. Municipale 743 (E. 74), fol. 103va.

[60] Huguccio, *Summa*, to C. 15 q. 6 c. 4, v. *fidelitatem*, B.N. Lat. 15397, fol. 11ra: 'Quod ergo servitium debent [vasalli] ei negare? Dico quod non debent eum visitare, vel ei curiam facere, vel cum eo conversari in equitando, in eundo,...sicut ab aliis excommunicatis, non facient ei exercitum, non ibunt cum eo ad bellum, non defendent eum, non auxiliabuntur ei et huiusmodi.'

pline.[61] Yet the construction of a theory of disobedience to orders that were defective as to authority or unjust in cause still lay in the future.

The Decretists only treated briefly the problems of conducting a just war. In general they agreed that faith once promised to the enemy must be maintained, especially when truces had been concluded.[62] Rufinus argued that even conduct of a just war should respect the solemn holy days of the Church, for during these times those against whom a just war was waged should be spared from their well-deserved punishment.[63] Against this opinion but in conformance with Gratian was the more common view, represented by Sicard of Cremona, that if necessity dictated a just war, it could be waged at all times and by means of ambushes.[64] Beyond this the Decretists did not sense the need to devote further attention to the proper procedures for waging war and to the legal consequences of the just war. The issue that provoked far more Decretistic debate was the problem of clerical participation in warfare.

CLERICAL PARTICIPATION

Gratian's discussion of clerical participation in wars of secular lords had merely opened the debate. He had stopped short of absolutely forbidding any clerical participation whatsoever in these matters, and had somewhat grudgingly allowed bishops with regalia to accompany the army of the emperor or their overlord provided they had received papal permission.[65] The Decretists expanded on Gratian's remarks in regard to three separate but allied issues: participation of clerics in war; fighting against pagans and infidels by clerics; and the military activities of prelates possessing temporal jurisdiction.

---

[61] The issues at stake here are far too broad to be treated here, for they involve basic relationships between *regnum* and *sacerdotium*. The basic presupposition of the Decretists was found in Gratian's contention (C. 15 q. 6 cc. 2–5) that the Church could forbid subjects and soldiers to fulfill their oaths of fealty to an excommunicated prince. Here I have only mentioned opinions that bear upon military obedience. For a discussion of the Decretist positions, see Baldwin, *Masters Princes and Merchants*, I, 211f.

[62] E.g. *Summa: 'Et est Sciendum,'* to D. 1 c. 10, v. *inducie*, Rouen, Bibl. Municipale 710 (E. 29), fol. 119va; Sicard of Cremona, *Summa*, to C. 23 q. 2, B.N. Lat. 14996, fol. 102v.

[63] Rufinus, *Summa*, to C. 23 q. 1 c. 4, p. 405; *Summa: 'Omnis qui iuste iudicat,'* to D. 1 c. 9, Rouen, Bibl. Municipale 743 (E. 74), fol. 103va.

[64] Above, n. 62. Cf. Stephen of Tournai, above, n. 9 and C. 23 q. 8 c. 15.

[65] Cf. above, ch. 3, nn. 79–92. For a treatment of the subject focused differently from what follows, see Benson, *Bishop-Elect*, pp. 315–34 and his earlier 'The Obligations of Bishops with "Regalia",' *Proceedings of the Second International Congress of Medieval Canon Law*, ed. S. Kuttner and J. J. Ryan (Vatican City, 1965), pp. 123–37.

In their definitions of the just war itself the Decretists had been unanimous in restricting professional military service to laymen, but this did not rule out occasional armed violence carried on by clerics under different circumstances. For Rolando Bandinelli and Stephen of Tournai the crucial distinction was between clerics in sacred orders and those in minor orders. Rolando argued that all clerics in sacred orders and those as well who wished to follow in the way of evangelical perfection were absolutely forbidden to use weapons, yet he permitted clerics in minor orders to use weapons on legitimate authority. He reasoned that as clerics in minor orders, not being ordained as priests or living under a rule, could be allowed to marry or return to secular pursuits, so an unordained cleric could on papal or princely order take up arms just as could an ordinary layman. Stephen of Tournai went so far as to allow an unordained cleric to take up arms in his own defense even without authority.[66] Rolando's attitude was a vestige of the older suspicion of military service in general that attempted to exclude Christians who aspired to perfection from using armed violence, while nonetheless tolerating military service by the less spiritually ambitious. Since penitents had often been considered as quasi-clerics, Rolando was able to include them in his discussion. However, his position was immediately attacked by Rufinus, who drily observed that 'certain of our predecessors more drunkenly than soberly have endeavored to distinguish which clerics are allowed to take up arms, and which are not.'[67] While he admitted that some clerics in minor orders might contract marriages, Rufinus 'most vehemently' denied that they could return to secular professions such as military service, for otherwise why was such service forbidden in the early Church when clerical marriage was permitted? And what would prevent those doing penance for sins committed in military service from returning to their profession? Rufinus answered that penitents could only use weapons for defending justice *casualiter*, that is, on those occasions for which their bishops had granted permission, and he concluded that no cleric, whatever his order, should be exempted from the pro-

---

[66] Rolando Bandinelli, *Summa*, to C. 23 q. 1, q. 8, pp. 88, 98. He was followed by the *Summa Parisiensis*, to C. 23 q. 8, p. 220, and Stephen of Tournai, *Summa*, to C. 23 q. 8, B.N. Lat. 14609, fol. 69ra.

[67] Rufinus, *Summa*, to C. 23 q. 8, pr., p. 412: 'Quidam de antecessoribus nostris magis ebriose quam sobrie distinguere nitebantur, qui clericorum arma possint movere, et qui non...'

hibition unless he fought in his own defense under urgent necessity against pagans, and then only by order of a superior authority.[68] He thereby tacitly reflected Rolando's assimilation of penitents and clerics in minor orders. Huguccio even more categorically insisted on strict adherence to the prohibition. No cleric could make military service his profession,[69] although no Decretist seriously entertained the thought. Moreover he prohibited clerical bearing of arms, without excepting self-defense or defense of the *patria*. A cleric could not use weapons on other men even on superior authority or if he had temporal jurisdiction or regalia.[70] Huguccio's position was even more rigorous than that of Rufinus. Others qualified the absolute nature of the prohibition in the face of practical necessity.

At the end of the period the *Summa: 'Omnis qui iuste iudicat'* allowed limited clerical participation in actual fighting, but the author presumed a more rigorous standard of conduct for clerics than for laymen. Should a cleric be faced with the problem of obeying a command that was of doubtful consonance with divine precepts, he was assumed to have a better awareness of right and wrong, and, unlike the ordinary layman caught in a similar position, the cleric was not excused from blame for his obedience to such a command.[71] The author unfortunately did not explain why the cleric was fighting in the first place. Elsewhere the author prohibited a cleric from killing either pagans or Christians,[72] but in other contexts he involved himself in contradictions and argued that a cleric could use weapons either in self-defense or in defense of the faith against pagans on superior authority. Yet a cleric or bishop in the

---

[68] *Ibid.* Cf. *ibid.*, to D. 50 cc. 5–6, p. 116; to C. 23 q. 1, pr., p. 403; to C. 23 q. 3, p. 405; to C. 33 q. 2 c. 8, v. *armis numquam cingere*, p. 499 and to De penit, dist. 5, p. 503. On this problem Rufinus was followed by the *Summa: 'Elegantius in Iure Divino,'* to C. 23 q. 2, B.N. Lat. 14997, fol. 142r and Johannes Faventinus, *Summa*, to C. 23 q. 8, pr., B.N. Lat. 14606, fol. 125va.

[69] Huguccio, *Summa*, to C. 23, pr., B.N. Lat. 15397, fol. 46rb.

[70] *Ibid.*, to C. 23 q. 8, pr., B.N. Lat. 15397, fol. 51vb: 'Ut de necessitate, puta propter defensionem proprii corporis, vel auctoritate maioris vel si iurisdictionem habeant temporalem, ut in his qui habent regalia, nos dicimus, quod in nullo casu licet clericis arma contra homines ferre in propria persona, nec etiam pro sui defensione vel patrie...possunt tamen contra feras vel homines, si vulnerentur arma portare et loricam induere, sicut faciunt episcopi in partibus transmarinis. Item possunt alios exhortari ad pugnam si ecclesia impugnetur.' That this passage lacks helpful clarity is due to its probable spuriousness.

[71] *Summa: 'Omnis qui iuste iudicat,'* to C. 23 q. 1 c. 4, Rouen, Bibl. Municipale 743 (E. 74), fol. 103va.

[72] *Summa: 'Omnis qui iuste iudicat,'* to D. 36 c. 3 and C. 23, pr., Rouen, Bibl. Municipale 743 (E. 74), fols. 17ra and 103rb.

service of a prince should join the prince's retinue but could not take up arms himself.[73] This summa did not arrive at a helpfully coherent position. The Decretists in general maintained Gratian's caution regarding clerical fighting, and while they could not agree among themselves as to the conditions that rendered such fighting tolerable on occasion they did agree to deny Christian burial to any cleric who went to war with the intention to fight or who fought for payment or booty or out of hatred.[74] It was easier to gain consensus about what was forbidden than it was about what could be permitted.

The Decretists showed a little less reserve in the matter of clerical participation in battles against enemies of the Church. Firmly entrenched in the Decretum was the conviction that it was necessary to defend the faith by every available means, a conviction that on occasion overrode the canonical prohibition. Most restrained was Rufinus, who only allowed clerics to take up arms against pagans under stringent restrictions.[75] He considered a cleric who killed a pagan without absolute necessity as a murderer who should be deprived of his clerical status. Clerics, however, who were forced to kill pagans in self-defense could remain in their prior clerical status but could not be further promoted.[76] While the *Summa: 'Omnis qui iuste iudicat'* allowed clerics to take up arms in defense of the faith against pagans on superior authority,[77] it was Huguccio's more moderate qualification of the prohibition that stood the best chance of acceptance, when he allowed clerics to carry weapons and wear armor for self-protection, as did the bishops in the Holy Land (*in partibus transmarinis*).[78] It was clear that clerics accompanying the crusades to the Holy Land were not armed for the purpose of fighting but to terrify the enemy and to protect themselves from flying arrows. Those clerics who did bear arms with the intention of fighting could not be excused even by papal authority.[79] With the pos-

---

[73] *Ibid.*, to C. 23 q. 8, pr., cc. 4, 26, Rouen, Bibl. Municipale 743 (E. 74), fol. 107ra.

[74] E.g. Johannes Faventinus, *Summa*, to C. 23 q. 8 c. 4, B.N. Lat. 14606, fol. 125va; *Summa: 'Omnis qui iuste iudicat,'* to C. 23 q. 8 c. 4, Rouen, Bibl. Municipale 743 (E. 74), fol. 107ra.

[75] Rufinus, *Summa*, to C. 23 q. 8, pr., p. 412.

[76] *Ibid.*, to D. 50 c. 5, p. 116.

[77] Above, n. 73. Sicard of Cremona allowed a cleric to use weapons in defense of the faith: above, n. 31.

[78] Above, n. 70.

[79] Huguccio, *Summa*, to C. 23 q. 8, pr., B.N. Lat. 15397, fol. 51vb: 'Item ierosolomitanos clericos inculpate credimus in armis cum induti loricis crucem dominicam portant, cum

sible exception of the *Summa: 'Omnis qui iuste iudicat,'* the Decretists only slightly qualified the prohibition on clerical fighting, but they did allow clerics to bear arms and to fight in cases of utmost necessity.

A most crucial issue for the Decretists was the conflict of loyalties and duties that faced a bishop who possessed regalia or some other sort of temporal jurisdiction. While Paucapalea's early treatise prohibited all prelates from participation in a public war except on papal authority,[80] the Decretists generally adhered to Gratian's distinction between clerics owing service to secular overlords and those who were free of such obligations. Without referring to this distinction the *Summa Parisiensis* required permission by higher prelates or the emperor before a bishop could accompany the military expeditions of his overlord, where his legitimate functions included comfort, counsel and prayers for the warriors but excluded his direct participation in battle.[81] Prelates possessing civil jurisdiction could licitly exercise the *iudicium sanguinis* only through their lay administrators and could command others to bear arms for them.[82]

Sicard of Cremona perhaps best expressed the Decretists' consensus when he argued that prelates with regalia must contribute their allotment of soldiers to the army, exhort the army to fight a just war, travel with the host, but they must not fight themselves.[83] This seems to be the first explicit link between the obligations of regalian bishops and a just war rather than simple military expeditions, and it reinforced the obligatory character of the bishop's duties to his overlord. Indeed, most of the Decretists saw the regalian bishop's obligations as binding unless the war was decidedly unjust.[84] A further

hoc non faciant ad pugnandum sed ad terrendum et ne ledantur a sagittis volantibus eos, autem qui arma portant ut pugnent non credimus excusari, nec auctoritate Romani pontificis. non credo posset etiam dominus papa constituere quod clerici ferent arma.' For Gerhoh of Reichersberg's earlier expression of a similar view, see his *Tractatus in Psalm LXIV*, 53–4; P.L. 194, p. 42.

[80] Paucapalea, *Summa*, to C. 23 q. 8 c. 26, v. *quo ausu...ad comitatum*, p. 103.

[81] E.g. *Summa Parisiensis*, to C. 23 q. 8 d. p. c. 27, p. 222. For the political context of episcopal duties in the Empire, see Benson, *Bishop-Elect*, p. 330.

[82] *Ibid.*, to C. 23 q. 5, p. 218. Rufinus, *Summa*, to D. 50 c. 15, v. *militare*, and C. 23 q. 5 c. 8, pp. 116, 409. Bishops had princely status under a ruler, especially in Germany. Rufinus distinguished between the *auctoritas* of a bishop and his administration: Benson, *Bishop-Elect*, pp. 59, 65, 297–302.

[83] Sicard of Cremona, *Summa*, to C. 23 q. 8, B.N. Lat. 14996, fol. 106r. For other expressions of the same view, see Benson, *Bishop-Elect*, p. 323, n. 26.

[84] E.g. *Summa: 'Et est Sciendum,'* to D. 36 c. 3, Rouen, Bibl. Municipale 710 (E. 29), fol. 126ra; *Summa: 'Elegantius in Iure Divino,'* to C. 23 q. 2, B.N. Lat. 14997, fol. 142r. Cf. above, nn. 73, 79.

reinforcement of the bishop's obligations was the silent treatment accorded by most Decretists to Gratian's ban on regalian military service without prior papal permission, although Sicard of Cremona with unwonted reserve warned regalian bishops that it was 'more advisable' not to serve without a papal mandate.[85] The issue was potentially important, for if the papacy were able to withhold such permission and prevent episcopal military service when it deemed the overlord's war unjust, it would have gained a powerful weapon for regulating warfare, since the lord waging an unjust war would be deprived of episcopal support and knightly contingents from Church lands. Without explicitly entertaining this consequence, Johannes Bazianus and the often-contrary Huguccio took exception to the Decretists' neglect of the requirement. Johannes' strict interpretation of Gratian insisted on special papal license for a bishop summoned to go on a campaign, but even the pope could not authorise the bishop to fight.[86] Although Huguccio did allow prelates to bear arms provided they either had temporal jurisdiction or were acting on higher authority and did not actually fight,[87] in other places he required a papal license for regalian and non-regalian bishops alike. Even if armed with such a license a bishop could not be compelled to serve against his wishes. Huguccio thus disregarded Gratian's distinction but maintained in full vigor his requirement of papal permission. Like Johannes Bazianus he placed the burden of the final decision squarely on the episcopal shoulders.[88] On the other hand, the *Summa: 'Omnis qui iuste iudicat'* restricted the necessity of prior papal permission to non-regalian bishops, who, lacking it, could stay behind.[89] By implication the author reinforced the unqualified obligation of the regalian bishop to serve his prince. Perhaps as a concession to the tensions inherent in the regalian bishop's position, the Decretists did not achieve a consensus of opinion about the necessity of papal permission.

---

[85] Above, n. 83.
[86] *Glossa Palatina*, to C. 23 q. 8 c. 19, v. *venire*, cited in A. Stickler, 'Sacerdotium et Regnum nei Decretisti e Primi Decretalisti,' *Salesianum*, xv (1953), 591. Cf. Benson, *Bishop-Elect*, p. 324.
[87] Above, n. 70.
[88] Huguccio, *Summa*, to C. 23 q. 8 cc. 26, 28, v. *nisi forte*, B.N. Lat. 15397, fol. 52ra.
[89] *Summa: 'Omnis qui iuste iudicat,'* to C. 23 q. 8 c. 26, Rouen, Bibl. Municipale 743 (E. 74), fol. 107ra.

If a papal license was seen as obligatory or at least advisable, what was a regalian bishop to do if he was summoned both to his secular overlord's expedition and to papal service? How could he resolve this agonising conflict of loyalties, where he was faced either with loss of his temporal or his spiritual office, depending on the displeasure of his superiors at his decision? Briefly, the Decretists and the early Decretalists agreed that the papal summons must always be obeyed in preference to the lay summons.[90] While this dilemma did not directly concern the just war so much as the relationships between *regnum* and *sacerdotium*, the agreement that a regalian bishop must obey the pope rather than his secular overlord gave the pope another instrument of control over warfare. Thus, hypothetically, if a prince were waging a war not to the pope's liking, the pope could call a bishop and perhaps also the bishop's troops away from the host of the prince. This hypothetical situation did not arise in the Decretists' commentaries, but the precedence of papal commands over royal ones was established as a principle for later elaboration.

The tortuous reasoning that the Decretists devoted to the problems of clerical participation in warfare resulted from the conflicting tensions they faced. On the one hand they had to prevent any suggestion that clerics possessed the right to kill, and yet Augustine's opinion that private Christians must allow themselves to be killed rather than kill in self-defense had already been rendered unpopular and unrealistic even for clerics by the violent tenor of medieval life. The authority of the pope over his bishops had to be balanced against the fact that almost all bishops had some fiefs or temporal jurisdictions and therefore had temporal overlords. To cope with these tensions the Decretists tried to distinguish between military service and the right to occasional and restricted use of weapons and between fighting and actually killing. Under the pressure of practicality, they cautiously justified the obligations of the regalian episcopacy while also trying to safeguard ultimate papal authority. Differences arose in determining the proper extent of these rights and duties, although little was said about ecclesiastical contributions of knights to princely armies and payment of the extraordinary taxes needed to support large-scale wars. Throughout the texture of their comments the Decretists showed a caution that became less apparent

[90] Benson, *Bishop-Elect*, pp. 325-32; see especially Huguccio's treatment at p. 328, n. 39.

when they allowed popes and prelates to undertake wars on behalf of the Church.

THE JUST WAR OF THE CHURCH

The Decretists' prohibition on personal clerical involvement in battles was most pointedly qualified in the instance of battles waged on superior authority, however that was understood, against enemies of the Church. In their eagerness to contribute canonical support to the crusading movement and to wars undertaken by prelates, they tolerated, sometimes enthusiastically, this major exception to the canonical ban. For many of them Gratian's Causa 23 served primarily as a florilegium of texts to justify the forcible conversion of heretics to orthodox faith,[91] and thereby they conferred their approval on the bellicose activities of the bishops portrayed in the preface to the Causa. The notion of a just war waged for the Church on its own authority underlay all their debates on the just war theory itself. However, unlike the ordinary causes of war arising from some form of unjust violence, the cause of the Church's just war was not necessarily linked to prior violent acts. Of course many heretics and infidels did commit acts of violence against Christians, but often their mere divergence from orthodox Christianity when coupled with *de facto* possession of property and dominion was sufficient to justify war against them. In their own minds the Decretists were often unclear as to whether heterodoxy or unbelief alone, or the resort to violence was the just cause. This ambivalence had a long history that stretched back at least to Ambrose and Augustine. Decretist debate on the definition of the just war had already laid the foundation for the war against enemies of the Church. The Decretists looked to the Old Testament wars as justification of their own wars, and linked their cause with that of the divinely chosen people of Israel. This was especially true in the crusade-mongering passages of the *Summa: 'Elegantius in Iure Divino'* and the *Summa: 'Omnis qui iuste iudicat.'*[92] In the minds of the canonists all pagans, infidels, heretics, schismatics and excommunicates posed an almost collective threat to Christianity from

---

[91] E.g. Paucapalea, *Summa*, to C. 23, pr., p. 99; Rufinus, *Summa*, to C. 23, pr., p. 403; Stephen of Tournai, *Summa*, to C. 23, pr., B.N. Lat. 14609, fol. 65va. Here the terms *hereticus* and *malus* are used interchangeably.

[92] Cf. above, nn. 18–21, 26.

within and without.[93] Defense of the Church was not always consciously distinguished from defense of the Holy Land, defense of hierarchy and clerics, and defense of the faith and faithful. It was with this attitude that the Decretists overrode their own cautious restraint in matters dealing with clerical involvement in warfare and went on to construct a theory of war based on the Church's initiative and authority.

Although most of the Decretists dealt with the reasons for which the Church could make war, Huguccio, writing on the eve of the Third Crusade, supplied the opinion perhaps most capable of broad interpretation. His fundamental assumption was that wars had a punitive function; just as the war wickedly waged by Nebuchadnezzar justly afflicted the Jews, so also did wars waged by Christians to punish Saracens for their sins, while Saracen attacks punished Christian sins.[94] Rufinus argued that St Paul's admonition to Christians that they not involve themselves in affairs of the flesh referred only to the treatment of peaceful pagans who did no harm to the Christian religion, and then invoked patristic approval of wars waged against men so evil they did not realise the danger they presented even to themselves.[95] Rufinus here at least implicitly distinguished between unbelief itself and violence inflicted by unbelievers. The *Summa: 'Tractaturus Magister'* considered the repulsion of wicked men as a just cause for war,[96] and, according to the *Summa: 'Omnis qui iuste iudicat,'* a war against heretics to compel their return to orthodoxy was justified as a defense of the faith.[97]

The Decretists developed in effect a religiously motivated just

---

[93] E.g. Huguccio, *Summa*, to C. 14 q. 4 c. 12, v. *ab illo*, B.N. Lat. 15397, fol. 5rb: 'scilicet hoste, sive sit paganus sive iudeus sive hereticus sive alius christianus.'

[94] *Ibid.*, to C. 23 q. 5 c. 13, B.N. Lat. 15397, fol. 50va. *Ibid.*, to C. 23 q. 4 c. 47, B.N. Lat. 15397, fol. 49va: '...et nota quod propter peccata contra nos deus mulceat sarracenos.' Cf. the same passage in B.N. Lat. 3892, fol. 272vb: '...et nota quod propter peccata nostra contra nos deus incidat sarracenos.' This passage is but one example of the difficulties encountered in delimiting Huguccio's positions in default of a critical edition of the *Summa*.

[95] Rufinus, *Summa*, to C. 23 q. 1 c. 1, p. 404. Cf. Johannes Faventinus, *Summa*, to C. 23 q. 1 c. 1, B.N. Lat. 14606, fol. 121r.

[96] *Summa: 'Tractaturus Magister,'* to C. 23 q. 2 c. 1, v. *propulsandorum hominum*, B.N. Lat. 15994, fol. 69rb.

[97] *Summa: 'Omnis qui iuste iudicat,'* to C. 23 q. 8 c. 11, Rouen, Bibl. Municipale 743 (E. 74), fol. 107rb and Luxembourg, Bibl. 144, fol. 335ra: 'Queritur ad hoc iudeorum melior est conditio quam paganorum, quia ad aliud deteriorem quod ad mensam paganorum rite accedimus...quia omnes tenentur esse de ecclesia. Sed nonne tali bello coguntur ad fidem?...Solutio: fides nostra incolumis conservetur.'

cause for war out of the Old Testament, Roman legal principles, and patristic writings. Since heretics by their false belief transgressed the divine law, equated by some Decretists with canon law, and also persecuted the Church, they were denied thereby the protection of human law. Hence they had no legal claim even to hold property, which was liable to suffer imperial confiscation in a just war.[98] Likewise Church property was unjustly possessed by heretics, so whatever was taken from them by orthodox Christians acting on authority became the property of the orthodox.[99] Huguccio justified wars against enemies of the Church on the grounds that they not only offended God by their unbelief but also usurped territories (*sedes*) legitimately held by Christians in accordance with divine law and the *ius gentium*. On the basis of divine law that took precedence over the *ius gentium*, pious men had the right to expel impious men from their territories, and just men similarly retained possession of territories captured without sinful intentions. Just as the Jews had expelled the enemies of God from the Promised Land, so now Christians licitly occupied the possessions of those who had offended God.[100] Peaceful coexistence with pagans was impossible so long as they retained rights over possessions belonging to Christians. Huguccio introduced a possible limitation on the right of Christians to make war on infidels merely because of their unbelief. Citing a law from Justinian's Code (Cod. 1.11.6) that forbade Christians to harass peaceful pagans, he asked why Christians should not coexist peacefully with infidels, and responded that the allegedly peaceful conduct of the infidels was not sufficient cause to refrain from war

<hr/>

98 Simon of Bisignano, *Summa*, to C. 23 q. 7 c. 1, v. *nisi vel iure divino*, B.N. Lat. 3934A, fol. 88va. Johannes Faventinus, *Summa*, to C. 23 q. 7, B.N. Lat. 14606, fol. 125va. Similar passages are found in the *Summa*: 'Quoniam Status Ecclesiarum,' to C. 23 q. 7, B.N. Lat. 16538, fol. 59ra; the *Summa*: 'Cum in Tres Partes,' to C. 23 q. 7, B.N. Lat. 16540, fol. 65r; and the *Summa*: 'Et est Sciendum,' to D. 1 c. 10, Rouen, Bibl. Municipale 710 (E. 29), fol. 118va.

99 *Summa*: 'Quoniam Status Ecclesiarum,' to C. 23 q. 3, B.N. Lat. 16538, fols. 62rb–va; *Summa*: 'Omnis qui iuste iudicat,' to C. 23 q. 7, Rouen, Bibl. Municipale 743 (E. 74), fol. 106vb; Huguccio, *Summa*, to C. 23 q. 7, pr., B.N. Lat. 15397, fol. 51va.

100 Huguccio, *Summa*, to D. 1 c. 9, B.N. Lat. 15396, fol. 4rb and B.N. Lat. 3892, fol. 3rb: 'Ergo interveniente auctoritate maioris, iuste pugnatur contra hostes, sive imperii sive ecclesie, scilicet hereticos, et tunc non solo iure divino de sedibus, que contrar ius usurpantur, vel ad iniuriam dei detinentur. Pius expellit impium et iustus iniustum, et ipsas occupat sine peccato.' *Ibid.*, to C. 23 q. 4 c. 40, B.N. Lat. 15397, fol. 49rb: 'ar. quod Christiani sedes inimicorum ecclesie possint occupari et tenere, similiter aliorum hostium. Unde sedium occupatio de iure gentium dicitur esse...et nota quod quidam sunt de iure gentium, que [*sic*] et de iure divino.'

unless the infidels surrendered the rights they were exercising. To this assertion Huguccio appended a dictum inspired by Roman law, that the occupant of a certain territory could fight to expel anyone seeking to dispossess him.[101] Huguccio was obviously referring to Saracen control over the Holy Land, which he considered as territory rightfully belonging to Christians. These passages show an attempt to distinguish between innocuous and hostile infidels, but perhaps imbued with crusading fervor and righteous indignation over Saracen control of the Holy Land, Huguccio hesitated to go the whole way and advocate toleration of peaceful non-Christians. What began as a counsel of moderation toward pagans in Roman law Huguccio turned into an ingenious and cogent justification of the crusades to the Holy Land.

Now armed with just causes for Church wars, the Decretists sought to delimit the necessary authority and chain of command. Augustine had justified ecclesiastical recourse to the coercive power of the Roman Empire in persecuting heretics, and in the early Middle Ages royal authority often undertook wars against infidels and pagans either on its own initiative or at the behest of the papacy. Gratian had interwoven both these strands in a complex matrix and had added examples of direct ecclesiastical initiative in wars against infidels, heretics, schismatics, and excommunicates. In the three decades before the Third Crusade it became the Decretists' urgent task to render more precise the role of authority in such wars. To do this they had to make use of the rapidly evolving canonistic analysis of jurisdictional prerogatives. Granted that the violent spoliation of heretics and other enemies of the Church required the intervention of a judge lest impure motives come into play,[102] but what judge? What roles did lay rulers and ordinary Christians have to play? Not surprisingly, the Decretists saw the Church as the repository of ultimate authority, and their cautious restrictions on personal participation of clerics in warfare did not prohibit prelates from initiating wars provided that they possessed either regalia or the *ius gladii*

---

101 *Ibid.*, to C. 23 q. 8 c. 11, B.N. Lat. 15397, fol. 51vb: 'Ergo iuste pugnatur contra paganos. Sed pone quod volunt quiete vivere, utrum non sit pugnandi contra eos, sicut nec contra iudeos, ut [Cod. 1.6.11]. quod verum est, si velint nobis reddere iura que occupant. Hic est arg. quid si aliquis velit alium expellere de sede sua, iuste potest contra eum pugnare.' Unfortunately, the authenticity of this perplexing passage is in doubt.

102 *Summa Parisiensis*, to C. 23 q. 7, p. 220. Cf. above, n. 99.

or both. For Stephen of Tournai the Church authorised public wars (*forinseca bella*) against its external enemies such as the pagans, while by conciliar decisions and judicial sentences the Church waged *ecclesiastica bella* on heretics and reprobate Christians.[103] With this the Decretists acknowledged the right of the Church on its own authority to initiate wars both within and without Christendom, although not all of them were as frank as Stephen. Rufinus related the example of a count who, passing fortuitously through territory controlled by schismatics, was encouraged by the pope to persecute them for their error and also to avenge his own injuries.[104] Rolando Bandinelli, Stephen of Tournai and the *Summa Parisiensis* even allowed unordained clerics to take up arms on apostolic mandate.[105] The *Summa: 'Elegantius in Iure Divino'* returned to the examples of Gregory the Great and Leo IV to justify papal initiative in preparations for war,[106] and Sicard of Cremona cited Alexander III's contemporary persecution of the Cathars and others to conclude that the pope and prelates authorised by him could summon princes and urge ordinary Christians to attack all those who disturbed the Christian faith, and the Peace of the Church or *patria*.[107] The Decretists were in agreement that the pope himself had the authority to declare war, but they did not specify the bases of that authority.

Even ordinary bishops shared with the pope the authority to declare war. Sicard of Cremona allowed bishops to take up arms on papal authority, provided of course that they did not actually shed

---

[103] Stephen of Tournai, *Summa*, to C. 23 q. 4 c. 48, B.N. Lat. 14609, fol. 71ra: 'forinseca bella vocat, que fiunt armis contra eos qui sunt foras ecclesiam. Ecclesiastica vero qui fiunt conciliis rationibus et diffinitivis sententiis contra hereticos et reprobos Christianos qui esse in ecclesia videntur. Vel utrumque bellum corporale intelligitur, ecclesiasticum contra hereticos, forinseca contra paganos.' The passage was repeated by Johannes Faventinus, *Summa*, to C. 23 q. 4 c. 48, B.N. Lat. 14606, fol. 123va.

[104] Rufinus, *Summa*, to C. 23 q. 5 c. 45, p. 411.

[105] Above, n. 66.

[106] *Summa: 'Elegantius in Iure Divino,'* to C. 23 q. 2, B.N. Lat. 14997, fol. 142r.

[107] Sicard of Cremona, *Summa*, to C. 23 q. 8, B.N. Lat. 14996, fol. 105v: 'Ita auctoritate pontificis vel principis arma movere...nunc alexandri tercii qui contra catharos et in ecclesia debachantes fideles christianos ut arma suscipiant, adhortatur ecclesia...Respondeo: licere apostolico et aliis eius auctoritate prelatis principes postulare et quoslibet exhortari ad defensionem et impugnationem contra adversarios sancte fidei pacis ecclesie et patrie.' Cf. above, n. 83. That Rolando Bandinelli as Decretist somewhat restricted clerical participation in war but as Pope Alexander III took the initiative in military action against heretics does not constitute a contradiction or change of conviction but rather indicates how seriously the Decretists took the distinctions between exhortation and action and between authority and execution.

blood.[108] Bishops and even ordinary clerics could exhort the faithful to take up arms in defense of the oppressed and to defend the Church against its enemies.[109] According to the *Summa: 'Et est sciendum'* and the *Summa: 'Elegantius in Iure Divino'* a bishop with regalia not only had the right to exhort others but also could actually wage war on heretics because he possessed the *ius gladii*.[110] Implicit in both passages is the assumption that the prelate's actual war-making power stemmed from the prince rather than the pope, and so it was unclear whether a bishop without regalia received from the pope the *ius gladii* necessary to make war.

The uncertain source of a bishop's *ius gladii* was portrayed forcefully in a hypothetical situation analysed in the anonymous *Quaestio Palatina*.[111] A certain vassal out of obedience to his lord had devastated lands belonging to the Church. Despairing of the prospects for the vassal's correction, the local bishop excommunicated him without a hearing and ordered his own ecclesiastical vassals to devastate the vassal's lands. The author took this opportunity to devote a full-fledged quaestio to whether a bishop could persecute the enemies of the Church by both spiritual and material swords. On one hand the usual texts from the Decretum were marshalled to exempt bishops from involvement in violence. Then the author adduced two very different lines of reasoning to justify the bishop's action. First, papal activities and writings proved that in the case at hand necessity forced the bishop to exercise his right to expel enemies of the Church. Second, the author, true to Gratian's treatment (C. 23 q. 8), declared that all the texts used to prohibit episcopal involvement in physical violence were irrelevant to the case at hand because they only applied to bishops without regalia. The conclusion allowed bishops, especially those who had secular power ('maxime illis episcopis, qui seculares habent potestates'), to become involved in violence when necessary, but only until blood was about to be shed, at which time the bishop should withdraw from the scene. This quaestio left unresolved the basic ambivalence: does a bishop have the right to make

---

108 *Ibid.*
109 E.g. Stephen of Tournai and the *Summa: 'Omnis qui iuste iudicat,'* above, nn. 66, 72.
110 Above, n. 84. Even Rufinus, otherwise so tenacious in his adherence to the prohibition, allowed clerics to order others to take up arms: above, n. 68.
111 *Quaestio Palatina*, Bibl. Apost. Vat., Cod. ms. Pal. 678, fols. 104rb–vb, cited in Stickler, 'Sacerdotium et Regnum,' 604f.

war simply because he is a bishop acting under papal jurisdiction, precept, and example, or must he also have temporal jurisdiction? The author appears to consider the bishop's position within the Church as a necessary but not sufficient authorisation of his war-making powers that must be complemented with his temporal position. If it was clear toward the end of the Decretist period that bishops had the right to direct just wars, the bases for that authority remained a matter of debate.

It was Huguccio's self-appointed task to supply the most prolix and profound legal justification of the Church's right to wage wars. Bishops acting on superior authority either ecclesiastical or temporal could urge others to do battle in defense of the Church.[112] At one point he argued that any Christian could declare war upon pagans wishing to impugn the name of Christ,[113] but in his more considered opinion, based on his understanding of divine law, wars against heretics and other enemies of Church and empire required superior authority.[114] Indeed, such wars could only be waged by the highest authority. This explains why Peter sinned mortally in defending, for he lacked authority. His zeal stemmed not from knowledge but from a desire to defend Christ. Condemning the desire to strike others without authority, Huguccio criticised those of his own day who punished heretics without authority as guilty of the same mortal sin as Peter. Yet when Phinehas (Numbers 25: 7) killed sinners he was not guilty of evil willfulness, because as a priest he possessed the necessary authority.[115] Here again Huguccio sought Old Testament support for a position that otherwise was difficult to justify. Of course the Old Testament example had to be brought up to date and placed within the context of ecclesiastical jurisprudence if it was to serve as a guide to action, so in another context Huguccio accorded to ecclesiastical judges the powers to declare war, although he was

---

[112] Above, n. 70.

[113] Huguccio, *Summa*, to C. 23 q. 2 c. 1, B.N. Lat. 15397, fol. 47rb: 'Item quod non solus ille qui habet ius imperandi possit bellum indicere, videtur ex eo quod Christiani possunt paganis bellum indicere, nomine Christi volentibus impugnare.'

[114] Above, n. 100.

[115] Huguccio, *Summa*, to C. 23 q. 3 c. 4, B.N. Lat. 15397, fol. 47ra: 'Nos dicimus quod Petrus peccavit mortaliter quia percutiendi non acceperat potestatem. Quod ergo dicitur in hoc capitulo, tales sunt qui percutiunt hereticos, qualis erat Petrus, etc. Item zelum habebat sed non secundum scientiam sed voluntatem defendendi Christum, secuta est voluntas percutiendi qui mala fuit. Phynees autem non peccavit, quia potestatem habebat, nam sacerdos erat.'

careful once again to point out that neither judges nor other clerics could personally participate in warfare.[116] In one terse statement Huguccio resolved the ambiguities inherent in earlier treatments of the same topic such as found in the *Quaestio Palatina* and the *Summa: 'Elegantius in Iure Divino.'* Now a churchman without any temporal jurisdiction whatsoever possessed the material sword necessary to wage just wars. Yet Huguccio did not mention whether an ordinary bishop was qualified to act as judge in these cases, although by implication the pope was certainly qualified. Huguccio even criticised the contemporary pope, Urban III, for insufficient efforts in support of the wars against the enemies of the faith.[117] He came very close to an explicit assertion that the pope was the single superior authority competent to declare a crusade. After Huguccio the Decretists recognised that papal initiative in promulgating crusades entailed papal direction in waging them. While this was already true in practice, Huguccio gave it a canonical seal of approval. It is no mere coincidence that Huguccio's most illustrious pupil was later to become Pope Innocent III.

At the end of the Decretist period the canonists began to follow Huguccio's lead and elaborate a theory of the crusade, but Huguccio's contribution did not end there. He provided a new and more carefully constructed foundation for the crusades to the Holy Land. Through him the pious wish of the Decretum that whoever died in a war against infidels merited eternal salvation was incorporated into the nascent theory of the crusade. Huguccio reasserted God's power to declare war and the rewards that accrued to Christians fighting in a divinely ordained war. God's war, the crusade, was now also a just war.[118] Yet Huguccio's attitude toward the Saracens was not so intransigent as to justify a total war against them. Since they had not

---

116 *Ibid.*, to C. 15 q. 6 c. 2, v. *materiali*, B.N. Lat. 15397, fol. 10va: 'non propria manu vel per clericos, sed per laicos, et est ar. quod iudex ecclesiasticus potest indicere bellum et hortari ad bellum et bello persequi hostes...[C. 23 q. 8]...vel distingue *in spirituali* clerico, *materiali* laico.' It should be pointed out that Huguccio cited the alternate and older view that the material sword belonged to laymen, although this complex issue cannot be discussed here. Cf. A. Stickler, 'Die Schwerterbegriff bei Huguccio,' *Ephemerides Iuris Canonici*, III (1947), 1–44.

117 *Ibid.*, to C. 23 q. 8 c. 8, v. *scire*, B.N. Lat. 15397, fol. 51vb: 'hoc non facit hodie urbanus [III?].'

118 *Ibid.*, to C. 24 q. 2 c. 3, v. *sed in Domini sui fide atque servicio*, B.N. Lat. 15397, fol. 46rb and B.N. Lat. 3892, fol. 278ra: 'forte in iusto bello...Hortamur quia Dominus habebat potestatem bellum indicendi. in aliis enim bellis, quicumque moritur servandus est.'

originally accepted the laws of the Roman Empire, they were not bound to live by them. They might sin in matters of faith, and perhaps they should be subjected to Roman rule, but Huguccio did not fully commit himself to this ambitious program. He even allowed the Saracens some legal standing, as in a court case between a Christian and a Saracen where the judge would follow either his own laws or those of the defendant.[119]

Huguccio also extended the notion of right conduct developed by earlier canonists to include wars with Saracens. Truces concluded between Christians and Saracens should be honored because of general obligations to maintain faith with an enemy.[120] Similarly other consequences of war derived from the *ius gentium* applied to wars between Saracen and Christian. If, Huguccio asked, those captured in a just war could be enslaved, as Roman law and the *ius gentium* held, what about captives taken during the crusades? Saracens so captured could be enslaved, but suppose that Saracens waged a just war, as when they were unjustly attacked by Christians? Huguccio was doubtful that this would ever actually happen, but if it did, Christians could be enslaved. However, by divine law no man could be enslaved. Huguccio's argument on this point is inconclusive, but he seemed to say that the captive should remain the property of his former master if he was not originally free, or, if he had been a free man, he should ultimately be allowed to return to his native region.[121] Inconclusive or not, that Huguccio even broached this

---

[119] *Ibid.*, to D. 1 c. 12, B.N. Lat. 15396, fol. 4va: 'Item quid de sarracenis? Resp. non ligantur legibus romanis, quia eas non receperunt. Unde secundum eas non tenentur vivere. Licet in aliis peccent, videtur tum quod et ipsi debeant subesse romano imperio, et ideo teneantur vivere secundum leges romanas, sed quid si non tenentur, et lis est inter sarracenos et Christianum? Iudex sequitur leges suas vel rei.'

[120] *Ibid.*, to C. 23 q. 1 c. 3, B.N. Lat. 15397, fol. 47ra: 'Hic est arg. quod quando Christiani pasciscuntur treugas vel redire ad vincula cum Sarracenis observare tenentur. Not. quod in illa est fides inter fidelem et infidelem.' For Decretist opinions of maintenance of fidelity in general, see above, nn. 62–4.

[121] *Ibid.*, to D. 1 c. 9, v. *servitutes*, B.N. Lat. 15396, fol. 4rb: 'sed numquid omnes capit in bello iusto vel iniusto efficiuntur servi. Non nisi in bello iusto sed nec tunc omnes, sed tantum capti ex illa parte ex qua est iustum bellum. Unde sarracenus captus a Christianis servus eorum efficitur, quod Christiani contra eos iuste pugnant, sed non econtra...Sed potest esse quod iustum bellum sit ex parte sarracenorum et non Christianorum, puta si Christiani iniuste impetant eos et illi iuste se defendant? Tunc in tali bello Christianus captus servus efficitur Sarracenorum, et non econtrario. Forte huic constitutioni iuris gentium derogator iure divino, scilicet ut secundum ius divinum Christianus captus ab hostibus vel econtra non efficiatur servus hostium sed remaneat liber vel servus illius cuius ante erat, et hic ea ratione quod si fugeret sive furtum committeret, et sic teneretur non

question indicates the change in attitude he initiated. While he shrank back from allowing Christians to be enslaved by Saracens, Huguccio came close to according to Saracens the legal rights of the *ius gentium*.

Other hypothetical cases relating to contacts between Christians and infidels received the benefit of Huguccio's casuistry. To the question of whether a Christian could serve in the army of an infidel lord he answered that such service was licit when absolutely necessary, as when an entire people was conquered. Rather than suffer death, the captives should obey all military commands except those contrary to God. As an example Huguccio mentioned a shadowy case in which the Milanese, having lost their city to the barbarians, fled to the side of the barbarians, who must have been pagans. Since Huguccio considered the Milanese submission voluntary, they were guilty of mortal sin and no Christian should have dealings with them.[122] In another passage Huguccio allowed Christians to perform military service for a pagan prince provided they were under his jurisdiction or were his captives and the war was just. Other Christians were guilty of sin if they were not in his jurisdiction or if they served voluntarily. Huguccio observed that many of these latter were serving under Saladin. When a Christian soldier was ordered by a pagan or apostate prince to make war on other Christians, which was illicit, he was to disobey, or rather obey an orthodox prince.[123]

---

fugere ab hostibus. Et si fugeret, debet reverti cum non remittitur peccatum nisi restituatur ablatum.' Cf. above, n. 94.

[122] *Ibid.*, to C. 23 q. 1 c. 5, B.N. Lat. 15397, fol. 47rb: 'Secundum est sub pagano milite. Verum si necessitate hoc fiat, puta quod captus est populus cum civitate a sarracenis; nolunt eos interficere sed servant eos ad serviendum sibi etc. Possint eos iudicare et eis precipere et debent eos obsequi in his que pertinent ad miliciam, dummodo non sit contra dominum . . . et hic est ubi salus summa lata ab homine alterius secte tenet. Si autem voluntate eis eis [sic] subiciunt ut fecerunt mediolanenses quando civitate amissa ad barbaros confugerunt. mortaliter peccant et nullius fidelis debet eis communicare.' It is difficult to understand why Huguccio considered the Milanese surrender a voluntary one. While it is difficult to locate the incident in question, it may have occurred during the early Middle Ages. The *Summa: 'Inperatorie Maiestati'* probably reflected more common Decretist opinion when it condemned the military service of Christians under infidel princes: above, n. 57.

[123] *Ibid.*, to C. 11 q. 3 c. 94, B.N. Lat. 15396, fol. 172ra: 'Item arg. quod Christiani licite possunt militare sub pagano principe . . . Si bellum est iustum et ipsi sunt de iurisdictione iuris, vel captivati vel captivitate ab eo et ita ex necessitate. Ad hoc inducuntur. Alii vero Christiani, scilicet qui non sunt de iurisdictione eius vel ab eo detenti in captivitate, quamvis bellum sit iustum, non tamen sine peccato militant sub pagano. Quales multi nunc sunt cum Saladino. *producite.* cum esset bellum illicitum. Nunc in tali casu plus est obediendo catholico principi quam apostate vel pagano.'

Huguccio's main point, however, was that Christian participation in a just war waged by a pagan prince was not inherently sinful. In a simple war without religious overtones Christians need not attribute more to the orthodox prince than to the pagan prince when he assessed the justice of the war. Yet while Christians who had not been captured could voluntarily fight under a catholic prince, they could not do so under a pagan prince. Huguccio left unresolved the case of a pagan prince who derived his authority from a legitimate Christian prince,[124] and once again he stopped short of according full legal equality to pagans.

The casuistry of Huguccio marked a departure from the views of the other Decretists and pointed toward the topics to be debated by the Decretalists. Huguccio was practically alone in allowing pagans to possess property by legal title. For him the major Saracen offense was not disbelief but occupation of the Holy Land claimed by Christians.[125] He almost extended to them the rights of the *ius gentium* relating to war and property. Infidels possessed certain indigenous rights and jurisdictions over persons and property that Christians could not take away by claiming violation of divine laws or ecclesiastical discipline. Before his time the Decretists and others assumed that all wars of the Saracens against Christians were automatically unjust and deserved to be countered by a Christian just war.[126] In this context Huguccio's assertion that infidels could wage just wars constituted a revolution in thought. Huguccio limited the scope of the crusades against the Saracens to the Holy Land, and realistically rejected Christian claims to territories formerly under Roman rule but now controlled by Moslems. Further, by so limiting the crusades Huguccio prohibited at least by implication wars of conquest, conversion and extermination waged against infidels

---

[124] *Ibid.*, to C. 11 q. 3 c. 98, v. *Iulianus contra illam gentem*, B.N. Lat. 15396, fol. 172ra: 'contra quam iuste pugnabatur. Aliter nunc catholico principi obediendum est. Non plus in talibus attribuitur principi catholico quam pagano, eo excepto quod Christiani non captivati sed spontanei possunt in iusto bello licite pugnare sub catholico de cuius iurisdictione non sunt. Quod non possunt sub pagano. Sed numquid habuit iste potestatem a domino, sic canonice sit electus, i.e. ab illis qui habent potestatem eligendi?'

[125] Cf. above, n. 100. This discussion supplements Herde, 'Christians and Saracens.'

[126] E.g. *Summa: 'Elegantius in Iure Divino,'* above, n. 19. The *Summa: 'Permissio Quᵈdam,'* composed between 1179 and 1187, did advocate toleration of peaceful Saracens while approving Christian wars against aggressive ones: Herde, 'Christians and Saracens,' 367, n. 29.

simply on account of their unbelief. In according certain rights even to infidels, however hesitantly, Huguccio placed himself at the forefront of later canonists and theologians who granted infidel kingdoms an increasing sphere of jurisdiction that was independent of the demands of Christian orthodoxy. Huguccio, who among the Decretists best expressed the theory of the crusade, also looked toward a limited toleration of unbelievers and infidel dominion that pointed toward the equality of sovereign states which underlies modern international law.

The Decretists' theory of the Church's just war evolved first within their more general discussion of the causes of the just war and then, able to stand on its own merits, received further special consideration. The Church possessed the requisite authority to declare a just war, although most Decretists hesitated to term such engagements explicitly as wars, and the pope gradually emerged as the official most suited to exercise this authority. Bishops also possessed this authority to a lesser extent, although the Decretists could not reach a definitive agreement as to whether their authority stemmed from the pope alone or needed to be supplemented with a delegation of princely authority. On some occasions ordinary clerics also were accorded the right to exhort others to fight in defense of the faith, but they did not really possess the authority to declare war, for this would have overextended the locus of authority. Within the narrow confines of their discussion of authority most Decretists devoted little attention to the sources of papal authority over the just war, and neglected to deal with the papacy's position as temporal overlord of central Italy. Once an ecclesiastical ruler had decided that a just war was necessary, his summons of lay princes to battle was binding on them. While Gratian's analysis had contained this obligation without clear emphasis, the Decretists were more forthright in asserting that a prince's compliance with an ecclesiastical order to wage a just war was not merely voluntary but stemmed from the duties of his office. The ecclesiastical judge's jurisdiction over the Christian also permitted him to urge ordinary laymen to take up the sword to defend the faith whenever it was felt to be threatened, but in this case the Decretists did not go so far as to claim that obedience to the judge's exhortation was binding on any specific individual. Still, the Church's authority to declare and wage wars was more strongly asserted than in Gratian, and was beginning to be expressed in the language of jurisdictional prerogatives.

By their justification of ecclesiastically motivated wars the Decretists were able to overcome any lingering suspicion of the morality of military service. Fighting in defense of the faith, as in the crusades, became laudable in theory as it had already become in practice. Imbued with the crusading ideal, one author came close to justifying clerical participation in wars against infidels by reference to the custom of those fighting in the Holy Land.[127] In this case, contemporary custom was used to construct legal opinion rather than, as was more frequently the case, traditional canon law texts serving to justify contemporary practice. The just causes for war, repulsion of injuries and preservation of peace now justified the crusades. The Decretist analysis of the crusades was, however, incomplete, for it did not construct a code of conduct (except Huguccio), although it can be assumed that all necessary means were to be employed, especially if the infidels had no legal rights. The Decretists also used the terms pagan and infidel very loosely to apply to all non-Christians who could conceivably threaten the Church. As yet no treatment of the special juridical status of the crusader had emerged.

Gratian had discussed the holy war waged for religious purposes alongside the just war, although he did not precisely show how one related to the other. By emphasising the necessity of ecclesiastical authority the Decretists transformed the more nebulous holy war into a species of the just war. The concept of holy war thus took on institutional solidity as the just war of the Church; but what, then, was the crusade? Since the end of the eleventh century the crusading movement had become an ecclesiastical institution. Neglected by Gratian, the elaboration of crusading theory was begun by the Decretists and completed by the Decretalists. In effect the Decretists, especially Huguccio, came close to viewing the crusade as that subspecies of the Church's just war waged solely on direct papal authority against internal and external enemies of the Christian

---

[127] *Summa: 'Omnis qui iuste iudicat,'* to C. 23 q. 1, pr., Rouen, Bibl. Municipale 743 (E. 74), fol. 103rb and Luxembourg, Bibl. 144, fol. 330ra: 'Nunquam vero militare debet quid si causa desit? Unde vero causa subsit semper potest, si dicatur clericis fratribus non licet alio casu militare. Sed aliis contra infideles permissum esse et hoc confirmetur ex consuetudine eorum qui insitant sepulturam.' Cf. Huguccio, above, n. 70.

religion.[128] The Decretalists would find it necessary to distinguish more precisely between the crusade and a just war declared by the pope or another prelate for more secular or disciplinary purposes, and they also had to relate the crusader and his vow to the Church's direct authority to promulgate and prosecute a crusade.[129]

That the texture of Decretistic thought on Church-related wars was so complex is difficult to explain. Most canonists were extremely reticent to denominate the use of violence for ecclesiastical purposes expressly as a war, and plainly intended for laymen to do the dirty work of actual fighting. On the one hand the Decretists recognised that the Church's earlier dependence on the willingness of secular princes to act as its intermediate agents in execution of Church requests for military aid had proved unreliable, while on the other hand they shared the general conviction that the crusades were absolutely necessary. In response they developed the notion of the Church's direct authority to promulgate crusades and in effect encouraged ordinary Christians as well as princes to forsake their normal duties and take the cross. Their enthusiasm for the crusading ideal did not translate into a marked enthusiasm for direct ecclesiastical involvement in fighting, so they limited the right to initiate crusades to the pope alone. Their positions would have been simpler had they been able to describe more clearly the many different types of involvement in warfare. What was lacking was an awareness of the subtle differences between authorising, promulgating, declaring, and directing hostile operations from afar. Instead they merely distinguished between the authority to declare war and the right to participate in fighting and killing. Had they employed the sword imagery more thoroughly their positions might have been easier to

---

[128] For the distinctions between holy war, just war, and crusade, see above, ch. 3, pp. 72ff.; Villey, *La croisade*, pp. 273–9; Bainton, *Christian Attitudes*, p. 14; and Brundage, *Canon Law and the Crusader*, ch. 1. Brundage is right to conclude, against Villey, that the crusades had received theoretical justifications long before Innocent IV and Hostiensis, although I reach this conclusion on the basis of somewhat different evidence. He is also correct in seeing the juridical status of the crusades and crusaders as gradually evolving out of earlier institutions, such as the pilgrimage vow, rather than Bridrey's and Villey's view that this status was a spontaneous creation of customary law. Yet it is going too far to claim that, like Gratian, his twelfth-century disciples neglected the crusades. Cf. Brundage, *ibid.*, pp. 114, n. 52, 192; E. Bridrey, *La condition juridique des croisés et le privilège du croix: étude d'histoire du droit français* (Paris, 1900), p. 9; Villey, *ibid.*, pp. 12, 256f., 263f.; idem, 'L'idée de croisade,' 567.

[129] For the canonistic treatment of the vow during this period, see Brundage, *ibid.*, ch. 2.

understand, although this imagery was and is capable of various interpretations. As it was, the sword imagery played a relatively minor role in the Decretists' analysis of the Church's role in warfare.

The Decretists set for themselves the task of explaining, systematising and bringing up to date the analysis of war they found in the Decretum. Their explanation of the terms contained in Gratian's text and comments led them to explore the functions and procedures proper to a just war, which they conceived as an instrumentality of justice that served to punish injuries both to God and to Christians and to repel illicit violence. Their functional approach was more useful in elucidating the purposes of warfare than it was in providing detailed applications to the contemporary institutional and jurisdictional relationships among kings, princes, popes and bishops. They said little about the rights of just and unjust warriors, and nothing about the warrior-monks of the military orders. Yet the Decretists' just war analysis contained the germs of later concepts of public authority, as contrasted with feudal right, and the legal personality of the state. In more precise legal fashion than had been found earlier they restricted the locus of authority to wage war, bringing to bear on it an awareness of the differing spheres of jurisdiction that existed within medieval Christendom, within which independent city-states and feudal principalities were accorded a secondary but vital legal status. By the time of Huguccio the principle was established that any use of violence was the monopoly of legitimate authority. The just war was the province of princes, popes and prelates; its use was justified when it was necessary to defend the *patria* against hostile force and to protect the Church from its many enemies. The Decretalists would devote their attention to the accommodation of the Decretists' just war to the political conflicts of the thirteenth century.

Chapter 5

THE JUST WAR
ACCORDING TO THE DECRETALISTS

Around 1190 the canonists' primary attention shifted from Gratian's Decretum to the contemporary papal legislation. As a Decretist Rolando Bandinelli had produced an early summa to the Decretum while as Pope Alexander III (1159–81) he formulated decretals or authoritative pronouncements on canon law. Papal decretals were gathered in numerous collections, of which the most important were the *Quinque Compilationes Antiquae* that appeared between about 1191 and 1226. This period witnessed the legislative reform activity of Huguccio's star pupil Pope Innocent III, the inclusion of many of his decretals in the *Compilatio Tertia* and *Compilatio Quarta*, and the massive penetration of Roman law into canonical jurisprudence that rendered the canonistic analysis of the just war at once more technical and more concrete. At the request of Pope Gregory IX the Dominican Raymond of Peñafort compiled a new and official decretal collection that was promulgated in 1234 and became known as the *Decretales Gregorii IX*. This collection was joined in 1298 by the *Sext* of Pope Boniface VIII that contained decretals issued since 1234.

Since they commented on these decretals, canonists of the thirteenth century naturally came to be called Decretalists. Their activities are usually divided into the Interim Period before 1234, which together with the Decretist period witnessed the most rapid development in the constitutional theory of the Church, and the period after 1234. This latter period was the golden age of canonical jurisprudence, when the Decretalists were able to overcome the lack in the decretals of a locus classicus dealing with warfare and accommodated the just war more effectively to canonical doctrines and contemporary politics.[1]

---

[1] For the latest general account of the history, literature and doctrines of the Decretalists, see LeBras *et al.*, *L'âge classique*, pp. 15f. *et passim*. On the relations between Roman law and canon law, see Legendre, *La pénétration*.

THE FORMULATION OF THE JUST WAR

The Decretists had attempted to define the just war and to delineate its sphere of application, although they did not always distinguish between warfare and other hostile acts. For their part, the Decretalists sought to render even more systematic the concept of the just war in preparation for their more detailed descriptions of how it should operate. Around 1210 Alanus Anglicus, an English professor of canon law at Bologna, first emphasised the just cause, which he considered the contumacious refusal of an opponent to submit a dispute to judgment, but then reverted to the more conventional formulations of his Decretist predecessors.[2] About the same time Laurentius Hispanus provided five criteria by which the justice of a war could be assessed: first, the person waging the war must be a layman; second, the object of the war had to be either the recovery of stolen goods or the defense of the *patria*; third, the necessity of waging the war constituted the just cause; fourth, the just intention of the belligerent excluded the desire to punish; and fifth, the war had to be waged on princely authority.[3] While Laurentius here added no new elements to the just war concept, his fivefold division of criteria into *persona*, *res*, *causa*, *animus* and *auctoritas* cast the mold for most later formulations. It was soon adopted without significant change by Johannes Teutonicus in his *Glossa Ordinaria* to the Decretum,[4] and in the version of Raymond of Peñafort it entered into general use. Raymond added to the formula the appropriate requirement that all five criteria must be met for a war to be just and expanded the material under the various headings.[5] In his version of

---

[2] Alanus Anglicus, *Apparatus: 'Ius Naturale,'* to C. 23 q. 2, pr., B.N. Lat. 15393, fol. 181va and Mazar. 1318, fol. 277rb: 'Quod bellum sit iustum vel iniustum ex causa bellandi precipue iudicatur. Causa autem una sola est legitima, scilicet contumacia iniuste resistentis. Tunc enim demum iuste bellatur cum aliter ab eo quo obnoxious est iustitia haberi non potest...' Cf. above, ch. 4, pp. 87–95.

[3] Laurentius Hispanus, *Apparatus*, to C. 23 q. 2, pr., B.N. Lat. 3903, fol. 180ra.

[4] Johannes Teutonicus, *Glossa Ordinaria*, to C. 23 q. 2, pr., B.N. Lat. 14317, fol. 181vb. Peter of Salins followed this formula substantially: *Lectura in Decretum*, to C. 23 q. 2, pr., B.N. Lat. 3917, fol. 173ra. In the printed versions of the *Glossa Ordinaria* as revised by Bartholomew of Brescia the formula is similar.

[5] Raymond of Peñafort, *Summa de Casibus* (Rome, 1603), 2.5.12.17, p. 184ab: 'Ut autem plene liqueat de bello, nota, quod quinque exiguntur ad hoc, ut bellum sit iustum, scilicet, persona, res, causa, animus, et auctoritas. *persona*, ut sit saecularis, cui licitum est fundere sanguinem; non autem ecclesiastica, cui est prohibitum...nisi in necessitate inevitabili...*res*, ut sit pro rebus repetendis et pro defensione patriae...*causa*, si propter necessitatem pug-

the formula certain conditions leading to war were described in unusual fashion. Thus for Raymond the *causa* was the immediate circumstances necessitating a just war. Necessity made warfare unavoidable since peace no longer existed, which suggested that hostilities had already begun. The fundamental or underlying causes of war, recovery of property and defense of *patria*, came under Raymond's criterion of *res*. The proper attitudes of those waging a just war, considered under Raymond's heading of *animus*, included piety, justice and obedience and excluded hatred, cruelty and cupidity. Although these qualities had been mentioned by earlier canonists in the context of their discussions on warfare in general, the Decretalists' inclusion of them in the very definition clarified their relevance to the just war.

It was the profound and prolix Hostiensis however who in the mid-thirteenth century produced the most extensive categorisation of warfare, for he was able to distinguish seven different types of wars.[6] The first he considered the Roman war, a just war waged by the faithful against infidels and so called because Rome was head and mother of the Christian faith. No mention was made here of the Roman Empire. The second type was a judicial war, also just, that

---

netur, ut per pugnam pax acquiratur...*animus*, ut non fiat propter odium, vel ultionem... *auctoritas*, ut si auctoritate Ecclesiae, praesertim cum pugnatur pro fide; vel auctoritate Principis...Si aliquod istorum defuerit bellum, dicetur iniustum.' Cf. Aquinas, S.T. 2-2, q. 40 art. 1, resp. Goffredus of Trani and Hostiensis in restating Raymond's formula reverted to the negative form used by Laurentius Hispanus and Johannes Teutonicus: Goffredus, *Summa in Titulos Decretalium* (Venice, 1570), to X. 5. 12. para. 18, fol. 205rb; Hostiensis, *Summa Aurea* (Venice, 1574), to X. 1. 34. para. 4, p. 357.

[6] Hostiensis, *Lectura in Decretales Innocentii IV* (Venice, 1581), to *De homicidio voluntario et casuali*, c. *Pro humani*, para. 34 (= Sext. 5.4.1), pp. 29–29A: 'Ad doctrinam autem huius materiae no. quod septem sunt bella. Primum potest dici Romanum quod faciunt fideles impugnando infideles, et hoc est iustum...et dicitur Romanum, quia Roma est caput fidei...Secundum iudiciale quod fit authorite iudicis legitimi habentis merum imperium non dicentis sibi ius, sed aliis ordinem iudiciarum observantis, et ex causa contumaciae hoc concedentis...Tertium praesumptuosum, quod scilicet faciunt iudices inobedientes... Quartum licitum quandocunque hoc fit authoritate iuris quo ad illum cui conceditur...et in proximi vel vicini iniuria repellenda, et in praelato qui contra iniuriantes ecclesiae utroque gladio (si utrunque habeat) authoritate propria uti potest...Quintum temerarium quo ad illos qui hoc faciunt contra authoritatem iuris, nam et qui defendit se contra authoritatem iuris temerariae se defendit: sapienter autem faceret si corrigeret vitam suam...Sextum voluntarium...quo scilicet principes nostri temporis seculares utuntur frequentius, et est iniustum...Septimum necessarium, et est iustum. hoc est illud quod faciunt fideles defendendo se authoritate iuris contra voluntarie impugnantes: nam vim vi repellere ad tuitionem sui corporis vel etiam rerum cum moderamine inculpatae tutelae omnia iura permittunt...' Cf. Hostiensis, *Summa*, to X. 1. 34. para 4, pp. 359f. The *merum imperium* was supreme jurisdiction in criminal matters: Berger, 'Encyclopedic Dictionary,' v. *imperium merum*, 494.

was waged by Christians on the judicial authority of someone who, possessing the *merum imperium*, was not judging in his own interest but was rather enforcing judicial order on those who contumaciously resisted it. The third type was the presumptuous and unjustly waged war of those Christians who contumaciously opposed the judicial authority of the second type. The fourth type of war was that waged by those who possessed legal authority to repel injuries to one's associates. Even a prelate with the use of the temporal sword could wage such a war, which was both just and licit. The fifth type of war, waged by adversaries of the fourth type, was rash and unjust. Hostiensis advised those who were unjustly defending themselves against legal authority to mend their ways. The sixth type was a war of attack waged on personal, that is private, authority, and as a willful war it was unnecessary and unjust. Hostiensis condemned contemporary princes for their frequent resort to this type of war, for they lacked the proper authority. The seventh type of war was waged on proper authority in self-defense against the attacks inflicted by those who waged the sixth type of war. This last type was necessary and justified by the right to repel violence with moderate use of violence.

Hostiensis' formulation may seem a mere virtuoso display of legal subtlety, but it is much more than that. By viewing situations of both parties in a single war Hostiensis was able to contrast just and unjust wars more effectively, and in so doing he harked back to the Decretists' definitions initiated by Stephen of Tournai while avoiding the legal difficulties of that view.[7] The seven-fold typology of warfare stood a better chance of clarifying prior ambiguities and of becoming a comprehensive formula for analysing actual wars than had earlier attempts to separate just from unjust wars.

Although they established concise and inclusive formulations of the just war, the Decretalists realised that these definitions raised more questions than they solved, and only served to open the debate. Common consensus as to the definition of the just war was no substitute for detailed theories about the operation of the just war. Definitions that contained all aspects of war were simply too broad to provide reliable guides for use in settling actual conflicts. Hence

[7] Above, ch. 4, nn. 9–14.

most of the Decretalists' discussions were focused on problems such as defense, authority, conduct, consequences and the roles of Church and churchmen.

THE CAUSES OF THE JUST WAR

Just as the Decretists had considered defense of the *patria* as the best example of a just cause for war, so the Decretalists further refined this notion and in the course of their debates added several other just causes to it. For Gratian and the Decretists the primary problem was that violence used in self-defense, however justified in Roman and canon law, appeared to contradict the canon (D. 46 c. 8) that prohibited avenging or punishment (*ultio*) of injuries done to oneself. While they never satisfactorily resolved the dilemma, their usual stance was to allow the avenging of injuries only when it was performed on judicial authority. In tension with this was the Decretists' toleration of violent self-defense in certain cases even when proper authority was lacking.[8] For their part the Decretalists took to heart the Roman law dictum that violence could be repelled by violence, and on the strength of this conviction they were able to reinterpret Gratian's pivotal phrase, 'iusta bella ulciscuntur iniurias.' Alanus Anglicus initiated this transformation when he argued that *ulciscuntur* meant *repulsion* of injuries or the recovery of goods unjustly seized performed under princely aegis. By contrast, the condemnation of *ultio* referred only to similar actions performed by persons acting without authority or to cases of unjust punishment.[9] Incorporating this differentiation into his *Glossa Ordinaria*,[10] Johannes Teutonicus

---

[8] Cf. above, ch. 4, pp. 95ff., and Kuttner, *Schuldlehre*, pp. 334–67.

[9] Alanus Anglicus, *Apparatus: 'Ius Naturale,'* to C. 23 q. 2 c. 2, v. *ulciscuntur*, B.N. Lat. 15393, fol. 181va; Mazar. 1318, fol. 277ra: 'vel repellunt vel quibus ablata repetuntur...ar. contra [D. 46 c. 8] ubi puniuntur suarum ultores. Sed istud locum habet in principibus, illud in subditis, vel illud de iniusta ultione.' *Ibid.*, to C. 23, pr., B.N. Lat. 15393, fol. 180va; Mazar. 1318, fol. 275vb: 'His dupliciter uti accidit, scilicet impetendo et defendendo. Impetare armis non licet, nisi iudici, militi et officiali...armis defendere licet omnibus laicis.' *Ibid.*, to D. 46 c. 8, v. *ultores*, Mazar. 1318, fol. 49ra: 'ex intervallo, scilicet bello renovato set non continuato. Hoc enim nulli privato licet, ut [Cod. 1.9.14]. Tanquam principi vero qui supra se iudicem non habet, in temporalibus etiam licet bello renovato iniuriam suam et suorum ulcisci...vim vi repellere bello continuato omnibus licet.' Cf. Laurentius Hispanus, *Apparatus*, to C. 23 q. 2 c. 2, v. *ulciscuntur*, B.N. Lat. 3903, fol. 180rb: 'i.e. repellunt. et sic non obstat [D. 46 c. 8].'

[10] Johannes Teutonicus, *Glossa Ordinaria*, to C. 23 q. 2 d. p. c. 2, v. *ulciscuntur*, B.N. Lat. 14317, fol. 182ra; Cod. Vat. 1367, fol. 186vb: 'i.e. repelluntur. sic non obstat [D. 46, c. 8]. Johannes. Jo.'

added a general theory of licit repulsion of violence. Someone who defended himself against violence when it was being inflicted on him, or when the adversary was about to strike again, was considered to be justly defending himself rather than wreaking vengeance or *ultio*. However, should the person attacked seek to strike his adversary after the immediate danger had passed, he was then guilty of acting out of vengeful motives. In this train of thought Johannes in effect assimilated *iniuria* to *violentia*, holding that injury or violence could be repelled *incontinenti* provided that the defense was moderate. The right to repel violence was valid whether the person or his property was attacked.[11]

Most of the Decretalists were content to follow the *Glossa Ordinaria* with little change, but Raymond of Peñafort's more lengthy analysis added the restriction that anyone who intentionally exceeded the limits of moderate defense should be excommunicated because he thereby acted out of vengeance, and he limited the right to defend one's possessions when he concluded that if a defender in expelling an attacker from his property had killed or wounded anyone, he should likewise be excommunicated.[12] Like Huguccio before him Raymond harbored moral suspicions about attempts to justify the right of a private person to resort to violence on his own behalf, however licit it was in Roman and canon law. He advised those Christians who aspired to perfection to avoid striking back under any circumstances.[13] Since it was not likely to meet with practical acceptance, his contention that private self-defense justified neither wounding nor killing an enemy found few followers among the Decretalists. At the end of the golden age Hostiensis argued that, according to both Roman and canon law, defense against injuries to one's person rendered licit the injuries committed by the person

---

11 *Ibid.*, to C. 23 q. 1, pr., v. *propulsandam*, B.N. Lat. 14317, fol. 180va: 'si tamen aliquis vim factam repellat, potius presumi debet quod defendendi non ulciscendi causa fecerit id, ut [Dig. 9.2.52.1]. et hoc si primus percussor volebat percutere denuo. Alioquin si nolebat denuo percutere, et alter repercussit, potius est vindicta, quam repulsio iniurie. Et sic intellige quod dicitur iniuriam incontinenti posse repelli. Requiritur ergo quod defendendo repercutiat non ulciscendo, ut infra [C. 23 q. 1 c. 4] et [Dig. 9.2.45] et cum moderamine se defendat...Item incontinenti debet vim repellere, ut [Dig. 43.16.3.9]. Si vis infertur rebus et illatam et inferendam licitum est repellere, sed potius illatam quam inferendam. Jo.' In effect Johannes skillfully combined Decretist and Romanistic analyses.

12 Raymond of Peñafort, *Summa de Casibus*, 2.5.12.18, pp. 185b–186b.

13 *Ibid.*, p. 187a.

attacked, and that repulsion of violence by violence *incontinenti* was not considered vengeful.[14]

As a result of this transformation the term *ultio* gradually disappeared from the Decretalists' vocabulary. There was however at least one exception to this trend. Peter of Salins, who around 1250 composed a *Lectura* to the Decretum long after other canonists had shifted their attention to papal decretals, saw fit to repeat the phrase *ulciscuntur iniurias* in a conventional restatement of the Augustinian statement upon which it was based.[15] He also attempted to resuscitate the notion, broached by Stephen of Tournai almost a century earlier, that a war could be just with respect to both belligerents, or just only for one party, or even unjust on both sides.[16] The distinguishing feature of this mode of thought justified war as a punishment for sin; Peter's formulation lacked references to an objective just cause and the requirement of authority. As these omissions placed Peter's view outside the mainstream of Decretalist debate that substituted objective and judiciable criteria for punishment as motives for the just war, his analysis received little if any attention. The thirteenth-century definitions of the just war detailed above omitted Gratian's phrase 'iusta bella ulciscuntur iniurias,' and the omission was justified by the Decretalists when they prohibited the term *ultio* from being understood as unlimited punishment or vengeance. When it was used, it took on the more restricted meanings of repulsion or defense. The Decretalists were now prepared to ascertain under what conditions legitimate defense rendered wars just, licit, and necessary.

Dropping a pivotal but vague concept from the just war vocabulary enabled the Decretalists to explore what was meant by defense. The *Glossa Ordinaria* to the Decretum expressed the common opinion that military service was not sinful when employed in defense of one's person and property, the *patria* or ancestral laws, and Johannes Teutonicus was only one among many who hesitated at the point of requiring princely authority for all such employment of military force.[17] He distinguished between an illicit war of attack, and a

---

[14] Hostiensis, *Summa*, to X. 1.34, para. 4, p. 358; idem, *Lectura* (as above n. 6), to X. 5.12.3, para. 3, v. *Hoc etiam*, p. 43A.

[15] Peter of Salins, *Lectura*, to C. 23 q. 2 c. 2, B.N. Lat. 3917, fol. 173va.

[16] *Ibid.*, to C. 23 q. 2, pr., B.N. Lat. 3917, fol. 173ra. Cf. above, ch. 4, nn. 9–14.

[17] Johannes Teutonicus, *Glossa Ordinaria*, to C. 23 q. 1, pr., B.N. Lat. 14317, fol. 180va.

defensive war that was licit and could be waged at all times.[18] Raymond of Peñafort justified recourse to war even in the absence of special princely or ecclesiastical authority. Defense of the *patria* and recovery of stolen goods were licit by reason of the right to repel violence with violence, provided it was carried out immediately and with proper moderation.[19] At this point the whole prior canonistic theory of the just war could have been sabotaged, for if the fundamental requirement of authority could be dispensed with, then the way was opened for each person to wage war on his own authority. Since authority was the means by which the just *causa, animus* and *persona* were maintained, lack of that authority could at least in theory encourage unlimited but still licit wars for recovery of property. The context of Raymond's remarks and his other opinions show that he did not intend to annul his own formulation of the just war and leave the way open to self-help, the vendetta or vigilante justice. A more likely explanation is that Raymond somewhat clumsily denied to this sort of violent self-defense the full status of a just war, for he did not explicitly term it a just war. The legal consequences of a just war, such as the right to take captives and spoils, were not operative in this type of war, and no action beyond the simple repulsion of violence was justified. It appears that Raymond was groping toward a distinction between a war waged only in self-defense and violence from a just war, and that he would accord only limited rights to a simple war of defense. His inconclusive treatment would stimulate others to make more precise the role of self-defense in warfare.

Subsequent discussion of a simple war of defense centered upon a decretal of Innocent III that concerned a case of disseizin or violent ejection from property illegally occupied (X. 2.13.12, *Olim causam*).[20] The proctor of a bishop had used violence to expel certain Templars from a property belonging to the bishop, and Innocent III had justified the proctor's action by the right to repel violence with violence. In the event that the bishop had exceeded the limits of moderation in

---

[18] *Ibid.*, to C. 23 q. 8 c. 15, v. *quadragesimali*, B.N. Lat. 14317, fol. 197rb: 'unde et machabei pugnaverunt in sabbato. Non obstat [x. 1.34.1] quia hic loquitur de defensore, ibi de inpugnatore.' Cf. Monaldus, *Summa Perutilis* (Lyons, before 1516), *de bello iusto*, fol. 19va.

[19] Raymond of Peñafort, *Summa de Casibus*, 2.5.12.18, p. 185a, and William of Rennes' *Glossa* to this summa, p. 185b.

[20] Innocent IV, *Commentaria. Apparatus in Quinque Libros Decretalium* (Frankfurt, 1570), to x. 2.13.12, paras. 7–8, fol. 231va; cited below, n. 58.

defending his possession, he was obliged to make restitution to the Templars for the excessive violence. While the actual violence used here was probably minimal by contemporary standards, the fact that all the parties were clerics provided Innocent IV with the opportunity to dwell at length on the rights of anyone, even a cleric, to use violence in his own defense. Innocent first asked how the cleric involved in the case could use violence without incurring the canonical penalties against clerical participation in war and violence, to which he replied that everyone was allowed to *movere bellum* in defense of self and property, though he did not consider this act a war, properly speaking, but a simple defense. Someone ejected forcibly from his property could fight back according to the Roman law right of self-defense. Since this right was conceded to everyone, no princely authority was necessary. Clerics who exercised this right did not incur excommunication unless they actually fought in hand-to-hand combat, nor even then if those in illegal occupation were unwilling to leave peacefully. Excommunication was incurred only if the violence used was excessive. In this passage Innocent IV proposed in effect a distinction between warlike acts and a legal state of war, a proposal that improved upon Raymond of Peñafort's more implicit statement. If a warlike act was to qualify as a war properly understood, recourse to authority was necessary. Whenever someone could not otherwise defend his property and protect his rights, he could employ armies and even declare war on superior authority. The proper authority was the prince who had jursidiction over him. In Innocent's view authority was thus necessary even for a defensive war, although he accorded the right to perform hostile acts in self-defense to everyone. Hostiensis evidently agreed with Innocent's treatment, for he repeated its essential features and did not elaborate elsewhere on the right of self-defense.[21] Innocent here was groping toward the construction of a hierarchy of violent actions in which each level of violence had its proper authority and extent. Further consideration of this crucial element of the Decretalists' analysis will be deferred until other relevant passages are brought to bear on it.

Other Decretalists detailed numerous instances in which a just defensive war was licit. In addition to assimilating defense of the *patria* into the formula of the just war under the criterion of *res*,

[21] Hostiensis, *Lectura*, to X. 2.13.12, para. 17, p. 52A.

Johannes Teutonicus held that someone could even kill his own father while defending his *patria*;[22] its defense even overrode a vassal's obligation to his lord;[23] and clerics could exhort others to defend the land.[24] Raymond of Peñafort considered a war in defense of associates licit if the war was just, but he naturally condemned defense of associates in the course of waging an unjust war.[25] The anonymous *Gloss: 'Ecce vicit Leo,'* a work of the French school written before 1210, introduced a new facet to the discussions of the just cause when it distinguished military occupations from invasions. Such an occupation was a just war waged by a prince, while an invasion was unjust because it was waged on the personal authority of someone who either lacked legitimate authority or who had no superior authority from whom he could seek legal settlement of his claim.[26] This passage portrayed the dilemma of a petty knight who was unable legally to wage a just war but who also lacked recourse to the jurisdiction of a superior court. The author prohibited the knight from taking up violence in his own cause, lest he be guilty of acting without authority. The knight was forced to swallow his grievance unless a competent authority was able to enforce his jurisdiction. The author in effect restricted the use of a just war as a legal process to superior authority. This passage came closer than most other Decretalists to making a distinction between just and unjust offensive wars that was based on possession of authority.

Yet in general the Decretalists contributed few innovations to the notion of defense as a just cause, but rather gave it more systematic expression. Unanswered with precision was what was meant by the *patria*, although recent research has concluded that the Decretalists variously considered the Empire, the Church, Italian city-states, and the national kingdoms of England, France and Spain as *patriae*

---

[22] Johannes Teutonicus, *Glossa Ordinaria*, to C. 23 q. 3 c. 5, v. *patriam*, B.N. Lat. 14317, fol. 182vb. Cf. William Durantis, *Speculum Iudiciale*, IV, partic. iii, para. 2 no. 32 (Venice, 1602), III, 321; cited in Post, *Studies*, p. 245, n. 161. Canonists and Romanists alike shared this opinion: *ibid.*, pp. 438 n. 11, 442, n. 35. Cf. above, ch. 2, nn. 36, 42.

[23] Johannes Teutonicus, *Glossa Ordinaria*, to C. 22 q. 5 c. 18.

[24] *Ibid.*, to C. 23 q. 8, pr.

[25] Raymond, *Summa de Casibus*, 2.1.7, p. 154a.

[26] *Gloss: 'Ecce vicit Leo,'* to D. 1 c. 9, v. *sedium occupatio*, B.N. Nouv. Acq. Lat. 1576, fol. 20vb: 'secundum hoc intelligere de iusta occupatione, qua fit positum bellum auctoritate principis iusta...Contra intelligitur de iniusta invasione que sit auctore propria vel quando non invenitur superior a quo ius petatur.'

worthy of defense in a just war.[27] While defense of the *patria* justified recourse to war, it constituted only a necessary and not a sufficient precondition, for without reference to authority the just cause of defense was incomplete. Seen in this light, Monaldus' opinion that moderate self-defense justified war was plainly unsatisfactory,[28] and so the Decretalists examined the other necessary preconditions when they came to discuss authority.

The Decretists had adduced a few causes of the just war other than defense, notably denial of free passage, recuperation of goods seized, and necessity. These causes were mentioned with little elaboration, but the Decretalists added several new conditions that qualified as just causes. According to Laurentius Hispanus a just war could be waged even without authority to enforce a right or debt that had been unjustly denied [29] although the nature of the debt was not specified. Alanus Anglicus saw contumacy as a cogent reason for going to war, as in the case of a city or people that had unjustly seized property and refused to restore it to its rightful owners.[30] When goods had been seized and held by violence, a just war could be waged to regain possession of them when the violent possessor contumaciously refused to submit the dispute to judgment.[31] Here Alanus only underscored the basic Augustinian just cause (C. 23 q. 2 c. 2) when he expressed it in the language of Roman legal procedures against contumacy, although elsewhere he considered the punishment of contumacy to be within the purview of Church courts at least in the first instance, rather than as cause for a just war.[32] In line with feudal custom Hostiensis preferred counts to settle disputes with their vassals in the comital court, but if the vassals remained contumacious

---

27 E.g. Kantorowicz, *King's Two Bodies*, pp. 232–72 and Post, *Studies*, pp. 435–53 and 568f.

28 Monaldus, *Summa, de bello iusto*, fol. 19rb: 'Item bellum iustum est quando fit auctoritate ecclesie vel principis vel alicuius persone cui licitum est pugnare...ex causa necessaria... pro defensione patrie vel propter iustam obedientiam vel caritatem. Similiter propter defensionem suam cum moderamine inculpate tutele, ut [x. 2.13.12].'

29 Laurentius Hispanus, *Apparatus*, to C. 23 q. 2 c. 3, v. *transitus*, B.N. Lat. 3903, fol. 180rb and B.N. Lat. 15393, fol. 181vb: 'argumentum quod etiam sine maioris permissu iuste bellum geritur ubi debitum negatur.' Peter of Salins, *Lectura*, to C. 23 q. 2 c. 3, v. *contra amorreos*, B.N. Lat. 3917, fol. 173rb.

30 Alanus, *Apparatus*: 'Ius Naturale,' to C. 23 q. 2 c. 2, v. *si gens vel civitas*, B.N. Lat. 15393, fol. 181va and Mazar. 1318, fol. 277va. Cf. Berger, 'Encyclopedic Dictionary,' v. *contumacia*, 415.

31 *Ibid.*, to C. 23 q. 2 c. 1, v. *rebus*, B.N. Lat. 15393, fol. 181vb and Mazar. 1318, fol. 277va.

32 Alanus, *Apparatus* to Comp. 1, 5, 6. 7, v. *confiscentur*, B.N. Lat. 3932, fol. 59va. For this decretal, see below, p. 189.

of the legal proceedings, then the count could attack them with full legal authority.[33] Closely allied with contumacy was negligence, for as contumacy was refusal to obey a judicial sentence, so was negligence a judge's refusal to render a just sentence. Alanus Anglicus perceived this connection when he held that when a city or people had unjustly seized property, it could be taken to court or if the judge neglected to render a decision he himself could be the target of a just war.[34] In agreeing with Alanus, Laurentius Hispanus added that a judge who rendered a fraudulent, injurious or sordid judgment could also become the target of a just war.[35] Hostiensis' opinion was more simply expressed: a city or territorial lord that neglected to render justice could be attacked and plundered.[36]

In these opinions the Decretalists drew out the juridical components of Augustine's definition of the just war and expressed them in the language of jurisdiction. The just war was increasingly seen as a quasi-legal process employed to settle disputes that could not be adjudicated by more normal legal processes, and here the causes of contumacy and negligence resemble *déni de justice* that sanctioned the right of a vassal to revolt against his overlord. The Decretalists did not consider at length the abstract or theological justice of a cause for war but rather emphasised the legal status of a violent act. In isolation their analysis of just causes was inconclusive, for the just cause could not be understood without reference to the specific authority entitled to invoke it. To have a just cause necessarily implied that the belligerent already possessed authority, or, to put it differently, only a legitimate authority was entitled to have a just cause for war.

AUTHORITY AND OBEDIENCE

The general trend of Decretist opinion stressed the necessity of proper authority for the just war and attempted to restrict the locus of that authority to princes. With varying success the Decretalists took the next step of specifying what sort of prince possessed the right to levy a just war. Their solutions usually turned on the extent of

---

[33] Hostiensis, *Summa*, to x. 1. 34, para. 4, p. 360.

[34] Alanus, *Apparatus*: 'Ius Naturale,' to C. 23 q. 2 c. 2 v. *neglexerit*, B.N. Lat. 15393, fol. 181va and Mazar. 1318, fol. 277vb. Cf. above, n. 30 and Berger, 'Encyclopedic Dictionary,' v. *negligentia*, 593.

[35] Below, n. 130.

[36] Hostiensis, *Lectura*, to x. 1.34.1, para. 6, p. 176A.

jurisdiction that princes of various levels were capable of exercising. Yet they did not achieve a unanimous consensus, and doubts remained as to how far the authority to wage a just war should be restricted. An exemplification of their dilemma was the approach of Peter of Salins, who in his summary included implicit references to both direct and indirect princely authority. Just wars were waged either by order or permission; by divine order the Israelites conquered the city of Ai, and through the intermediary of canon law God permitted men to wage war in defense of their own persons. Secular and ecclesiastical princes ordered just wars by human laws that also permitted wars of self-defense.[37] This view left the authority to wage war where it had been with the Decretists, restricted only to princes. Clearly further restraints were necessary if warfare was not to be the prerogative of any knight whatsoever.

To prevent this consequence Alanus Anglicus, Johannes de Deo and Hostiensis tried by various means to limit the authority to wage just wars to kings, the Emperor, and the pope. For his part Alanus saw the *ius merum* as limiting authority to someone who had no secular superior. Although he did not mention the Emperor explicitly in this context, it is likely that he had him in mind when he brought Roman law with its emphasis on imperial authority to bear on the problem. Other princes regardless of their actual power lacked the authority to declare war.[38] Yet in another context Alanus saw God, the pope, and any princely authority as the necessary superior authorities,[39] and elsewhere he even accorded the right to declare war to the Italian cities, for although they indeed had superior authorities over them they still had the right to wage war in pursuit of their own rights.[40] Provided that a prince had the right to declare

---

[37] Peter of Salins, *Lectura*, to C. 23 q. 2 c. 2, v. *deus imperat*, B.N. Lat. 3917, fol. 173rb. For the problems of authority and obedience treated from a different point of view, see F. Russell, 'Innocent IV's Proposals to Limit Warfare,' *Proceedings* of the Fourth International Congress of Medieval Canon Law, to appear in *Monumenta Iuris Canonici*.

[38] Alanus, *Apparatus*: '*Ius Naturale*,' to C. 23 q. 1 c. 4, v. *penes principes*, Mazar. 1318, fol. 276vb. Cf. above, n. 6.

[39] *Ibid.*, to C. 23 q. 4 c. 36, v. *superiori*, B.N. Lat. 15393, fol. 186va and Mazar. 1318, fol. 282vb: 'summi principis. ibi accipiunt a superiori scilicet deo...vel a papa, vel ab eis qui eos eligere ad principatum, qui quantum ad hoc eo maiores sunt.'

[40] *Ibid.*, to C. 23 q. 5 c. 13, v. *miles*, B.N. Lat. 15393, fol. 190vb: 'Consuetudo quorundam locorum etiam aliis principibus qui super se habent alios concedit ius indicendi bellum sua auctoritate in civitatibus italie, et pro eis facit istud [C. 23 q. 2 c. 2].' Alanus may have come to this conclusion because Augustine's definition focused on the right of a city to avenge its own injuries.

war he could do so even without a formal edict, to redress an injury done to him, or in proper exercise of his authority when other means were of no avail. Here Alanus interjected his opinion that the pope as ordinary judge of all matters spiritual and temporal had jurisdiction over quarrels between Christian princes, and thus by papal authority a prince could declare war. He then cited the alternate opinion that recourse to the pope was unnecessary, and concluded somewhat lamely that any pursuit of one's own rights without princely authority was delinquent.[41] While he clearly favored papal authority over warfare, Augustine and Gratian had accorded this authority to all princes, so Alanus was unable to reconcile the conflict between his notion of papal jurisdictional primacy and prior canonistic positions.[42]

While this lack of precision in limiting authority to certain officials could have been a serious defect in the Decretalists' analysis, their opinions became somewhat bolder when they came to discuss unjust wars. Perhaps the most extensive treatment of this problem was found in the confessional manual of Johannes de Deo, written around 1245, in which he considered the sins that were likely to arise in pursuit of different professions. The simple knight often fell into sin not only by his license and rapine, but also when he attacked his own *patria* or did not maintain fealty to his lord.[43] It is noteworthy that in this passage the private obligations of feudalism were placed on the same level as the public obligation to defend the *patria*.[44] Barons were similarly liable to fall into sin through violence and homicide and devastation of property committed while waging unjust wars.[45] Kings sinned when they impressed priests into their

---

[41] *Ibid.*, to C. 23 q. 2 c. 1, v. *ex edicto*, B.N. Lat. 15393, fol. 181va–vb and Mazar. 1318, fol. 277rb: 'principis qui habet ius indicendi bellum. Ipse autem princeps sine edicto licite gerit bellum in quo est specialissimum, quod potest iniuriam suam vindicare et sua auctoritate quod sibi competit occupare...sed hoc ita demum potest et licet, si aliter iustitia consequi non possit...et secundum opinionem nostram qui dicimus papam esse iudicem ordinarium omnium principum quoad spiritualia quoad temporalia. ad eum antequam indicat bellum tenetur recurrere ut per eum iustitiam consequatur si potest. Vel eo auctoritate prestante bellum indicat.' Cf. J. A. Watt, *The Theory of Papal Monarchy in the Thirteenth Century* (New York, 1965), p. 50.

[42] Cf. Huguccio, above, ch. 4, n. 46.

[43] Johannes de Deo, *Liber Poenitentiarius*, 6, 8, B.N. Lat. 14703, fol. 110ra; quoted, partially, from another manuscript, in Post, *Studies*, p. 438, n. 14.

[44] Johannes Teutonicus (*Glossa Ordinaria*, to C. 22 q. 5 c. 18, v. *honestum*) placed the duty to defend the *patria* above fealty to one's lord.

[45] Johannes de Deo, *Liber Poenitentiarius*, 6, 7, B.N. Lat. 14703, fol. 109vh.

armies and occupied territories belonging to others instead of remaining content within their own borders. Although they might govern these territories well, their possession of them was nevertheless illicit.[46] Johannes' simplified view was symptomatic of the common ecclesiastical opinion that most wars waged by the feudal nobility and even kings were unjust because they lacked a just cause, were waged out of greed for the property of someone else and lacked the requisite authority. Even kings were at least implicitly confined to waging wars only in self-defense. The opinion of Johannes, a Spanish confessor, was shared by the international diplomat and bureaucrat Hostiensis, who as canonist considered rash those unauthorised wars waged between Christian princes, for in such wars one party's possession of his territory was peaceful and of long standing, while the other party attempted to usurp the possession of it. To this observation Hostiensis added a condemnation of those confessors who, desirous of receiving pious donations from princes' illicit gains, absolved these patrons from their sins. For this practice Hostiensis found no excuse, and he advised such confessors to be careful lest they drag the whole mass of people committed to their care down with them into Hell.[47]

Hostiensis also introduced a new dimension to the problem of authority by extolling the solidarity of the Roman people. Commenting on a decretal of Innocent IV with his customarily copious use of Roman law citations, he asserted that the Roman people, by whom he meant all Christians, were bound together by nature in an indissoluble relationship that was reinforced by the Golden Rule and the Roman *ius cognationis*. Hence no one Christian nor any groups of Christians could renounce this bond and make war on one another. Since all civil laws that justified this resort to war were invalid, the only licit wars were those waged by Christians united against other peoples. On this basis Hostiensis condemned all wars waged between

---

[46] *Ibid.*, 6. 2, B.N. Lat. 14703, fol. 108rb–va.

[47] Hostiensis, *Lectura*, to x. 3.34.8, para. 8, p. 128A: 'sed cum hodie princeps [*sic*] Christiani inter se bella et guerras propria temeritate moveant, et quod unus iuste et pacifice possidet, et possidet ab antiquo, alius de novo occupet et usurpet, et nihilominus a suis confessoribus et eorum peccata quamvis notoria palpantibus et dissimulantibus, et ab eisdem castra, possessiones et alias eleemosinas scienter recipientibus absolvantur, et per consequens praescribi nequeant...Quis excusabit ista? Nescio. Respondeo, caveant ipsi sibi, et consulant, alioquin timendum est, ne catervatim ad inferos innumerabiles populos secum trahant.' *Ibid.*, to x. 5.12.18, para. 17, p. 48A.

Christian princes, whose rupture of their common bond he termed *diffidentia*. And since only the Emperor had the authority to wage war and grant permission to bear arms, all such princes were guilty of treason. Against these princes who had broken their faith or harbored assassins, the Roman people could promulgate a sentence acknowledging that a *diffidatio* had taken place and could then wage a just war against them and occupy their possessions.[48] For Hostiensis then the *diffidatio* sanctioned earlier in the Middle Ages as a feudal right of rebellion now became a breach of the faith that held Christian society together, so wars that formerly were waged in accordance with feudal custom were now condemned as unjust, anti-social and lacking in authority. Such princes by their *diffidentia* or *diffidatio* had placed themselves beyond the pale of peaceful Christian society and were now no more than mere brigands and thieves. Having thus made a frontal assault on contemporary practice Hostiensis then turned to consider the problem of the proper authority for waging wars against such offending princes. He required a judge who had the *merum imperium* to exercise jurisdiction over the offending princes,[49] and was inclined to attribute such authority to the pope, for he alone had no earthly superior.[50] When war was waged on such proper authority, the adversaries had no right to defend themselves, since their temerity and contumacy had rendered such defense an illegal and presumptuous rebellion. They would be better advised to mend their ways. But if proper authority for a war waged against them was lacking, they then could justly defend themselves.[51] In the case of a disputed possession the Emperor or a competent judge could authorise an injured person to wage war on the contumacious offender.[52] In Hostiensis' view then, the just war could only be waged on the full authority that he allowed variously to the Emperor, the pope, or a judge. The competent authority must either possess the *merum imperium* or have no judicial superior.[53] In stressing the role played by authority Hostiensis limited its exercise to very few officials.

[48] *Ibid.*, to *De homicidio*, c. 1, *pro humani* [= Sext 5.4.1], para. 8, v. *per assissinos*, pp. 28–28A and *ibid.*, paras 32–3, v. *diffidatus*, p. 29. Cf. idem, *Summa*, to x. 1.34, para. 4, p. 358.

[49] Hostiensis, *Summa*, to x. 1.34, para. 4, pp. 359–60 and *ibid.* to x. 2.2, para. 2, pp. 454f. Cf. above, n. 6.

[50] Hostiensis, *Lectura*, to x. 2.13.12, paras. 18–19, pp. 52A–53.

[51] Hostiensis, *Summa*, to x. 1.34, para. 4, p. 359.   [52] *Ibid.*, to x. 2.13, para. 1, p. 548.

[53] Durantis, *Speculum*, II, partic. i, de 2 decreto, para. 5, nos. 1–2 (3 vols., Venice, 1585).

The Decretalist positions thus far described indicate two different tendencies. Peter of Salins represented the older view of the Decretists that tended to allow almost any prince regardless of the nature or extent of his jurisdiction to wage war, while Alanus Anglicus and Hostiensis tended to restrict the authority and the right to perceive a just cause to either the Emperor or the pope. In effect the choice so far was between a position that regarded almost all contemporary princely wars as just wars and one that condemned almost all such wars as flagrantly unjust. There was a clear necessity for a middle position that took into account not only contemporary practice and Christian–Roman legal norms but also the evolving differentiations between the various levels of jurisdiction.

From different vantage points William of Rennes and Innocent IV constructed this middle way based on a more precise and subtle analysis of the limits of actual jurisdictions. In his gloss to the *Summa de Casibus* of Raymond of Peñafort, William of Rennes at first allowed kings, princes, and, in somewhat circular fashion, anyone else who had the right to bear arms to wage war against disobedient vassals and external enemies.[54] Presumably realising that this was too broad, William launched a lengthy discussion of authority.[55] He

---

II, 489, also restricted the right to wage a public war to a prince with no superior; in practice this usually meant the king. Cf. Keen, *Laws of War*, p. 77.

[54] William of Rennes, *Glossa*, 2. 4, para. 1, v. *ex edicto*, p. 165a. Cf. above, n. 28.

[55] *Ibid.*, 2. 17, v. *auctoritate principis*, p. 184b: 'Quid si barones subditi comitis, vel ducis, habent guerram contra eum, aut comes contra regem suum, vel econverso, cuius principis est auctoritas requirenda? Respondeo: princeps, qui nullum habet superiorem, sive sit rex, sive imperator, auctoritate propria si iusta causa subsit, potest movere bellum, tam contra subditos, quam contra extraneos; potest etiam subditis suis dare auctoritatem movendi bellum, tam contra principem extraneum, quam contra subditos eius si causa subsit, et viderit expedire; sed non contra proprios subditos quamdiu potest iniurantem iustificare, vel quamdiu vult stare iuri coram eo, et coram iudice suo si est iudex medius inter huiusmodi principem, et iniurantem...Si autem non potest eum iustificare, aut si ille non vult stare ibi iuri, potest, non solum princeps huiusmodi, sed etiam ille princeps, qui habet super se superiorem, auctoritate sua movere bellum contra huiusmodi iniurantem, si subest ei mediate, vel immediate, et dare licentiam iniuriam passo movendi contra eum arma; si autem iniurans non subest mediate, vel immediate principi habenti super se superiorem, princeps ille non potest auctoritatem dare subdito suo movendo contra eum arma; sed auctoritas superioris principis est requiranda, maxime si ille iniurans pertinet mediate, vel immediate ad iurisdictionem superioris principis: cum ergo vasallus comitis habet guerram contra comitem regis, est auctoritas requirenda. Si autem comes contra regem, et rex noluit ei ius exhibere per pares curiae humiliter requisitus, credo, quod si ius suum armis defendat cum moderamine inculpatae tutelae, non peccat; impugnare tamen regem autoritate sua non poterit: papa tamen facta denunciatione de excessu regis, si rex nollet a peccato desistere, posset regem excommunicare, et crescente contumacia dare auctoritatem movendi arma contra eum. Cum autem rex habet causam guerre, et contra

asked whether barons of a count or duke or counts of a king had the authority to make war on their superiors. He answered that the Emperor, a king, or a prince with no superior could wage war on both his own subjects and external enemies provided his cause was just, and could also authorise his subjects to fight just wars. Even this prince could not make war on his own subjects if he could peacefully judge the case or submit the dispute to an impartial judge. However when a prince was unable to adjudicate the dispute or when the offender was unwilling to submit his case to judgment, even a prince with a superior who nevertheless had mediate or immediate jurisdiction over the offender could make war on him. He could also authorise one of his other subjects who had suffered injury to take up arms against the culprit. In case the offender did not come under this prince's jurisdiction, only a superior prince having jurisdiction over the offender had the right and the duty to make war on him. For example, a vassal wishing to make war on his count first had to secure permission from the king as the count's superior, and if the count wished to make war on his king, the latter being unwilling to render judgment in the court of the count's peers, then the count could without sin defend his rights by resort to moderate use of arms. He could not however directly attack the king on his own authority; his court of last resort was the pope, who could first denounce the king for his excesses, and then in the face of royal contumacy excommunicate him and grant the authority to take military action. In the more difficult case where the king had cause to make war on the Emperor, or vice versa, William did not see how either one could submit his case to judgment, since there was no judge with suitable competence. That William was unwilling to grant the pope this competence suggests that he considered the feudal monarchs of his day as immune to imperial jurisdiction. Not even the pope possessed jurisdiction over quarrels between Christian princes with no temporal superior. William concluded his analysis with the opinion that whoever suffered injustice and on that account made war was guilty of sin if the offender had offered to submit the case to just arbitration.

imperatorem, vel econverso, non credo quod uterque vel alter uter teneatur ius suum prosequi in forma iudicii, cum neuter eorum habeat super se superiorem: peccaret tamen movendo bellum passus iniuriam, si iniuriator offerret ei debitam satisfactionem ad arbitrium bonorum virorum, de plano et sine strepitu iudiciorum.' Cf. Monaldus, *Summa, de bello iusto*, fol. 19va and *de restitutione damnorum in bello iusto facienda*, fol. 217rb–va.

Elsewhere William also drew a distinction between defensive and offensive wars: without special authority a war could only be waged in self-defense, while full authority was needed to attack someone else.[56] Here William probably based his distinction on the difference between a knight's right to defend himself in petty feudal violence and the wars of great princes. In his view the king emerged as the primary but not the sole authority for waging war.

The complex casuistry of this passage demonstrates the canonists' transition from the emphasis on the just cause to the concern for authority and jurisdiction. A war was just if waged by an authority with sufficient jurisdiction, for a just cause to be sure, but now the just cause included the opponent's refusal to act in accord with ordinary judicial procedures. Even a prince with no superior could not settle his dispute by recourse to arms when his opponent was willing and able to seek a peaceful means of settlement. William at once preserved the right of a vassal to self-defense through battle on his own authority, but prohibited that right from extending to a war of attack on someone over whom he had no jurisdiction. The feudal noble still possessed a large sphere of legitimate violence, but his military action was limited to *guerrae* or small-scale violence.[57] Implicit in William's treatment were distinctions between the knightly *guerra* in self-defense and the *iustum bellum* of a prince with no superior, and between a lord's military actions against his rebellious vassals and warfare against enemies foreign to his jurisdiction.

It was Innocent IV who in his commentaries on the restitution of spoils rendered more explicit William's implicit distinction between a just war against external invaders and armed exercise of jurisdiction over one's own subjects. In commenting on the passage from Innocent III that dealt with violent dispossession (X. 2.13.12, *Olim causam*) Innocent IV proposed distinctions between the various levels of licit violence that were appropriate to various levels of authority.[58] In a case of simple defense against attack the intended victim could

---

[56] William of Rennes, *Glossa*, 2.18, v. *sine auctoritate speciali*, p. 185b. Cf. above, nn. 31, 33.

[57] For the range of medieval usages of *guerra*, see C. DuCange, *Glossarium Mediae et Infimae Latinitatis* (10 vols. in 5, Paris, 1883–7) v. *guerra*, IV, 129–31. While in general *guerra* could mean both a royal war and petty violence, the canonists seem to have used *bellum* for an openly-declared war and *guerra* for petty and illicit wars.

[58] Innocent IV, *Commentaria*, to X. 2.13.12, paras. 7–8, fols. 231va, 232ra. Cf. above, n. 20 and Hostiensis, in *Lectura*, to X. 2.13.12, para. 24, p. 53: 'Bellum autem verum in quo capti servi fiunt, et quod vere et proprie bellum dicitur solus princes [*sic*] qui superiorem non

repel the attack *incontinenti*. This was not a real war however, but a simple defense that was everyone's right even without the intervention of authority. Whenever a person could not otherwise defend his rights and recover his property, he could wage war only on the superior authority of his prince. The legal status of violent defense was more complex when a lord or prelate was faced with a revolt of his subjects, in which case the lord could exercise his right to declare war, but his actions did not really constitute a war but rather an exercise of jurisdiction (*executio iuridictionis*) or justice. Properly speaking war could only be declared by a prince with no superior against enemies over whom he had no ordinary jurisdiction. Princes and prelates could wage a just battle against enemies within and without their normal jurisdiction, but a just war became the prerogative solely of an independent prince. Elsewhere Innocent similarly distinguished between a just war waged by an independent prince and a war that was just in every other respect, such as one waged for defense of one's property against external invaders or as an exercise of jurisdiction.[59]

These passages indicate Innocent's conscious effort to distinguish simple defensive actions, those that did not qualify as just wars since they did not require license by a legitimate authority, from the full just war that only an independent prince could declare. All violent actions except those waged in immediate self-defense required the right to exercise jurisdiction or, preferably, a license from a prince with no superior, and even these actions were not really just wars. The Decretists had made the right to take up arms the monopoly of legitimate authority. Now Innocent IV restricted the right to wage just wars to the monopoly of superior authorities while still preserving the right of lords to use violence in their own defense. Military actions of inferior princes remained licit but they did not qualify as just wars. Innocent had at last found a way to remove the ambiguity

---

habet potest indicere, etiam contra eos, contra quos locum iurisdictionis executio non haberet, verbi gratia contra illos, qui essent in possessione iuris alicuius alterius principis inferioris.' The careful wording here indicates the awareness of the complexities of the practical problems.

[59] Innocent IV, *ibid.*, to x. 2.24.29, para. 5, fol. 288va: 'Si vero non sit bellum ex edicto principis, sed alias sit iustum, puta quia est ad defensionem rerum suarum, vel pro executione iuris sui... Si autem ille, qui tale bellum iuste agit, nullam habet iurisdictionem super eo, pro quo bellum agitur, et tamen quia iuste pugnat, puta quia alius invadit ipsum, et ipse et res suas defendit, et tunc licet vim vi repellere.'

that had plagued canonistic debates ever since Gratian. Now wars were clearly set apart from military actions in general, and Innocent and his colleagues could now turn to advantage this newly restricted concept of the just war when they came to discuss the practical operation of the just war. While vassals could still wage their petty warfare when it was justified, the Decretalist analysis found in the concept of superior jurisdiction the basis on which to restrict the locus of authority for waging just wars to kings, the Emperor, and, *in extremis*, the pope.

The notion concomitant with authority was that of obedience. If war could only be justly waged on superior authority, it remained to determine the duties of the belligerents. The Decretists had focused upon the knight or soldier who was to follow the orders of the *dux belli*, and concluded that only in the event that such orders contradicted divine or canon law was disobedience to be countenanced. Accepting this conclusion, the Decretalists expanded their analysis to cover especially difficult situations. On the authority of both Roman and canon law the Decretalists condemned as an infamous traitor any soldier who deserted in a public war, unless he was unable to defend his lord.[60] On the other hand Peter of Salins asked whether a soldier should fight in a war waged out of cupidity. Such a war could be licit because of an objective complaint justifying recourse to war, yet illicit because of the sinful intentions on the part of the prince who undertook the war. In such a war, just in cause but unjust in intention, he concluded that a soldier could fight so long as the prince's orders did not contravene God's precepts. Here Peter merely subscribed to Gratian's position, but he then went on to argue that if a war was also unjust by reason of the subject who was called upon to fight, then he was not obligated to obey his lord.[61] Peter did not mention what this might mean, but he probably had in mind such disqualifications as clerical status or service not obligatory in the feudal contract. Elsewhere he added that even a catholic prince need not be obeyed in an unjust war,[62] although he did not mention how the knight should

[60] *Gloss: 'Ecce vicit Leo,'* to D. 1 c. 10, v. *si locus deseratur*, B.N. Nouv. Acq. 1576, fol. 20vb. Johannes Teutonicus, *Glossa Ordinaria*, to D. 1 c. 10, v. *deseratur*, B.N. Lat. 14317, fol. 1va; *ibid.*, to C. 6 q. 1 c. 17, v. *publicis*, B.N. Lat. 14317, fol. 119vb. Cf. Post, *Studies*, p. 438.

[61] Peter of Salins, *Lectura*, to C. 23 q. 1 c. 4, v. *non nocet sanctis*, B.N. Lat. 3917, fol. 172va: 'sed si bellum est iniustum ex causa, subditus non tenetur domino precipienti in tali bello pugnare.'

[62] *Ibid.*, to C. 11 q. 3 c. 94, v. *cognoscebant*, B.N. Lat. 3917, fol. 116vb. The more traditional

determine that the war was unjust and how the disobedience could be expressed.

It was in their analysis of feudal obligations that the Decretalists provided their most trenchant analysis of obedience. With the Decretists, Alanus Anglicus held that faith once promised to an enemy must be maintained, but he limited this obligation to the prince on whose authority the war was waged. Consequently vassals could not make any treaty with their lord's enemy without the lord's permission, and if they nevertheless did so and then attacked the lord's enemy on his order, they were guilty of contumacy. Alanus asked but unfortunately did not answer whether a vassal caught in this conflict of loyalties could licitly harm the enemy.[63] In discussing the *ius militare* the author of the *Gloss: 'Ecce vicit Leo'* added to the requirement of authority the necessity of indicating the prince's warlike intentions as was prescribed in Roman law. Hence, if without license from his prince a knight should invade the lands of his enemies and forcibly eject them, he should be punished for acting against princely authority.[64] His statement belies an increasing Decretalist reliance on Roman law as well as awareness of contemporary feudal custom and private wars. In describing the obligation of a vassal to serve his lord the gloss asserted that a vassal should not fight a war for his lord unless he was certain of its justice. Since this contradicted the earlier attitude that obligated a soldier to fight unless he was certain of a war's injustice, the author added that, just as a vassal should be deprived of his fiefs when he acted against his lord, so the lord no longer commanded obedience when he broke his faith with the vassal.[65] Significantly, the author did not grant the vassal permission to make war on his lord in the latter case but in his train of thought the author implied that when a lord commanded the

view that enjoined obedience unless the soldier was convinced of the injustice of the war was expressed by Vincentius Hispanus: *Apparatus in Decretales Gregorii IX*, to x. 5.39.10, v. *mandato*, B.N. Lat. 3967, fol. 204va and B.N. Lat. 3968, fol. 170ra; see also *Glossa Ordinaria*, to x. 5.39.10, v. *mandato*.

63 Alanus, *Apparatus:* 'Ius Naturale,' to C. 23 q. 1 c. 3, v. *promittitur*, B.N. Lat. 15393, fol. 181ra and Mazar. 1318, fol. 276va: 'de eo, qui ius indicendi bellum habet, i.e. a principe; vassallus enim sine principis auctoritate fedus cum hoste inire non poterit [C. 23 q. 5 c. 13; Cod. 1.38.1; Dig. 49.16.6]. Contumacia sed si miles prius fedus cum hoste inierit et post sub principe ipsum impugnante militare ceperit. Quero an hosti licite nocere possit.'

64 *Gloss: 'Ecce vicit Leo,'* to D. 1 c. 10, vv. *signo dato, egressio in hostem*, B.N. Nouv. Acq. 1576 fol. 20vb.

65 *Ibid.*, to C. 22 q. 5 c. 18, v. *domino suo*, B.N. Nouv. Acq. 1576, fol. 232rb.

waging of an unjust war he broke his faith with the vassal, who was thereby released from his obligation to participate. In this context Johannes Teutonicus required a vassal to refrain from giving aid to his lord's enemy lest he render himself guilty of the Roman concept of treason as well as rupture of the feudal bond, but he also prohibited a vassal from obeying his lord's command to commit atrocities. Johannes showed himself aware of the conflict of loyalties vassals often encountered for while he considered the vassal's oath to his lord as generally valid, the vassal was not bound to serve his lord against his own *patria*, the pope or his own son unless the latter was excommunicated. Most importantly, the vassal was not bound to aid his lord when the latter unjustly attacked someone or when obedience would lead to sinful activities.[66] Durantis was more specific: in case of a war by the *patria* against a foreign enemy, allegiance to a vassal's king took precedence over his obligation to his feudal overlord.[67]

While common opinion released a vassal from his obligations to aid his lord in unjust activities, the Decretalists thus far had not explored the consequences of their opinion for warfare. Was a vassal prohibited from participating in his lord's unjust war, or was he merely not bound to do so? Could he fight in an unjust war if he so desired, and if so, what risks did he take? And what were the risks if he chose to disobey his lord? After all, disobedience in an unjust war clearly opposed feudal custom that obligated a vassal to fight in his overlord's wars to the limit of the duties specified in the feudal contract, and exposed the vassal to such drastic consequences as disinheritance, forfeiture of fiefs, conviction as a felon or a traitor, dishonor and even capital punishment.[68] It was Innocent IV, followed by Hostiensis, who provided a more precise and comprehensive formulation of the right of knights to refuse to fight that took into account the established and still evolving feudal customs. Innocent took upon himself the task of translating the canonistic prohibition on participation in an unjust war into terms specific

---

[66] Johannes Teutonicus, *Glossa Ordinaria*, to C. 22 q. 5 c. 18 v. *honestum*, B.N. Lat. 14317, fol. 179rb. Cf. *ibid.*, to C. 22 q. 5 c. 1, v. *et miles*.

[67] Durantis, *Speculum*, IV, pt. 3, para. 2, no. 31, III, 321; cited in Kantorowicz, *King's Two Bodies*, p. 251, n. 180.

[68] Cf. Baldwin, *Masters Princes and Merchants*, I, 211; F. Ganshof, *Feudalism* (2nd ed., New York, 1961), pp. 99–101; R. Boutruche, *Seigneurie et féodalité* (2 vols., Paris, 1959–70), II, 199, 201, 208f. For the Romanistic positions, see above, ch. 2, nn. 34–7.

enough to endow a vassal's disobedience with effective legal leverage. As his point of departure Innocent IV took a decretal of Innocent III (X. 2.24.29, *Sicut*) that concerned an unjust war a certain Hugh had waged on a certain John. In the course of the war John had lost many of his possessions and was taken captive. Hugh had moreover exacted an oath from John that John would neither seek restitution of his possessions nor attempt to recover them by force. Innocent III had pronounced the oath invalid because it was exacted under duress, and had further ordered Hugh to restore without delay the property he had unjustly seized. The case appears to be a fairly typical example of a petty feudal war, but it did not stimulate significant commentary before Innocent IV.[69]

Limiting his observation on the actual justice of the war to a brief preliminary comment, Innocent turned to consider a hypothetical situation in which a vassal was summoned to fight in an unjust war. In the event that he obeyed the summons and consequently suffered damages and incurred expenses, he was not entitled to bring an *actio mandati* against his lord.[70] In Roman private law, mandate or agency was a consensual contract by which the *mandatarius* or agent agreed to perform a service gratuitously for the *mandator* or principal for whose benefit the service was performed. Since the contract was an honorable one for both parties, its gratuitous nature was essential to its validity. Thus if the *mandatarius* should incur damages and expenses in the performance of the service, he had the right to petition the *mandator* for compensation by means of an *actio mandati*

---

[69] Johannes Teutonicus did claim that the Church possessed the jurisdiction to pass judgment on the justice of a particular war: *Apparatus* to Comp. IV, to 2.9.2, (= X. 2.24.29), v. *iniuste*, B.N. Lat. 3931A, fol. 241va; B.N. Lat. 12452, fol. 122vb; and B.N. Lat. 14321, fol. 226rb: 'Istud autem spectat ad iudicium ecclesie, bene in hoc casu potest iudicium dare.' Yet he did not mention a specific judicial procedure, nor did he discuss the problem of obedience. In describing the details of the decretal I have consulted the *Glossa Ordinaria* and the commentary of Abbas Antiquus (Bernard of Montemirato), *Lectura in Decretales Gregorii IX*, in *Perillustrium tam Veterum quam Recentiorum in Libros Decretalium Aurea Commentaria* (Venice, 1588), fol. 81vb. Knowledge of the particular circumstances in Ireland that occasioned this 1205 decretal would be illuminating. The full text is found in Innocent III's *Registrum*, VIII, 114; P. L. 215, pp. 681f.; cf. A. Potthast, *Regesta Pontificum Romanorum* (2 vols., Berlin, 1873–5), no. 2556.

[70] Innocent IV, *Commentaria*, to X. 2.24.29, v. *iniuste*, para. 1, fol. 288rb: 'secus si iuste [C. 23 q. 5 c. 25]. quod sit iustum bellum, et quando licet alicui alium iuste impugnare, no. supra [X. 2.13.12]. Et not. quod nunquam vocati ad iniustum bellum habent actionem mandati, vel aliam contra vocantem ad impendia vel damna contingentia sibi occasione vocationis vel mandati; qui in re turpi obligatio non contrahitur [Inst. 3.26.7; Dig. 17.1.6; Dig. 17.1.22.6].'

contraria. In Roman penal law a *mandator* was a person who ordered the commission of a crime.[71]

The line of argument Innocent pursued was an attempt to employ this Roman law concept of mandate as a description of the feudal relationship between lord and vassal, whereby the *dominus* was assimilated to the *mandator*, and the vassal was seen as a *mandatarius*. In this instance Innocent denied to a vassal fighting in an unjust war the redress offered by an *actio mandati*, supporting his contention with Roman legal references that prohibited the contraction of valid obligations for the pursuit of wicked activities ('obligatio non contrahitur in re turpe').[72] Furthermore, no *mandatum* need be obeyed when it affronted established customs. Hence Innocent equated the lord whose mandate commanded participation in an unjust war with the *mandator* in Roman penal as well as civil law. Consequently, if the vassal did perform these services and losses or damages resulted, he could seek no legal compensation from his lord. If, on the other hand, the vassal refused to obey his lord, he could escape punishment by his lord for his disobedience, since the lord had no legal right to order him to perform wicked acts. More concretely, the lord could not legally disinherit his vassal for non-participation in his unjust war, for the vassal's obligations in that instance were invalid. Innocent made quite clear that a vassal could not be forced by his contractual obligations to participate in an unjust war, and that if the vassal nevertheless did choose to fight, he did so at his own risk with no possible legal recourse to secure compensation for his eventual losses.

In a just war the vassal's legal position was very different, in that he had the right to institute an *actio mandati* against his overlord to recover his damages and expenses, unless he fought out of a special debt to his lord or for pious, humanitarian or familial motives. Here Innocent probably had in mind either special pacts or conditions that vitiated the voluntary and gratuitous nature of the vassal's mandate, or perhaps fighting a war against enemies of the Church. If the vassal fought out of his own motives of piety, humanity or family interest,

---

[71] Cf. Berger, 'Encyclopedic Dictionary,' vv. *mandator, mandatum,* 574; B. Nicholas, *An Introduction to Roman Law* (Oxford, 1962), pp. 187–9.

[72] Innocent IV could also have cited canons from Gratian's Decretum, C. 22 q. 4, that prohibited the fulfillment of oaths to perform illicit activities. Cf. also *Glossa Ordinaria,* to x. 2.24.27 (*Casus*).

he then was acting as his own agent and thus his mandate and his lord's obligations pertaining to it ceased entirely. Innocent then returned to a consideration of an unjust war in which a vassal fought out of a special duty not part of his feudal contract. Here the vassal was excused from culpability unless the war was manifestly wicked. Innocent buttressed his opinion with relevant texts from the Decretum that condemned the performance of evil acts in warfare.[73]

Encouragement of vassals' disobedience in an unjust war contradicted feudal custom, even as expressed in the Decretum itself (C. 22 q. 5 c. 18, *De forma*), that obligated vassals to render aid and counsel to their lords and prohibited them from doing harm to them. Taking cognisance of this objection, Innocent replied that knights and lawyers were bound to perform their services only when so obligated by contracts, feudal custom, or other laws. Here Innocent seemed to mean that once the vassal had entered into the feudal contract, the lord thereby incurred the obligation to render compensation for losses and expenses sustained in his service, unless that service was illicit. According to another objection a lord under whose command a war was waged was not obligated to compensate his knights because he was not responsible for fortuitous disasters. Innocent countered with the sensible observation that the lord could easily foresee eventual losses in warfare since the outcome was always uncertain.[74] Further on, Innocent drew the logical consequence of his argument when he asserted that the vassal had the right to bring an *actio mandati* to compensate for the loss of his horse in fighting a just war, since loss of horses and weapons in warfare could easily be predicted. Here the vassal's right to bring the action was all the stronger when he had more than adequately performed his services without fraud or other culpability.[75]

---

[73] Innocent IV, *Commentaria*, to x. 2.24.29, v. *iniuste*, para. 1, fol. 288rb: 'Vocati autem ad iustum bellum, actionem mandati habent contra vocantem nisi ex debito teneantur, vel nisi causa pietatis, vel humanitatis, vel parentelae faciunt [C. 23 q. 3 c. 7; C. 11 q. 3 cc. 93–94]. et videtur quod illi qui ex debito faciunt excusantur, nisi bellum esset malum manifeste [C. 11 q. 3 c. 99; C. 23 q. 1 c. 4].'

[74] *Ibid.*, para. 2.

[75] *Ibid.*, para. 4, fol. 288va. Hostiensis' more clearly stated opinion confirmed Innocent's tacit assumption that certitude of compensation for their losses encouraged vassals to participate in their own lord's campaign: *Lectura* to x. 2.24.29, paras. 5–6, fol. 136b.: 'Et quod certum est, quod vix aut nunquam possunt milites venire cum armis in guerris, quin magnas

Possessed of perhaps the finest jurisprudential mind of any medieval pope, Innocent IV was able to make a significant contribution to the Decretalist theories of the just war. The underlying logic of his transformation of the Roman law *actio mandati* suggests that by it Innocent meant to construct a theoretical limitation of warfare. Thus in an unjust war, or at least one that the vassal suspected was tainted with injustice in view of generally recognised criteria, Innocent allowed the vassal to obey his lord, but he was warned that he obeyed at his own risk. Innocent did not absolutely prohibit a vassal from participating in his lord's unjust war, for the tradition of obedience to authority was too strong for Innocent to contradict flatly even if he so desired. To champion the unqualified right of a vassal to disobey a superior's command when the vassal on his own subjective assessment deemed the command unjust could have undermined the whole structure of authority that Innocent otherwise took such great pains to uphold. After all, he could hardly have countenanced a right of disobedience so broad that enemies of papal authority could employ against the papacy itself. Instead, Innocent chose to deny the vassal caught in such a dilemma the opportunity to profit from or at least to minimise his losses incurred in such an unjust venture. Correspondingly, a lord who contemplated waging an unjust war was forewarned that his vassals might choose what they perceived to be in their own material best interest over obedience to his own unjust command, with the result that they would refuse to heed his summons and use the fact that his war was unjust as a means to evade both the performance of their feudal duties and the dire feudal consequences of their disobedience. Vassals were noted more for their contentiousness in seeking to minimise their duties and maximise their rights than they were for unflinching and unquestioning obedience to their overlords.

The legal status of a just war entailed very different legal consequences for both vassal and lord. The vassal's duty to fight was balanced by his right to compensation for damages and expenses

expensas faciant, et multa damna incurrant. et sic hoc dicat ignorare se in lata culpa est...

Sed dices eodem modo videtur imputandum vocato ad bellum, si veniat, et expensas faciat, vel aequos et arma amittat, quia et praescire potuit hoc evenire posse. Rn. verum est. Sed et sciebat, quod et de natura contractus erat, ut a vocante, sive mandatore per actionem mandati impendia sua et damna recuperaret, et ideo sub hec spe securius veniebat.'

incurred in his lord's service. For his part the lord was made cognisant of his full legal liability to compensate his vassals for their losses sustained in his just war. Threatened with lack of forces if his war was unjust and with the prospect of lawsuits if it was just, the lord was well-advised to determine whether his chances of handily winning his just war and of taking extensive plunder were so propitious that he could thereafter afford to indemnify his vassals. Innocent in effect proposed a two-stage limitation of war. First, a lord contemplating a war had to ensure that it would not appear manifestly unjust and unpropitious to his vassals, so that he could count on their obedient service. Then the lord still had to calculate whether he could afford to pay off his vassals from the spoils he was likely to gain.

Within this framework vassal and lord alike were forced by their own self-interest to confront both moral and material considerations. The vassal had to weigh the spiritual dangers of fighting in an unjust war and the eventual loss of property against the duties enforced both by feudal custom and his overlord's power. The vassal might then decide that his self-interest dictated a course of action that succeeded in evading his feudal duty but at the same time enabled him to maintain his feudal tenure.[76] It was clear that no one could be obligated to fight in an unjust war, but canonists had come to this conclusion before Innocent IV, whose innovation was rather to endow this conclusion with concrete legal consequences based on the judicial procedures of Roman private law. Innocent chose Roman private law as the vehicle for his opinion, since it better described the feudal relationship than did Roman public or criminal law. In addition to the incalculable dangers to his soul, the lord who waged

[76] One way for a vassal to evade fighting in his lord's unjust war and still maintain possession of his fief was to choose to go on a crusade. For some specific cases, see Baldwin, *Masters Princes and Merchants*, I, 211. While a careful study of feudal disobedience from this point of view lies outside the scope of this study, England provides a case study of how feudal lords could by their reluctance to serve ensure the failure of royal military campaigns. At the time of Innocent IV's pontificate, Henry III's plans to campaign in France and Sicily were thwarted by lack of baronial support. The English kings constantly faced baronial attempts to limit overseas service that were only overcome by the lure of profit offered during the Hundred Years' War. Cooperation of the baronage was necessary for a successful campaign; cf. M. Powicke, *Military Obligation in Medieval England. A Study in Liberty and Duty* (Oxford, 1962), esp. pp. 61, 227f., 231f., 235, 260. It would be unwise to underestimate the role played by baronial perceptions of self-interest in the mounting of campaigns and even just wars. One facet of this self-interest was the weighing of the material risks involved even in subsidised warfare against the potential profits.

an unjust war was threatened with a shortage of warriors, and even a just war with its unpredictable outcome might bankrupt him in the long run. Innocent thus attempted to limit wars by limiting participation in them and profits to be gained from them. In appealing to the well-developed sense of self-interest of lords and vassals alike Innocent grounded his proposal on the strength and the elasticity of the feudal bond. For a vassal caught in a dilemma involving duty, selfishness and observance of Christian morals Innocent provided the feudal contract with an escape clause that was doubly sanctioned by Roman law and papal jurisprudence. The broader significance of self-interest so reinforced was manifested when the Decretalists discussed the proper conduct and the legal consequences of warfare.

The Decretalists concluded that the just war could only be waged on superior authority, although they did not agree on the precise locus of that authority. Since defense of the *patria* overrode defense of other persons and property, the ruler charged with defense of the *patria* had first claim on the obedience of the subject. Only on superior authority could war be waged against external enemies, and only the superior who had jurisdiction over an internal defender had the right to make war on him in the absence of effective peaceful procedures. The Decretalists enlarged upon earlier and less explicit notions of the just war as a quasi-legal process by seeking to transfer settlement of disputes off the battlefield and into the courts.

CONDUCT AND CONSEQUENCES

The Decretalists' conclusions about just cause, authority and obedience led them to an extensive consideration of the legal aspects of waging a just war, and it was in this context that the just war theories were most clearly outlined. The fundamental assumption underlying their views was that hostile acts were deemed praiseworthy or sinful, licit or illicit, according to whether the war itself was just or unjust. The conditions under which the act was performed, rather than the act itself determined its legal status. In certain cases the Decretalists considered licit the use of military force but nevertheless denied it the legal status of the just war.

The Decretists allowed the waging of war by whatever means were necessary to gain victory, provided that the war was just, hence the just war could be fought openly and also by means of ruses, ambushes and other deceptions. The Decretists had, however, limited this right when they maintained that fidelity once promised to an enemy must be observed as long as the enemy observed it. The Decretalists partially removed this restriction when, for example, Alanus Anglicus contended that fidelity ought not even to be promised to enemies of the Emperor or the pope,[77] and Peter of Salins considered the maintenance of promises made to the enemy as obligatory only when such promises were for good and licit purposes.[78] These and other Decretalists inclined to the position, most clearly expressed by the *Gloss: 'Ecce vicit Leo,'* that all manner of stratagems were licit means of avoiding the perils of war.[79] If war could be waged by any means, could it also be waged at any time? Johannes Teutonicus merely confirmed the opinion of Gratian and the Decretists when he argued that the Truce of God (X. 1.34.1) applied only to wars of attack, and so a just defensive war could be waged at all times.[80]

A more pressing problem was the interpretation of a canon from the Second Lateran Council of 1139 that barred the use of crossbows, bows and arrows and siege machines against Christians, although presumably their use was licit in wars against infidels and heretics. These were the twelfth-century version of 'ultimate weapons' because they pierced or crushed armor, struck without discernment, and the tips of arrows and crossbow bolts could be poisoned. Since they were usually manned by non-nobles, often mercenaries, the nobles considered them both lethal and unfair. While the Decretists, lacking the text in Gratian, had been silent on the issue, the prohibition had been renewed by several councils and by the Decretalist period the canon took on new vigor by its inclusion in the *Compilatio Prima* (5.19.1) and the Gregorian decretals (X. 5.15.1).[81] Opinion was divided over the effect of the Decretal, with Richardus Anglicus, Damasus, Raymond of Peñafort and Johannes de Deo

[77] Alanus, *Apparatus*, to Comp. I, 1.24.1, v. *precipimus*, B.N. Lat. 3932, fol. 10vb.

[78] Peter of Salins, *Lectura*, to C. 23 q. I c. 3, v. *promittitur*, B.N. Lat. 3917, fol. 172rb.

[79] *Gloss: 'Ecce vicit Leo,'* to C. 22 q. 2 c. 21, v. *simulationem*, B.N. Nouv. Acq. Lat. 1576, fol. 229vb. Cf. Johannes Teutonicus, *Glossa Ordinaria*, to C. 23 q. 2 c. 2, v. *insidiis*, B.N. Lat. 14317, fol. 182ra.

[80] Johannes Teutonicus, *ibid.*, to C. 23 q. 8 c. 15, v. *quadragesimali*, cited above, n. 18. For further discussion of truces, see below, pp. 183–8.

[81] Cf. Baldwin, *Masters Princes and Merchants*, I, 223f. The Decretists had been silent on this issue, perhaps because Gratian had not included this canon in the Decretum.

maintaining that the prohibition must be interpreted literally even in a just war. Raymond did, however, expressly allow the use of these weapons against pagans and persecutors of the faith.[82] Decretalists of the earlier generation generally permitted the use of such weapons against Christians in a just war on the conventional grounds that all means of waging a just war were licit,[83] while according to post-Gregorian Decretalists the prohibition remained valid in an unjust war for the same reasons.[84] In his *Summa* Hostiensis first considered the prohibition valid for judicial or voluntary wars, corresponding to the second and sixth of his types of war, while dispensing with it in the first type, the Roman war against the infidels, especially Saracens. But like most of his colleagues he concluded that in a just war or battle all means were licit, and condemned all such means used in an unjust war. He added that in a just war clerics should not use these weapons, but that laymen could.[85] In his *Lectura* Hostiensis inquired whether by this decretal the pope was to be considered a murderer, for he often permitted the use of such weapons, and answered somewhat lamely in the negative by holding that the pope could not incur canonical irregularity and that many generally licit actions were often prohibited in specific instances. Thus while a pope neither granted nor denied the use of such weapons against pagans

---

[82] Damasus, *Summa Decretalium*, to Comp. I. 5.19 (= x. 5.15), B.N. Lat. 14320, fol. 169ra; Richardus Anglicus, *Apparatus*, to Comp. I. 5.19.1, v. *christianos*, Reims, Bibl. Municipale 692, fol. 104vb; Raymond of Peñafort, *Summa de Casibus*, 2.4.1, fol. 165a; Johannes de Deo, *Summa super Certis Casibus Decretalium*, to x, 5.15, B.N. Lat. 3971, fol. 28vb and B.N. Lat. 3972, fol. 41ra. It was Raymond who decided to include the prohibition in the Gregorian decretals. If use of such weapons against Christians was illicit, what was the moral status of their makers and sellers? To this question Raymond replied that such activities were not sinful when the weapons promised to be useful in a just war, but he cautioned against making or selling such items against the dictates of conscience: *Summa de Casibus*, 2. 8. 6, pp. 248b–249a. Raymond's opinion is puzzling, for if such items were not to be used, their manufacture likewise would appear illicit. One possible way to resolve the dilemma is to interpret Raymond's approval of the prohibition as applying only to wars against Christians. Hence these weapons could be useful against pagans, although Raymond does not explicitly so state.

[83] E.g. Alanus, *Apparatus*, to Comp. I. 5.19.1, vv. *Christianos, exerceri*, B.N. Lat. 3932, fol. 65ra. Tancredus, *Apparatus*, to Comp. I. 5.19.1, v. *catholicos*, B.N. Lat. 3931A, fol. 72va and B.N. Lat. 14321, fol. 66va. Tancredus was seconded by Vincentius Hispanus: *Apparatus*, to x. 5.15.1, v. *artem*, B.N. Lat. 3968, fol. 156va.

[84] *Glossa Ordinaria*, to x. 5.15.1 (*Casus*); Bernard Botone, *Summa Titulorum*, to x. 5.15, B.N. Lat. 3972, fol. 68vb and B.N. Lat. 4053, fol. 111ra. Cf. Goffredus, *Summa*, to x. 5.15, para. 1, fol. 207rb–va. William of Rennes even dissented from the opinion of his master Raymond of Peñafort: *Glossa*, 2.4.1, vv. *nequaquam, prohibemus, Dicunt quidam*, p. 165a.

[85] Hostiensis, *Summa*, to x. 5.15, para. 1, pp. 1571–2.

and heretics, he sometimes should and did exhort others to fight and even granted indulgences.[86] The sense of this difficult passage is that the pope could tolerate the use of especially deadly weapons without guilt, provided that he did not expressly command their use. Hostiensis' conclusion was thus consonant with the conventional canonistic opinion that any weapons could be used in a just war and that clerics should not directly order killing. The Decretalists thus rendered the prohibition on certain deadly weapons a dead letter despite its inclusion in the Gregorian decretals.

If any means of waging a just war were licit, then how was the prince able to afford these means? Both the size of armies and the level of violence had increased significantly by the mid-thirteenth century. Kings were no longer able to conduct wars with their feudal levies alone, if indeed they ever had been earlier. They were thus forced to employ mercenaries, who often manned these terrifying new and costly weapons. To meet their greatly increased expenses kings were forced to develop such financial expedients as scutage or shield money, and extraordinary taxes such as *tributum* (the Roman war tax) and new taxes (*nova vectigalia*). With its crusading tithes the Church spurred the development of national taxation. In response, by the thirteenth century Roman and canon lawyers were holding that in an emergency or urgent necessity kings could take extra-ordinary measures to defend the *patria*, such as the levying of new taxes.[87] The decretal collections, however, only briefly touched upon the right to levy new taxes,[88] and the Decretalists for the most part did not take up the opportunity to consider the question at length in relation to warfare, although they limited the authority to impose new *pedagia* or taxes to kings and princes.[89] The *Glossa Palatina* suggested that the right of princes to exact tribute was justified by their military service in defense of the Church,[90] and Raymond of

---

[86] Hostiensis, *Lectura*, to x. 5.15.1, paras. 1–2, pp. 51A–52.

[87] Since these broad topics only tangentially concern the just war, they are treated briefly here. Cf. Kantorowicz, *King's Two Bodies*, pp. 235f., 250f., 276, 284–9; Post, *Studies*, p. 440; Baldwin, *Masters Princes and Merchants*, I, 215–20; Berger, 'Encyclopedic Dictionary,' v. *tributum*, 745; v. *vectigal*, 759; J. R. Strayer and C. H. Taylor, *Studies in Early French Taxation* (Cambridge, Mass., 1939), pp. 89f.

[88] x. 3.39.10; 3.49.4 and 7; 5.40.26.

[89] E.g. *Glossa Ordinaria*, to x. 3.39.10 (Casus) and v. *regum*. *Pedagia* were taxes paid by travellers to the prince of the territory: *ibid.*, to x. 5.40.26, v. *pedagia*.

[90] *Glossa Palatina*, to C. 23 q. 5 c. 20, v. *principes*; cited in Stickler, 'Sacerdotium et Regnum,'

Peñafort considered both old and new taxes licit when the prince was faced with the necessity to defend public order, the faith and the *patria* against pagans, heretics and others who confounded order and security. He however cautioned princes not to levy such taxes unless there was a clear necessity for extraordinary expenses. If a lord who went on a campaign ordered by the Church or his prince against pagans or heretics was unable to meet his expenses from his own resources, he could demand moderate aid from his subjects.[91] This is as close as the Decretalists came to justifying extraordinary taxes for a just war. It appears that the jurist Oldradus da Ponte in the early fourteenth century first admitted that extraordinary taxes for military purposes had now become ordinary ones.[92]

Granted that a prince should employ whatever means were useful in achieving victory in a just war, what then was the moral and legal status of the combatants? True to their basic assumptions the Decretalists viewed hostile acts as licit in just wars, although they sometimes limited the legal consequences of those acts. No one disagreed with Johannes Teutonicus when he claimed that when a knight killed in a just war he was not guilty of homicide, while he deemed culpable the same action in an unjust war.[93] Similarly Peter of Salins held that a knight in protecting his own people and property might justly kill an enemy in war.[94] The *Glossa Ordinaria* to the Decretals compiled by Bernard Botone of Parma even granted a spiritual dispensation to someone on his way to fight a just war: even during an interdict and even if the soldier was excommunicated, he could receive penance and eventually absolution. These were usually denied to persons living in territory under ecclesiastical interdict, but as there was obviously danger of dying in a just war, the Church granted the exception.[95] While the practical effect of the exception

---

590. This work is now attributed to Laurentius Hispanus: Stickler, 'Il decretista Laurentius Hispanus,' *Studia Gratiana*, IX (1966), 463–549.

[91] Raymond of Peñafort, *Summa de Casibus*, 2.5.13, pp. 178b–179a. Cf. *ibid.*, 2.5.15, pp. 181b–182a.

[92] Kantorowicz, *King's Two Bodies*, pp. 287–9.

[93] Johannes Teutonicus, *Glossa Ordinaria*, to C. 23 q. 5 c. 8, v. *miles*, B.N. Lat. 14317, fol. 191vb.

[94] Peter of Salins, *Lectura*, to C. 23 q. 5 c. 19, v. *subveniendi*, B.N. Lat. 3917, fol. 185rb.

[95] *Glossa Ordinaria*, to X. 5.38.11, v. *poenitentia*. Johannes Teutonicus maintained that a knight who had done penance for his military sins had a quasi-clerical status and therefore could not return to fighting. Should this impediment threaten to cause him loss of his fief, he could send a substitute to perform his knight-service for him: *Glossa Ordinaria*, to De penit.,

cannot be calculated, that it was made at all indicates how seriously the Church considered the difference between just and unjust wars.

Raymond of Peñafort defined as incendiaries condemned by canon law to excommunication (C. 23 q. 8 c. 32) those who burned houses or towns with evil intent rather than authority, but whoever performed these same acts while acting on authority was not culpable.[96] William of Rennes enlarged the definition of incendiaries to include all those who robbed, ravaged, wounded and killed in an unjust war, but in a just war such acts were licit when performed in good faith. In this passage William exemplified the Decretalists' emphasis on both the legal situation under which violent acts were committed and on the legal consequences of war with regard to spoils and damages. The belligerent in a just war had the right to confiscate goods and property from the enemy as compensation for losses suffered by himself and the men serving under him. Then William asked whether a person who had pillaged, burned and destroyed the property of his adversary within the latter's own territory should be obliged to make restitution. On the basis of customary practice William thought not, if the warrior had acted in good faith and was unable to avoid such destruction. If destruction resulted from love of violence, greed or malice, the warrior was bound to render compensation above and beyond the amount of damages he and his men themselves had suffered, although William did not specify whether this obligation was moral or legal.[97]

William here directly related the Augustinian analysis of motives proper and improper to fighting to the conduct of even a just war,

dist. 5, c. 3, v. *ad militiam*; C. 33 q. 2 c. 15, v. *arma*. His opinions were carry-overs from the suspicions of military service found in the earlier penitential literature and maintained by some of the theologians.

[96] Raymond of Peñafort, *Summa de Casibus*, 2.5.5, p. 168b. Hostiensis, *Summa*, to x. 5.39.14, p. 1924.

[97] William of Rennes, *Glossa*, to 2.5.12.19, v. *sibi dato*, p. 188a: 'et suis. etiam iuste, tam in depraedationibus et rapinis, quam incendiis, et fracturis, et vulneribus, et caedibus, et aliis quibuscunque. Quid sit ille, qui iustum habet bellum, fecerit incendia, vel effracturas, vel arborum, vel vinearum extirpationes in terra propria adversarii sui, et hominum eius, numquid pro his tenetur in aliquo? Resp. De illis damnis non tenebitur, quae bona fide intulit, aut a quibus commode abstinere non potuit secundum industriam, et consuetudinem bona fide pugnantium. Si autem grassandi animo et malitiose ea intulit, cum alias posset sibi consulere commode, tenebitur et compensabuntur illa damna cum damnis sibi datis, et hominibus suis usque ad concurrentes quantitates, et de eo, quod super excreverit, tenetur satisfacere illis, quos damnificavit.' Vincent of Beauvais included this passage in his *Speculum Doctrinale*, xi, 75.

whereby the motives with which the war was fought helped to determine both the conduct of the war and the legal and moral consequences resulting from it. The phrase 'industria et consuetudo bona fide pugnantium' indicated his recognition of certain commonly accepted contemporary customs. Contravention of these customs, such as wreaking immoderate destruction, necessitated compensation for the excessive damages. Furthermore William considered as established the principle that even in the just war needless destruction must be avoided. This limit was vague, however, since it was based on the good faith of the warrior, his observance of customary practice, and the demands of the specific hostile situation. Yet in providing compensation for needless violence it was a distinct advance in precision over the Roman and canon law principle that violence was to be limited by moderation (*moderamen inculpatae tutulae*).

Content to lay down general principles, the Decretalists provided few specific prescriptions for the proper conduct of the just war. The profession of mercenary was tacitly tolerated rather than explicitly analysed. Kings were permitted to use mercenaries since Roman soldiers had been paid wages. The Decretalists were more concerned to condemn the abuses perpetrated by the various unemployed mercenary bands or *routiers* that roamed throughout Europe.[98] Of course non-combatants and property remained at the mercy of marauding armies waging both just and unjust wars. Rules of conduct, whether customary or canonical, were based more on military expediency and moral justification than on the rights of bystanders.[99] Recognising these circumstances, the Decretalists brought to their discussion an increasing concern to limit the destruction of warfare by legal means.

While the common opinion of Romanists, Decretists, and Decretalists saw violence in self-defense as justified by every law, this basic agreement did not prevent many different attempts to distinguish simple violence from the just war, whereby each type of self-defense involved separate legal consequences regarding persons, property, and jurisdictions. According to both Roman law and

---

[98] The full force of ecclesiastical opprobrium was levied on these groups, though the relevant canon did not find its way into the Gregorian decretals; cf. Comp. 1, 5. 6. 7 and below, n. 175.

[99] Cf. Keen, *Laws of War*, pp. 19, 121, 140, 190f., 243.

feudal custom, that all three groups of scholars recognised, spoils taken in war became the property of the victor or at least of the warrior who seized them and was able to maintain possession. Roman law allowed prisoners of war to be enslaved, while feudal custom allowed them to be held for ransom.[100] Building on these principles the Decretalists' analysis of the consequences of war contained their most precise discussions of the just war. Prior canonistic opinion had provided warriors with little precise guidance about the right to kill or capture enemies and to confiscate their properties and those of their subjects. The Decretalists recognised that these questions loomed large for princes, knights, lawyers and confessors alike.

Johannes Teutonicus represented common opinion when he limited the right of capture to those who waged a just war. Since a captive taken in an unjust war was not legally a captive, he could not legally be reduced to servitude and was encouraged to escape.[101] Raymond of Peñafort went further in prohibiting the payment of ransom by someone who was captured while fighting a just war.[102] The Decretalists' analysis thus contradicted both the Roman law right to enslave prisoners and the feudal right to exact ransom, probably because the Church barred Christians from enslaving other Christians. Yet they did not expressly prohibit Christians captured in a just war to come under the lordship of others, perhaps as serfs or men-at-arms. Recognising the difficulty of reconciling Christian doctrine with pagan Roman law and contemporary patterns of lordship, they shrank back from devoting a necessarily careful treatment to the subject. Instead they chose to concentrate on how property rights were affected by warfare, and here their treatment was more satisfactory than it was for the effects of war on personal status.

Ever since Gratian the title *res recuperandae* or recovery of goods had been a principal reason for waging a just war. Using this principle the Decretalists examined the rights to booty and spoils that were ultimately derived from Roman law. For Alanus, property seized and held by violence could be repossessed by a just war, and he even allowed capture of booty to function as a licit though secondary

[100] Dig. 49.15.24; 50.16.118. Cf. Boutruche, *Seigneurie et féodalité*, II, 191f.
[101] Johannes Teutonicus, *Glossa Ordinaria*, to D. I c. 9, v. *servitutes*, B.N. Lat. 14317, fol. 1rb; cf. below, n. 106.
[102] Raymond of Peñafort, *Summa de Casibus*, 2.5.11, p. 181b.

motive for such a war.[103] Laurentius Hispanus added that in a war waged on princely edict the warrior could rightfully despoil the enemy of his goods, which then became part of the warrior's own domain.[104] Conversely all property seized in an unjust war must be restored to its rightful owners, and all oaths sworn in pursuance of injustice became void.[105] In further concurrence Johannes Teutonicus added that in a just war heretics and all other enemies could be despoiled,[106] and while according to the *ius gentium* all spoils belonged to the captor, in practice the prince waging the war was bound to divide the spoils among his warriors according to their merits.[107] The *Gloss: 'Ecce vicit Leo'* was more precise in distinguishing the prince's portion from the total spoils. By contemporary feudal custom the prince granted equal portions to his men.[108] Feudal custom was not so firmly committed to this conclusion, and although few if any Decretalists would agree to equal division of spoils, they did agree with feudal custom that the prince was bound to share the booty in some way or other. To proceed beyond the elementary conclusion of the Decretists the Decretalists needed to relate restitution and division of spoils to the different types of wars.

Alanus Anglicus opened the discussion with his distinction between

---

103 Alanus, *Apparatus: 'Ius Naturale,'* to C. 23 q. 1 c. 5, v. *propter predam*, B.N. Lat. 15393, fol. 181rb and Mazar. 1318, fol. 277ra. Cf. above, n. 31.

104 Laurentius, *Apparatus*, to C. 23 q. 7, pr., B.N. Lat. 15393, fol. 194va.

105 Johannes Teutonicus, *Apparatus*, to Comp. IV. 2.9.2, v. *restituat*, B.N. Lat. 3931A, fol. 241va; B.N. Lat. 3932, fol. 214rb; B.N. Lat. 12452, fol. 122vb; B.N. Lat. 14321, fol. 226rb: 'contra. si enim in iusto bello occupasset res eius statim facta esset sua...et ita est arg. quod petenti restitucione obstat excepcio.' Evidently there was some difficulty in understanding this gloss, for the *Glossa Ordinaria* to the same decretal (x. 2.24.29) omitted the last portion of Johannes' gloss as being obscure. Hostiensis, in *Lectura*, to x. 5.7.13. para. 14, v. *domini principales*, p. 39: 'nam si fideles sunt hi, qui iniustum bellum fecerunt, universa restituere compelluntur.' For Johannes de Deo's opinion, see above, n. 46.

106 Johannes Teutonicus, *Glossa Ordinaria*, to C. 23 q. 7, pr., v. *nunc autem*, B.N. Lat. 14317, fol. 195vb: 'non solum heretici set omnes hostes licite possunt spoliari rebus suis, dummodo bellum sit iustum. Et ille qui rem abstulit iuste factus est dominus illius rei... Hereticis autem licitum est auferri ea que habent...Melior est tamen hic qui hoc auctoritate iudicis facit.' Raymond of Peñafort, *Summa de Casibus*, 2.5.12.17, p. 184a: 'Circa principes vel milites habentes guerras adinvicem, distingue, quia aut ille de quo queritur, habet iustam guerram, vel bellum, aut non. In primo casu, scilicet cum habet iustum bellum, et non exercet illud, nisi contra nocentes, et non habet intentionem corruptam; quidquid capit ab hostibus, suum est, nec tenetur restituere [D. 1 c. 9, et C. 23 q. 7 c. 2], et require supra [1.5.2].' Note how rights over heretics' property are assimilated to those over enemy property; cf. *ibid.*, 1.5.2, pp. 38b–39b.

107 Johannes Teutonicus, *ibid.*, to C. 23 q. 5 c. 25, v. *omnia*, B.N. Lat. 14317, fol. 192vb; *ibid.*, to D. 1 c. 10, v. *principis*, B.N. Lat. 14317, fol. 1va.

108 *Gloss: 'Ecce vicit Leo,'* to D. 1 c. 10, v. *principis porcio*, B.N. Nouv. Acq. Lat. 1576, fol. 21ra.

a *bellum renovatum* and a *bellum continuatum*. A prince with no superior might wage a *bellum renovatum*, a war recommenced after an interval of time had elapsed since the injury had been committed. This Alanus contrasted with a *bellum continuatum*, an immediate and legitimate defense licit for all men.[109] From Alanus' opinions expressed in other contexts, it seems reasonable to conclude that he did not grant to every private individual the right to wage war on his own authority. Then what were the rights proper to someone waging a just *bellum continuatum*? A possible suggestion was later provided by Peter of Salins, who argued that invaders and unjust possessors ought to be despoiled in a *bellum continuatum*, but if they were despoiled of the possessions they seized unjustly in war after the war had ceased, these possessions should be restored to them.[110] From this it appears that in a simple case of self-defense, a *bellum continuatum* waged without superior authority, the right to take spoils was limited to recuperation of property unjustly seized, but that without judicial authority even these goods could not be recovered after cessation of hostilities. The passage lacked only an explicit discussion of the authority required for seizure of the invader's property in a *bellum renovatum*. Goffredus of Trani considered defense of one's property so important that he allowed someone whose property was violently occupied to use violence to repel the invader by a *bellum continuatum*. Here the lawful possessor had no obligation to make restitution to the violent possessor for any damages suffered in the course of his expulsion.[111] Thus in a *bellum continuatum* these Decretalists limited the right to take spoils to immediate recovery of goods lost. The defender could take no further booty after hostilities had ceased, but he was exempted from making restitution for damages he did during them.

Hostiensis pursued an independent course when he analysed legal consequences of his sevenfold list of wars.[112] In the second type of war, that waged on judicial authority, adversaries were not enemies in the legal sense, for enemies were those at war with the Roman people. Lacking such status and considered merely as outlaws, whatever the opponents could unjustly seize became only their *de facto*

109 Alanus, cited above, n. 9.
110 Peter of Salins, *Lectura*, to C. 3 q. 1 d.p.c. 6, B.N. Lat. 3917, fol. 83va.
111 Goffredus, *Summa*, 2. rubric: *De restitutione spoliatorum*. para. 38, fol. 86va.
112 Hostiensis, cited above, n. 6.

possessions, while those waging war on authority became *de jure* possessors of whatever property they captured.[113] In a war between Christians, the just party could take possession of all property that he seized, including properties held in fief, provided that papal rights were respected. Immovable property occupied unjustly by Christians or infidels returned to its former domain when it was recovered, but movable property seized by infidels became their own.[114] Hostiensis extended the Roman legal right of conquest to cover feudal territories whose tenants had rendered themselves unworthy to hold feudal tenures. Restitution was obligatory for those who waged presumptuous, rash or voluntary wars, which in Hostiensis' mind comprised most contemporary wars that were waged against their own vassals by counts who lacked superior authority. These counts should rather bring the vassals to court, and only if the latter contumaciously resisted the judgment could the count then attack them. By contrast, in Roman, judicial, licit and necessary wars (which any other canonists would consider simply as just wars), restitution was unnecessary unless the warrior had exceeded the limits of moderation by killing his captives.[115] Hostiensis of course considered most wars unjust, and never tired of blaming contemporary princes for them. On the authority of Roman law he even called them mere robbers and brigands. His solution to endemic wars was to limit the licit violence of most minor lords to simple defense, and he preferred to submit even simple defense to judicial arbitration.[116] On the other hand he invoked the Roman right of unlimited conquest against those who waged egregiously unjust wars.

At the other extreme Raymond of Peñafort evidently considered one knight to have the proper authority to wage war against another, for in his view a knight could make his own the property he captured from an enemy and the latter's accomplices. He was

---

113 Hostiensis, *Lectura* (as cit. above, n. 6). De homicidio. c. 1, *pro humani* (= Sext, 5.4.1), para. 34, p. 29.

114 *Ibid.*, to x. 5.7.13. para. 14, v. *domini principales*, p. 39: 'Vel dic quod ubi inter Christianos iustum est bellum ex parte una, ex altera vero parte iniustum, is, qui iuste pugnat, omnia occupata sua facit, quae tamen ab alio in feudum non tenentur...sed et feudalia iure occupare possunt, salvo tamen iure domini Innocentis, a quo tenentur, ut hic. Ubi vero infideles vel Christiani iniuste pugnantes bona immobilia iuste pugnantium occupant, et postea recuperantur, ad antiquum dominium revertuntur...mobilia vero, quae infideles occupant, sua sunt.'

115 Cf. idem, *Summa*, to x. 1.34. para. 4, p. 360.

116 Hostiensis, *Lectura*, to x. 2.13.12. para. 2, v. *bellum*, p. 136.

entitled to confiscate as much as his conscience dictated was proper in compensation for his labor and the damages suffered by himself and his accomplices. He was obliged, however, to cease seizing property when his enemy capitulated and petitioned for a settlement. The victor's right to spoils was further limited regarding the property belonging to the subjects of his defeated foe. Those pious subjects who did not aid their lord in his unjust and illicit war should not be punished by confiscation of their property, for the penalties resulting from an unsuccessful war should only be levied on the guilty in satisfaction for crimes committed.[117]

Raymond here did not extend his focus beyond simple wars of defense to cover wars between independent princes, but his opinion bears witness to the growing importance attached by the Decretalists to the condemnation of unrestrained vengeance. His glossator William of Rennes elaborated on Raymond's limitation of the right of spoils. Before William's time the canonists had not provided an explicit definition of *res* as applied to warfare. William explained that the common phrase *pro rebus repetendis* applied not only to material possessions but also to incorporeal *res* such as *iura* or rights. Infractions of rights or *iniuriae* justified recourse to war, such as when someone's movable or immovable property rights were violated. The war was just so long as it was waged with proper motives to secure satisfaction for damages and injuries.[118] Armed with this clarification William then considered the case of a war in which four of Raymond's five criteria – cause, intention, person and authority – were lacking, but where the requirement of *res* or goods to be recovered was valid. He inquired whether restitution should be made by the person seeking to recover his own property. He replied that while such a person was not obliged to restore property seized in the war, he still should not cause damages to his adversary beyond the amount the latter had himself caused, lest the person be guilty of inflicting excessive punishment. Adjudication of these problems William considered the task of the confessional forum, not a court

---

[117] Raymond of Peñafort, *Summa de Casibus*, 2.5.12.19, fol. 188ab. Cf. above, n. 19.
[118] William of Rennes, *Glossa*, to 2.5.12.18, v. *pro rebus repetendis*, p. 185b: 'nomen rerum credo hic large accipi. non solum, ut comprehendat res corporales, sed etiam iniurias; sicut enim pro rebus mobilibus, vel immobilibus ablatis potest moveri bellum, ita pro iniuriis illatis ad consequendum de his satisfactionem, non libidine vindictae, sed zelo iustitiae, vel quantum ad interesse.'

of law. For example, if the defender confessed to having seized a tenth of the goods of his adversary who himself had previously taken a tenth of the defender's property, custom enjoined restitution only if the unjust adversary had restored the stolen tenth, but nevertheless penance was required of the victor for his theft.[119] This situation was obviously not a full just war, nor was it termed such, and the right to take spoils was more limited than the Decretalists tolerated in a full just war. William apparently felt that the full canonical privileges did not apply to this case of a limited just war. His example referred to the use of violence to recover one's rightful property rather than to a just war of public and political importance. Since this case exemplified private violence rather than a public war, the property settlement was a matter for the confessional.

In another case William inquired whether a cleric was bound to make restitution for property he acquired as a result of participation in a just war, and he replied that if such property was given to a cleric by someone who had licitly plundered it, then he could retain it. But if the cleric himself had plundered, he had thereby sinned and must undergo penance and make restitution. As a cleric he lacked the authority to capture and keep property. Since a lord was forbidden to order clerics to fight, so he likewise could not authorise them to take plunder. Yet William concluded that property plundered by consent of the cleric's lord could be kept, provided that the lord consented in time of war, because this instance was just as if the lord had given him the property.[120] It is evident that William esteemed highly the practice of the lord's rewarding a portion of legitimate spoils to his associates, even clerics.

The problem of taking spoils was more difficult when someone who was unjustly plundered was unable to make recovery, as for

---

[119] *Ibid.*, to 2.5.12.17, v. *defuerit*, p. 185ab: 'quid si defuerit aliquod istorum, numquid tenebitur restituere quicquid adeptus est de huiusmodi bello ille, qui movit illud? Respondeo quamvis bellum sit iniustum ex causa, et ex animo, et ex persona, et ex auctoritate: si tamen res subsit, quia pro rebus repetendis factum est, non tenetur qui movit bellum restituere quod ibi ceperit, vel damnificaverit adversarium suum, ultra quod habuerat ille de suo iniuste, aut damnificaverat eum; et hoc dico secundum iudicium fori paenitentiali confiteatur se per furtum habuisse decimam de rebus illius, qui manifeste abstulerat ei decimam, facere consuevit, et bene, iudex paenitentialis conpensationem nec iniunget ei restitutionem illarum decimarum, nisi adversarius eius postmodum restitueret ei decimam ablatam; iniunget tamen ei paenitentia de furto commisso.' Cf. above, n. 5 and Monaldus, *Summa, de restitutione damnorum*, fol. 217rb.

[120] *Ibid.*, to 2.5.12.17, p. 185b.

example when the plunder was stored in an impregnable place. In such cases the injured party could seize as an indemnity property of the same value belonging to his adversary or the latter's accomplices, just as he would from a thief.[121] This case corresponded to many actual incidents of violent plundering and counter-plundering that did not qualify as full just wars. It was more likely that a confessor would be confronted with such cases than with manifestly unjust wars. William's use of *nobilis* in such contexts indicates that he had in mind not only kings and those with superior authority but also any petty knight with a small armed retinue. This *nobilis* William considered to possess sufficient authority to recover his property by violence, and the phrase *indemnitati suae consulere* showed the despoiled lord as an agent of his own defense. The military action was seen not as repulsion of violence by violence but as defense of rights, a title perhaps more congenial to feudal attitudes. As a confessor William was more likely to accord to local lords the defense of their property than would a canonist concerned with the more theoretical justification of violent self-defense and warfare. William's analysis of this case however prefigured the jurisprudential discussions of marque and reprisal that became current in the fourteenth century.

Even in a just war the right to damage the enemy's property was not unlimited, and the just warrior was bound to make restitution for the damages he caused in excess of the damages done to him.[122] In an unjust war damages caused by the unjust party had to be compensated. Furthermore, all damages suffered by the knights who fought in an unjust war, even those damages justly caused by the adversaries, had to be compensated by the lord of the unjust war himself. He, rather than his adversaries, was liable to suits for indemnities brought by his own men, but if his knights on the unjust side should themselves inflict damages on their just opponents, they could not seek compensation for damages from their own lord, since the damages they suffered resulted from their own culpability. A noble who fought justly, on the other hand, was not held liable to compensate his own men for the damages they had suffered at the hands of their unjust adversaries, for they were bound to offer themselves and their resources in the service of their lord, who was only bound to com-

---

[121] *Ibid.*, v. *incontinenti*, pp. 186b–187a.
[122] *Ibid.*, to 2.5.12.19, v. *sibi dato*, p. 188a; cited above, n. 97.

pensate them when he was negligent in defending them.[123] It is doubtful that William's approach was influenced by Innocent IV's similar analysis based on the *actio mandati*. In fact William arrived at the opposite conclusion that the lord of an unjust war was ordinarily liable to provide compensation for damages suffered by his vassals, while he absolved the lord of a just war from any such liability.[124] William's opinion betrayed the feudal outlook that a lord was duty bound to defend his vassals, which in his opinion resulted in the obligation of the lord to indemnify them in case of his negligence.

From a consideration of damages William was led to discuss the proper methods of concluding a peace treaty when he asked whether two lords at war could settle their differences without making restitution for damages to their own respective knights. He answered that it was only licit to do so when those knights who had suffered damages agreed to the settlement, because the person who was guilty of waging war unjustly could otherwise prejudice the interests of those who had fought under him. But in the event that his men were equally guilty, he was bound to make restitution to them in open court (*forum contentiosum*), since they had knowingly participated in his crime. On the other hand, if the lord had persuaded his hesitant knights to participate, he was bound by confessional practice to make restitution to them.[125] Noteworthy here is William's expression of the ideal of feudal solidarity and the reciprocal relationships that should prevail between lord and vassals. If both were guilty together, then the vassals could exact no damages from him, but if only the lord was guilty, he was liable to them. The lord was barred from making a peace settlement that infringed upon the property rights of his vassals.

A lord who had waged a just war likewise had to respect the interests of his own men. William advised him to compensate his men for damages even if he was not obliged to do so, and to procure for them the indemnity surrendered by the defeated adversary. By damages William meant only those losses suffered by fire and plunder, not the expenses of fighting itself, for according to custom, princes could disregard such expenses in their settlements. If the

---

[123] *Ibid.*, p. 188ab.
[124] Cf. Innocent IV, cited above, nn. 70, 73–5.
[125] William of Rennes, *Glossa*, to 2.5.12.19, p. 188b.

princes considered the payment of damages preferable to renewing the war, then by so doing they usefully served the interests of their subjects. In this case the subjects, here meaning the vassals, were obliged to ratify the settlement agreed upon by their princes. Yet the decision to halt the war, as the decision to commence it, belonged to the princes alone.[126] Thus if the vassals did not agree to the settlement of their lords they were still entitled to seek indemnities, but they were prohibited from continuing the war called to a halt by their leaders. At the same time William maintained the requirement that lords alone had authority to make war, while preserving the rights of vassals. He also made a plea to halt open hostilities even if all problems of restitution and damages had not been settled. Here as elsewhere Monaldus followed William's treatment closely, adding only that an invader or unjust possessor was bound to make restitution for all the gains he acquired as a result of his invasion and also for all the gains the rightful possessors would otherwise have realised from the time of the invasion.[127]

The lengthy casuistic position expressed by William of Rennes and Monaldus, feudal in outlook, defined and limited the conditions under which spoils could be taken and restitution for damages made. Authority for waging war was conceived broadly as the prerogative not only of Church and princes but also of feudal lords, who were, however, bound to respect their vassals' rights. The theoretical effect of their position approximated that of Innocent IV regarding the vassal's loyalty to his lord, for both views would force a lord to think twice before waging a manifestly unjust war if he were threatened with disobedience on the part of his vassals, who even if they served could sue him for recovery of damages after the war was over. Even in a just war the lord would be wise to consider whether his chances of acquiring spoils seemed so favorable that he could absorb without great loss the claims to indemnification advanced by his vassals.

Yet to many Decretalists writing at a greater distance from feudal custom a position like that of William and Monaldus would appear highly unsatisfactory, for it allowed too many lords with limited authority to wage just wars, allowed vassals entirely too many rights

[126] *Ibid.*, pp. 188b–189a.
[127] Monaldus, *ibid.*, *de restitutione spoliatorum*, fol. 226ra: 'Item restituere tenetur invasor sicut male fidei possessor omnes frucius perceptos de re invasa et que percipi potuissent a tempore invasionis.'

over the terms of peace treaties, and did not clearly limit excessive taking of spoils. Consequently other Decretalists not only limited the locus of authority as previously discussed, but also developed positions that prevented vassals from jeopardising peace treaties with their selfish demands for compensation. Thus Hostiensis allowed a king to renounce in advance the restoration of damages inflicted on his people by an enemy when peace could be secured by no other means. This was, to be sure, the single instance in which a king without the assent of his subjects was permitted to execute a legal act that redounded to the disadvantage of his subjects, but in Hostiensis' view the desirability of peace that was equitable on both sides overrode the absolute necessity for consent of the subjects.[128]

Another facet of the deficiencies of William's position was that the limitation on taking spoils and the claims for restitution of spoils and damages were couched in terms of feudal customs and moral intentions such as good faith. As such these limitations and claims could only be enforced in the confessional, a conclusion that a confessor such as William of Rennes or a moralist such as Monaldus could consider suitable and proper, but to which other Decretalists more attached to the procedures of an open court had to find an alternative that was based on the precision of Roman and canonical procedures. Alanus Anglicus strictly adhered to the letter of the Roman law position on spoils when he allowed the wronged party in the course of waging a just war to seize not only property of the same value as that unjustly seized, but also all other property belonging to the guilty party. He reasoned that since the adversary had refused to return the goods he unjustly seized, he was guilty of contumacy, as well as of his original theft, and in Roman law unlimited suits could be brought against contumacious persons. While moderation suggested that the just party take no more than the amount of damages done him, Alanus did not see this as obligatory. In case the unjust party after the war wished to make satisfaction for his original misdeed, Alanus asked whether the just party was obliged to restore the property he received and accept his foe's offer to make good his damages. Alanus refused to obligate the just party to do so, for all that he took in a just war became his rightful property by the *ius*

---

[128] Hostiensis, *Summa*, to X. 5.38, para. 62, v. *sed posse*, pp. 1864f. Cf. L. Buisson, *Potestas und Caritas. Die päpstliche Gewalt im Spätmittelalter* (Cologne and Graz, 1958), p. 294.

gentium.[129] Strictly speaking then, even though moderation was laudable, Alanus refused to restrict the right to take spoils in a just war. Laurentius treated the same problem at greater length in discussing a case in which someone who by means of a just war had recovered all property unjustly seized from him. Could he then bring suit before a judge for the same damages and also continue the war further, as was possible by feudal custom? Laurentius cited numerous texts that affirmed the right to pursue both avenues, violent and non-violent. Since legitimate satisfaction had been denied by the contumacious foe, whatever the just warrior could capture was considered not as payment of a debt but as the legitimate spoils of war, and his foe was exposed also to unlimited judicial proceedings to recover the same goods. Laurentius based the contrary argument on the Roman law principle that in good faith the same thing could not be sought twice, and concluded that once satisfaction for the damages had been arrived at in the war, the just party could seek no more either in court or on the field of battle.[130] On the basis of Roman law this position in effect significantly restricted the feudal right to unlimited use of violence by an aggrieved lord, a limitation that William of Rennes was unable to construct on the basis of feudal custom and moral exhortation.

It was Innocent IV, followed by Hostiensis, who most systematically linked the limitations on violence and spoils to the just war itself by specifying how property rights and personal status were affected by the various levels of licit violence. The major theme of Innocent's analysis was the close connection between warfare and

---

129 Alanus, cited above, n. 30.
130 Laurentius Hispanus, *Apparatus*, to C. 23 q. 2 c. 2, v. *civitas*, B.N. Lat. 3903, fol. 180rb: 'Iudex ergo qui non vult facere iustitiam potest conveniri...et ita iudex facit litem suam non solum si per dolum vel gratiam vel iniuriam iudicet set etiam si alie sordes intraveniant [= interveniant]...set quod si aliquis in bello consecutus est totum suum interesse, nunquid adhuc ipsum in iudicio? de hoc potest convenire vel an potest adhuc licite bellum habere contra ipsum? videtur quod sic, quia penam contumacie sue prestitit. unde adhuc potest agere ad estinationem rei ablate, ut [Dig. 43.5.3.13 and 15]. Item res ista non est soluta ei pro precio debito set in bello sua est facta, ut [C. 23 q. 5 c. 25; C. 23 q. 7 c. 2; Dig. 41.1.5.7], quia contra contumacem in infinitum potest iurari, ut [Dig. 6.1.68]. ar. contra quia bona fides non patitur, ut idem bis petatur [Dig. 50.17.57]. credo quod non potest iterum agere vel movere bellum.' Johannes Teutonicus followed Laurentius' argument closely, although in the printed version *estinationem* was changed to the more appropriate *restitutionem*. More significantly, Johannes tacitly refused to subscribe to Laurentius' conclusion: *Glossa Ordinaria*, to C. 23 q. 2 c. 2, v. *civitas*, B.N. Lat. 14317, fol. 182ra. Cf. Horoy, *Droit international*, pp. 123, 137.

jurisdiction. He distinguished between an exercise of jurisdiction that princes could levy against their own subjects, in which captives could not be enslaved, and a just war that, properly speaking, only a prince with no superior could wage. He confined such a war only to enemies who with their possessions properly belonged to the jurisdiction of another but inferior prince. Against these enemies the prince could also wage war in defense of the ancestral laws of his *patria*.[131] This just war Innocent contrasted with a *iustum praelium* or just battle that could be waged even against his own rebellious vassals and subjects who were aiding an external enemy. In the course of this just battle the prince could take spoils and capture his adversaries. Innocent then cited an alternative opinion that prohibited the prince from taking spoils and captives except in war or when his own subjects were using their fortified sites to harm him. And if actual war had not been declared but the prince intended to punish enemies outside his ordinary jurisdiction, he should first seek justice from the judge having jurisdiction over them. Lacking this recourse, the prince could recover his own property on his own authority. Without expressly considering this objection Innocent stated that a prince could punish persons and seize their property located within his jurisdiction provided that their crimes against him were committed there.[132] While closely following Innocent's treatment Hostiensis emphasised the contumacy of the enemy or rebellious vassal and the necessity incumbent on the prince to punish his adversary only for crimes committed within the territory belonging to his proper jurisdiction. Hostiensis did not however distinguish between a just war and a just battle, so for him a just war could also be waged against a prince's own vassal and the latter's accomplices after the promulgation of a formal sentence against him, a war that corresponded to the judicial war, his second type. A prince could wage war on someone outside his proper jurisdiction only after failing to secure redress from the authority having jurisdiction over the offender, a war that approximated the licit war, Hostiensis' fourth type.[133]

The analysis put forth by Innocent IV and Hostiensis represents the most serious Decretalist attempt to distinguish between a full

---

[131] Innocent IV, *Commentaria*, to x. 2.13.12, para. 8, fols. 231vb–232ra; cited above, n. 58.
[132] Cf. Hostiensis, *Lectura*, to x. 2.13.12, para. 27, p. 53.
[133] Hostiensis, *ibid.*, para 26.

state of war, the just war proper, and the less drastic forms of legal violence that were proper to a prince's jurisdiction over his own recalcitrant subjects. The prince had the right to punish those who perpetrated crimes within his territory, but such an exercise of jurisdiction usually entailed a just battle rather than a full just war. In this commentary on the restitution of spoils Innocent did not fully explain the prince's obligation to those of his subjects who aided him in his wars and battles, and his legal rights over his enemies.

Innocent's most detailed analysis of these rights and duties occurred in the context of the maintenance of oaths. First, Innocent took pains to indicate the liability of the prince to indemnify his vassals by the *actio mandati* for all the damages they suffered in his just military engagements.[134] But what then were his obligations to others who aided his cause? Here Innocent limited himself to those who either gratuitously loaned horses for use in war or leased them out for the same purpose. If horses were lost, captured or killed, as was likely to happen, then the lender or lessor was denied any action to secure compensation for them, because they were used for purposes specified in the contract. The borrower or lessee, in this case the prince, was therefore immune from liability unless he was guilty of fraud, and the lessor was obliged to be content with his fees.[135] Since loans and leases were voluntary while the vassals' services were mandatory in a just war, the vassal unlike the lender or lessor was entitled to seek compensation for damages. By his contrast between lenders and lessors on the one hand and vassals on the other Innocent may have intended to deprive ambitious princes prone to waging unjust wars the advantages of gratuitous loans or inexpensive leases of horses and weapons, for the owners of these war materials stood to lose their property without hope of compensation. The prince was in effect advised to make sure that the prospects of winning his war were so propitious that he could afford to pay off the debts he incurred to the lessors. Unfortunately Innocent did not take this golden opportunity to discuss the role of mercenaries in the just war, for it would have been interesting to have his comments on whether mercenaries could disobey their employer when he commanded them to fight in an unjust war.

---

[134] Innocent IV, cited above, nn. 70, 73–5.
[135] Innocent IV, *Commentaria*, to x. 2.24.29. paras. 3–4, fol. 288rb–va.

Innocent then shifted his attention to the rights of a prince faced with the necessity of taking military action to defend the territory under his jurisdiction.[136] Again his differentiation of the just war from exercise of jurisdiction and simple defense remained crucial. When a prince waged war as an exercise of jurisdiction, he could promulgate a statute to the effect that whenever one of his subjects was invaded, that subject could seize the property of the invader and even detain him for judgment by the lord. Even without such a statute the prince could still condemn the invasion of his territorial jurisdiction. Innocent apparently considered the person whose territory was invaded to be a knight of subordinate rank who possessed neither the superior authority to wage a just war nor even jurisdiction over the invader or substantial territory, but who nevertheless exercised some petty jurisdiction. When the invader was a foreign lord not subject to the jurisdiction of the knight he invaded, this knight could legally defend himself and his property by violence, provided that he acted with due moderation. Consequently, he could if necessary kill his foes in the heat of battle, but he had no right to capture them, nor was he entitled to seize and occupy their possessions. Here Innocent reasoned that the defender lacked sufficient authority to wage a full just war with all its attendant legal rights and consequences, such as the right to exact punitive damages. By the same token the invader's liability to suffer capture and confiscation of his property was limited. Hostiensis clarified several overly terse portions of Innocent's analysis, and considered adversaries over whom the prince had jurisdiction as rebels guilty of contumacy. Once captured the rebels were to be detained until they could be transferred to his custody.[137]

The position constructed here by Innocent IV and Hostiensis gave legal substance and precision to the just war seen as a legal procedure, and thereby limited the incidence of licit violence more concretely than had the earlier attempts of Alanus Anglicus, Laurentius Hispanus and Johannes Teutonicus. A full just war between enemies each having no superior entailed full rights, consequences, and penalties. On the other hand a simple armed defense by a petty lord with subordinate jurisdiction carried with it a lesser legal significance, and

---

[136] *Ibid.*, para. 5, fol. 288va–vb.
[137] Hostiensis, *Lectura*, to x. 2.24.29. para. 6, p. 136b.

so the rights and penalties appropriate to it were correspondingly diminished. In a full just war men and property captured came immediately under the jurisdiction and possession of the captor without further legal formalities, but in a war of defense against an invader under one's own jurisdiction, such as a rebel, the invader could be detained but not reduced to servitude, while his property was legally confiscated. In a war of even more narrowly circumscribed legal limits, where the invader was not previously subjected to the jurisdiction of his present enemy, all measures necessary to repel the invasion, including killing, were licit, but capture and confiscation were denied. The only legal consequences of this type of war were the invader's loss of his right to compensation for damages sustained during the invasion, but he still retained his right to sue for recovery of his property that was unlawfully seized during the hostilities or afterward.

In effect Innocent and Hostiensis were proposing three different levels of the just war. The highest level, a full just war corresponding to the Roman law doctrine of the just war, was waged between independent adversaries and carried with it the full legal consequences of the Roman just war. The second type was waged by a prince with some jurisdiction over his enemy, but without superior authority. Here the prince was denied the full rights of Roman law but could exercise the more normal rights of jurisdiction over the offender. The third and most restricted type of just war was waged in simple defense against an invasion inflicted by an opponent outside the sphere of one's own jurisdiction. The only right open to the defender was simple repulsion of the attack. While he was not liable to the invader for damages, he was prohibited from confiscating the invader's property.

If it was Innocent IV's purpose to limit the violence of warfare, then why did he apply Roman law to the seemingly incongruous practices of feudalism? While a general answer might be that a Romanised canon law enforced by ecclesiastical courts was the only legal system that stood a chance of becoming a European common law, the explanation may be more precise. Innocent chose to apply Roman private law rather than public law, for feudalism in its diversity and its confusion of public office and private right could not suitably be described in terms of Roman public law with its jurisdic-

tional centralisation. Roman law moreover emphasised the requirement for justice more formally and coherently than did feudal law.
If Roman private law could be skillfully grafted onto existing feudal
custom, a common law of war could develop. Without the beneficial aid of Roman law actions and principles of justice, feudal
custom and even canon law were unable effectively to withhold
compensation for losses that vassals sustained in fighting an unjust
war, as is shown by the treatises of William of Rennes and Monaldus.
For this reason Innocent IV incorporated the Roman legal principle
that obligations were not contracted in wicked activities in an attempt
effectively to deny to unjust warriors the favorable legal consequences available to just warriors. Innocent discarded as unrealistic
an attempt to prevent all acts of warfare between feudal lords, and
instead attempted to limit the incidence of violence in these wars by
clarifying the structures of authority and violence found in feudal
customs. Hence there was less emphasis on the abstract justice of a
war and more on its consequences. In just wars the vassal was as much
the prince's agent in a legal procedure as was a lawyer in the prince's
court, and so his service created similar responsibilities for the prince.
When vassal and prince sharply disagreed over their respective rights
and duties, Innocent urged them to seek peaceful legal settlement.
He attempted to apply Roman and canon law to the bewildering
array of feudal rights and duties in order to render them more precise
and susceptible to judicial action.[138]

It was the necessity to explain the legal consequences of war,
especially regarding property rights, that stimulated the Decretalists
to produce their most extensive formulations of the requisite
authority for a just war. After all, the old adage that 'money is the
sinews of war' was as true in the thirteenth century as it is in the
twentieth. The Decretalists' formulations can best be divided into
three groups. The first formulation, that put forth by Alanus
Anglicus and perfected by Hostiensis, restricted the locus of authority
so narrowly that only the pope and the Emperor could declare a just
war. The second group, including perhaps the majority of the
Decretalists and perhaps best represented by Innocent IV, extended
the right to declare a just war more broadly to those princes who had

---

[138] For similar conclusions about the canon law theories arrived at by a different approach,
see Keen, *Laws of War*, pp. 68f. *et passim*.

superior authority, and referred best to the sovereigns of the rising national states. The third group, more feudal in outlook and represented by William of Rennes, extended the right to declare and wage war most broadly so as to include any feudal lord with vassals under him, although William had kings primarily in mind. Here the authority carried with it the right to wage war to its conclusion and to pursue its legal consequences, which included the rights to take captives and spoils and to exact compensation for damages, and the rights of vassals to seek indemnities from their lord for damages sustained. While an individual author often supported several of these formulations in his diverse comments, the Decretalists as a group responded to the hardening of territorial boundaries and jurisdictions, which has also been termed the closing of the medieval frontier, by increasingly viewing the just war as a defense of territory against external invasion. On this score the emergence of the concept of superior authority was crucial to the Decretalist analysis.[139] The prince and his subordinate officials, or the lord and his vassals, were considered to be united in common cause to defend their territory and also to have reciprocal rights and duties that each must respect. This conception implies the existence of a whole network of legal and moral relationships between the realm, its ruler and its subjects that paved the way for the emergence of the modern notion of the state.

There were several other broad purposes of the Decretalist consequences of warfare. The personal status of a warrior was now more protected, for not only could he not be killed save in the heat of battle, but unless he was captured in an unjust war he also could not be reduced to servitude. The requirement of superior authority denied any right of any previously uninvolved party to meddle in a troubled situation. The just war now was more clearly seen as an extraordinary legal procedure designed to supplement more normal procedures that were also envisaged as means to reduce the incidence of violence by bringing disputes off the battlefield into the courtroom. By a casuistry that only a lawyer or zealous confessor could love, private wars were transformed into court duels and wars of conquest had at least to appear just for their waging to be profitable.

---

[139] For Hostiensis' view of the solidity of territorial jurisdiction that was a necessary prerequisite for this position, see his *Summa*, to x. 2.2. para. 2, pp. 454f., cited above, n. 49.

In an attempt to cope with the shifting mosaic of conflicting jurisdictions that characterised power politics in the high Middle Ages the Decretalists constructed this body of casuistry that rendered significant service to the monarchs of the rising national kingdoms and city-states.[140]

It may seem puzzling that the Decretalists seldom even mentioned the most obvious consequence of war, death. It was as if they felt that wars could be fought without killing, and while that was sometimes the case in petty feudal wars where peasants outside the feudal system bore the brunt of the violence, it was becoming less so in the large-scale wars between great princes. The Decretalists realised that knights often fought primarily for booty in spite of the canonical prohibitions against this attitude, and in sensible response they sought to regulate this practice rather than condemning it outright, which in any case the Roman law of spoils prevented them from doing. In effect they recognised that feudal wars were a profitable business, as the well-known example of William the Marshal shows. Hence their treatment of the consequences of warfare bore close resemblance to their treatment of the mercantile profession. Just as the merchant was entitled to profits for his labor, losses and expenses, so the knight was entitled to the wages of war, spoils of real and movable property, in recompense for his labor, expenses and damages, and when the merchant or knight felt that his profits did not adequately cover his losses, he could bring suit at the conclusion of the contract or war. When on the other hand the merchant's profit or the knight's spoils were excessive or gained by illicit means, then the Decretalists enjoined him to make restitution as compensation and even punishment for his misdeeds.[141] Their analysis of the consequences of war was directed to implementing the principle that in warfare, crime did not pay.

[140] For a recent description of how this casuistry aided in the extension of royal jurisdiction, see F. Cheyette, 'The Sovereign and the Pirates, 1332,' *Speculum*, XLV (1970), 40–68.

[141] For William Marshal's profiteering, and his attitude and that of his contemporaries toward it, see S. Painter, *William Marshal* (Baltimore, 1933), esp. ch. 3 and pp. 285f. The canonistic attitudes toward mercantile profits are discussed in J. W. Baldwin, 'The Medieval Theories of the Just Price,' *Transactions of the American Philosophical Society*, XLIX[4] (1959), esp. 47–9; and J. Gilchrist, *The Church and Economic Activity in the Middle Ages* (London and New York, 1969), pp. 53–8. On the Church's economic doctrines in general, see *The Cambridge Economic History of Europe*, III, ed. M. Postan, E. Rich and E. Miller (Cambridge, 1963), ch. 8, esp. pp. 560, 574.

THE CHURCH AND THE JUST WAR

The Church could hardly escape involvement in the many thirteenth-century wars, for Church property was seen to be in constant danger from the violence of lay lords, and prelates were bound up in political strictures in countless ways. The Decretists had responded by condemning violation of ecclesiastical persons and property and by allowing prelates with regalia to accompany the military expeditions of their secular overlords. Under certain conditions prelates could command secular lords and ordinary laymen to take up the sword in defense of the Church, and clerics could in exceptional cases participate in fighting. The Decretalists sought to enlarge and systematise the opinions they had received, and thus they focused on ecclesiastical regulation of wars of lay lords and on the authority of churchmen to declare war.

The first problem that confronted the Decretalists was how to establish the competence of Church courts in bellicose affairs. In support of this attempt they could draw upon the recent extensive development of the Church's judicial institutions. Wars and other disputes came within the purview of these institutions when they involved the commission of sinful acts. Thus Alanus Anglicus, for whom contumacy was a just cause for war, argued that any crime that was contumaciously pursued became an ecclesiastical crime,[142] and claimed that the papacy as judge-ordinary of princes in both spiritual and temporal affairs was the court of last resort for princes ready to declare war.[143] In an often repeated opinion Johannes Teutonicus claimed for the Church the competence to pronounce judgment on the justice of a particular war. It is significant that he based his claim on a decretal of Innocent III (X. 5.40.26, *Super quibusdam*) that detailed ecclesiastical initiative in ordering secular princes to persecute heretics and confiscate their property.[144] Other Decretalists also based this competence on the Church's jurisdiction *ratione peccati* over secular affairs (X. 2.1.13, *Novit*).[145] Traditionally

---

[142] Alanus, *Apparatus*, to Comp. I, 5.6.7; cited above, n. 32.
[143] Alanus, *Apparatus:* '*Ius Naturale*,' to C. 23 q. 2 c. 1; cited above, n. 41.
[144] Johannes Teutonicus, cited above, n. 69.
[145] E.g. *Glossa Ordinaria*, to X. 2.24.29, v. *iniuste*: 'et ideo saltem indirecte ratione peccati spectat hoc ad iudicium ecclesie, ut [X. 2.1.13].' *Ibid.*, to X. 2.2.10, v. *vacante imperio*: 'iudex ecclesiasticus potest se immiscere saeculari iurisdictione, scilicet cum superior non invenitur.

the Church had a mission to serve the interest of peace, and a canon of the Decretum provided Johannes Teutonicus with the point of departure for his assertion that bishops should band together to maintain peace within their dioceses. Those who were negligent of this duty could be deposed from office.[146] In glossing the Gregorian decretals Bernard Botone maintained that a count must answer in the ecclesiastical forum for matters concerning the peace of his county.[147] Hostiensis provided for Church competence in case of the deficiency of secular justice to maintain peace, and allowed the pope to pronounce judgment in certain matters in which it was dubious whether they pertained to ecclesiastical or secular courts.[148] Of all the Decretalists Hostiensis came closest to according to the pope the right to act as supreme judge of wars within Christendom, but even he shrank back from a full commitment to that position.

It was one thing for the Decretalists to claim ecclesiastical competence over warfare but quite another to detail procedures by which the Church could actually pronounce judgment on a particular war. On this latter problem the Decretalists provided some pertinent elaboration. Innocent IV considered a papal sentence about a violent dispute to have the force of law binding both parties to its observance. After such a sentence had been delivered neither party should do any violence since a Roman law interdict prohibited any legal or physical action after a sentence had been rendered in the case. If anyone exceeded the limits of moderation in waging his own defense, he should suffer excommunication and temporal penalties. While the decretal upon which Innocent was commenting concerned defense of clerics against other clerics, the tenor of his remarks indicate that he considered his opinion as binding also on laymen.[149]

Alius est cum iudex saecularis negligit facere iustitiam.' Cf. J. Watt, *The Theory of Papal Monarchy*, pp. 52f.

146 Johannes Teutonicus, *Glossa Ordinaria*, to D. 90 c. 11 and v. *praecipimus*.

147 *Glossa Ordinaria*, to X. 5.40.26, v. *personarum*.

148 Hostiensis, *Lectura*, to X. 2.1.13. para. 28, v. *contra pacem*. fol. 6A. Ibid., to X. 2.2.8, pr., v. *sunt remissi*, fol. 11A. Ibid., to X. 4.17.13. para. 21, v. *certis causis*, fol. 39. Ibid., to X. 4.17.13. para. 33, v. *ad iudicium*, fol. 39A: 'quo ad ecclesiastica indistincte et regulariter, quo ad secularia casualiter...sicque spectat ad papam declaratio dubiorum.'

149 Innocent IV, *Commentaria*, to X. 2.13.12. para. 9, v. *decernentes*, fol. 232ra–rb: 'id est reservantes, nisi enim reservasset eis quod post sententiam istam possent agere, si modum excessissent, non potuissent postea agere, cum agentes interdicto unde vi omnia haec induxissent in iudicium...[Cod. 7.51.3]. dic quod hoc decretum non fuit sententia, sed iuris declaratio. *Excessistis*. non enim licet modum excedere, et si excesserit incurrit excommunicationem, et poenam temporalem et irregularitatem.'

Hostiensis was more specific in suggesting a concrete means by which the Church could aid in keeping the peace. Suppose, he said, a lord who was immediately subjected to a prince with full authority was faced with a rebellion of one of his own vassals. While this lord did indeed have the authority, even in Hostiensis' restrictive view, to take up arms against his vassal, Hostiensis counseled another course of action that posed less danger to his soul. He could enlist the aid of the vassal's bishop, who in turn would warn the vassal, and if the vassal spurned the episcopal admonition, the bishop could then excommunicate him *ratione peccati*. Should the vassal remain excommunicated for more than a year, the bishop could then expose him and his property to his lord's military attack. Evidently Hostiensis had seen this arrangement work to his satisfaction in Lombardy, where counts and bishops cooperated in such matters.[150] Noteworthy here is the locus of authority for the attack on the vassal, for while the dispute originally concerned the temporal lord, the authority for the eventual military action lay with the bishop. In such cases the delay encountered by the lord would naturally encourage him to seek settlement with his vassal that avoided perilous and costly hostilities, and even the eventual military action did not constitute a full just war with all its drastic consequences.

Hostiensis strongly favored such appeal by secular officials to the Church, for in another passage he provided a technical formula by which a Church court could judge a particular war. In judging a war just or unjust the burden of proof was placed on the party that claimed the war was just. To settle the conflicting claims to restitution the total list of damages had to be studied, after which it could be determined which party initiated the hostilities, since liability for all damages sustained in the war were his liability. The fact that he started the war Hostiensis considered to be *prima facie* evidence that he had acted unjustly and was therefore bound to make restitution, but if the party could prove he was justified in commencing hostilities, he incurred no guilt and all property he had seized became his own. This placed as great a burden on his lawyers as it did on his soldiers. Hostiensis argued that this procedure lay within the proper competence of Church courts.[151] The passage is significant for a

---

[150] Hostiensis, *Summa*, to x. 1.34. para. 4, p. 360.
[151] Hostiensis, *Lectura*, to x. 2.24.29. para. 2, v. *movit*, p. 136.

number of reasons. It shows how important the problem of restitution had become to the canonistic theories of war, but the citations Hostiensis adduced to establish standards to determine where justice lay came from the Roman law condemnation of illicit violence. Hostiensis of course put these citations to uses never envisaged by the Roman law. The proceedings he described could only take place after hostilities had ceased and the conflict had moved into the courtroom. This appears to be the only Decretalist passage that assumed the unjust party to be that one who opened the hostilities unless proved otherwise.

Lacking a decretal that would encourage them to elaborate on papal activity promoting peace within Europe, the Decretalists did not comment on its role in condemnation of unjust wars, orders for free passage of troops on their way to fight a just war, and conferral of occupied territories to the victorious party.[152] An aspect of the Church's role in maintaining peace that did draw the attention of the Decretalists was the Truce of God. At issue was whether wars could licitly be waged during the times of the Truce. On the basis of a canon from the Decretum (C. 23 q. 8 c. 15) the Decretists had concluded that if a war was just, it could be waged at all times.[153] In the interim, canon 21 of the Third Lateran Council of 1179 promulgated the Truce of God for all Christendom. The canon took on additional importance by its inclusion as a decretal in the *Compilatio Prima* (1.24.1) and the Gregorian collection (X. 1.34.1), and it was in this form that it came to the Decretalists' attention. The decretal prohibited all fighting from Thursday through Sunday and during the periods from Advent through Epiphany and from Septuagesima through Easter Week. Those who broke the truce were first to be warned by their bishop, and should they continue, the local bishop was to excommunicate them and in case of need seek the aid of other bishops. Recalling the duty of bishops to maintain peace, the decretal closed with the admonition that bishops who neglected their duties in this regard should be removed from office. The issue was thus joined: did Gratian's canon take precedence over the decretal; or did

---

[152] Cf. Ullmann, *Growth of Papal Government*, p. 450; G. B. Pallieri and G. Vismara, *Acta pontificia juris gentium* (Milan, 1946).

[153] For a fuller exposition of the canonistic analysis of the Truce of God, see Hoffmann, *Gottesfriede und Treuga Dei*, pp. 217–43. Cf. also the discussion of Gratian and the Decretists on C. 23 q. 8 c. 15, above, ch. 3, nn. 25, 52 and ch. 4, nn. 63–4.

the more recent decretal demand literal interpretation and strict enforcement?

Laurentius Hispanus first recognised the conflict between the Decretum and the decretal, and attempted to reconcile it by considering the Truce of God as applicable to a situation where personal rancor was involved. Since war was unnecessary in this case anyway, it was therefore unjust and should not be fought at all. The canon from Gratian he interpreted as referring to just wars against Saracens and heretics that could be waged by any means and at any time.[154] But Laurentius neglected to solve the problem of whether a war between Christians was to be interrupted during periods of the Truce. Damasus applied the truce only to private wars, such as those in which a prince wished to recover property unjustly seized when judicial redress was unavailable. Such a war, since it was not really a war, was unnecessary and therefore in it the periods of truce should be observed, although Damasus allowed use of violence in self-defense even on Easter Day. Had his strict position attracted more followers, it could have opened the way to widespread condemnations of feudal violence waged in time of truce. As it was, when Bernard Botone appropriated this passage, he made a significant change: for the 'prince' waging a voluntary war, he substituted 'private person.' Since no private person should wage war at all, much less a voluntary one during time of truce, Damasus' potentially significant opinion was still-born.[155]

The solution that ultimately gained favor during the Interim Period before 1234 was based on a distinction between canonical and conventional truces. The canonical truce was the Truce of God in the decretals, while a conventional truce was that struck by the warring parties. They solved the conflict by holding that an unjust war should never be waged, much less in times of truce either canonical or conventional, and they considered most wars to come under this category. When a war was just, it was licit to wage it even during the canonical truce, and in their opinion even the pope respected this situation. And if canonical truces could not be maintained, bishops who did not compel their observance were not culpable because such

---

[154] Laurentius, *Apparatus*, to C. 23 q. 8 c. 15, v. *quadragesimali*, B.N. Lat. 15393, fol. 195vb.
[155] Damasus, *Summa Decretalium*, to Comp. I. 1.24, B.N. Lat. 14320, fol. 153vb; *Glossa Ordinaria*, to X. 1.34.1. Cf. X. 5.41.4.

truces had not won the approval of the warriors to whom they applied. It might even be necessary for someone to break the canonical truce to prevent something worse from happening.[156] Most other canonists of the period accepted this conclusion. Raymond of Peñafort seems to have been alone in favoring a strict interpretation of the canonical truce.[157]

Succeeding Decretalists added certain additional qualifications to the applicability of the canonical truce. Innocent IV thought that bishops should make special efforts to enforce the truce in unjust wars, but conceded that when it was doubtful whether the war was unjust they need not attempt to enforce compliance.[158] Johannes Teutonicus considered waging defensive war licit even during Lent, and applied the Truce of God only to unjust wars of attack.[159] After Raymond of Peñafort the only significant departure from the common opinion of the Decretalists was Hostiensis, for whom unceasing war was in order against those who had ruptured the bond of faith with Christian society.[160] This type of war corresponded to the war of the Roman people against enemies who were outside the boundaries of legal protection. But in all the six other types of war, whether just or unjust, Hostiensis enjoined observance of the canonical truce, giving as his reason the long established desire of the Church for peace. In prohibiting the waging even of just wars during the truce periods, the pope did not intend to approve the unjust cause of enemies, but, realising that he could not effect a total correction of the conflicts, the pope wished to restrain the hostilities carried out by both sides.[161]

Hostiensis' position came too late, and was perhaps too closely bound up with his own typology of war to fit in logically with the common opinion of the Decretalists. The Truce of God had become

---

[156] Vincentius, *Apparatus*, to x. 1.34.1, v. *treugas*, B.N. Lat. 3967, fol. 53va–vb and B.N. Lat. 3968, fol. 46ra; idem, *Lectura*, to x. 1.34.1, v. *treugas*, B.N. Lat. 3967, fol. 53va; Damasus, *Apparatus*, to Comp. I. 1.24.1, B.N. Lat. 3930, fol. 1rb; Tancredus, *Apparatus*, to Comp. I. 1.24.1, B.N. Lat. 3931A, fol. 11vb; B.N. Lat. 14321, fol. 11rb; and B.N. Lat. 15398, fol. 14ra; *Glossa Ordinaria*, to x. 1.34.1, v. *frangere*.

[157] Raymond of Peñafort, *Summa Juris*, ed. J. Ruis Serra (Barcelona, 1945), p. 140.

[158] Innocent IV, *Commentaria*, to x. 1.34.1, fol. 161rb.

[159] Johannes Teutonicus; cited above, n. 18.

[160] Hostiensis, *Lectura* (as above, n. 6), para. 31, p. 29.

[161] Hostiensis, *Summa*, to x. 1.34. para. 4, pp. 360f. The *Glossa Ordinaria*, to x. 1.34.1, v. *frangere*, hinted at Hostiensis' eventual position.

a dead letter long before his time. In their efforts to apply the Truce to unjust and private wars they were careful not to diminish the rights attendant upon the waging of the just war. Their position followed logically from their conviction that if a war was just, it was also necessary. Gratian's canon came to be preferred to the decretal that Raymond of Peñafort had carefully defended and included in the Gregorian collection.

The Peace of God received very little attention at the hands of the Decretalists. Gratian had included several canons that prohibited violent attacks to clerics, peasants and other unarmed non-combatants (C. 24 q. 3 cc. 21-5), and canon 22 of the Third Lateran Council of 1179 which similarly granted such security was included in *Compilatio Prima* (1.24.2) and the Gregorian decretals (X 1.34.2). That the canonists paid scant attention to this medieval expression of non-combatant immunity, the Peace of God, may seem puzzling at first, but their lack of significant commentary indicates that they considered the decretal valid as it stood. In their view wars were usually waged by persons to whom fighting was licit, that is, soldiers, and all other were *hors de guerre*. For a just war to remain a just war, it had to be conducted properly, which meant that it could only be waged on other soldiers. And an unjust war should not be fought at all, so there was no need to specify that it should not attack non-combatants. In never ceasing to bewail the indiscriminate violence of the *routiers* and marauding knights,[162] the decretals and their commentators only confirmed the Peace of God, which was as taken for granted in canon law as it was violated in practice.

The Church's efforts to limit wars of secular lords did not prohibit churchmen from limited participation in just wars of secular lords under certain conditions nor did it prevent prelates from declaring just wars on their own authority. During the Decretist period canonists conceded that prelates could exhort laymen to fight in just wars to defend the faith but barred clerics from personal participation in combat except in extreme circumstances. Similarly, bishops without regalia were permitted and bishops with regalia were obliged to perform military service in their lord's just wars but could not actually fight. Certain Decretists cautiously required prior papal license for their performance, for they considered obedience of

---

[162] E.g. Comp. I. 5.6.7; cf. below, n. 175.

prelates to the pope to take precedence over loyalty to secular overlords.[163]

The Decretalists' treatment clarified most of the hesitations found in prior opinions on clerical participation in warfare. Like the Decretists, Alanus Anglicus allowed clerics to exhort others to fight a just war, but prohibited clerical participation in the campaign unless the cleric went to make peace or administer penance. He added that if a cleric ordered the killing of a certain person, whether deserving of death or not, he was guilty of homicide.[164] Innocent IV allowed prelates to declare and wage wars while barring them from fighting. Rather he should urge soldiers on with commands to capture and fight, but not to kill. When he was ignorant of any deaths resulting from the execution of his orders, he was not guilty of homicide and was left to his own conscience. A cleric could fight to defend himself and others by throwing stones, and did not incur irregularity unless he thereby killed someone.[165] Hostiensis barred clerical use of especially deadly weapons, but naturally he allowed laymen to use them.[166] On the other hand Raymond of Peñafort allowed clerics actually to fight in a just war when it was absolutely necessary.[167] Abbas Antiquus at the end of the period chose to straddle the issue, for while he claimed that a cleric could not fight to repel violence, he also joined Hostiensis in allowing a cleric to defend the rights of his Church by violence.[168] The Tertiary Franciscans presented another facet, for their rule explicitly prohibited them from bearing arms and taking oaths except to defend the Church, the faith or their own land.[169] Had the Decretalists seen fit to comment

---

[163] Cf. above, ch. 4, nn. 84–90.

[164] E.g. Alanus, *Apparatus:* 'Ius Naturale,' to C. 23 q. 8 c. 10, v. *adriani*, B.N. Lat. 15393, fol. 195va and Mazar. 1318, fol. 290va; Laurentius, *Apparatus*, to C. 23 q. 8 c. 19, v. *omnium*, B.N. Lat. 15393, fol. 196ra.

[165] Innocent IV, *Commentaria*, to X. 2.13.12. para. 8, fols. 231vb–232ra: 'Satis etiam credimus, quod praelatus ecclesiae, pro iure ipsius possit indicere bellum, et ei interesse, sed non debet pugnare sed potest clamare: capite et pugnate, sed non occidite. Nec obstat ei de homicidio...sed nesciebat utrum aliquem occidisset, et ideo fuit suae conscientiae relinquendum...Sed quid etiam si clericus sit in praelio contra raptores, vel ad defensionem suam vel aliorum, licet ibi pugnet, et lapides iaciat, dummodo de suis ictibus neminem occidat, non est irregularis.'

[166] Hostiensis; cited above, n. 85.

[167] Raymond of Peñafort; cited above, n. 5.

[168] Abbas Antiquus, *Lectura*, to X. 5.25.3, fol. 141va; to X. 2.13.12. para. 2, fol. 67ra; Hostiensis, *Lectura*, to X. 3.50.9. para. 6, v. *praeponatur*, fol. 182A.

[169] F. Duval, *De la paix de Dieu à la paix de fer* (Paris, 1923), p. 30.

on the bellicose acts of these quasi-clerics devoted to furthering social peace, their analysis of clerical violence would have been more relevant. As it was, they unanimously prohibited killing by clerics but nevertheless allowed them to fight defensively and to urge others to do battle.[170] They were less interested in this problem than had been the Decretists, perhaps because secular lords less frequently took clerics on military expeditions. Hence the Decretalists were able more clearly to distinguish between licit and illicit clerical participation. What interested them more were the rights and duties of prelates in warfare.

The Decretalists reinforced the duty of prelates with regalia to follow their lords into a just war.[171] Johannes Teutonicus added that when a bishop was required to defend his vassals, he was not guilty of avenging injuries, and allowed a prelate to send the specified number of knights to his prince.[172] Yet the Decretalists devoted little attention to the duties of bishops with regalia, for since the time of the Decretists the Church had succeeded in rendering the ecclesiastical confirmation of a bishop-elect as the constitutive act by which the candidate entered into full possession of his jurisdictional powers. The consequence of this development was double-edged: the importance of the investiture with regalia for the bishop's authority was 'eclipsed' by confirmation, and the distinction between a bishop's temporalities, his regalian holdings, and his spiritual jurisdiction tended to break down. Thus the temporal powers of a bishop became a mere annex dependent on the spiritual jurisdiction he held from the pope, and his jurisdiction became indivisible.[173] Since the episcopal office and jurisdiction owed more to the pope and less to the prince than before, no conflict of loyalties need arise and the Decretalists were thereby spared from having to follow the tortuous opinions of the Decretists. Furthermore, the right of bishops to

---

[170] Johannes Teutonicus summarised canonistic opinion on this matter: *Glossa Ordinaria*, to D. 50 c. 6, vv. *de his, defendo*, B.N. Lat. 14317, fol. 38ra; *ibid.*, to C. 23 q. 1, pr., v. *propulsandam*, B.N. Lat. 14317, fol. 180va.

[171] *Glossa Palatina*, to C. 23 q. 8 c. 19, v. *venire*; cited above, ch. 4, n. 86.

[172] Johannes Teutonicus, *Glossa Ordinaria*, to C. 23 q. 8 c. 8, v. *presentialiter*, B.N. Lat. 14317, fol. 197ra. The passage was repeated by Peter of Salins, *Lectura*, to C. 23 q. 8 c. 8, B.N. Lat. 3917, fol. 190rb. Cf. *Glossa Ordinaria*, to C. 23 q. 8, pr., v. *clericis*, B.N. Lat. 14317, fol. 196va and Laurentius, *Apparatus*, to C. 23 q. 8, pr., B.N. Lat. 3903, fol. 193ra.

[173] This is a mere summary of Benson's excellent treatment of the evolution of episcopal confirmation; cf. *Bishop-Elect*, ch. 10 and pp. 377f.

make war now was part of their spiritual jurisdictions and so the Decretalists were able to concentrate on the purely ecclesiastical authority to declare and wage war, based on the Church's right as a juridical institution to intervene in temporal affairs in pursuit of its spiritual mission. Alanus Anglicus expressly attributed this authority to the Church, especially the pope,[174] but neglected to explain how this authority was to be exercised. At issue here was whether ecclesiastics on the basis of their possession of both spiritual and material swords could directly wage wars. The intrusion of the sword imagery ensured that differences of opinion would arise in the Decretalists' discussions. Under Alexander III's direction, the Third Lateran Council of 1179 (canon 27) condemned the *routiers* who were then ravaging many parts of Europe. This rather motley list of persons were likely to find employment as mercenaries and often lapsed into brigandage, especially when unemployed. Thus Brabançons, Aragonese, Basques, Cottereaux and Traverdines were excommunicated, anathematised and considered equivalent to heretics because they attacked churches and defenseless folk, sparing neither age nor sex. Alexander provided for their repression by secular princes acting at the behest of prelates. To princes so engaged were granted privileges similar to those enjoyed by crusaders.[175] The decretal further complicated the nature of the Church's authority to wage war, for it left unclear whether that right extended to direct involvement of Church officials as well as ecclesiastical commands to lay princes to take up the sword. Most Decretalists conveniently if confusingly straddled the issue. For example, Tancredus laconically observed that war could be waged on ecclesiastical authority, and Peter of Salins ascribed to an ecclesiastical judge the authority to declare war.[176]

The more complex view was signaled by the *Glossa Palatina* when

---

[174] Alanus, *Apparatus*, to Comp. 1. 5.6.7, v. *consilium*, B.N. Lat. 3932, fol. 59va: 'ar. ecclesie auctoritate bellum committi posse'; idem, *Apparatus: 'Ius Naturale,'* to C. 23 q. 1 c. 4, v. *sive deo*, B.N. Lat. 15393, fol. 181rb and Mazar. 1318, fol. 276vb: 'i.e. ecclesia que habet potestatem indicendi bellum...Iussit enim dominus iosue et multis aliis.' Cf. *ibid.*, to C. 23 q. 4 c. 36; cited above, n. 39.

[175] Comp. 1. 5.6.7. On this perplexing canon 27, cf. G. Sicard, 'Paix et guerre dans le droit canon,' *Paix de Dieu et guerre sainte en Languedoc* (Cahiers de Fanjeaux, IV, 1969), pp. 86, 89, nn. 14, 37. For the theologians' treatment, see below, ch. 6, nn. 78–87.

[176] Tancredus, *Apparatus*, to Comp. 1. 5.6.7, v. *consilium*, B.N. Lat. 3931A, fol. 66va; Peter of Salins, *Lectura*, to C. 23 q. 2 c. 2, v. *deus imperat*; cited above, n. 37.

it argued both that a bishop could declare a just war and that when the pope conferred the power of the sword on the prince he ordered him to punish and kill criminals according to the laws. Since the pope however ultimately possessed both swords he could exercise them both directly, especially in his capacity as ruler of Rome and the papal states.[177] Laurentius Hispanus followed Huguccio in granting the right to declare war to an ecclesiastical judge,[178] to which Johannes Teutonicus added the right of an ecclesiastical prince or prelate to persecute enemies and to order a secular judge to punish malefactors.[179] Raymond of Peñafort enlarged upon a view current earlier in the Middle Ages, when he encouraged bishops and ecclesiastical judges to invoke the secular arm, but these officials were not to command the killing or mutilation of violent men, heretics and pagans but rather to encourage defense of the faith and *patria* and return territories occupied by infidels to the Christian faith. He brought this attitude more up to date when he mentioned the many remissions of sins granted by the Church pursuant to these purposes. The Church and its officials were not responsible for the deaths that resulted; on the contrary, officials who were delinquent in urging such defensive measures deserved to be deposed from office. Raymond praised those who responded to the Church's call for military aid and suggested that all their sins were forgiven. Princes who in spite of their God-given authority did not so respond on the other hand could be forced by ecclesiastical censures to purge their territories from the wickedness of heretics and to defend the Church.[180] Even

---

177 *Glossa Palatina*, to C. 15 q. 6 c. 2, v. *simul et materiali gladio*; to C. 23 q. 8, pr., v. *hactenus tibi*; to C. 23 q. 8 c. 7, vv. *igitur, cum sepe*; cited in Stickler, 'Sacerdotium et Regnum,' 590f.

178 Laurentius, *Apparatus*, to C. 23 q. 1 c. 4, v. *tributa*, B.N. Lat. 3903, fol. 179vb: 'principis... nullus ergo bellare potest sine auctoritate principis...Similiter ecclesiasticus iudex potest indicere bellum.' *Ibid.*, to C. 15 q. 6 c. 2, v. *materiali*, B.N. Lat. 3903, fol. 153ra: 'ar. quod iudex ecclesiasticus potest indicere bellum.' Cf. Huguccio, *Summa*, to C. 15 q. 6 c. 2, v. *materiali*; cited above, ch. 4, n. 116.

179 Johannes Teutonicus, *Glossa Ordinaria*, to C. 15 q. 6 c. 2, v. *materiali*, B.N. Lat. 14317, fol. 159vb: 'ar. quod iudex ecclesiasticus bene potest indicere bellum, et in bello sequi hostes...Item est arg. quod iudex ecclesiasticus bene potest precipere iudici seculari ut puniat maleficos...Jo.' *Ibid.*, to C. 23 q. 1 c. 4, v. *principes*, B.N. Lat. 14317, fol. 181va: 'nullus ergo bellare potest sine auctoritate principis, ut hic et [Cod. 11.47.1]. Similiter princeps ecclesiasticus potest indicere bellum...Johannes.'

180 Raymond of Peñafort, *Summa de Casibus*, 2.1.10, p. 157ab. For the historical background of this view, see Choderow, *Christian Political Theory*, pp. 223–5, 244f. Raymond wrote against the background of the Reconquista.

in the first quarter of the thirteenth century this passage had an antiquarian ring to it, for the newer theories allowed the Church to exercise violence directly on its own independent authority without recourse to the aid of secular princes. Yet Raymond's opinion also contained indirect reference to the Church's practice of encouraging lay military aid through the grant of indulgences. Indeed the *Glossa Ordinaria* to the Gregorian decretals itself justified the granting of exceptional remissions of sins to those who had been guilty of immoderate self-defense when they were fighting in the service of the Church, in order to encourage such service.[181] Thus far the Decretalists had insisted to a man that the churchmen did indeed possess the authority to initiate wars in defense of the Church, but they had explained neither the basis for this right nor who should exercise it nor whether a layman could disobey an ecclesiastical command to fight in a just war.

In an attempt to anticipate the latter contingency Johannes Teutonicus proposed a hypothetical situation in which a layman who had previously sworn to defend the Church now felt in his conscience that the Church was promoting an unjust war. Johannes allowed the layman caught in this dilemma to follow the dictates of his conscience, but nevertheless allowed the Church to prosecute him for perjury when he did not fulfill his oath.[182] In effect his solution placed the individual conscience in conflict with ecclesiastical discipline, and, since the Decretalists to this point had constructed no theory of licit disobedience to an unjust command, it could not be considered as coherent law. Apparently realising the deficiency of Johannes' solution, Bernard Botone omitted it from the *Glossa Ordinaria* to the same decretal that was incorporated into the Gregorian collection (X. 2.24.17). The problem resurfaced in Hostiensis' condemnation of a priest who promoted an unjust war, although neither he nor any other Decretalist seems to have confronted this problem of obedience directly.[183]

---

[181] *Glossa Ordinaria*, to x. 5.38.3, (*Casus*) and v. *retardentur*.

[182] Johannes Teutonicus, *Apparatus*, to Comp. III. 2.15.2 (= x. 2.24.17), v. *requisitus*, B.N. Lat. 3930, fol. 140vb: 'si vero ecclesia ei fidem non servavit in suis necessitatibus, nec ipse tenetur iuvare ecclesiam...vel si remordet conscientiam quod ecclesia movet iniustum bellum...sed licet ipse tunc non teneatur sequi conscientiam suam, ecclesia tamen eum habebit pro periurio.'

[183] Hostiensis, in *Lectura*, to x. 5.39.23, pr., vv. *non propulsando, sed inferendo iniuriam*, fols. 110–110A: 'subaudiendum est maxime, vel hoc dicit ad notandum, quod idem sacerdo

The more fundamental problem from the point of view of the Church was taken up by Innocent IV, who provided a more specific opinion on the right of ecclesiastical officials when he allowed any prelate with temporal jurisdiction or the right to declare war to invoke military force against disobedient subjects. Innocent however considered this action an exercise of jurisdiction rather than a proper war.[184] He confirmed the right of a prelate to coerce those subjects belonging to his jurisdiction by references to the Church's coercive power over its manifold enemies, but he was unwilling to grant the jurisdiction necessary to declare war to just any prelate. Indeed, he was so adamant about the necessity of princely authority that he denied a papal judge-delegate the power to declare war. In default of ordinary justice, be it ecclesiastical or secular, the judge-delegate had the right to prosecute sentences and confer possession of ecclesiastical property, but when recourse to military force was necessary to execute a sentence the judge-delegate was forced to invoke the aid of a secular judge-ordinary.[185] Innocent reasoned that while a judge-delegate was indeed a prelate, he was not a prince and hence lacked the proper jurisdiction directly to declare war. In concurring, Hostiensis added that even when the case at hand concerned any sort of ecclesiastical property the judge-delegate was bound to invoke the aid of the secular arm.[186]

[sic] iniustum bellum moverat...et quicquid ex illo bello ex parte sua secutum est, videtur fecisse non propulsando, sed iniuriam inferendo.'

[184] Innocent IV, *Commentaria*, to x. 2.13.12. para. 8, fol. 231vb: 'Item quilibet praelatus, si habet iurisdictionem temporalem contra subditos inobedientes licite moveret arma... dummodo iurisdictionem indicendi bellum habeat, vel in casibus supradictis, et etiam si non habent ius indicendi, quia in his casibus non proprie dicitur fieri bellum, sed melius executio iurisdictionis, vel iustitia...nec in his casibus capti fient servi.' *Ibid.*, to x. 5.37.5, para. 2, v. *incitant*, fol. 542rb: 'Nos credimus, quod licet episcopus ratione iurisdictionis temporalis possit bellum indicere et antequam sit in percussionibus hortari ut utiliter pugnent et bellis interesse, et possit semper hortari ad capiendum.' Cf. Hostiensis, *Lectura*, to x. 2.13.12. para. 22, fol. 53; and *ibid.*, to x. 2.13.12. para. 28, fol. 53: 'Qualiter autem licet vim vi repellere, et qualiter nedum papae, vel episcopo, sed etiam inferiori prelato temporalem iurisdictionem habenti bellum movere ad defensionem iurisdictionis sue ecclesie, et suorum, et utrunque gladium exercere;' *ibid.*, to x. 2.34.9. para. 8, v. *inhabiles ad pugnandum*, fol. 129A: 'No. expressum, quod non licet clericis arma sumere, nam arma clericorum consistunt in censura ecclesiastica, orationibus...Solutio. ex officio clericatus solo hoc non licet...Ratione autem iurisdictionis temporalis competentis hoc licet...et posset dici quod in propria persona non licet...sed per subditos.'

[185] Innocent IV, *Commentaria*, to x. 1.29.7, v. *executioni*, fol. 121vb. On this general problem, see J. Rogazinski, 'Ordinary and Major Judges,' *Studia Gratiana*, xv (1972), 591–611.

[186] In *Lectura*, to x. 1.29.7. para. 2, v. *coercere*, p. 134; *ibid.*, to x. 5.12.18. para. 17, fol. 48A. Cf. Hostiensis, *Summa*, to x. 1.34. para. 4; cited above, n. 150. For x. 5.7.13, cf. below,

The question of whether a prelate could directly declare and wage war on his own authority was thus resolved in the affirmative when the prelate's spiritual jurisdiction included both temporal jurisdiction and the right to declare war. In case he had only temporal jurisdiction he could execute a sentence by recourse to violence but was restrained from declaring war. When he was only a prelate, such as a judge-delegate with no temporal jurisdiction, then his authority to take up the sword was limited to invoking the aid of the secular power and reflected the older theory of the Church's indirect authority to command laymen to take up the sword in defense of the Church and its property. Innocent and Hostiensis were able to accomplish this limitation and clarification of the right of prelates to make war on the basis of their distinction between the just war proper and other forms of licit violence. The way was made easier by the notion that the jurisdiction of a confirmed bishop was inseparably bound up with his spiritual office, such that he had the right to declare war when that right was included in his jursidiction. Innocent was thus able to avoid even the mention of prelates' regalian obligations that had so vexed earlier canonists, and by reference to the different levels of jurisdiction he rendered irrelevant the thorny issue of whether the prelate had both swords that had obscured the opinions of earlier canonistic commentators. For the first time a bishop with temporal jurisdiction was clearly set apart from his fellow prelates who lacked it. Innocent's complex position was a response to the increased sophistication of the ecclesiastical jurisdictional machinery, and he was the first to draw these consequences from the 'eclipse' of the regalia by episcopal confirmation. Yet his analysis did not go unchallenged: after close paraphrase of Innocent's opinion Durantis reopened the issue when he expanded the locus of authority to declare war to include both ecclesiastical judges-ordinary and judges-delegate.[187] Even Hostiensis elsewhere reintroduced the confusion over the swords when he allowed a prelate who possessed either the spiritual or material sword to make

p. 196. Since the *exposition en proie* was not necessarily a war, I have not considered it as fully in this context as did Pissard, *La guerre sainte*, pp. 95–9. In view of the position of Innocent and Hostiensis, and of Benson's analysis of episcopal jurisdiction, Pissard erred in concluding that only in the fourteenth century could prelates declare war on their spiritual authority alone; cf. *ibid.*, p. 100.

[187] Durantis, *Speculum*, cited above, n. 53.

war on those who caused injury to the Church.[188] Evidently here he considered either sword as sufficient authority without explaining the sort of jurisdiction the prelate possessed, for he did not bring to bear the indivisibility of that jurisdiction.

A major problem that occupied Innocent IV as pope more than as canonical jurisprudent was the endemic war between the papacy and Holy (Roman) Emperor. Hostiensis, in bringing to bear his vivid memory of papal condemnations of the imperial claims by *dominus noster*, as he called his master Innocent IV, asked whether a war declared by the Emperor on the Church was a just war, for it was waged by a prince with no superior. According to a theory he adduced, it was indeed just since while both temporal and spiritual jurisdictions proceeded immediately from God, temporal jurisdiction was superior and therefore not subject to spiritual jurisdiction. Hostiensis rejected this argument out of hand as remote from the hearts of the faithful and closer to heresy, for the Emperor was the advocate and protector of the Church, not its oppressor. When the Emperor did make war on the Church, all catholics were obligated to cling to the cause of the Church, and imperial vassals were loosed from their bonds of fealty to the Emperor.[189] In addition to making temporal jurisdiction dependent on spiritual, Hostiensis implicitly accorded to the papacy the supreme authority within Christendom to declare war.

The Decretalists viewed the Church's role in warfare as twofold. First, through its superior jurisdiction the Church was to bring settlement of disputes between Christians off the battlefield and into the ecclesiastical courtroom, and through enforcement of the Truce of God and the Peace of God it hoped to discourage private and illicit war. Second, prelates who exercised temporal jurisdiction as part of their spiritual jurisdiction could wage war for the same reasons of defense as those invoked by their secular counterparts, while the papacy was the supreme judge of war within Christian society. Still to be discerned was the juridical status of wars waged in defense of the faith and the Church against those who operated outside the bonds of Christian society.

[188] Hostiensis; cited above, n. 6.
[189] Hostiensis, *Lectura*, to x. 2.13.12. paras. 24–5, fol. 53.

THE CRUSADES

The Church's experience during the twelfth and thirteenth centuries indicated to the Decretalists the need for a special kind of war against enemies of the Church and orthodox Christians. Crusading expeditions to the Holy Land, poorly organised by feudal nobles, seldom accomplished their stated goals and often dissolved into chaotic raids that the Church was unable to control, such as the conquest of Constantinople during the Fourth Crusade. In its reliance on the good offices of secular princes the Church had been unable to stem the tide of heresy that was flowing across Europe. During the long conflict with Frederick II the papacy was embarrassed by his successful Crusade to the Holy Land carried out while he was under papal excommunication and the target of its own crusade. From this period dates the Decretalist recognition of the need for the construction of the juridical basis for crusades to the Holy Land and against the Church's enemies within Europe. When Innocent IV in practice and Hostiensis in theory called all Christians to the aid of the Church and freed imperial vassals from their oaths of fidelity, they were demonstrating the judicial theory of wars waged on direct papal initiative for the sake of the faith. Earlier in the Middle Ages a war or crusade was deemed sufficiently justified when it was waged on behalf of God and His faith, as was shown by the cry 'Deus vult' that allegedly arose spontaneously from those in attendance at Clermont in 1095. To the unsophisticated it may have seemed impious to question holy wars that they assumed to be inspired by a divine command, just as the sons of Levi in Exodus 32 had not questioned the divine command to slay their fellows, but as good lawyers the Decretalists could not be content with Peter of Salins' simple conviction that military activities could be undertaken on divine inspiration.[190] Gratian and the Decretists had been familiar with the many texts referring to God's wars, and they had produced lengthy discussions of the right of the Church to punish infidels, heretics and excommunicates through the agency of secular princes, but, Huguccio excepted, they only hinted at a theory of direct ecclesiastical authorisation for wars devoted to such an end. Although the Gregorian decretals were moot on the reservation of the right to

---

190 Peter of Salins, *Lectura*, to C. 23 q. 1 c. 5, v. *non est delictum*, B.N. Lat. 3917, fol. 172rb.

proclaim the crusade to the pope, the Decretalists produced a more systematic development of ecclesiastical judicial machinery and elaboration of a theory of papal monarchy that paved the way toward their consideration of the relations between holy war, crusade and just war. The treatment here does not attempt a comprehensive survey of crusade theory but rather considers it only in so far as it relates to the just war.[191]

Recent papal and conciliar legislation provided the basis for Decretalists' comments on the crusades. Basic decretals that found their way into the Gregorian collection included the famous constitution *Ad Liberandam* of the Fourth Lateran Council that forbade Christians to aid the Saracens or enter into commerce with them (X. 5.6.17). Strangely, those extensive portions dealing with the juridical status of crusaders were not included in Gregory's collection, thereby denying the Decretalists a convenient point of departure for discussion of the operations of the crusades.[192] The virtually unlimited extension of the concept of heresy to include all those contemptuous of ecclesiastical discipline led to a spate of decretals dealing with the persecution of heretics, of which perhaps the most important was canon 3, *Excommunicamus*, of the Fourth Lateran Council (X. 5.7.13). According to this decretal heretics were to be excommunicated and then punished by secular justice and their property was to be confiscated. Secular princes were further required to purge their territories of heresy under penalty of excommunication. Should a prince remain excommunicated for more than a year, the pope should free his vassals from their oaths of fealty to him and expose his territory to conquest, confiscation and expulsion of heretics by orthodox catholics who could make the territory their own as long as they respected the rights of its superior lord. These orthodox catholics, whether princes or ordinary laymen, in acting as agents of papal authority were entitled to the privileges accorded to crusaders to the Holy Land. Princes who did not persecute heretics were in effect treated as heretics themselves. Other decretals in the

---

[191] Among the copious bibliography on the subject several useful works may be cited: Bridrey, *La condition juridique des croisés*; Pissard, *La guerre sainte*; Villey, *La croisade*; idem, 'L'idée de croisade,' *Storia del medioevo*. (*Relazione del X. Congresso Internazionale de Scienze Storiche*, vol. 3, 1955), 565–94; Brundage, *Canon Law and the Crusader*.

[192] For the most recent discussion of the fate of this constitution, see Brundage, *ibid.*, pp. 82f. Other decretals condemning trade with the enemy include x. 5.6.6, 11, 12, the first canon coming from Alexander III, and the others from Innocent III.

same title detailed the punishment of heretics, those who associated with them and princes who refused to cooperate with the Church.[193] From this brief survey of crusading legislation it appears that the Decretalists were provided with few specific statements that could serve as points of departure for a treatment that related the crusades to the just war. Warfare itself was not even mentioned. The Decretalists would have to make their own way through this problem without legislative aid.

Since the Decretalists saw the crusades as a form of repression appropriate to Saracens and heretics, legitimation of the idea of the crusade was not a difficult task. Indeed, the just war itself had been nourished in the seedbed of ecclesiastical persecutions of heresy during the late Roman Empire. The general principles of such persecutions were found in Roman law and Augustine's writings as excerpted in Gratian's Decretum. Still, the problem remained whether Saracens and other infidels and pagans deserved to suffer a crusade merely because they were non-Christians, or because they committed overt crimes against Christians. At stake was whether Saracens could be tolerated in their own territories outside the Holy Land. The early Decretalists often could not agree on the reasons why Saracens deserved to be the targets of Christian crusades. Alanus Anglicus gave as a vague reason their contumacious resistance to Christians, and went on to explain that Saracens merited spoliation and corporal punishment. Any means short of killing them could be employed to accomplish their conversion, and Christian princes licitly waged war on them and expelled them from their territories. Then Alanus cited without comment the divergent opinion that Christians should merely defend themselves from Saracen attacks rather than attacking them.[194] Significant here is Alanus' express use

---

[193] x. 5.7.8–10. The first decretal was taken from the famous canon 27 of the Third Lateran Council of 1179 that also prescribed the punishment of routiers. This latter portion was included in the Compilatio Prima (5.6.7) but not in the Gregorian collection. Had the two portions been included together, the connection between punishment of heresy and repression of illicit violence might have been more coherently discussed. Cf. above, n. 175. The two other canons were from Lucius III and Innocent III. The basis of the right to confiscate the property of heretics came from Augustinian passages contained in the Decretum, C. 23 q. 7.

[194] Alanus, *Apparatus: 'Ius Naturale,'* to C. 23 q. 4 d. p. c. 36, v. *rationabiliter*, B.N. Lat. 15393, fol. 186va and Mazar. 1318, fol. 283ra: 'quidam nobis resistunt contumaciter, ut Saraceni ...resistentes vero bonorum subtractione et flagellis corporalibus citra mortem ad fidem possumus compellere...unde Christiani principes licite bella indicunt et a sedibus eos

of *bellum* to apply to the crusades. He went on to deny Saracens and heretics the right to hold property, exercise jurisdiction, use force or enact laws. Only Christians had the right to wage war, and by this right they despoiled infidels and heretics.[195] Alanus was inconsistent, however, for in another passage he himself subscribed to the restriction that Saracens should only be fought when they had just attacked Christians, while peaceful Saracens should be left alone. He betrayed a similar tolerant attitude in allowing Christian knights to serve under infidels when they had been enslaved in a just war, or if such knights held territories from them.[196] Alanus here answered, in contradiction to his other statements, that Saracens could govern territories and wage just wars. Thus was the issue joined: Saracens either were entitled to certain temporal rights, or their power had no legal standing and their holdings were denied legal protection. While Alanus tacitly straddled the issue, Raymond of Peñafort and William of Rennes were inclined to tolerate Saracen control over their own territories, although they emphatically denied the legitimacy of Saracen jurisdiction over territories formerly under Christian control.[197] Since much of Saracen territory had been ruled by the Roman Empire, their toleration was of a limited sort, although the

expellere...alii tamen dicunt quod ab eis nos debemus defendere et non impetere.' *Ibid.*, to C. 23 q. 7 c. 2, v. *possident*, B.N. Lat. 15393, fol. 194va and Mazar. 1318, fol. 389va.

[195] *Ibid.*, to C. 23 q. 7 c. 1, v. *appellatis*, Mazar. 1318, fol. 389rb–va: 'ecclesiasticis, in quibus nichil iuris habent heretici...immo nec proprias habent nec habere possunt...Item ius de sarracenis dici potest. quid utique non enim habent vim quibus eis quicquam habere liceat, cum potestatem condendi iura non habeant, nec iurisdictionem...Sic ergo eis qui ius indicendi bellum habent, licet ab omnibus talibus tamquam iniustis possessionibus auferre ea que possident...solis fidelibus debentur...vel dicatur quod omnes predicti dominium habent rerum que sue dicuntur quousque eis iuste auferantur. Auferri autem possunt ab his qui habent legitimam potestatem.'

[196] *Ibid.*, to C. 23 q. 8 c. 11, v. *pellunt*, B.N. Lat. 15393, fol. 195va: 'aliter non debemus pugnare bellum. Enim debet esse necessitas.' Cf. the variant reading: *ibid.*, Mazar. 1318, fol. 290va: 'Alii dicunt quod non nisi se suaque ab illis defendendo vel recuperando.' *Ibid.*, to C. 11 q. 3 c. 94, v. *Christianos*, B.N. Lat. 15393, fol. 137vb and Mazar. 1318, fol. 199vb: 'Queritur an hodie Christianis militibus liceat sub infidelibus principibus militare. Respondeo utique si legitima obnoxietate eis sint obligati, puta sunt capti ab ipsis in iusto bello, vel tenent ab ipsis territorias, ut [x. 5.6.2.].' Laurentius, *Apparatus*, to C. 23 q. 8 c. 11, v. *dispar*, B.N. Lat. 3903, fol. 193rb: 'videtur ergo quod Sarraceni non sequantur Christianos, quod non possumus eos.' *Ibid.*, to C. 23 q. 8 c. 11, v. *Sarracenorum*, B.N. Lat. 15393, fol. 195va: 'si Sarraceni vellint vivere in quiete et nobis subditi esse, non debemus eos expugnare vel sua eis auferre. [Cod. 1.11.6 and Cod. 1.9.14], La.'. For a more detailed consideration of the problem of toleration, see Herde, 'Christians and Saracens.' Cf. Huguccio's earlier treatment, above, ch. 4, nn. 119–24.

[197] Raymond of Peñafort, *Summa de Casibus*, 2.5.14, p. 180ab. William of Rennes, *Glossa*, to 2.5.14, v. *persolvere*, p. 184b.

Decretalists did not use this historical fact to justify crusades against all Saracen territories.

Johannes de Deo expressly considered the crusades to the Holy Land as meriting the title of a just war. He changed the term *pro rebus repetendis* to *pro rebus defendendis*, thus rendering just a war waged in defense of property. By this means a war against the Saracens was supremely just (*bellum iustissimum*), for Saracens were unjustly occupying lands that rightfully belonged to Christians. He even saw the threat that Saracens were plotting to seize more Christian territories. Perhaps with the example of Frederick II in mind, he extended his *bellum iustissimum* to include wars against excommunicates.[198] Thus Johannes de Deo rendered explicit the conclusion, logically implicit in the writings of other canonists, that the crusades to the Holy Land were justified not by the infidelity of the Saracens but by their *de facto* possession of territories that rightfully belonged to Christians, yet he did not explain just what were these territories. After him and Alanus Anglicus, however, the Decretalists admitted that the crusades qualified as just wars rather than as some other sort of legitimate violence.

It was Innocent IV and his pupil Hostiensis who provided the conclusive discussion of Christian claims to territories ruled by infidels. Innocent denied that Christians could make war on Saracens merely because they were infidels, and expressly prohibited wars of conversion. But when Saracens invaded Christian territories or attacked Christians, both the Church and the Christian prince of the territory could wage a just war to avenge their injuries and losses. If Saracens refused to render customary tribute to a Christian prince, he could wage a just war on them, but he lacked Church support when Saracens neither polluted Christian territories with their sordid practices nor attacked Christians. When Saracens occupied the Holy Land the case was very different, for then either the Church or any Christian prince could make war on them since Saracen possession of the Holy Land was an offense to Christ and all Christians.[199]

---

[198] Johannes de Deo, *Liber Poenitentiarius*, 6. 2, B.N. Lat. 14703, fol. 108va: 'Sed iustum bellum... ubi describitur iustum bellum, scilicet pro rebus defendendis vel etiam repetendis. Cum sit iustum bellum contra saracenos immo iustissimum qui vestras terras per iniusticiam detinent occupatas... et intendunt occupare si possent... Cum sepe est enim iustum bellum contra excommunicatos.'

[199] Innocent IV, *Commentaria*, to X. 3.42.4. para. 5, fol. 456rb.

Innocent thus left to the prince of a threatened territory the authority to wage a defensive war, but this war was not a crusade. Since as a *res sancta* the Holy Land belonged to all Christians, any prince could wage war in its defense for the benefit of all. Outside of the Holy Land infidels could hold property and territory without sin, and neither the pope nor other Christians had the right to take these away. Yet the pope as vicar of Christ retained a measure of *de jure* authority over infidels by which he could punish them for actions committed contrary to natural law, just as God had punished the Sodomites.[200]

While Saracens and other infidels could exercise legitimate dominion without sin, the Holy Land belonged without question to Christianity, for it was so consecrated by the life and death of Christ and there only Christ, not Mohammed, was to be worshipped. After the death of Christ it was conquered by the Roman Emperor in a just war, whence the pope by reason of his accession to the Empire could return to his own jurisdiction both the Holy Land and even other territories formerly under Roman dominion. Even if the objection that the Church only had *imperium* in the West were granted, the pope could still exercise dominion over the Holy Land in his capacity as vicar of Christ, and similarly the Emperor as rightful king of Jerusalem could secure his jurisdiction there. (Innocent was careful not to distract attention from his main theme by injecting a polemical discussion of the conflicting papal and imperial claims to jurisdiction into the argument.) In other lands held by infidels but which formerly had been ruled by Christian princes the pope could order infidel princes not to molest their Christian subjects unjustly, but when they flagrantly did so the pope could depose them from their jurisdictions. The pope further had the right to command infidel princes to allow the preaching of Christian missionaries, within their territory, and when such missionaries were hindered the pope could punish the princes. In all these cases of papal jurisdiction over infidels Innocent safeguarded the papal right in the last resort to declare war on them.[201] Throughout this passage Innocent's cautious attitude was evident, for while he safeguarded the pope's universal jurisdic-

[200] *Ibid.*, to X. 3.34.8. paras. 3–4, fol. 430rb. For further discussion of papal jurisdiction over non-Christians, see J. Muldoon, ' "Extra Ecclesiam non est Imperium." The Canonists and the Legitimacy of Secular Power,' *Studia Gratiana*, IX (1966), 553–80.

[201] *Ibid.*, paras. 7, 10, fol. 430rb-va.

tion in theory, he clearly intended to withdraw papal support from rash Christian attacks on Saracen territories other than the Holy Land.[202] In his caution Innocent also refused to justify a papal monopoly over military expeditions to the Holy Land by allowing the Emperor and other Christian princes to wage their own just wars there. Hostiensis' attitude was somewhat less cautious, for although he followed Innocent's commentary to this decretal, elsewhere he considered any war waged between Christians and infidels to be just on the Christian side by the merit of their faith alone.[203] Yet in his final opinion Saracens who lived peacefully within the Empire were to be left alone, while those who refused to recognise the dominion of the Roman Church and the Roman Empire merited Christian attacks.[204]

The common opinion emerging from these debates was that peaceful Saracens and infidels outside of the Holy Land were to be left in peace provided they neither infringed upon Christian territories nor hindered the Church in the pursuit of its mission. In practical terms a crusade against infidels was limited to those who occupied the Holy Land itself. The Decretalists thus chose to build the toleration of infidels first broached by Huguccio rather than to elaborate on the unqualified intolerance of Saracens that the *Summa: 'Inperatorie Maiestati'* advanced as justification for the Crusades.[205]

Quite different was the Decretalist attitude toward crusades against heretics, for as wicked Christians they were not entitled to any toleration or legal rights whatsoever. Peter of Salins contrasted the tolerance to be shown toward peaceful Saracens with the denial of rights to property and jurisdiction to heretics of his own day, whom he compared to the enemies of imperial Rome.[206] By the thirteenth

---

[202] Innocent showed little enthusiasm for the crusade of Louis IX: E. Berger, *Saint Louis et Innocent IV*, cited in Villey, *La croisade*, p. 266.

[203] Hostiensis, *Lectura*, to x. 3.34.8. paras. 8–17, pp. 128–128A; and idem, *Summa*, to x. 1.34. para. 4, p. 358: 'notabis quod multiplex est bellum. Unum, quod est inter fideles et infideles, et hoc iustum est, respectu fidelium.' (x. 5.7.13.)

[204] Hostiensis, *Summa*, to x. 5.6. para. 3, p. 1523: 'Qualiter ergo ipsos Christiani debeant se habere? Et quidem degentes sub imperio, non debent impugnare nec in eos saevire, alias puniuntur. alii autem, qui dominium Romanae ecclesiae non recognoscunt, sive imperii Romani, impugnandi sunt.'

[205] For the varying Decretist attitudes toward Saracens, see above, ch. 4, nn. 91–101, 119–24.

[206] Peter of Salins, *Lectura*, to C. 23 q. 8 c. 11, B.N. Lat. 3917, fol. 190va; *ibid.*, to C. 23 q. 7 pr., c. 2, v. *alioquin*, c. 4, v. *res hereticorum*, B.N. Lat. 3917, fols. 188vb–189vb; *ibid.*, to C. 23 q. 4 c. 48, B.N. Lat. 3917, fol. 182va. Cf. Johannes Teutonicus, *Glossa Ordinaria*,

century the concept of heresy had become so broad that any distinction between brigands, criminals and heretics, and between peaceful and aggressive heretics had become purely theoretical and academic and was therefore disregarded by the Decretalists.[207] Thus to a canon that detailed papal efforts against enemies of the faith (*inimici sanctae fidei*) Johannes Teutonicus supplied a gloss that portrayed the pope as exhorting others to fight against the enemies of the Church (*inimici ecclesiae*). The Church indeed felt itself to be threatened by countless enemies within its own midst, and had already waged the bloody Albigensian Crusade. Only Innocent IV sounded a note of caution when he counseled the papacy to use discretion in its legitimate punishment of Christians, refusing to inflict such punishment when it lacked sufficient resources or when it was feared that punishment might result in danger or scandal.[208] Thus, while canonists had for a long time justified corporal punishment of heresy and confiscation of heretical property on ecclesiastical authority, they had yet to relate these punishments to the crusades. Hostiensis provided what passed for a formula of the crusades when he justified the unlimited Roman war waged by Christians against infidels,[209] but nothing of the sort was forthcoming for crusades against heretics. To this point theory had lagged far behind practice, and it remained to be seen what distinguished crusades against infidels and heretics from ordinary just wars waged on ecclesiastical authority.

While it was generally recognised that the pope alone could declare and direct a crusade, the Gregorian decretals were silent on the question. After more than a century of crusading activity the Decretalists were still faced with the necessity finally to take an unambiguous position on the authority necessary to initiate a crusade. Innocent III was clearly displeased when the crusaders attacked Constantinople without his permission during the Fourth Crusade, and so he took a more direct command over the Albigensian Crusade.[210] Innocent IV had justified the crusades waged on

to C. 23 q. 7, pr., v. *nunc autem*, B.N. Lat. 14317, fol. 195vb; Laurentius, *Apparatus*, to C. 23 q. 7, pr., v. *nunc autem*, B.N. Lat. 3903, fol. 192rb.

[207] Indicative of this conflation of categories is of course canon 27 of the Third Lateran Council. Cf. above, nn. 175, 193 and Pissard, *La guerre sainte*, pp. 31f.

[208] Innocent IV, *Commentaria*, to x. 3.34.8. para. 6, fol. 430rb.

[209] Hostiensis, cited above, n. 6.

[210] Innocent III, *Registrum*, VI, 102, P.L. 215, p. 107f. Cf. Duval, *De la paix de Dieu*, pp. 58–60. Gregory IX considered himself 'dux et magister' of armies defending the catholic faith:

papal initiative against the Holy Land; since he had not explicitly restricted the right to direct a crusade to the pope, it was still theoretically possible that a prince or bishop could undertake a crusade on his own initiative, as had Frederick II. Could the impetus for a crusade stem from a specific divine revelation to an especially holy person such as Bernard of Clairvaux, or did the initiative derive solely from papal legislative omnicompetence? Peter of Salins' unsophisticated view was more appropriate to the period of the First Crusade, for he likened wars waged on divine authority or inspiration to the spoliation of the Egyptians by the Jews, where the warriors merely exercised God's will, although they should also have prior public authority.[211] With Laurentius Hispanus and Johannes Teutonicus he required the authorisation of lords and kings to despoil heretics, for otherwise the people of God would be suspected of cupidity.[212]

The *Glossa Ordinaria* to the Gregorian decretals restricted the authority to declare war on enemies of the faith to the Church that alone could promote such wars by granting indulgences for crusades against both Saracens and heretics.[213] It was thus in the context of indulgences that the Decretalists formulated their position on authority. For Raymond of Peñafort the duty to defend Church property and the faith rested with bishops and ecclesiastical judges, who could invoke the secular arm to purge their territories of heretics and to recover territory in infidel hands. Two sorts of pressure were available to prelates to force compliance from secular lords, for they could both censure princes and grant them remission of sins. Bishops who failed to invoke both the carrot and the stick sinned and should be deposed from office.[214] Raymond evidently feared that if the position of Laurentius, Johannes Teutonicus and Peter of Salins were

---

Ullmann, *Growth of Papal Government*, p. 306, n. 5. On the basis of this authority he ordered certain bishops on the pain of censure to hasten to Rome with troops to defend the Roman church against attack by Frederick II: *ibid.*, p. 296, n. 1.

[211] Peter of Salins, *Lectura*, to C. 23 q. 2 c. 2, v. *novit quid*, B.N. Lat. 3917, fol. 173rb; *ibid.*, to C. 23 q. 5, pr., B.N. Lat. 3917, fol. 183vb; cf. *ibid.*, to C. 23 q. 1 c. 5, cited above, n. 190.

[212] Above, n. 206.

[213] *Glossa Ordinaria*, to X. 5.7.13, v. *accinxerint*: 'arg. quod auctoritate ecclesiae bellum fieri potest...quod verum est contra inimicos fidei et contra illos qui ecclesiam impugnant... *si qui vero*...Item auctoritate ecclesiae bellum fieri potest. Item pari privilegio et indulgentia gaudent cruce signati contra haereticos, cum illis qui vadunt contra Sarracenos.' Cf. Durantis, *Speculum*, 4, partic. 3, para. 7, III, 489f.

[214] Raymond of Peñafort, *Summa de Casibus*, 2.1.10, p. 157ab; quoted above, n. 180.

not qualified, secular princes would see in the canon *Excommuni-camus* (X. 5.7.13) a general authorisation for them to undertake wars on their own authority. This would have the effect of assuming secular control over crusades against heretics, whereas the canonists assumed without question that such punishment was within the sphere of ecclesiastical jurisdiction. In response to the possibility that all catholics could despoil heretics on their own authority without regard to orderly legal procedures, Raymond required a special edict of the prince or the Church to prevent wars waged out of greed and cruelty.[215] Still, this did not sufficiently limit the authority to wage crusades, and Hostiensis, in citing Raymond's opinion, unambiguously restricted that authority to ecclesiastical judges, and barred secular princes from confiscation of heretical property.[216] While the locus of authority was now confined solely to the Church, it remained to determine what distinguished a crusade from a mere war against heretics and infidels.

It was when the doctrine of indulgences was linked to the just war that the juridical theory of the crusades was born. The canonists' theory of indulgences had developed independently of the just war theories before the thirteenth century, and only now were indulgences seen explicitly as an aspect of the Church's promotion of wars waged on its own authority.[217] At the hands of Innocent IV and Hostiensis this juridical theory underwent its maturation. For Innocent, only the pope had the right to grant indulgences to promote crusades in defense of the Holy Land and the Christians dwelling there.[218] Hostiensis limited authority for the crusades even more strictly to the pope when he asserted that the authority to grant full indulgences was based on the pope's singular possession of the *plenitudo potestatis*.[219] The preaching of the cross thus became the symbolic act by which the pope initiated a crusade; without it no Church war, however justified, could rightfully enjoy the status of the crusade. Hostiensis then turned to the question of whether a

[215] *Ibid.*, 1.5.3, pp. 39b–40a. Goffredus (*Summa*, to x. 5.7 para. 4, fol. 220ra) and Monaldus (*Summa, Qua pena hereticus punitur*, fol. 83) were also in agreement. Cf. Pissard, *La guerre sainte*, p. 114.
[216] Hostiensis, *Summa*, to x. 5.7. para. 5, pp. 1534–5.
[217] For a closer examination of the development of crusade indulgences, see Brundage, *Canon Law and the Crusader*, pp. 145–55.
[218] Innocent IV, *Commentaria*, to x. 3.34.8. para. 9, fol. 430va.
[219] Hostiensis, *Lectura*, to x. 5.6.17. paras. 19–20, p. 34.

lesser prelate could preach a crusade on papal authority.[220] The length of his exposition indicates the importance he attached to the problem.

Hostiensis' discussion focused first on the general justification for waging crusades and thus included crusades against heretics, schismatics and rebels. He cited the objection, current in German imperial circles, that crusades should not be waged against Christians because explicit legal justification was lacking. (The unnamed proponents of this view obviously recognised that the Church's right to wage such crusades was the very basis for papal efforts to combat Frederick II.) In rejecting this opinion Hostiensis first observed, somewhat curiously, that since the legal vocabulary of his time was insufficient to describe every situation, an explicit law authorising such crusades was unnecessary. Authorisation was forthcoming by analogy with similar situations explicitly treated in law, and furthermore even natural reason showed that such criminals should be punished.[221] Hostiensis then distinguished between the *crux transmarina* proper to crusades to the Holy Land and the *crux cismarina* as the authoritative initiative for crusades within Europe. He deemed these latter crusades even more necessary than those to the Holy Land, since Christ taught Christians to expend more diligence for the care of their souls than for the sake of material possession, and the threat to Christian souls was all the more pressing where heresy was concerned. To support his point Hostiensis even adduced a Roman law citation.[222] Similarly the crusade waged against an excommunicated prince was called for if after a year of excommunication and interdict he remained contumacious, for such a situation encouraged the extension of heresy. Hostiensis admitted that a crusade to the Holy Land appeared more favorable to simple souls, but still concluded that the crusade against European enemies of the Church was more reasonable and just.[223]

Only after extensive discussion of the justification did Hostiensis state conclusively that the single locus of authority for the crusade

220 *Ibid.*, to x. 5.7.13. para. 15, v. *accinxerint*, p. 39: 'Ar. quod authoritate ecclesiae bellum fieri potest...quod verum est contra inimicos fidei, vel contra eos, qui ecclesiam impugnant, secundum B[ernard Botone; above, n. 213]. vel ei rebelles existunt... crux tamen praedicari non potest, nisi de papae licentia speciali, sicut nec nomen ipsius redimi.'

221 Hostiensis, *Summa*, to x. 3.34. para. 19, p. 1141.

222 Id., *ibid.*, pp. 1141f.

223 Id., *ibid.*, p. 1142.

was the pope in his capacity as the chief agent and vicar of Christ responsible for the faith. But then, what about wars waged against heretics by other bishops who had temporal and spiritual jurisdiction? Were these wars not deserving of the status of the crusade? Hostiensis indeed granted such bishops the right to declare war, but denied their wars the status of the crusade. Bishops lacked the authority to preach a crusade for three reasons: they were not empowered to grant the remission of sins by indulgence; the pope alone had the duty to respond to such great threats to the faith; and he alone had jurisdiction over the crusaders' vow. Any prelate's war that was proper to his spiritual jurisdiction was an ordinary just war waged without the seal of the cross (*sine crucis signaculo*).[224] Too occupied with his crusade against Frederick II, Innocent IV was unable to elaborate systematically its juridical status. Enjoying the leisure denied his papal teacher, Hostiensis accomplished the task and thereby merits Villey's opinion that he was the father of the juridical theory of the crusade.[225] He went straight to the crux of the theory when he reserved the right to proclaim the crusade to the pope alone. In a sense Hostiensis' position served to limit recourse to a crusade, and its awesome arsenal of rights and privileges, although his extension of the purposes for which the pope could proclaim a crusade ensured that the crusade would continue to be invoked as the papacy's ultimate weapon against any and all of its enemies. Heresy seemed as the paradigmatic case that justified any ecclesiastical resort to warfare against its European enemies.

The theoretical shape of the crusades had thus become more clearly defined, and the scattered opinions of earlier Decretalists took on sharp focus. Princes were obligated to obey the Church's call to conduct a crusade to protect the Church and the faithful within their territories, and should they refuse obedience they themselves were in danger of having a crusade preached against them in which every catholic who participated acted as a justiciar or special papal agent. The Church was thus freed from its earlier obligation to use the secular arm as its intermediary in exterminating heresy, especially when a territory ravaged by heresy lacked a suzerain, as in the case

---

[224] Hostiensis, *Summa*, to X. 3.34. paras. 19–20, pp. 1142f.
[225] Cf. Villey, *La croisade*, pp. 256f.; Brundage, *Canon Law and the Crusader*, p. 114, n. 152. Hostiensis was of course not the first to discuss the crusades juridically.

of the Albigensian Crusade. The papacy had the right to seize the initiative itself and dispose of contaminated territories that it offered as booty. The fighting of wars out of lust for booty that the Church ordinarily condemned, it now, ironically, invoked to encourage participation in its own crusades even without the consent of a suzerain, who was consequently forced to accept those Christian soldiers as new vassals by right of conquest. Whereas earlier persecution of heretics had been only internal operations undertaken by individual princes, now the whole panoply of papal prerogatives was employed. The crusade thus served as the papal just war, where the pope directly exercised all those rights over the participation, conduct and consequences that sovereign lords employed in ordinary just wars.[226]

As a special type of warfare the crusades ideally required some modification of the usual modes of conduct and legal consequences. Thus the pope and his prelates, however deeply they were involved in a crusade, were neither to order the death or mutilation of anyone nor to fight themselves. All means of waging war were licit, although truces were to be maintained with Saracens. Since heretics were effectively outlawed there could be no truces made with them. While the Gregorian decretals prohibited Christians from selling war materials to Saracens, they differed over whether Christians could carry on commerce in non-military items with the Saracens in time of truce.[227] Raymond of Peñafort did condemn Christians who seized Saracen property during a truce and obliged them to make restitution. They could also be punished by the Christian prince who had concluded the truce, from which punishment Raymond curiously exempted the Templars.[228] In keeping with the Decretalist tolerance of peaceful infidel dominion Raymond allowed Christians to pay taxes and tolls to infidel rulers in return for their protection. On the other hand when Christians conveyed the prohibited goods

[226] Johannes Teutonicus, *Glossa Ordinaria*, to C. 23 q. 4 c. 39, v. *pacatam*; x. 5.7.13; Goffredus, *Summa* (Lyons, 1519), to x. 5.7. para. 5, fol. 207vb. Cf. Pissard, *La guerre sainte*, pp. 27f., 37–9, 89, 113. In view of these papal rights over the crusades as well as the right of prelates with jurisdiction to direct just wars, it appears that Pissard (*ibid.*, p. 92) understated the Church's direct role when he concluded that the canonists denied the Church the right to execute a war. Cf. above, nn. 178–80, 184–6.

[227] Cf. above, n. 192 and Goffredus, *Summa*, to x. 5.6, fol. 199rb. I have not found any discussion that dealt explicitly with the question of truces with heretics. There was no locus classicus for such a discussion.

[228] Raymond of Peñafort, *Summa de Casibus*, 2.5.12.18, p. 187b. This is the only mention I have found of the military orders.

to Saracens even in time of truce, they were not bound to make any restitution or pay any taxes, but were rather to undergo penance and contribute their profits either for redemption of Christian captives or to aid those who were fighting for the Christian faith.[229] By contrast, an apparatus to a canon in the *Compilatio Quinta* included in the Gregorian collection condemned as a perjurer any Christian who, after swearing not to trade with the Saracens unless there was peace, nevertheless carried on commerce with them in time of truce. Other Christians who had not taken the oath were, however, obliged to observe the truce.[230] The Decretalist opinions on proper Christian conduct toward Saracens did not constitute a full and systematic treatment but rather mirrored their ambiguous attitudes.

In keeping with the spiritual purposes of the crusades the Decretalists constructed a system of beneficial spiritual consequences for crusaders that were set in motion by the vow the crusader took when he assumed the cross. The crusader's vow, which had evolved from the pilgrimage vow, was similar in function to a vassal's feudal oath, for by it the papacy was able to require his participation and obedience in a crusade. Such vows could be inherited, or in some cases commuted to the performance of another task, and thus the papacy was able to exert its authority over crusaders in even more ways, as when the papacy commuted vows to fight in the Holy Land to vows to go on a crusade against heretics. Just as a vassal had certain rights attendant upon his participation in his lord's war, so also the crusader enjoyed special privileges pertaining to his status, such as the privilege of the Church forum, exemption from taxes and protection of his lands from armed aggression by his neighbors. While the canonists attempted to construct a theory of obligations that crusaders must fulfill, they were more concerned with the dispensation, commutation or redemption of the vow rather than with its fulfillment.[231] Raymond of Peñafort did give cursory attention to the

---

[229] *Ibid.*, 2.5.14.10, p. 180ab. Alternatively Raymond allowed Christian princes to confiscate contraband property and enslave those dealing in it: *ibid.*, 2.33.10, pp. 387b–388a. Raymond's toleration of taxes paid to infidels was quoted in Vincent of Beauvais, *Speculum Doctrinale*, XI. 65.

[230] *Apparatus*, to Comp. V. 5.17.1, v. *pacem*. Douai. 596, fol. 28vb. Cf. *Glossa Ordinaria*, to X. 5.6.11, vv. *post treugam, non absolvit*.

[231] The crusade vow, its obligations and its spiritual and temporal privileges have most recently been treated by Brundage, *Canon Law and the Crusader*, chs. 3-6. Tancredus first

remission of sins for those who fought to defend the faith and the *patria*, although he did not expressly link these remissions with the crusade vow,[232] and on the strength of a decretal of Innocent III the *Glossa Ordinaria* permitted crusaders preparing to depart for the Holy Land to undergo penance even when the territory in which they were located was under interdict.[233]

It was obvious that Christians could seize the Holy Land and hold it as their own, but what about heretical territory? Departing from the universally recognised principle that the property of heretics, like that of all other enemies, could be confiscated in a just war, Johannes Teutonicus accorded to the pope the jurisdiction over captured heretical property. In glossing a decretal that did not find its way into the Gregorian collection, he noted that the pope had gained control over spoils acquired during the Albigensian Crusade, but according to the general principle he was bound to share them with the knight who captained the battle, in this case Simon de Montfort.[234] In such crusades even a whole city could be put to the torch if it contained some heretics.[235] The Decretalists somewhat clumsily grafted their sketchy views on the conduct and consequences of the crusades onto their more general analysis of the same problems in the just war. They were more explicit when they considered the general problem of heresy and rebellion against ecclesiastical authority. After all, the crusade was only one means among many of dealing with the pest of heresy. While it would have been less disappointing if they had devoted more attention to the purpose and limits of the crusades against heretics, the relative silence of the Decretalists indicates beyond the shadow of doubt that they viewed such crusades as a special category of the just war entitled to its full legal status.

Yet in confounding just war and crusade the Decretalists raised fundamental questions about the role force should play in the return

expressly linked the vow to the crusade: *ibid.*, p. 74, n. 22. Cf. Villey, 'L'idée de croisade,' pp. 582-8.

[232] Raymond of Peñafort, *Summa de Casibus*, 2.1.10, p. 157ab; quoted above, n. 180.

[233] *Glossa Ordinaria*, to X. 5.38.11, (*Casus*) and v. *poenitentia*.

[234] Johannes Teutonicus, *Apparatus*, to Comp. IV. 5.5.1, v. *Montis fortis*, B.N. Lat. 3931A, fol. 253va; B.N. Lat. 3932, fol. 229vb; and B.N. Lat. 12452, fol. 133vb: 'sed nonne ea que capiuntur in licito bello cedunt occupanti?... Respondeo immo illi cedunt qui est princeps exercitus, scilicet papa, et ille tenetur dividere inter alios secundum merita eorum, ut (C. 23 q. 5 c. 25; D. 1 c. 10). Jo.' Cf. Johannes and Laurentius, cited above, n. 206.

[235] Johannes Teutonicus, *Glossa Ordinaria*, to C. 23 q. 5 c. 32, v. *omnes*, B.N. Lat. 14317, fol. 193ra.

of heretics to the orthodox fold. The problem had tormented Augustine, and in their makeshift adaptation of the crusades against heretics to the just war they neglected to consider thoroughly the efficacy and the advisability of the use of force for spiritual purposes. In their conception, concerted persecution of heresy operated at the nebulous boundary between the just war and a holy war waged by anyone in his own interpretation of divine inspiration. The holy war was domesticated by its submission to papal authority, but under this veneer of authority the war of extermination, unlimited violence and greed continued to lurk. When they did not expressly restrict the crusade against heretics as they had other just wars or even the crusades against the Saracens, the Decretalists created a monster in theory as papal policy was doing in practice. Ironically, by denying or at least by not affirming that such crusades were subsumed under the normal laws of war and by considering heretics as outside the law, they sabotaged the development of those laws upon whose observance they had otherwise insisted so strongly. In effect they did not give the crusades the treatment they deserved, but rather expressed opinions that dwelt at length on general principles to the detriment of practical deductions from those principles. They did not even have in their vocabulary a word that corresponded to 'crusade,' and were content to use such circumlocutions as 'pilgrimage,' 'journey,' and 'expedition,' or, in the case of heretics, 'extermination.' For the most part it was canonistic commentary on the decretals that clarified the just war theories, but for the crusades against heretics the military rhetoric of the decretals themselves was more indicative of canonistic attitudes.

While the theory of the crusades only appeared after crusading activity had lost much of its importance, at least in expeditions to the Holy Land, the essential features of the crusade were recognised much earlier, even if the definitive formulation only emerged with Hostiensis. In effect there were three levels to the Church's wars against its enemies. It could first invoke the secular arm, then prelates could take the initiative and direct the operations, and finally the pope could preach and direct the crusade.[236] While the Decretalists had portrayed the just war as one waged with full legal consequences by a sovereign prince, Hostiensis portrayed the crusade as

[236] Cf. Pissard, *La guerre sainte*, pp. iii, n. 2, 83–90, 94.

that war which was waged against infidels and heretics on the authority of the pope who recognised no superior save God Himself.

The Decretalists saw in the just war a legal procedure to achieve a just situation when the *patria* or the Church was threatened with grave harm, and so allowed the use of any means that promised to be effective. The Decretists had rendered the just war the monopoly of legitimate authority, and the Decretalists brought this view more into line with contemporary politics as well as patristic opinion when they made just warfare the monopoly of superior authority. This conclusion was stated succinctly in the early-fourteenth-century *Summa Astesana* that distinguished between two kinds of princes. Those with a superior could not make war against their suzerain but were limited to simple defense against attack and punishment of rebels. Princes with no superiors enjoyed full rights to make war limited only by the elastic dictates of Christian morality. Thus was the Christian just war doctrine accommodated to the emerging public feudal law.[237] When the war was just, the sovereign had a right to expect obedience from his vassals and subjects, and in turn he had responsibility to them for the conduct of the war and for its consequences. Churchmen armed with their own proper jurisdiction had the right to execute wars without any intermediaries when it was incumbent on them to protect the Church, its followers, its property and its faith. To be successful the just war needed manpower, so the just war theories depended in practice on the two factors of authority and spoils. Authority compelled obedience, and the lure of property made such obedience attractive. The prospect of confiscation on a grand scale when coupled with spiritual and legal benefits granted by the papacy made the crusades possible. Realising that it was unrealistic to eliminate warfare in the contemporary context, the Decretalists sought to limit it to purposes useful to obedient princes and Church prelates. The texture of their debates is permeated with the thought of a canonist who never took the opportunity to write a summa, Innocent III, and the climax of those debates came with Innocent IV and Hostiensis. In a sense Hostiensis summed up the debates when he observed with impeccable legal logic that in these cases of warfare he who uses the sword uses it justly, and consequently he who defends himself against such use defends himself

[237] Hubrecht, 'La juste guerre dans la doctrine chrétienne,' p. 117.

rashly.[238] The Decretalists sought to endow the champions of the just cause with abundant spiritual and material advantages and to deprive the unjust warrior of the manpower and resources necessary to render attractive his pursuit of injustice and sin.[239]

[238] Hostiensis, *Summa*, to x. 1.34. para. 4, p. 359.
[239] Cf. Pissard, *La guerre sainte*, p. 115.

Chapter 6

THE MEDIEVAL THEOLOGY OF THE JUST WAR

The twelfth and thirteenth centuries witnessed the maturation of medieval theology into a comprehensive intellectual edifice constructed in the urban cathedral schools of the twelfth century and the universities of the thirteenth century. By about 1140 such luminaries as Abelard and Gilbert de la Porrée had endowed Paris with a reputation as the foremost center for theological study. Through the use of dialectic and the pedagogical method of *lectio–questio–disputatio* Parisian theologians advanced the understanding of Christian doctrine with such success that in the thirteenth century theology attained the status of queen of the sciences. Their study of Christian ethics led them to formulate at length general principles of morality and to apply these formulations to contemporary political activities. The theologians brought to their task not only a knowledge of authoritative texts but also a background of practical experience. Like their canonistic colleagues they were often from the knightly class, and frequently served as prelates. As bishops possessing temporal authority, they owed allegiance and knight service to their overlords, and as church officials they served as papal legates to secular lords and as advisers to popes, councils, and crusades. With a cosmopolitan outlook stemming from their diverse geographical origins and experience, they had more than a passing familiarity with the various feudal, royal, imperial and papal wars of the time.

The basic sources for theological elaboration of just war theories included the Old and New Testaments, the writings of the Church Fathers, and the Sentences of Peter Lombard that appeared about 1150. The formative inspiration for shaping the theories was provided by Augustine and the early medieval ecclesiastics writing within the Augustinian frame of reference, hence most questions on warfare raised by the theologians were posed and resolved by Augustinian texts. The most comprehensive collection of Augustinian and other texts relating to war was Gratian's Decretum, which thereby molded the opinions of the theologians on warfare just as strongly as it did those of the canonists. Another reason for the theologians' dependence on Gratian was that the basic medieval text used for systematic theological exposition, the Sentences of Peter Lombard, did not discuss warfare *ex professo*. Lacking their own locus classicus for consideration of the just war, the theologians were forced to borrow that of the canonists, even continuing to draw upon Gratian's text long after the canonists had shifted their attention to decretal collections. Divergences between canonical and theological opinion were not marked in the twelfth century when the two disciplines were closely allied, but after 1200 theology and canon law became more strictly delimited spheres of competence. These divergences were further accentuated after 1250 when Aristotle joined the Bible and Augustine as a fundamental *auctor* for theological commentary.

Theological thought on war took shape in several literary forms, including commentaries on the Scriptures and the Sentences, theological, disputed and quodlibetal questions and sermons, and commentaries on the works of Aristotle. This chapter studies the major trends in the just war theories, especially the changes in the direction of the theories. Where the theologians agreed substantially with the canonists and Romanists their positions will be more briefly noted.[1]

ATTITUDES TOWARD WAR AND KILLING

The justification of corporal punishment so abundantly prepared by earlier ecclesiastical writers and so conveniently summarised in Gratian's Causa 23 relieved the theologians of the necessity of further

---

[1] This chapter draws heavily on the treatment and citations in Baldwin, *Masters Princes and Merchants*, ch. 10. For surveys of the development of theology in the high Middle Ages, see especially E. Gilson, *History of Christian Philosophy in the Middle Ages* (New York, 1955), which contains extensive biographical and bibliographical footnotes. Cf. also M. D. Chenu, *La théologie au douzième siècle* (2nd ed., Paris, 1966); partially translated into English as *Nature, Man and Society in the Twelfth Century*, trans. J. Taylor and L. Little (Chicago, 1968); idem, *La théologie comme science au xiiie siècle* (Paris, 1957); A. Forest, F. Van Steenberghen and M. de Gandillac, *Le mouvement doctrinal du xie au xive siècle* (Paris, 1956); B. Smalley, *The Study of the Bible in the Middle Ages* (2nd ed., Oxford and New York, 1952); G. de Lagarde, 'La philosophie sociale de Henri de Gand et Godefroid de Fontaines,' *L'organisation corporative du moyen âge à la fin de l'ancien régime*, VII (1943), 55–134. Information about editions and manuscripts of individual authors can be found in P. Glorieux, *Répertoire des maîtres en théologie de Paris au xiiie siècle* (2 vols., Paris, 1933–4); idem, *La littérature quodlibétique de 1260 à 1320* (2 vols., Paris, 1925–35); F. Stegmüller, *Repertorium biblicum medii aevi* (7 vols., Madrid, 1950–61).

protracted consideration of the basic issues. Hence they were able merely to repeat such common assumptions as the motivation of killing by love, and yet their attitudes toward military service and its moral pitfalls influenced the ways in which they approached the just war and led to certain differences of opinion with the canonists. For example, the theologians placed more stress on the moral dimensions of warfare. Writing at the end of the thirteenth century, Henry of Ghent viewed divine inspiration as the motive for David's war with Goliath, since God revealed His will in the outcome of the battle,[2] and other theologians admitted that wars formed part of God's providential plan for mankind. Peter the Chanter a century earlier had viewed warfare as an example of God's punishment of sinful mankind.[3] Bonaventura saw wars as a consequence of the concupiscence that God permitted in order to ruin the wicked and stimulate the good.[4] Peter of Poitiers, however, cautioned against an overly indulgent interpretation of man's duty to wage wars on divine command when he observed that men might sin even when doing God's will,[5] and Robert Pullen saw the avenging hand of God in the Roman conquest of the Jews, but refused to praise the Romans because they were motivated by avarice and other impure motives. God was pleased with the punishment of the Jews, but nevertheless was displeased with Roman intentions and actions.[6] Peter and Robert were especially concerned to prevent the divinely ordered punishment of guilty persons from serving as a pretext for wicked actions. Even justly deserved punishment had to be meted out with good intentions.

At the outset of their discussions of warfare the theologians thus betrayed a more pronounced suspicion of military service than did the canonists, a suspicion that was given even greater force by its inclusion in the Sentences of Peter the Lombard. His only text that dealt expressly with military service, a passage taken from Gregory

[2] Henry of Ghent, *Quodlibetum* 5, 32, *Aurea Quodlibeta* (2 vols., Venice, 1613), I, fol. 315rb.
[3] Peter the Chanter, *Distinctiones Abel*, v. *arma*. B.N. Lat. 455, fol. 60va.
[4] Bonaventura, *Expositio in Lucam* 21. 17 (to Luke 21: 9), *Opera Omnia* (11 vols., Quaracchi, 1882–1902), VII, 526. The *Speculum Conscientiae*, I, 30, dubiously ascribed to Bonaventura, considered wars to arise out of cruelty, a branch of wrath: *ibid.*, VII, 629. Cf. L. Di Fonzo, 'De belli liceitate. Quid censeat S. Bonaventura?' *Miscellanea Francescana*, XLI (1941), 34–48.
[5] Peter of Poitiers, *Sententiarum Libri V*, 4, 4, P.L. 211, p. 1152.
[6] Robert Pullen, *Sententiarum Libri VIII*, 6, 19, P.L. 186, p. 877.

VII, argued that the soldier like the merchant could not exercise his office without sin.[7] Rather than condemning military service as such, however, the passage was concerned to show the falseness or invalidity of a penance undergone by a soldier who had either committed grievous sins, or unjustly seized and held property, or who still harbored hatred in his heart. Only by abandoning his profession and his hatred and by restoring property unjustly seized could his penance be true and valid. He was advised to perform good works so that God would lead him to true penance. On its face the passage did not levy a blanket condemnation of military service but only condemned the opportunities for sinning that often arose during its performance. In essence the viewpoint of the passage was consonant with the tradition, stretching back to Augustine, that condemned the abuse rather than the use of military service. Yet the passage could be seen as ambivalent, for while it cast suspicion on military service it still did not unequivocally forbid war. Subsequent commentators were to use this passage as a major point of departure for discussion of the morality of warfare. The stigma attached to military service and killing remained part of the theological attitude into the thirteenth century. For example Alain of Lille cited a canon taken from Burchard of Worms that enjoined penance for killings committed even on princely authority.[8] Bartholomew of Exeter and Robert of Flamborough condemned someone who in contempt of God attempted to curry the favor of his temporal lord by intentionally committing an unnecessary homicide, and repeated the penitential canons that prohibited return to military service after penance.[9]

The opinions of the penitentials had become outmoded however,

---

[7] Peter the Lombard, *Libri Sententiarum IV*, 4, 16, 3 (2 vols., Quaracchi, 1916), II, 842. The same passage is found in Gratian, De Penit., dist. 5 c. 6. Gratian and his canonistic successors interpreted the passage in the narrowest sense of forbidding a penitent to return to military service after penance except on license from his bishop. As such, the passage did not really condemn warfare or even military service in general, but merely prohibited participation of penitents. Since the Lombard's version did not contain the provision for returning to military service with episcopal permission, it appeared to cast suspicion on the morality of military service itself. Cf. above, ch. 1, n. 73; ch. 3, n. 17; ch. 4, n. 68; ch. 5, n. 95.

[8] Alain of Lille, *Liber Poenitentialis*, 2, 53, ed. J. Longère (2 vols., Louvain and Lille, 1965), II, 74f.

[9] Bartholomew of Exeter, *Penitentiale*, cc. 54, 117, 130, ed. A. Morey, *Bartholomew of Exeter, Bishop and Canonist* (Cambridge, 1937), pp. 221f., 280, 289. Robert of Flamborough, *Liber Poenitentialis*, paras. 239, 269, 348–9, ed. J. J. Francis Firth (Toronto, 1971), pp. 207, 228, 272f.

and theologians were forced by patristic opinion and contemporary practice to attempt a reconciliation between their suspicions and the need to justify military service and warfare. While warfare did not particularly interest Abelard, in his *Sic et Non* he did marshal texts that justified corporal punishment and killing, citing along the way Isidore's definition of the just war and pseudo-Cyprian's imperative that kings had the duty to punish thieves, adulterers, impious men and perjurors. Writing before the appearance of Gratian's Decretum, Abelard did not cite Augustine's crucial definition of the just war, but he did repeat Nicholas I's assertion that war could if necessary be waged at any time.[10] Thomas of Chobham represented more mature theological opinion when he contended that killing was sometimes meritorious, as when it was ordered by a secular judge to safeguard the peace of Church and kingdom. Leaning heavily on Gratian's texts, he went on to say that since judgments of capital punishment were licit, churchmen should encourage secular officials to exercise this judgment provided that they did not single out a specific individual to be killed. It was also licit to kill enemies in a just war in defense of kingdom and justice.[11] William of Auvergne justified killing in a just war when he feared that worship of God would be destroyed if His enemies were spared a just death.[12] The Dominican Hugh of Saint Cher qualified Gregory VII's suspicious attitude when he said that soldiers could exercise their office without sin when they did so with righteous intention and in case of necessity, but that when moved by vainglory or cupidity they were guilty of sin. Yet he could not entirely divest himself of suspicion, for he observed that few soldiers of his time actually did fight for proper motives and thus they were condemned unless they did penance.[13] The Franciscans Jean de la Rochelle, Alexander of Hales and Bonaventura overcame Gregory's suspicion when they interpreted the Sixth Commandment

[10] Abelard, *Sic et Non*, chs. 155, 157, P.L. 178, pp. 1603–9. For the texts he cited, see above, ch. 1, nn. 46, 70. The passage from Pseudo-Cyprian was also cited by Alain of Lille, *De Fide Catholica adversus Haereticos*, 2, 23, P.L. 210, pp. 398f.; idem, *Liber Poenitentialis*, 2, 73, II, 86; also Robert Pullen, *Sententiarum*, 7, 7, P.L. 186, p. 920.

[11] Thomas of Chobham, *Summa Confessorum*, ed. F. Broomfield (Louvain, 1968), pp. 422f., 430.

[12] William of Auvergne, *De Legibus*, 1, *Opera Omnia* (2 vols., Paris, 1624; rep. Frankfurt, 1963), I, 28A.

[13] Hugh of St Cher, *In IV Libros Sententiarum*, to 4, 16, 3, B.N. Lat. 3073, fol. 128rb and B.N. Lat. 3406, fol. 115vb.

as applicable only to killing out of vengeance or lust for killing. The New Testament objections to warfare in general were only to be taken seriously by those Christians who desired to attain perfection, whom they equated with clerics.[14]

Content to assert received opinions on the morality of warfare rather than undertaking their own independent analysis, the theologians cast aside their suspicions of warfare and military service only to have them re-emerge in the form of a denial that men who sought perfection, especially clerics, could undertake such activities without grave danger to their aspirations. While they were unwilling to condemn military service out of hand, their lingering suspicions caused them to place greater emphasis on the individual soldier's responsibility to determine the justice of his acts and correspondingly less emphasis on obedience to authority than did the canonists. More concerned with the spiritual condition of the individual soul, the theologians took greater care in constructing theories of the just war that placed in the forefront the moral purity of the motives and acts with which it was waged.

THE JUST WAR AND ITS FORMULATION

The durable Augustinian definition of the just war as that which avenged injuries passed into theological commentaries by way of the Decretum and continued to serve as point of departure for most subsequent attempts to define the just war. Thus even as late as the 1260s William of Antona saw fit to repeat it.[15] Yet the Augustinian definition appeared as elastic and generalised to the theologians as it had to the canonists, and so both groups felt constrained to advance formulae of greater precision that placed more emphasis upon the motivations of the belligerents. Since Peter the Lombard had not defined the just war, the theologians did not give the definition much attention before the coming of speculative theology in the middle third of the thirteenth century. William of Auvergne emphasised the distinction between just and unjust wars when he deemed one side

---

[14] Jean de la Rochelle, *Summa de Vitiis, utrum bellare licet*, B.N. Lat. 16417, fol. 158vb; Alexander of Hales, *Glossa in IV Libros Sententiarum*, to 3. 37. 5 (4 vols., Quaracchi, 1951–7), III, 465, 487; idem, *Summa Theologiae*, para. 466, resp., ad 2, 4 (4 vols., Quaracchi, 1934–1948), III, 685; Bonaventura, *Commentarium in Evangelium Lucae*, 3, 34 (to Luke 3: 14), *Opera Omnia*, VII, 77.

[15] William of Antona, *Postilla in Josue*, 8, v. *pone insidias*, B.N. Lat. 526, fol. 215vb.

unjust in a war between two peoples,[16] and no other theologian challenged the general opinion that a war could only be just on one side. What, then, were the precise conditions that distinguished just from unjust wars? The Dominican Roland of Cremona pursued an independent course when he deduced a definition based on an interpretation of both Testaments. From the Old Testament he derived the notion that God justified a particular war waged by the Jews, who were obliged to consult Him before joining battle. The Gospel provided Roland with the examples of royal punishment of murderers and marshaling of armies, and he noted that the New Testament contained no unqualified censure for armies but only for armies engaged in an evil war. For a just war Roland constructed three requirements: authority of a prince; maintenance of faith, by which he seemed to mean the Christian faith; and the righteous consciences of both the prince and his warriors. This conviction of conscience must be informed by wise counsel. While Roland deemed many other requirements necessary, he did not elaborate.[17] His view was thus unfortunately incomplete, and evidently inspired little elaboration by others, but it did emphasise the requirement that a war could not be justly fought when conscience dictated otherwise. The Cistercian master Gui de l'Aumône similarly condemned wars that were unjustly fought and then proposed a hybrid formula that combined the definitions of the canonists Rufinus and Raymond of Peñafort. A war was just when it met the requirements of authority, attitude (*affectus*), condition and merit or cause. As such his formula contained no new elements, but Gui did stress the moral rectitude and legal suitability of the just belligerents and the moral culpability of the adversary who thereby deserved to suffer a just war against him.[18]

It remained to the Franciscan theologians to contribute the most extensive formulations of the just war. Taking the lead, Jean de la Rochelle repeated Raymond of Peñafort's five requirements: person, thing (*res*), cause, intention (*animus*), and authority, and

---

16 William of Auvergne, *De Legibus*, 24, *Opera Omnia*, I, 76B.

17 Roland of Cremona, *Summae Liber Tercius*, 264, paras. 1–5, ed. A. Cortesi (Bergamo, 1962), p. 730. In another passage Roland required princely authority to be free of error: *ibid.*, 465, p. 1349.

18 Gui de l'Aumône, *Summa de Diversis Questionibus Theologiae*, 127, B.N. Lat. 14891, fol. 207ra–va. For Rufinus' definition, see above, ch. 4. n. 3; for Raymond's, see above, ch. 5, n. 5.

added that when all five requirements had not been met the war was not only unjust but rapacious. Proper authorities for declaring warfare included kings and the Emperor, as well as the leaders of the ancient Israelites, and just causes included protection of the *patria*, the faith, and peace.[19] Jean strongly influenced his pupil and successor Alexander of Hales, whose massive *Summa Theologiae*, considered to be the compilation of several authors, contained the most extensive list of requirements for a just war.[20] Alexander was able to distinguish six requirements for a just war – authority, attitude, intention, condition, merit and cause – but his explanation of the first five criteria hewed to the conventional Augustinian outlook of his colleague. Departing however from the earlier formulations that considered the avenging of injuries and the necessity of defense as just causes, Alexander's just causes became those overriding moral purposes of Augustine's just war, the alleviation of good men, the coercion of the wicked, and peace for all.[21] In essence Alexander's just causes were overarching moral goals rather than prior legitimating conditions that gave rise to just wars. The just cause was thus elevated from the avenging of injuries suffered to the pursuit of a supreme moral ideal. It is significant that Alexander placed his just cause at the end of his list of criteria rather than in the middle, for this placement emphasised the teleological view of the just war that Thomas Aquinas under Aristotelian influence would soon develop more fully. The greatest luminary of the thirteenth-century Franciscans, Bonaventura, was only minimally interested in the just war, and so after arguing that military service did not contradict the prohibition on avenging one's own injuries he was content to appropriate Jean de la Rochelle's definition of the just war as his justification of military service.[22]

---

[19] Jean de la Rochelle, *Summa de Vitiis, de hiis rapiuntur in bello*, B.N. Lat. 16417, fol. 151ra. Cf. above, n. 14. In the 1280s Gervais du Mont-Saint-Eloi attempted to restate Raymond's fivefold requirements in negative form, thus providing a definition of the unjust war that was the mirror image of Raymond's formula: *Quodlibet* 1, 84, B.N. Lat. 15350, fol. 290ra: cited below, p. 309. The reverse statement had earlier been expressed in the *Glossa Ordinaria*, to C. 23 q. 2 c. 1, v. *quod autem*.

[20] In two Assisi MSS., passages from an anonymous quaestio entitled *De Justo Bello* and from a known work of Jean de la Rochelle contained arguments similar to those advanced by Alexander of Hales: *Summa Theologiae*, III, 678, n. 1 and 683, n. 2. The attribution either to Jean or to Alexander is not crucial for the present discussion.

[21] *Ibid.*, para. 466, resp., ad 3, III, 684f.

[22] Bonaventura, cited above, n. 14. The *Speculum Conscientiae* did contain the three criteria

Thus far the theologians had effected few changes in the definition
of the just war that they borrowed wholesale from the canonists.
Whether they enumerated four, five, or six requirements was of
little consequence, as were the superficial differences in terminology.
Most theologians conventionally assumed that some wars were
justified, but they did insist more strongly than the canonists that
pursuit of perfection was incompatible with military service. Their
insistence on including within the very formulations the requirements of the pure motives and actions of the just warriors and the
prior guilt of the adversary indicated that they considered the just
war to have the moral function of punishing sin as well as injustice.
Unlike the canonists they continued to see war as the avenging
(*ultio*) of injuries, and hence maintained the punitive function of warfare after the canonists had all but discarded that function in favor
of the repulsion of injuries.[23] More emphatically than the canonists
they saw the just war as a moral instrumentality in pursuit of the
ideal of peace.

Included within the theologian's formulations were conventional statements of just causes, and perhaps Henry of Ghent best
summarised the just causes as the recovery of lost goods or the
repulsion of an injury by which the enemy endeavored to take away
such material and spiritual goods as life, liberty, *patria*, laws and
faith.[24] This common opinion did not mean that the just cause was
easy to determine in a complex hostile situation. That the legitimacy
of actual conflicts was often morally suspect was due in part to the
broad nature of the just cause. Solution of the many difficult cases
that the theologians discussed often turned on the question of proper
authority, for after all, the determination of the just cause usually lay
with the legitimate authority who was party to the issue. In a section
of his *Summa* dealing with perplexing questions Robert of Courson
raised the problem of whether denial of the right of free passage was
a just cause for war (C. 23 q. 2 c. 3). While the case concerned the
Israelites who had justly invaded the Amorites and taken possession

of 'auctoritas principis,' 'iusta causa' and 'intentio recta' that were probably taken from
Aquinas, S.T. 2–2, q. 40 art. 1 resp.: *Opera Omnia*, VIII, para. 30, 629. Unless Bonaventura
copied this from his Dominican competitor, which is unlikely, this passage lends weight
to doubt about the authenticity of the treatise.

23 For the Decretalists' reinterpretation of *ulciscuntur iniurias*, see above, ch. 5, nn. 9–10.

24 Henry of Ghent, *Quodlibetum*, 15, 16, *Aurea Quodlibeta*, II, fol. 395ra.

of their territory, Robert interjected the case of the Edomites, who, even though they had denied a similar request from the Israelites, still were not faced with an Israelite attack. The difference between the two cases, according to Robert, was that God had promised the Amorite land to the Israelites, but not that of the Edomites. Thus an invasion of the Edomites would have been an unjust war, while the actual Israelite conquest of the Amorites and their land was a just war both because it had divine authority and because the land belonged to the Israelites by hereditary right.[25] From this it appears that Robert considered, albeit rather vaguely, that defense of hereditary right was a legitimate cause for war. This was not really a new just cause, but a specific example of the just cause of defending one's rights that have been denied by an enemy. The primary issue was not the cause but the divine legitimating authority. Robert then asked whether biblical examples of conquests authorised by divine commands justified the contemporary wars in which princes invaded others' lands, expelling legitimate heirs, turning the lands into their own fiefs and enfeoffing knights as they wished.[26] His answer involved a complex series of distinctions, but the essential point was that when princes such as Alexander the Great and Nebuchadnezzar and Sennacherib and their medieval counterparts occupied others' lands out of hatred, in an unjust war, and by dispossessing heirs, their conquest was unjust and they should restore their gains.[27] However, the main problem remained not the abstract justice of a certain war but the authority who declared the war.

While there was no doubt in the minds of canonists and Romanists alike that proper authority was required for a war to be just, the problem remained as to just what constituted legitimate authority. The Decretalists had taken great pains to restrict the right to declare a just war to superior authorities. Lacking the canonists' expertise in matters of conflicting jurisdictions, the theologians were less able to provide a full-scale discussion of the problem. With the Augustinian definition in mind, Peter the Chanter asked what princes possessed

---

[25] Robert of Courson, *Summa*, 26, 10, B.N. Lat. 14524, fol. 92rb–va; cited in Baldwin, *Masters Princes and Merchants*, II, 146, n. 23. Cf. *ibid.*, I, 208.
[26] Robert of Courson, *Summa*, 15, 3, B.N. Lat. 14524, fols. 63vb–64ra; cited in Baldwin, *ibid.*, II, 147, n. 24.
[27] Robert of Courson, *Summa*, 15, 3, B.N. Lat. 14524, fol. 64va–vb; cited in Baldwin, *ibid.*, II, 147, n. 25.

the requisite authority, observing that in wars of his time a judge had to find for one of the contending parties. Peter obviously had in mind the vassal's duty to seek justice at his overlord's court before embarking on a war, thereby fortifying his actions with a judicial mandate, just as Philip Augustus was soon to do in the conflict between Hugh of Lusignan and King John. In case the opposing lords had no temporal superiors, such as the Emperor or the king of France, then they should first go to the pope as their common superior before going to war. Recourse to the papacy was justified because the situation was fraught with moral peril.[28] The common suspicion of the injustice of most contemporary wars resulted in a position similar to certain Decretalists such as Alanus Anglicus and Hostiensis, who tended to consider the pope as judge ordinary in cases of wars between independent princes. Albeit tacitly, Peter also acknowledged the legal equality of kings with the Holy (Roman) Emperor.

A similarly practical question, raised by Roland of Cremona, was whether the Italian city-states, specifically those in Lombardy, possessed the requisite authority to declare and wage a just war. Roland obviously was referring to the wars of the Lombard League against the Emperor. After all, the Emperor was their prince, and while each city had its *podestà*, Roland concluded that these 'quasi-princes' lacked the requisite authority to make war, especially war against the Emperor.[29] He then shifted his attention to the problem of whether infidels could wage just wars, at first denying the possibility because infidels, lacking faith, could not fulfill his second requirement for the just war. Upon further consideration he seemed to understand faith in the sense of maintaining faith with the enemy. Since even infidels had the right to defend their lives and *patria*, they could repel an unjust attack with a just war, just as Christians could. In this case faith must be maintained by unjust infidel attackers but not by infidels unjustly attacked. Roland's solution was obviously unclear and unsatisfactory, as he himself suggested, but by implication at least he allowed infidels to exercise the legitimate dominion necessary to wage just wars, and he anticipated, however unclearly,

---

[28] Peter the Chanter, *Postilla in Josue*, 8, v. *pone insidias*, MS. Oxford, Balliol College 23, fol. 118va–vb; cited, with discussion, in Smalley, *Study of the Bible*, p. 213. Cf. Baldwin, *ibid.*, I, 208; II, 146, n. 20.

[29] Roland of Cremona, *Summae*, 264, para. 2, p. 730.

the more extensive analyses of Innocent IV and Thomas Aquinas that accorded legitimate dominion even to infidels.[30]

These two theologians alone attacked the problem of authority directly, and even then their solutions were not supported by full argumentation. Other theologians were content to adhere to the conventional requirement of legitimate authority without attempting precisely to specify what officials possessed this authority. The main thrust of their analysis was directed more to the problems posed by obedience to these authorities.

OBEDIENCE

The moral sensitivities of the theologians were never more evident than when they discussed the propriety of obedience to authorities who were waging wars. The basic theoretical dilemma for canonists and theologians alike was whether obedience to princes, the prima facie duty of every subject, was to be withheld when the princely command contradicted Christian morality or divine truth. More practical questions stemmed from this posing of the problem: should a subject or vassal go to war in the service of an infidel or excommunicated prince; had the subject any right to evaluate a prince's claim to wage a just war; and must a prelate with fiefs or regalia obey the command to aid his lord's unjust war?

Around 1200 the Parisian circle of Peter the Chanter produced the most extensive treatment of these problems as they affected the individual knight or prelate. At one point Peter himself upheld the right of a knight to refuse to obey commands of his lord that did not involve duties pertaining to the knight's fief, even if he had sworn to perform them.[31] While Peter's meaning is unclear here, the context, a prohibition of a regalian bishop's contribution of knight service to

---

[30] *Ibid.*, 264, paras. 3, 5, p. 730. Roland's opinion was thus in accord with Huguccio before him as well as with Innocent IV and Aquinas later: cf. above, ch. 4, nn. 119–24; ch. 5, nn. 200–1; and below, ch. 7, nn. 102–4.

[31] Peter the Chanter, *Summa de Sacramentis et Animae Consiliis*, para. 155, ed. J. A. Dugauquier (vols. I, II, III (1), III (2a), III (2b), Louvain and Lille, 1954–66), II, 383, 465: 'Si enim iniustum [bellum] est, non debet [episcopus] ei obedientiam in huiusmodi mandato, quod exemplo militum secularium est videre. Si enim precipiat dominus militi aliquid quod non pertineat ad foedum suum, dicet quod non faciet, etsi preciperit ei ut faciat per iuramentum quod ei facit.' Cf. Baldwin, *Masters Princes and Merchants*, I, 209f., who interprets Peter as obliging bishops to disobey a summons to an unjust war to set an example for the lay lords. The passage, however, seems to indicate that the bishops should rather be inspired by the practice of the lay vassals.

his overlord in the latter's unjust war, suggests that Peter intended to champion a vassal's right to refuse to serve in his lord's unjust war. Well aware of the tendency of vassals to disobey their lords when it suited their own purposes, Peter probably intended to build upon this practice to deprive princes of manpower for their unjust wars.[32] In another passage the Chanter returned to the conventional notion that prelates with regalia ought to furnish knight service. Just as misuse of governmental funds did not excuse non-payment of taxes, so an unjust cause for war did not excuse prelates from providing their contingents of knights.[33] Peter thus straddled the issue, making a more consistent treatment incumbent on other theologians.

For Robert of Courson, a war was obviously just when waged in obedience to a divine mandate, such as in the Israelites' war against the Amorites,[34] but contemporary conflicts posed more complex problems because constituted authority by itself was insufficient to render a war just or holy. In such a case Robert opened up the possibility that subjects had the right to debate the justice of a war commenced by their lord, and then eventually to refrain from participation. Robert's inconclusive opinion juxtaposed the human law tradition prohibiting subjects from discussing the prince's war with the superior divine law right of subjects to discuss such questions, although Robert did not point out precisely who were appropriate 'subjects.'[35] Elsewhere Robert stated more clearly that soldiers were not bound to obey their terrestrial lords in wars they themselves considered unjust,[36] and even in the more difficult case where a knight knew a war was unjust or only partially just, he should not obey the lord's command. In so doing of course he exposed himself to loss of his temporal possessions and disinheritance, yet he must not under any circumstances carry out his lord's command to burn churches and perform other misdeeds. Robert's advice to a knight

---

[32] In intent if not in argumentation Peter's advice bears a similarity to the attempts by Innocent IV, William of Rennes and Monaldus to encourage vassals to abstain from participation in their lords' unjust wars. Cf. above, ch. 5, nn. 70-4, 123-6.

[33] Peter the Chanter, *Summa*, para. 270, III (2a), 290.

[34] Robert of Courson, *Summa*, 26, 10, B.N. Lat. 14524, fol. 92rb-va; cited in Baldwin, *Masters Princes and Merchants*, II, 146, n. 23.

[35] *Ibid.*, 26, 10, B.N. Lat. 14524, fol. 92rb; cited in Baldwin, *ibid.*, II, 147, n. 26. For the difficulties of interpreting this passage, see *ibid.*, I, 208f., II, 146, n. 23, and II, 147, n. 26.

[36] Robert of Courson, *ibid.*, 30, 9, B.N. Lat. 14524, fol. 107ra; cited in Baldwin, *ibid.*, II, 147, n. 32.

caught in such a bind was to choose the middle way of taking the crusader's vow and set out in defense of the Holy Land. Indeed some barons had recently done just this in order to avoid both participation in an unjust war and the personal perils of disobedience.[37]

The debate over obedience was continued by Stephen Langton, later to become archbishop of Canterbury, who held that whenever a prince sought the advice of his court and received its consent to go to war, the 'people' had no right to discuss the judgment even if it were palpably unjust. In his opinion, Stephen seems to have distinguished between persons eligible to discuss the justice of the proposed war, that is, the court, and those outside the court who had no place in the discussions.[38] In the case of an unjust war waged by the king of France against the king of England, what course should the individual French knight choose, and what was the French host to do? To follow the king was to sin against divine precepts, but to refuse rendered the knights liable to charges of treason and scandal. In a rather tortuous discussion Stephen observed that while disobedience of a single knight was not likely to cause scandal, the withdrawal of the entire force certainly would, but if the individual knight were allowed to withdraw, then all knights should be so obligated. The individual and the whole force were therefore equally guilty and innocent, an obviously unviable solution. Stephen's solution allowed the individual knight to go to war but enjoined him to withdraw at the beginning of battle or at least to refuse to fight,[39] still an unworkable solution. In another question Stephen attempted to solve the dilemmas of obedience by reference to the analogous situation of administration of the sacrament: just as a priest served a communicant guilty of mortal sin in public but not in private; so also a knight might aid his king in public but not in private if the king was waging an unjust war.[40] Realising that this solution ob-

---

[37] Robert of Courson, *ibid.*, 10, 15, B.N. Lat. 14524, fol. 50va–vb; cited in Baldwin, *ibid.*, II, 148, n. 37. Robert may have had in mind the example of the counts of Flanders, Blois and Perche, who had departed on the Fourth Crusade in order to avoid the wrath of Philip Augustus against whom they had earlier allied themselves with Richard the Lion-Heart: *ibid.*, I, 211.

[38] Stephen Langton, *Questiones*, MS. Cambridge, St John's College 57, fols. 334vb–335ra and B.N. Lat. 14556, fol. 242rb–va; cited in Baldwin, *ibid.*, II, 112, n. 33.

[39] Stephen Langton, *ibid.*, MS. Avranches 230, fol. 261v; B.N. Lat. 16385, fol. 69va–vb; MS. Vatican Lat. 4297, fol. 62va; cited in Baldwin, *ibid.*, II, 147f., n. 33.

[40] Stephen Langton, *ibid.*, MS. Cambridge, St John's College 57, fol. 204rb; B.N. Lat. 14556, fol. 220va; cited in Baldwin, *ibid.*, II, 148, n. 35.

viously raised practical difficulties, Stephen posited the extreme case in which the king was surrounded and outnumbered by his enemies. Was the knight then guilty of treason in deserting the king? Stephen attempted to devise a solution by the introduction of a distinction between several sorts of offensive acts. In a simple defense of his king, the knight must fight, but must not join the king in attacking enemies armed with a just cause, and if the knight should defend his king solely to curry favor, he was guilty of sin. In distinguishing between public and private acts and offensive and defensive acts, Stephen attempted without notable success to accommodate the principles of the just war to the complexities of contemporary military practice.

The question of obedience similarly vexed Thomas of Chobham, who at one point followed Roman law in condemning as infamous those vassals who fled from the public wars of their lords.[41] In another passage he expressed the common conviction that knights should follow a king to a just war to defend the *patria* or to prosecute justice, and then turned to the more difficult case in which a king waged war on Christians without the judgment and counsel of his realm. Basing his answer on canons from Burchard of Worms and Ivo of Chartres and on the penitential manuals of Bartholomew of Exeter and Robert of Flamborough, he concluded that knights in this case should obey divine commands rather than the wicked orders of terrestrial princes, and added that prelates had the duty to warn their charges not to shed innocent blood in fulfilling their prince's command.[42] Thomas seemed to hold that a king could wage a just war without the advice and consent of his realm, but in order to wage an unjust war he had first to make the realm party to his misdeed, a conclusion Thomas obviously would not accept. In the same passage Thomas again upheld the right of a subject people to disobey their prince in his unjust war, unanimously if possible. It was preferable however that knights follow their lord in an unjust war only so long as they avoided shedding blood and rapine in merely defending themselves against attack. When these knights returned home from an unjust war, their priests should diligently inquire of them whether they had killed, committed rapine, or offered aid to their lord. If the knights confessed guilt, they should submit to the penances for

---

[41] Thomas of Chobham, *Summa*, p. 432.
[42] *Ibid.*, p. 430. For a different interpretation of this passage, see Baldwin, *ibid.*, I, 209.

homicide and rapine.[43] Thomas did not specify those members of the realm who possessed the right to discuss the justice of the proposed war with any more precision than had Stephen Langton, nor did he have more success in delineating precisely how a knight should act in an actual unjust war, but rather threatened the knight with ecclesiastical penalties after the fact.

The Dominican Roland of Cremona, writing around 1230, took up once again the problems of obedience that the Chanter's circle had faced without finding satisfactory solutions. At one point in his *Summa* Roland stated that subjects should not fight a war that contravened their consciences,[44] and then he devoted a full-fledged if somewhat disorganised question to the problem of obedience in an unjust war. He asked whether a people was bound to obey its king when it was convinced that the king unjustly attacked a city. Advancing arguments for and against, Roland first cited the opinion of some unnamed masters that the people were bound to obey lest the Church hierarchy be destroyed. Passing over this opinion without discussion, Roland referred to Moses' prohibitions on following a crowd bent on doing evil or on serving demons, foreign gods or the devil and concluded that the people should rather kill a king commanding them to do evil than obey him.[45] The case became more complex, however, when the city unjustly attacked by the king actually merited punishment for its sins, as when wicked Jerusalem was unjustly attacked by the Babylonian king Nebuchadnezzar. Should the Babylonians have obeyed their king when he was maliciously serving the devil? In response Roland cited the unjust and tyrannical Babylonian attack upon Tyre, for which crime among others Babylon itself was later destroyed. Yet in attacking Tyre the Babylonian king was serving as God's chastising instrument and therefore the war was just. Admitting that this conclusion contradicted every authority, Roland explained the later destruction of Babylon as the consequence of the Babylonians' attribution of their God-given victory over Tyre to their own idols.[46] In spite of his clumsy exposition, Roland was clearly of the opinion that an unjust

---

[43] Thomas of Chobham, *ibid.*, p. 432.
[44] Roland of Cremona, *Summae*, 264, para. 4, p. 730.
[45] *Ibid.*, 263, pr. and paras. 1–3, p. 727.
[46] *Ibid.*, 263, paras. 4, 5, 12, pp. 727–9. For similar canonistic argumentation, see above, ch. 4, nn. 9–14.

war could not be rendered just either by the moral failings of its intended victims or by the unjust warrior's function as an avenging instrument of divine wrath. Carried to its logical conclusion as it was not in Roland's treatment, this position could have rendered a war unjust even when it was divinely authorised. Roland's use of Old Testament examples demonstrates that canonists and theologians alike required that a war be justified on the part of both attackers and victims.

Returning to the case of a contemporary king unjustly attacking a city, Roland introduced several special conditions that clarified his opinion. First, if one of the king's men knew the king was attacking maliciously or without the right to attack, and recognised that this right was difficult to discern, as long as the king's other subjects were unaware of the injustice, the doubting subject could obey him. Roland seemed to suggest that one doubting subject need not heed his own hesitations when other subjects agreed that the war was just, but then he advised such doubters not to exert themselves to the limit of their capabilities while participating in the campaign. The reasoning employed here was based on an analogous situation in which a judge knew the truth of a case but the contrary was sufficiently proved in court and the judge was forced to condemn an innocent man. Thus Roland's advice to the solitary doubter was to swallow his doubts and obey orders in lukewarm fashion, but when the whole body of the king's men knew that the attack was unjust, then each man was bound to disobey the king even on pain of death, for God must be obeyed before men. The next condition Roland proposed concerned a war considered just by the king's royal council or by the counsellors of a *podestà*, in which case the individual subject was free to obey without sin for he could content himself with the thought that he was ignorant of all the facts of the matter. If, however, a subject still had insuperable doubts after learning of the allegedly expert counsel, these doubts must have been revealed to him by the Holy Spirit and he was thus bound by divine command to refrain from participation. To this point Roland's treatment obliquely but firmly limited the authority of a prince to force a subject to obey his command to wage war when the subject had autogenous doubts as to the justice of the war; Roland then returned directly to the crucial statement that a just war must be waged on princely authority. Now Roland commented that authority was insufficient to render a war just because many other conditions had to be met, and that arguments for the justice of a war based solely on authority were fallacious both in the simple terms of the requirement and for certain other reasons that he did not mention.[47] In summary, Roland's often cryptic treatment of the problem of obedience indicates a profound and agonising groping toward a solution that would limit the authority of a prince to make war by granting to all the king's subjects, or at least to those liable to be called to fight, the right to weigh the moral merits of the proposed war and to follow the dictates of their consciences without sin. Had Roland's often clumsy approach received coherent refinement in the writings of later theologians, the effect upon the just war theories and perhaps even practice would not have been far short of revolutionary. The fact is, however, that Roland's attempt to grant the individual the right to assess the justice of particular wars inspired few if any of his theological successors.

A major reason for the hesitation or, better perhaps, refusal on the part of other theologians to develop at greater length the solicitude for the individual conscience in matters of war was the very real and concrete disadvantages incurred by a disobedient vassal. Strict adherence to the advice of the theologians would have entailed the eventual loss of possessions for the knights and bishops with regalia, whose sensitivities were often less than well-informed about the fine points of moral judgments. Furthermore there was little objective agreement about the locus of justice in a particular conflict that usually contained a hopeless mixture of just and unjust elements.[48] Thus it is evident that while the theologians' attempts to advise knights caught in these quandaries added little to the formal theories of the just war, the goal of these attempts was to provide knights with advice on how to escape the dilemma without actually having to face up to the bald alternatives of serving either his eternal or his temporal lord.

The canonists wrestled with similar problems when they discussed

---

[47] *Ibid.*, 263, paras. 6–8, p. 728. Roland's solicitude for the individual subject caught in a moral quandary about the justice of a war is reminiscent of a similar approach on the part of Stephen Langton and Thomas of Chobham: cf. above, nn. 39, 40, 43, 45.

[48] For these disadvantages of non-obedience, see above, ch. 5, n. 68.

the question of fealty owed to an excommunicated lord.[49] For example, Huguccio's extensive treatment concluded that a vassal must avoid performing military service to an excommunicated lord and must not defend him. His solution was adopted by the theologian Master Martin,[50] but Peter the Chanter and Robert of Courson did not fully go along with it. When a vassal was summoned by an excommunicated lord under penalty of forfeiture of fiefs, Peter decided that he was free to obey the summons,[51] and when a city placed under interdict was unjustly besieged by enemies, its citizen defenders did not incur personal excommunication.[52] Scarcely consonant with the goal of clerical discipline of the laity, his opinion taken at face value allowed even excommunicated lords or cities under interdict to wage just wars that required the participation of their vassals or citizens, who were caught in the impossible dilemma of obeying either their temporal or their spiritual superiors. Admitting that this was indeed a difficult moral situation, over which the canonists disagreed, Robert of Courson attempted to resolve it by reference to the just war theory. For him, the duty of vassals to fight for their realm rested on the three grounds of oath, obligation to defend the realm, and duty to defend and protect the Church. He held that vassals should not follow their excommunicated lord when he was defending his own error, attacking the Church, or disinheriting someone unjustly, but when the king called upon his vassals for aid in fighting a just war in defense of the realm or even the Church, the vassals were bound by their threefold obligation to obey him.[53] Vassals were thus obligated to fight a just war whether or not their lord was excommunicated because their obligation was justified by its function in defense of Church or kingdom although the question of whether an excommunicated lord could wage a just war in defense of the Church was left open. Robert also discussed a perplexing case in which the pope had ordered his legate to France to excommunicate all knights fighting in the war 'between the kings' of England and France, and also to command the bishops to punish

---

[49] Cf. C. 15 q. 6 cc. 2–5; above, ch. 4, n. 61.

[50] Huguccio, cited above, ch. 4, n. 60. Master Martin, *Summa*, B.N. Lat. 14526, fol. 102va–vb; cited in Baldwin, *Masters Princes and Merchants*, II, 150f., n. 49; cf. *ibid.*, I, 212.

[51] Peter the Chanter, *Summa*, para. 24, III (2b), 740.

[52] *Ibid.*, para. 317, III (2a), 370.

[53] Robert of Courson, *Summa*, 4. 12, B.N. Lat. 14524, fol. 29ra–va; cited in Baldwin, *Masters Princes and Merchants*, II, 151, nn. 53, 55; cf. *ibid.*, I, 213.

disobedient knights with excommunication and interdict under pain of their own excommunication. The essential problem here was whether the bishops should obey the pope or their secular overlord, the king. To resolve this dilemma Robert again had recourse to the just war theory, according to which neither the bishops nor the barons should serve the king if the war was clearly unjust, but if the war was just, the bishops should not dissuade their knights and others from participation, since not even the pope could override the Pauline injunction to obey one's lord.[54] Thus in Robert's view the instrumentality of the just war took precedence over the particular papal command to levy excommunications, and permitted him to resolve the dilemma after a fashion.

In the complexities of feudal tenure a vassal often owed military service and allegiance to several overlords and when his overlords were at war with each other the vassal was caught with conflicting loyalties. The theologians do not seem to have approached this problem in relation to the just war, but Roland of Cremona did discuss a hypothetical case in which the pope had ordered certain Christians within the Empire to fight but the Emperor had forbidden them to fight. The subjects were then liable to excommunication if they fought on imperial command, and as excommunicates they could perform no legitimate acts, hence they could not wage a just war on imperial orders. Roland's solution allowed them to fight in a just war declared by the Emperor, for in this case the pope had no secular jurisdiction over them unless their lands were located in the patrimony of St Peter over which the pope did have secular jurisdiction. In the opposite case of an unjust war of the Empire where the pope had prohibited the subjects from fighting, they must obey the pope. Yet if the pope should unjustly excommunicate these subjects, could they then fight a just war? Defining uniquely the penalties of excommunication as abstention from the sacraments and from entering churches, Roland answered that if the subjects observed these penalties they could nevertheless perform legitimate acts such as fighting a just war because God Himself watched over those who were unjustly excommunicated. He admitted that his not wholly

---

[54] Robert of Courson, *ibid.*, 26, 9, B.N. Lat. 14524, fol. 92ra–rb; cited in Baldwin, *ibid.*, II, 152, n. 56. Robert's conclusions were summarised by Geoffrey of Poitiers: *ibid.*, II, 153, n. 58, For fuller discussion of the actual case, cf. *ibid.*, I, 214.

satisfactory solution should not prejudice a better opinion.[55] Roland's line of reasoning is interesting for it inclines toward the imperial right to wage a just war even in defiance of papal command. For him, as for Peter the Chanter and Robert of Courson, the justice of a war took precedence over specific papal commands and Church discipline in determining whether obedience was to be rendered.

Most of the theologians thus far studied brought a practical and casuistic approach to the question of obedience, but with the coming of speculative theology with Alexander of Hales, theological opinion returned to the terms employed by Augustine and Gratian. Alexander asked whether someone should obey sacrilegious kings when they declared war. Stating that the order of power had two aspects, authority and execution, he in turn divided the order of execution into the intention (*affectus*) of execution which was inordinate in sacrilegious kings, and the effect of execution that was proper when the king's orders were licit and did not contravene divine precepts. Furthermore, a king's evil intention did not free subjects from obeying a constituted but sacrilegious authority. In effect Alexander returned to Augustine's view that even a sacrilegious or apostate king must be obeyed in a just war. The theoretical simplicity of Alexander's view of course camouflaged the concrete dilemmas faced if not resolved by the earlier, more practically minded theologians. Alexander closed the door on the right of subjects to disobey their lord in an unjust war provided the war was not directed ultimately against divine truth. To the objection that a sacrilegious king might be moved by cupidity, lust for domination or love of inflicting punishment, Alexander answered in effect with a distinction between two elements of the just war formula: a war could be unjust with regard to the king but still be just for the knights whose duty it was to obey.[56]

From the foregoing analysis it appears that theological opinions concerning obedience in war were strenuous if fragmentary and inconclusive attempts to adapt traditional views to the complexities of contemporary practice that ultimately defied comprehensive casuistic treatment. These realities were simply too varied to be

---

[55] Roland of Cremona, *Summae*, 264, paras. 7–9, p. 731.

[56] Alexander of Hales, *Summa*, para. 467, c. 2 ad 1, ad 2, III, 687. Augustine's view, strangely not cited by Alexander, is found in C. 11 q. 3 c. 94.

incorporated into a general theoretical position. Most theologians writing after 1250 directed their attention toward speculative formulations of licit authority and dutiful obedience; in this sense Alexander of Hales indicates the future direction of theological debate that would find its most comprehensive expression in the writings of Thomas Aquinas. With Alexander the theologians had come full circle, returning the requirement of obedience to its pristine patristic position. In so doing the ability of the just war theories to prevent participation in unjust wars that earlier theologians had struggled to develop was now seriously compromised.

Motivated by a sensitive concern for the moral dilemmas of the individual knight or prelate, the Chanter's circle and Roland of Cremona had made the justice of a war rather than the authority by which it was waged their paramount concern. From this they came close to a justification of licit disobedience in an unjust war that would encourage a subject to look to his spiritual welfare when weighing the conflicting claims upon his loyalties. By contrast, the canonists' concern for the legal consequences of the justice or injustice of a war led them to construct a doctrine of disobedience that appealed to the material welfare of a vassal similarly perplexed. In their own way the theologians maintained their concern for justice in their opinions on the licit conduct and consequences of warfare.

CONDUCT AND CONSEQUENCES

Some of the most interesting and valuable theological discussion on war centered on the proper conduct of a just war and the different consequences resulting from just and unjust wars. Employing Augustine as usual, the theologians maintained that faith once promised must be maintained with an enemy, yet there was no moral necessity to promise the enemy anything. The sole restriction was that outright fraud be avoided,[57] although an anonymous sermon dating from about 1225 advanced the notion that in a just war men could even dress in women's clothes in order to defeat an enemy, the passage from Deuteronomy (22:5) forbidding transvestism notwithstanding.[58] Whether this tactic constituted an effective fraud was perhaps problematical, but most theologians were

[57] *Ibid.*, para. 470, III, 689.
[58] *Quodlibet*, II, 15, MS. Vatican Lat. 782, fol. 28rb–va.

more concerned to justify ambushes. Their task was made easy by the example of God ordering Joshua to ambush the city of Ai (Joshua 8: 2) and also by Augustine's declaration that ambushes were licit in a just war. On the basis of several Old Testament passages one author observed that warning an enemy of imminent attack was neither necessary nor desirable.[59] While no theologian strongly challenged the legitimacy of ambushes, Roland of Cremona did attempt a dialectical discussion when he offered the contention that use of ambushes was a deceit of the sophistical and hated men condemned in Ecclesiasticus 37: 23. Seen another way, someone using ambushes was treacherous, as were the Israelites under Joshua, for ambushes were illicit even in just wars. Roland answered these objections by contending that ambushes were sophistic and treacherous in unjust wars, but some ambushes stemmed from prudence, such as the aforementioned ambush of Ai and the ambushes of heretics and infidels undertaken by the contemporary Church. Roland also pointed out that Joshua had raised his shield against Ai, that is, he had declared war, and thus was innocent of breaking faith with the city. In contemporary times, the shield of Christians against heretics and infidels was the faith of Christ, and furthermore the enemies of God's people were not truly harmed by ambushes for they were thereby prevented from completing their days in sin. Roland concluded that prudent ambushes were licit,[60] although one would like to know just what special sort of ambushes he had in mind for infidels and heretics.

As the theologians discussed at length the conditions for obedience in war, so they were also concerned to enumerate the ways in which this obedience could legitimately be carried out. Here the crucial problems were military service and finance, for the increasing incidence of organised violence in the high Middle Ages required more knights and became ever more expensive. Hard-pressed princes developed a whole complex of expedients to raise the revenue for their wars. Aware of these measures, the theologians turned their attention to the moral dimensions of providing knight service and of

---

[59] *Biblia Pauperum*, 82, printed in the Vivès edition of Bonaventura's *Opera Omnia* (15 vols., Paris, 1864–71), VIII, 586. This treatise, also entitled *De Exemplis Sacrae Scripturae*, is attributed to Nicholas of Hanape, O.P., who was papal penitentiary between 1277 and 1285: Stegmüller, *Repertorium*, IV, 48–50.

[60] Roland of Cremona, *Summae*, 263, paras. 9–11, p. 729.

tributa or war taxes.[61] Robert Pullen for example declared that kings had the duty to collect tribute from their subjects in order to repel external invaders and to suppress intestine wars, but he cautioned rulers against demanding tribute when they were incapable of defending their subjects.[62] Likewise, Radulphus Ardens declared that tribute was owed to kings so that they might fight for the common protection,[63] and Roland of Cremona invoked Paul's justification of tribute paid to princes for defending the *patria*.[64] Like Raymond of Peñafort, Jean de la Rochelle upheld the right of a prince to demand taxes from his subjects when he fought on their behalf, adding that if the prince was captured in fighting to defend the *patria* and was unable without grave damage to raise his ransom out of his own resources, then he was entitled to seek moderate tallages according to his subjects' ability to pay.[65] For Bonaventura, funds from the public treasury could be expended on payments to soldiers and for waging battles when the utility or necessity of the community so warranted.[66] In basing his opinion on common utility Bonaventura anticipated the more extensive treatment Aquinas accorded to the common good. Similarly, at the end of the century Godfrey of Fontaines based the prince's right to levy extraordinary taxes on his authority to direct wars waged to defend the good of the polity; yet since the prince had only the principal authority for waging war and paying soldiers, in difficult cases he could only levy such exactions with the consent of his subjects.[67]

Robert of Courson focused more specifically on the contemporary royal practice of levying extraordinary aids and taxes on movable property for crusades and other wars, when revenues from regalian lands were obviously insufficient. These levies posed a moral dilemma, for while the royal cause was just and necessary, the

---

[61] Cf. above, ch. 5, nn. 87–92 and Baldwin, *Masters Princes and Merchants*, I, 215f.

[62] Robert Pullen, *Sententiarum*, 7, 9 P.L. 186, pp. 921f.

[63] Radulphus Ardens, *Speculum Universale*, 10, 6, B.N. Lat. 3240, fol. 27va and Mazar. 709, fol. 186rb.

[64] Roland of Cremona, *Summae*, 456, para. 6, p. 1350.

[65] Jean de la Rochelle, *Summa de Vitiis, de questis et taliis*, B.N. Lat. 16417, fol. 151ra. For Raymond's view, see above, ch. 5, n. 91.

[66] Bonaventura, *Commentarium in IV Libros Sententiarum*, to 4, 20, *Opera Omnia*, IV, 537.

[67] Godfrey of Fontaines, *Quodlibetum*, 11, 17, *Les Quodlibets onze-quatorze de Godefroid de Fontaines*, ed. J. Hoffmanns (Louvain, 1932), pp. 76, 78. The main thrust of Godfrey's Aristotelian argument was the limitation of the prince's right to act without consent of his subjects.

revenues thus acquired were tainted because they were levied on wealth illicitly gained through usury or other illicit commercial activity. In Robert's view the moral necessity of waging just wars took precedence over moral suspicion of commercial wealth, since he allowed the king to accept the taxes as a loan or concession, but he obligated the king to make full restitution upon his return from the Holy Land or after the war was over.[68] Contemporary French and English kings most likely welcomed Robert's justification of extra-ordinary taxes, but on the other hand they would be strongly tempted to neglect the requirement that they ultimately refund such taxes.

The theologians thus justified wholeheartedly the feudal and royal custom of demanding tribute for engaging in just and defensive warfare. Yet they did inject moral cautions into their approval. For some of them the moral dilemmas were most acute for regalian prelates who were sometimes confronted with demands to render knight service and tribute to a prince waging an unjust war. In one passage Peter the Chanter discussed the case of a regalian bishop who was obligated to contribute the services of archers, crossbowmen and knights to a royal war and pay for them out of funds destined for the poor. The question Peter raised was how the bishop could calculate the resources he could legitimately spend on military affairs without using funds that should go to the poor. His advice to the bishop was to estimate what he owed the king from his regalian possessions and pay only that sum, leaving the rest for his own expenses and for poor relief.[69] In this passage some rather vague limits were placed on the amounts of knight service and money a regalian prelate could contribute to his overlord, although Peter did not distinguish between just and unjust wars. Also discussing episcopal allocations for the royal host, Robert of Courson's first opinion held that all such expenditures including those incurred from regalian holdings were illicit, and the bishop who gave his wealth to kings was guilty of mortal sin. The bishop's sin was even more grave when the war

---

[68] Robert of Courson, *Summa*, 10, 11–12, B.N. Lat. 14524, fol. 49ra–va; cited in Baldwin, *Masters Princes and Merchants*, II, 157, nn. 95–7. For the moral dilemma posed by this issue, cf. *ibid.*, I, 220.

[69] Peter the Chanter, *Summa*, MS. W, B.N. Lat. 3477, fol. 125vb; cited in Baldwin, *ibid.*, II, 154, n. 74.

was unjust or only partly just, since it was his duty to upbraid the king for such actions rather than to indulge him.

Like Gratian and Huguccio, Robert wished the priesthood of his time to be free of all tribute, but Robert went further when he cast doubt even on the legal status of rendering tribute, since he declared regalian lands were in fact freely conveyed to the Church by Constantine. Only the fawning cowardice of prelates toward princes had allowed this servitude of the Church to become entrenched.[70] Robert then alluded to the princely practice of demanding aid from prelates to support both just and unjust wars. When this aid was denied, princes often plundered the episcopal or monastic under-tenants. Faced with this threat, Robert remarked, prelates often tallaged their manors and rendered the proceeds to the prince rather than to the poor, thereby considering themselves absolved of further responsibility. Robert objected that since prelates were not allowed to do evil in order that good might come of it, they should rather launch ecclesiastical censures against the prince, who alone then bore the responsibility for his continued and tyrannical pillaging of the undertenants. Yet the total elimination of regalian contributions was too radical a solution even for Robert, for he drew back to the more moderate position that a prince could require churches to contribute to his wars against pagans, heretics, and even other Christians. The prince's rights were limited to collecting only the exact amounts of tribute and knight service owed him by churches with regalian holdings.[71] In effect Robert felt forced to acquiesce to established custom provided that the prince did not violently pillage under-tenants. His grudging concession of regalian contributions was echoed by Jean de la Rochelle, who cautioned princes against the violent extortion of unnecessary tallages from their poor subjects which he considered the worst sort of rapine.[72]

Even if tribute and knight service were licit but limited duties of prelates with regalia, the problem remained whether these contributions could be withheld when the prince commenced an unjust war. Peter the Chanter detailed two contradictory positions on the issue

---

[70] Robert of Courson, *Summa*, 10, 16, B.N. Lat. 14524, fols. 50vb–51ra; cited in Baldwin, *ibid.*, II, 154, n. 75.

[71] Robert of Courson, *ibid.*, 15, 13, 16, B.N. Lat. 14524, fols. 66va–67ra; cited in Baldwin, *ibid.*, II, 154f., nn. 77, 79. For a fuller consideration, cf. *ibid.*, I, 217.

[72] Jean de la Rochelle, cited above, n. 65.

of whether the prelate was obligated to contribute to an unjust war. In one passage he asked whether a prelate with regalia was bound to render knight service owed to a prince whose war was egregiously unjust. One opinion Peter advanced held that the prelate was not so bound, by the analogy that a prelate should not entrust the use of the sword to madmen, but then Peter countered with the argument that since Christ Himself had ordered His followers to render unto Caesar the things of Caesar, the prelate owed tribute even when he knew that the king wished to put it to evil uses. Peter concluded here that the prelate must send the soldiers, and added that the prelate was also obligated to find knights to serve the prince, and if he so inade-quately compensated them such that they plundered others in the prince's army, then the prelate himself was obligated to make restitution to those thus despoiled.[73] In this passage Peter denied the prelate any right to withhold knight service even in an unjust war but then held the prelate responsible for the misdeeds of his knights. In other words, the prelate was liable to make restitution even though he had no choice but to send knights. Peter's conflicting opinion was that a bishop with regalia was not obligated to render military service to a prince commencing an unjust war on Christians, and moreover the bishop had the right to inquire into the justice of the war. Peter's reasoning for declaring the bishop free of his regalian obligation was based on the example of secular knights who could refuse obedience to a command when the lord attempted to force them to perform acts not pertaining to their feudal tenures, even if the lord attempted to coerce their compliance by invoking the feudal oath.[74] The discussion is interesting for two reasons: Peter seemed to approve the feudal custom buttressed by Roman and canonical jurisprudence that freed the vassal from the obligation to perform nefarious acts for his lord; and Peter evidently felt that part of a regalian bishop's duties was to determine the justice of his overlord's wars.

The obligations of prelates to render tribute from non-regalian lands was much less firmly entrenched, for these holdings were normally immune, but in a state of emergency princes often de-manded contributions for a just war. The Chanter's circle generally

[73] Peter the Chanter, *Summa*, para. 270, III (2a), 290.
[74] *Ibid.*, para. 155, II, 383, discussed above, n. 31.

saw the prelate's choice in this case as not entirely free. Peter himself discussed the issue without providing an answer,[75] but Stephen Langton attempted to provide a full answer. When a prelate was called upon to contribute money to the king's unjust war from his non-regalian lands, he was faced with the uncomfortable choice of rendering the money to avoid the mortal sin of scandal, but in so doing he committed the mortal sins of aiding an unjust cause and depriving the poor. In this case Stephen advised the prelate to refuse the king, but when the king had a just cause, then the prelate was free to aid him if he wished, provided that the aid established no precedent. Stephen here cited the contributions of English churches to Richard the Lion-Heart's ransom.[76] In a similar opinion Robert of Courson observed that monasteries often supplied princes with horses and wagons from funds destined for the poor and bishops also contributed excessive war subsidies that enabled knights to pillage and burn towns and monasteries. In his opinion such prelates shared responsibility for the illicit acts of war that they helped make possible. They also sinned mortally in dispensing wealth allocated for poor relief to wars against Christians. Since these wars were of no utility to the Church, the prelates were bound to make full restitution. However, in a just war to defend Church and kingdom against pagans and heretics, Robert qualified his condemnation when he obligated prelates to render contributions to the limit of their resources.[77] Once again the necessity of a just war won out over Robert's moral scruples.

The theologians thus provided prelates with contradictory and confusing advice about how to act when called upon to supply men and money to their overlords' wars. This advice showed, perhaps better than any other facet of the theology of the just war, just how sharply theological debate was focused upon the problems clergymen themselves faced. The rights and obligations of lay subjects in these matters received only passing mention and little analysis. This sharp focus on the clergy itself influenced the kind of questions the theologians asked and the solutions they found, thus limiting their perspec-

---

[75] Baldwin, *Masters Princes and Merchants*, I, 218; II, 155, n. 84.

[76] Stephen Langton, *Questiones*, MS. Cambridge, St John's College 57, fol. 195va–vb and B.N. Lat. 14556, fol. 250ra; cited in Baldwin, *ibid.*, II, 155f., n. 85.

[77] Robert of Courson, *Summa*, 15, 6–7, B.N. Lat. 14524, fol. 65rb–va; cited in Baldwin, *ibid.*, II, 156, n. 88.

tives on lay society that, after all, was most directly involved in warfare, and hence also limiting any practical effects the theories might have had.

Another reason why the questions of tribute money loomed so large for the theologians was that this money usually went to hire mercenaries for royal service. At the Third Lateran Council in 1179 persons who were likely to find employment as mercenaries were condemned to excommunication. The specific designations of the Third Lateran Council could and did easily become general and ill-defined terms of abuse for any warrior who lapsed into overtly sinful activities. It was clear that the strictures of the Council did not *eo ipso* condemn all mercenaries, but rather only those who abused their office. The task of the theologians was thus to distinguish use from abuse, that is, to justify the mercenaries' *métier* while detailing the specific moral dangers faced by mercenaries and their employers.[78]

Alain of Lille presented the strict interpretation of the Third Lateran Council when he repeated the strictures of the Council without comment.[79] Robert of Courson likewise felt that a prince should not use mercenaries like the Cottereaux even to defend the realm, since they were automatically excommunicated and also evil men infected with sacrilege.[80] Mercenaries were, however, considered too important by warring monarchs to be categorically condemned by the theologians. The Parisian theologians sought to justify the role of the mercenary while cautioning him against the usual abuses. Peter the Chanter opened up this way when he held that mercenaries could accept employment without incurring excommunication even from a city under interdict, provided that the city was being unjustly attacked and that the mercenaries were dependent on these wages for maintenance when there was no other available employment.[81] Again, it seems that defense against unjust

---

[78] For discussion of this canon 27, see above, ch. 5, n. 175 and Baldwin, *ibid.*, I, 220–4.

[79] Alain of Lille, *Liber Poenitentialis*, 3, 31, II, 145f.

[80] Robert of Courson, *Summa*, 4, 13, B.N. Lat. 14524, fols. 29vb–30ra; cited in Baldwin, *Masters Princes and Merchants*, II, 158, n. 104.

[81] Peter the Chanter, *Summa*, para. 317, III (2a), 370f. In other passages Peter was not so tolerant of mercenaries, for he placed them on his list of sinful professions and would deny them the Eucharist because they made their living by killing innocent people: *ibid.*, para. 361, III (2b), 525. He also changed the 'knight' of Gregory VII's condemnation (Peter the

attack took precedence in Peter's view over excommunication and the moral stigma attached to the profession. Robert of Courson himself admitted that knights could receive wages provided they sought no more than was due them. If they extracted higher wages from their employer they were guilty of robbery and should make restitution of their ill-gotten gains.[82]

The problem of mercenaries was complicated by the common practice of paying salaries or rewarding knights from spoils captured in war. The general opinion as stated by Bonaventura allowed soldiers to be paid wages for fighting to defend the *res publica* but considered plunder of the poor to be illicit.[83] Peter the Chanter held that knights should not fight in order to receive salaries, but nevertheless he recognised that they could not fight unless they were compensated by salaries.[84] Robert of Courson considered cross-bowmen and other salaried knights morally suspect because they attempted to profit from their bloody violence at the expense of the poor. Even in a just war these men were wont to plunder churches and to commit other acts of rapine while fulfilling their oaths of obedience. If they refused to obey their lord they were guilty of perjury, faced disinheritance and ejection from their lands. Robert advised knights caught in this dilemma to disobey their lords when ordered to plunder the Church, lest realm and Church be destroyed.[85] Robert obviously found it difficult, in this passage at least, to distinguish between vassals following their lords in a just and justly-waged war from hired brigands, but elsewhere he gave hired knights the conventional advice to obey God rather than man.[86] Robert could not overcome his skepticism regarding the moral worth of the hired knight, for he believed that even just wars inevitably resulted in illicit plundering of the Church and the poor under any circumstances, even though he did not go so far as to

Lombard, Sentences, 4, 16, 3) to 'mercenary knight' and advised mercenaries to desert their profession and undergo penance: *ibid.*, para. 116, II, 216f. Cf. Baldwin, *ibid.*, II, 44, n. 100.

[82] Robert of Courson, *Summa*, 15, 4, B.N. Lat. 14524, fol. 64vb; cited in Baldwin, *ibid.*, II, 158, n. 109.

[83] Bonaventura, *Commentarium in Evangelium Lucae*, 3, 32 (to Luke 3: 14), *Opera Omnia*, VII, 77.

[84] Peter the Chanter, *Postilla*, to Genesis 14: 24, MS. British Museum Royal 2 C 8, fol. 16ra; cited, with similar passages, in Baldwin, *Masters Princes and Merchants*, II, 158f., n. 112.

[85] Robert of Courson, *Summa*, 10, 15, B.N. Lat. 14524, fol. 50rb; cited in Baldwin, *ibid.*, II, 159, n. 116.

[86] Robert of Courson, *ibid.*, fol. 50va; cited in Baldwin, *ibid.*, n. 117.

condemn all contemporary wars. Thomas of Chobham shared Robert's suspicion of the mercenary, whose office he considered dangerous to the soul, since the mercenary tended to do as little as possible to earn his wages, while committing as much rapine as possible, thus receiving more than the just price for his labors and meriting reproach by his priests.[87] It is obvious that the Parisian theologians could not banish all doubts in their minds and unequivocally justify the office of mercenaries and absolve it from moral suspicion.

Another problem arose concerning the knightly sports of tournaments and duels. The theologians generally looked with disfavor on professional duelists as vicious men,[88] but Roland of Cremona and Alexander of Hales, while condemning most tournaments as mere outlets for ostentation, vainglory and greed, saw a limited usefulness in them when they were used to keep knights in fighting trim for wars in defense of the Church, provided of course that the violence used was not excessive.[89]

The theologians also considered whether the use of certain weapons was licit in war, primarily the crossbow that could be used by non-noble mercenaries.[90] Robert of Courson considered crossbowmen tainted with the same moral stigma as the Cottereaux and hired knights.[91] The Parisian theologians went beyond the canonists in levelling criticism on the profession. Peter the Chanter considered crossbowmen as not worthy of salvation, for they made their living by killing innocent victims, but observed with resignation that such men were favored because of their usefulness to princes.[92] Peter must have been so horrified at the effectiveness of the crossbow that he made no attempt to reconcile his condemnation of crossbowmen with his more tolerant view of other aspects of the military profession.[93] He also listed manufacture of crossbow bolts among useless

---

[87] Thomas of Chobham, *Summa*, p. 294.

[88] E.g. *ibid.*, pp. 293f.

[89] Roland of Cremona, *Summae*, 456, para. 6, p. 1350; Alexander of Hales, *Summa*, para. 471, III, 689f.

[90] For discussion of this canon 29, and for canonistic comment on the legitimacy of crossbows, see above, ch. 5, nn. 81–6, and Baldwin, *Masters Princes and Merchants*, I, 223.

[91] Robert of Courson, *Summa*, 10, 15, B.N. Lat. 14524, fol. 50rb; cited in Baldwin, *ibid.*, II, 159, n. 116.

[92] Peter the Chanter, *Summa*, para. 242, III (2a), 242; *ibid.*, para. 361, III (2b), 525.

[93] Baldwin, *Masters Princes and Merchants*, I, 224.

professions, and advocated burning their manufactures, yet like the canonists he did still allow Christians to use crossbows against pagans, Saracens and heretics in a just war.[94] Robert of Courson agreed with this sentiment of his teacher, adding that in a war to defend the Holy Land or the realm, the use of crossbows could be tolerated.[95] Yet in spite of their attempts to endow crossbowmen with a moral stigma, the Parisian theologians did not pursue these attempts whole-heartedly. In the end they decided that use of crossbows was licit in a just war. This conclusion was stated without comment or elabora-tion by Jean de la Rochelle in his section on useless professions, when he stated that manufacture of weapons was licit when they were destined for use in a just war.[96] On this issue the theologians came to agree wholeheartedly with the canonists.

A recurrent problem of medieval warfare was the observance of truces. Gratian had held that wars could be fought at any time in case of necessity, but the Third Lateran Council of 1179 declared truces to be in effect throughout much of the year. Subsequent canonists modified this canon such that a war for defense could legitimately be fought at any time provided only that the war was just and neces-sary.[97] Peter of Poitiers held that while fighting was prohibited on Sunday, defense against attack was licit even then,[98] and Peter the Chanter hinted that wars could be waged even on the Sabbath when common utility required, but neither he nor other members of his circle seem to have explicitly discussed truces.[99] Jean de la Rochelle and Alexander of Hales substantially agreed that wars could be waged at any time in case of necessity,[100] and for Gui de l'Aumône the example of the Maccabees justified waging war in self-defense at any time.[101] The theologians thus added no new insights to the canonistic positions on weapons and truces.

Like their canonistic colleagues, the theologians endowed war with

---

94 Peter the Chanter, *Summa*, MS. W, B.N. Lat. 3477, fols. 101va–vb, 136va, cited in Baldwin, *ibid.*, II, 160, nn. 125, 128.
95 Robert of Courson, *Summa*, 10, 10, 12, B.N. Lat. 14524, fols. 48vb, 49va; cited in Baldwin, *ibid.*, II, 160, n. 127.
96 Jean de la Rochelle, *Summa de Vitiis, de inutilibus officiis*, B.N. Lat. 16417, fol. 146rb.
97 For the views of Gratian and the canonists on truces, cf. above, ch. 3, nn. 52–3 and ch. 5, nn. 153–61.
98 Peter of Poitiers, *Sententiarum*, 4, 4, P.L. 211, p. 1150.
99 Peter the Chanter, *Summa*, para. 199, III (2a), 130.
100 Alexander of Hales, *Summa*, para. 469, III, 688.
101 Gui de l'Aumône, *Summa*, 128, B.N. Lat. 14891, fol. 207va.

inseparable moral, legal and material consequences. Foremost among these was the legitimate retention of spoils taken in a just war; conversely, plunder taken unjustly required penance and restitution enforced in the confessional and in Church courts. The status of plunder loomed so large since a major reason for going to war was often to plunder an adversary. Knights were concerned to know whether they legitimately possessed the spoils of war in the eyes of the Church. Peter the Chanter raised an issue debated at length by Romanists and canonists when he asked whether a knight in justly defending himself could legitimately retain as much plunder as his enemy had earlier taken from him, but Peter's answer was inconclusive.[102] In his *Liber Poenitentialis* Robert of Flamborough constructed a dialogue between a confessional priest and a knightly penitent in which the priest advised the knight that he could keep plunder acquired while fighting a just war on princely authority unless the plunder had been taken from the helpless poor or from clerics.[103] In concurring Thomas of Chobham added, however, that if the poor or the clerics had resisted with weapons the knight could keep what he took from them.[104] Peter the Chanter's opinion was more complex, for at one point he held a prelate responsible for the plunder committed by knights he furnished to his overlord, although it was not clear whether this stricture applied to plunder taken during a just war,[105] while another opinion allowed payment of legitimate wages out of wealth acquired as spoils in a just war.[106] Robert of Courson had difficulty in separating licit wages from illicit plunder taken by knights when they despoiled churches and the poor, but he nevertheless acquiesced in the taking of plunder lest knights refuse to fight to defend the Church or the realm, presumably because they would be deprived of the chance to take booty.[107] In a more general statement Robert expressed the common opinions that spoils taken

---

102 Peter the Chanter, *Summa*, para. 209, III (2a), 163.

103 Robert of Flamborough, *Liber Poenitentialis*, 4, 6, pp. 185f.

104 Thomas of Chobham, *Summa*, p. 502.

105 Peter the Chanter, *Summa*, para. 270, III (2a), 290. Cf. the Chanter's *Verbum Abbreviatum*, 6, P.L. 205, p. 201, where he related the incident in which Bohemund, king of Jerusalem, forced Count Raymond of Saint-Gilles to return plunder taken illicitly from passing merchants.

106 Peter the Chanter, *Postilla* to Genesis 14: 24, MS. London, British Museum Royal 2 C 8, fol. 16ra, cited in Baldwin, *Masters Princes and Merchants*, II, 158, n. 112.

107 Robert of Courson, *Summa*, 10, 15, B.N. Lat. 14524, fol. 50rb; cited in Baldwin, *ibid.*, II, 159, n. 116.

in a just war became the property of the captor, and that mercenaries might receive salaries drawn from these spoils, but they must not usurp more than their stated wages, for to do so made them guilty of rapine and bound to do restitution.[108] Robert seemed unable to divest himself of the suspicion that wages drawn from plunder were morally tainted, but in the end he grudgingly allowed the practice.[109] Radulphus Ardens distinguished four types of rapine among which were licit rapine committed in a just war and an illicit sort taken on one's own illicit authority during an unjust invasion in time of peace.[110]

For Roland of Cremona, the moral issue turned on whether tithes based on profits acquired in a just war were licit. He first considered such profits just because of the example of David distributing booty, but for priests actively to seek such tithes would cause a scandal among simple people who believed all such booty to be rapine. After all, was not the Church bound to reject the tithes of prostitutes? Roland answered this objection by recalling that booty taken in a just war was licit according to the laws of war. He advised priests to inform people of this fact to avoid scandal.[111] Roland here showed keen awareness of what must have been popular resentment against plunder taken by knights in war, although he discounted that resentment as an objection to the receipt of tithes. He then discussed the objection that since Abraham had not taken spoils from the king of Sodom in a just war, such spoils must be illicit, otherwise Abraham would have accepted them for distribution to the poor. Roland's response to the objection is based on his interpretation of the Genesis passage (14: 21–4) that held the spoils to be illicit in the first place since Abraham had not given his men permission to accept such plunder, lest he give the king of Sodom the opportunity to say that he himself had enriched Abraham to his own detriment. Somewhat lamely Roland approved Abraham's action, reasoning that if Abraham had accepted the spoils many people would have reproached him and his descendants for allowing the vile Sodomite

---

108 Robert of Courson, *ibid.*, 15, 4, B.N. Lat. 14524, fol. 64vb; cited in Baldwin, *ibid.*, II, 158, n. 109.
109 Baldwin, *ibid.*, I, 223.
110 Radulphus Ardens, *Speculum Universale*, 12, 64, B.N. Lat. 3240, fol. 126va: Mazar. 709, fol. 306va; Mazar. 710, fol. 190rb.
111 Roland of Cremona, *Summae*, 456, paras. 1, 2, 4, pp. 1349f.

king to enrich him with evil gain, a reputation deemed unworthy of a saintly patriarch.[112] Roland's statement in the end approved without qualification the capture and appropriation of plunder in a just war, but Jean de la Rochelle's simple statement that property captured in a just war became one's own and not subject to restitution was more readily comprehensible.[113]

Jean's opinion, shared by most theologians, did not provide specific guidance in the frequent and difficult cases of wars waged with dubious justice by both parties, but toward the end of the thirteenth century several theologians devoted lengthy discussions to this issue. One approach was proposed around 1290 by Godfrey of Fontaines in a discussion of restitution to be made for the spoils of war.[114] According to one argument, knights who fought their prince's just war in fulfillment of their feudal oath were innocent of any wrongdoing when they attacked the enemies in body and property, but on the other hand they lacked just title to what they took because they lacked princely authority and were bound to restore their plunder. Having thus established a dialectic Godfrey attempted to resolve it by reference to the right of a prince waging a just war to confiscate the property of those who invaded his territory. On his own authority the prince could transfer legitimate title to confiscated property to his knights as a reward; however, those who fought on his side not out of the necessity to render obedience but out of voluntary lust were guilty of homicide and rapine. The prince had the right only to summon certain of his subjects to war, lest he leave other parts of his land unprotected and unduly burden the populace. In order to defeat his enemies more handily he could then decree that whoever responded even to his implicit summons could keep what they captured without having to make restitution, especially if they came voluntarily to aid their prince and the common good. Realising that this opinion without qualification opened the way for freebooters from outside his territory to participate in hopes of taking spoils, Godfrey cautioned

---

[112] *Ibid.*, paras. 3, 5.

[113] Jean de la Rochelle, *Summa de Vitiis, de questis et taliis*, B.N. Lat. 16417, fol. 151ra. Jean followed Raymond of Peñafort (above, ch. 5, n. 96) in allowing the burning of houses in a just war: *ibid., de rapina rerum*, fol. 149vb.

[114] Godfrey of Fontaines, *Quodlibetum* 13, 17, *Les quodlibets...de Godefroid de Fontaines*, pp. 298f.; text compared with B.N. Lat. 14311, fol. 229va–vb.

against greed as a motivation for fighting and required such soldiers of fortune to restore their ill-gotten gains even when they had established some sort of title to it, since they had taken spoils with wicked intent and without princely authorisation.

At about the same time Henry of Ghent attacked the problem of spoils from the opposite side by inquiring whether subjects could be punished in body and estate for the delicts of their prince.[115] Observing that the delicts of a prince were directed against either equals, superiors or subjects, Henry asserted the duty of superiors to render justice in case of disputes between their subjects, and the concurrent principle that inferiors of the same rank must not prosecute their own cause but rather must have recourse to superior judgment. When princes with inferior authority took matters into their own hands by killing their enemy and his subjects, and by devastating his property and that of his subjects, they were guilty for all the evils perpetrated in the war and were bound to make full restitution, and all those subjects who had aided them were likewise culpable. When the fact of their misdeeds was made generally known, they were furthermore cut off from the sacraments of the Church until all of them individually and publicly made satisfaction for their unjust war by devoting all their resources to the task of restitution. When, however, it was at least possible that the prince's war was in fact a just war, the subject knights, having been obliged to obey the prince, were excused from any wrongdoing. At the last moment, then, Henry retreated from his position that rendered subjects liable to punishment for their lord's unjust war. The traditional obedience to authority of some sort, reinforced by at least a probable just cause, overrode moral objections to subjects' participation in war and absolved them from subsequent punishment. Unresolved at the end was Henry's fundamental question, the possession of requisite authority to wage war, although he certainly intended to limit authority to major princes.

The relatively obscure theologian Gervais du Mont-Saint-Eloi, writing about 1290, wrestled with the problem of plunder in a complex quodlibetal discussion of two princes who were fighting each other without the license of their common overlord (see

---

[115] Henry of Ghent, *Quodlibetum* 8, 26, *Aurea Quodlibeta*, II, fols. 47va–48ra.

Appendix).[116] Gervais inquired whether one prince was bound to make restitution to the other for the damages he caused. One opinion he advanced absolved the prince of the duty to restore his spoils because his right to defend himself justified doing damage to his foe to prevent damages to himself, but on the other hand both princes were culpable in not taking their grievances to their superior and thus were bound to make restitution for damages lest they profit from their malice. Gervais used the two conflicting opinions as a point of departure for an extensive and complicated discussion of the legal and moral status of plunder. If one prince actually waged a just war he was excused from guilt because the malice of his adversary necessitated causing excessive damage, and in a just war the dominion of the vanquished party could be transferred to the victor on superior authority. At this point Gervais interjected the definition of an unjust war taken from the *Glossa Ordinaria* to the Decretum and used it to obligate a prince to make restitution for plunder he maliciously took from a third party who was not threatening to cause damage to himself. Gervais buttressed this opinion by reference to a Gregorian decretal forbidding persons from profiting from their own malicious acts. Perhaps the prince's rapine was justified when he plundered those who had caused damage to him since no other just means of recovering his property were available to him, but Gervais still considered such rapine sinful because the prince had usurped the office of judge in his own cause and even given vent to his avarice. Yet if he knew that certain property he had seized was rightly his, then he should not be enjoined in the penitential forum to make restitution but in the external forum he should be so obligated on the overriding principle that persons despoiled must be restored in their possessions. Gervais' reasoning here is difficult to follow, partly because it is based on references to two Gregorian decretals whose direct relevance to the case is not immediately obvious. He seemed to feel that in the confessional forum the prince should be allowed to retain his plunder since it was rightly his in the first place, but in the external forum he could not seek restitution since he himself had committed an injurious act against his adversaries in making war and

---

[116] Gervais du Mont-Saint-Eloi, *Quodlibetum* 1, 84, B.N. Lat. 15350, fols. 289vb–290rb. The text is reproduced in the Appendix to this book. For the similar treatment of William of Rennes, written also from a feudal point of view, see above, ch. 5, n. 125.

taking plunder. The proper course for him was to make amends to his adversaries for his wrongdoing. Gervais himself did not seem to find a clear solution to the case, for he concluded that in some such cases restitution was necessary, while in others it was not. Returning to a consideration of the underlying justice of the war, Gervais finally concluded that such a war waged without authority was not a licit means of securing compensation for damages, but also that full restitution was unnecessary, for otherwise it would be necessary in effect for one prince to restore to the other prince items of property that latter had earlier taken from him and that he himself had subsequently recovered.

The opinions of Godfrey, Henry and Gervais, taken together, reflect rather accurately both the feudal context in which the theology of the just war developed and the basic attitudes of that theology, yet because of their complexity these opinions did not provide clear principles to be applied in specific cases. It is evident, however, that the major concern of these theologians was the moral and legal status of plunder, while killing and violent attacks on persons were relegated to a decidedly secondary importance. Only Godfrey and Henry even mentioned killing, and even they did not place much emphasis upon it. Perhaps the most frequent activity of knights was mutual plundering as an expression of hostility that usually fell short of full-scale war. In this case few knights could claim to be fighting on superior authority and with just cause. Since both sides were usually tainted with wrong-doing, resolution of conflicts turned upon the two means of settling conflicting claims to seized property most clearly expressed by Gervais. First, a knight guilty of malice or avarice was obliged by the confessional forum to restore his evil gain lest he profit from it. Realising that application of these categories of sin was extremely difficult in such cases, Gervais proposed, albeit in clumsy fashion, the alternative of legal remedies of canon law enforced by ecclesiastical courts. The judicial process was viewed as a reinforcement for the moral suasion of the confessional. In fact, these passages are more commentaries on canon law than on speculative problems of political theology. Yet property laws themselves were difficult to apply accurately to such wars, since it was unclear who had just title to property that had often changed hands several times in the course of the war. Did the property rightly belong to the prince physically possessing the property he had seized or to the prince who claimed proprietary right over it? It took an expert and patient judge backed by his own coercive authority to effect resolution of such disputes. These types of wars only declined when and where such superior authorities as national monarchs considered such litigation to be in their own best interests. Like Peter the Chanter's circle, Roland of Cremona and many Decretalists, Godfrey, Henry and Gervais focused their attention less upon abstract moral categories and more on the concrete problems of authority, jurisdiction and plunder. In this sense they indicated the directions that the theory and practice of the just war would take in the late Middle Ages.

CLERICAL PARTICIPATION AND ECCLESIASTICAL WARS

The legitimate roles that canon law assigned to clerics drew the theologian's attention to some considerations of the extent to which clerics could participate in hostilities and of the conditions under which prelates could direct just wars on their own authority. The theologians' awareness of these issues resulted only in *ad hoc* comments on specific items rather than in full-scale treatments. Alain of Lille and Robert of Flamborough repeated the temporal and spiritual penalties clerics incurred by fighting, although Robert tacitly exempted members of the crusading orders whom he considered clerics.[117] Thomas of Chobham however allowed clerics to bear arms in self-defense and even change their clerical garb to avoid being attacked merely because of their clerical status.[118] While clerics could not themselves legally shed blood, they did have the right to demand that princes kill evil-doers in defense of the peace of the Church,[119] and they could exhort princes to make war although they could not urge the killing of specific persons.[120] For Jean de la Rochelle the prohibition on clerical participation was based not so much on the canons as on the clerical duty to attempt to lead perfect lives.[121] Nevertheless the papacy was justified in sending legates to princes informing them of God's law according to which evil men

---

[117] Alain of Lille, *Liber Poenitentialis*, 3, 32, II, 146; Robert of Flamborough, *Liber Poenitentialis*, paras. 105, 148, pp. 121, 150. Cf. C. 23 q. 8 c. 4.

[118] Thomas of Chobham, *Summa*, p. 228.

[119] *Ibid.*, pp. 426f.   [120] *Ibid.*, p. 423.

[121] Jean de la Rochelle, *Summa de Vitiis, utrum bellare licet*, B.N. Lat. 16417, fol. 158va.

must not be allowed to live, and in so doing the legates were not guilty of directly encouraging the death of sinners.[122] Alexander of Hales returned to the question, posed by the canonists, of whether bishops could authorise war, but he differed from them in holding, on the strength of a quotation from Bernard of Clairvaux, that while prelates could urge princes to take military action, they themselves lacked the required authority.[123] In similar fashion Roland of Cremona cast doubt upon the right of bishops to declare war when he asked whether subjects were obliged to obey their bishop when he commanded them to fight. If so, then in effect the bishop possessed both temporal and spiritual swords, but since princes also possessed the temporal sword, then both bishop and prince possessed the same sword, a situation Roland found unsuitable although he then allowed the pope to order Christians to fight.[124] Alexander and Roland, writing shortly before the middle of the thirteenth century, still were imbued with the concepts used a century or more earlier. A theory more consonant with contemporary practice awaited the attention of Thomas Aquinas and his circle.

If the theologians added no new elements to the problem of clerical participation in temporal just wars, they did devote some attention to crusades and other religious wars. Cautious as ever, Alain of Lille cited a canon that barred Christians from killing Jews or pagans on pain of a light penance, and Thomas of Chobham forbade clerics from killing pagans even in defense of the faith.[125] In the Parisian circle only Robert of Courson seems to have discussed the moral issues posed by the crusades against infidels and heretics, for he raised the fundamental question whether the copious Old Testament examples of Israelite wars against alien tribes served to justify contemporary wars of conquest. While the normative influence of these examples on current wars had usually been implicitly assumed rather than explicitly justified by canonists and theologians stretching back at least to Augustine and Ambrose, Robert in questioning the connection attempted an original viewpoint on the theology of the just war. He considered the conquests of the Israelites, such as that of Joshua, as just wars rather than as blatant cases of rapine, because God

[122] *Ibid., utrum clericis licet interficere pro necessitate*, B.N. Lat. 16417, fol. 156vb.

[123] Alexander of Hales, *Summa*, para. 469, III, 688.

[124] Roland of Cremona, *Summae*, 264, paras. 6–7, pp. 730f.

[125] Alain of Lille, *Liber Poenitentialis*, 2, 58, II, 77; Thomas of Chobham, *Summa*, p. 78.

had authorised them to fulfill His promises to His chosen people. Robert then inquired into the justice of a contemporary war in which a prince conquered a territory, expelled its legitimate heirs, and granted out the territory as fiefs to his vassals.[126] Robert's answer turned on a set of distinctions: was the prince acting on his own authority or on that of the Church to make war on its enemies; and were the victims infidels or Christians? Unfortunately he did not provide specific solutions for these questions, nor did he here explicitly refer to the just war, but he did hold unambiguously that a prince was justified in conquering infidel territory when armed with ecclesiastical authorisation. Robert justified the paradigm case of wars to reconquer the Holy Land, on the grounds that the Holy Land was the Church's rightful inheritance, just as Amorite territory belonged rightfully to the Israelites.[127] More pointedly, he declared that crusades in the Holy Land were just wars, because infidels there attacked the faith and usurped the rightful inheritance of Christians who as God's latter day chosen people were the rightful heirs of the ancient Israelites. The pope granted crusaders remission of their sins in order that they rid the Holy Land of its enemies and avenge attacks on Christian cities and fortifications. The crusaders were entitled not only to take usury from the infidels but also to keep spoils and conquests since they were only seizing property that right-fully belonged to the Church and Christians by heredity.[128] In agreement with other theologians and canonists, Robert concluded in effect that the examples of Old Testament wars were indeed normative for contemporary crusades. He was clear that a con-temporary war of conquest could only be justified by prior ecclesias-tical authority that rendered it a holy war or crusade. Robert thereby implicitly condemned as unjust those wars directed toward purely temporal conquest.

Robert's view thus endowed the Church of his day with the same authority to declare war on infidels that God Himself had exercised in the Old Testament wars. For Alexander of Hales the Church had the right to authorise the conquest of the Holy Land but the right to

---

[126] Robert of Courson, cited above, n. 26. Cf. Baldwin, *Masters Princes and Merchants*, I, 208.

[127] Robert of Courson, *ibid.*, 15, 2–4, B.N. Lat. 14524, fol. 64va–vb; cited in Baldwin, *ibid.*, II, 147, n. 25. Cf. Herde, 'Christians and Saracens,' 366.

[128] 'Le traité "De Usura" de Robert de Courson,' ed. G. Lefèvre, *Travaux et Mémoires de l'Université de Lille*, x, 30 (Lille, 1902), 9, 11.

kill infidels belonged to civil authority, although Alexander did not specify the appropriate official. By contrast, both ecclesiastical and royal officials had the proper authority to kill heretics.[129] Robert and Alexander were in general agreement with the canonistic position that crusades against infidels and heretics were legitimate operations of papal authority, although of course the authority for such actions came ultimately from God. In disagreement, Jean de la Rochelle denied that the Roman Church itself possessed the authority to punish pagans and heretics since that authority belonged to God alone.[130] Jean probably insisted on this point in order to absolve the Church of any culpability in the shedding of blood that would result from exceeding its authority. What was missing in his treatment was a clear reference to a theory of authority delegated by God to the pope and in turn to the papal legates who exhorted princes to make holy war on infidels and heretics, and who often directed those wars. Even Robert of Courson noted that since the Roman Church often sent legates and bishops out to enlist knights for combat duty in the Holy Land, prelates so occupied were themselves involved in the shedding of blood.[131] The problem obviously called for a more juridical treatment than the theologians were prepared to provide.

These somewhat confused positions concerning the locus of authority did not provoke extensive debate however, for the theologians admitted that in practical terms the papacy had the right to initiate and prosecute holy wars and crusades. More interesting to them was the proper conduct of crusades against infidels and heretics. Robert of Courson obligated bishops with or without regalia to aid princes in these wars, and allowed princes to collect crusading tithes to support their crusading efforts.[132] Bonaventura approved promulgation of indulgences and disbursement of the wealth of the Church for the common utility of defending the Holy Land and the faith.[133] Alexander of Hales upheld the spiritual benefits of the

---

[129] Alexander of Hales, *Glossa*, to 3. 37. 5, III, 465, 487.

[130] Jean de la Rochelle, cited above, n. 122.

[131] Robert of Courson, *Summa*, 30, 1, B.N. Lat. 14524, fol. 104rb–va; cited in Baldwin, *Masters Princes and Merchants*, II, 125, n. 87.

[132] Robert of Courson, *ibid.*, 15, 16, B.N. Lat. 14524, fols. 66vb–67ra; cited in Baldwin, *ibid.*, II, 154, n. 77. Cf. Robert of Courson, *ibid.*, 10, 11–12, B.N. Lat. 14524, fol. 49ra–va; cited in Baldwin, *ibid.*, II, 157, nn. 95–7.

[133] Bonaventura, *Commentarium in IV Libros Sententiarum*, to 4.20, pars 2, art. unic., q. 4, *Opera Omnia*, IV, 537.

crusader's vow that absolved him of sin while placing him in danger of dying in combat for the Christian faith against its enemies.[134] The pope was able to promulgate a plenary indulgence for crusaders out of his plenitude of power in the Church militant.[135] In actual combat the crusader's expropriation on princely authority of Saracen or heretical property was not considered rapacious but rather virtuous.[136] Not only offering the lure of spoils, conquests and usury, Robert of Courson provided knights with added encouragement to go on a crusade when he advised them to take the cross when faced with the difficult choices of either fighting in their lord's unjust war or running the risk of disinheritance and confiscation, in case of their lord's unjust command.[137] Taken together, the theologians offered three inducements to knights debating whether to go on a crusade: a plenary indulgence; the chance to take spoils; and the opportunity to escape from a feudal situation that threatened their spiritual and temporal welfare.

Christian possession of the Holy Land was conventionally seen by the theologians as a supremely worthy and righteous goal meriting the most strenuous measures in its pursuit, but could crusades be waged against other territories under Saracen control? Roland of Cremona had tentatively put forth the suggestion that infidels could exercise legitimate dominion outside territory belonging rightfully to Christians,[138] but other theologians neither pursued his suggestion nor commented specifically upon Christian campaigns against Saracen territories outside the Holy Land. Taking his lead from the canonists, Jean de la Rochelle did allow Saracens to exercise certain legal rights over Christians in time of truce. For example, when Christians journeyed in Saracen lands they were obligated to pay the ordinary tolls (*pedagia*) to support Saracen efforts to protect their safety against robbers and pirates, and if Christians did not render such tolls to Saracen rulers, they should give equivalent sums to the poor under Church supervision. Of course in time of wars between Christians and Saracens Christian travelers were not bound to make

---

134 Alexander of Hales, *Glossa*, to 4.20. 4, 32, 2, IV, 360, 509.

135 *Ibid.*, to 4.38.6, IV, 562.

136 Alexander of Hales, *Summa*, para. 475, III, 699.

137 Robert of Courson, *Summa*, 10, 15, B.N. Lat. 14524, fol. 50va–vb; cited in Baldwin, *Masters Princes and Merchants*, II, 148, n. 37. For Robert's position on spoils, see above, n. 128.

138 Roland of Cremona, *Summae*, 264, para. 5, p. 730.

such payments.[139] Christian captives held by Saracen enemies of the faith could be rescued at any time, and this action did not contradict the Augustinian injunction to maintain faith with the enemy, for the injunction in Jean's opinion only applied in times of truce. If the captives were rescued during a truce, their rescuers owed restitution to the Saracens but must not return the captives unless the Saracens had forced them to commit idolatry or other mortal sins, in which case the rescuers owed no restitution.[140] The Chanter went so far as to champion the right of a Christian captured by Saladin to escape even if he had taken an oath not to escape, for if he were to return he would probably be tortured into denying his faith.[141] Henry of Ghent, writing around 1290, explicitly applied the just war analysis to wars waged against infidels outside the Holy Land when he discussed Saracen ravages of the March of Ancona,[142] but of course such an attack from whatever quarter could be repulsed.

The theologians showed rather less restraint when they discussed crusades against heretics. For Alexander of Hales heretics could be killed both by royal and ecclesiastical authorities since their obstinacy had separated them from the Church,[143] and Bonaventura considered wars against heretics a species of civil war.[144] Roland of Cremona considered ambushes of heretics to be the most prudential means that orthodox Christians could employ against them.[145] These writers no doubt had in mind the recent Albigensian crusade that had redounded to the glory and power of the Capetian monarchy. This crusade was specifically mentioned in an anonymous postill written around 1230, in which the author was concerned to show the lawfulness of slaying heretics on judicial authority. When Christians were inadvertently killed in such crusades, the crusaders were not guilty of sin because the slain Christians had received sufficient warning to be able to escape from the mass of the heretics.[146]

---

[139] Jean de la Rochelle, *Summa de Vitiis, de rapinis contra pedagia*, B.N. Lat. 16417, fol. 150vb. Jean may have borrowed his opinion from Raymond of Peñafort: above, ch. 5, n. 229.

[140] *Ibid., de furantibus captivis a sarracenis*, B.N. Lat. 16417, fols. 151vb–152ra.

[141] Peter the Chanter, *Summa*, para. 116, II, 219.

[142] Henry of Ghent, *Quodlibetum* 15, 16, *Aurea Quodlibeta*, II, fol. 395ra.

[143] Alexander of Hales, *Glossa*, to 3.37.5, III, 465, 487.

[144] Bonaventura, *Expositio in Psalterium* (to Psalm 106: 39), *Opera Omnia* (Vivès edition), IX, 286b. This is probably a spurious work; it does not appear in the Quaracchi edition.

[145] Roland of Cremona, *Summae*, 263, para. 11, p. 729.

[146] Cited in Smalley, *Study of the Bible*, p. 278, n. 2. Alain of Lille cited the canon of the

Taken as a whole, the theologians provided only partial and inconclusive analysis of the morality and means of the crusades. They did not justify Christian wars against Saracen territories outside the Holy Land, but neither did they specify to what extent infidels could exercise legitimate dominion. The juridical chain of command in the crusades was not made explicit, nor was the distinction made clearly between holy wars and crusades. These problems received more extensive and coherent treatment in the works of the Decretalists and of Thomas Aquinas.

The defects of the theologians' treatment of the just war are palpably obvious. Some were more concerned with broader Christian political and moral issues. Thus, for example, John of Salisbury in the sixth book of his *Policraticus* gave a by-then thoroughly conventional portrait of the Christian soldier who faithfully and virtuously fought for the welfare of Church, *patria* and public utility. John frequently lamented the many contemporary conflicts and insisted on the need to maintain the peace and unity of the Church. Yet, despite his familiarity with the works of Cicero, Augustine, Isidore and Gratian, his works contain no references to the doctrine of the just war itself. The fragmentary or *ad hoc* approach of others reflected received opinion more than a systematic treatment based on the solid theoretical foundations of the just war in Christian moral thought. The Parisian circle grouped around Peter the Chanter forsook the systematic approach for a casuistic one that attempted to render the just war theories relevant to practical problems faced by ordinary knights and princes. While their high-minded casuistry was ultimately a failure that yielded place to the systematic and speculative approach of Thomas Aquinas, on the basis of their analysis of the moral dimensions of the just war, it is too much to claim that in the fifty years before the advent of the friars in the second quarter of the thirteenth century theological study had made little progress.[147] Even without the great Scholastics, theologians had established the just war as a moral punishment that incorporated both moral and legal consequences for just and unjust warriors and their respective supporters.

Council of Tribur (895) that absolved Christians of serious guilt when they killed other Christians who could not be distinguished from the mass of pagans: *Liber Poenitentialis*, 2, 59, II, 77.

[147] Southern, *Western Society and the Church*, p. 296.

Chapter 7

THOMAS AQUINAS AND HIS CIRCLE

By the middle of the thirteenth century leadership in theological study at Paris and other university centers had passed from casuistic and penitential theologians to the systematic and speculative philosophers whose major interest was the compilation of compendious theological summae. The most influential of this latter group were the Dominicans Albertus Magnus and Thomas Aquinas. These thinkers, their associates, and their direct pupils produced works of encyclopedic length that attempted to provide a synthesis of traditional thought and new innovations on current topics of discussion. Thus, in the thoughts on war scattered throughout his works, Aquinas fused the Aristotelian political theory to the traditional Augustinian outlook of his predecessors. His comprehensive treatment incorporated such Aristotelian tenets as the naturalness of political authority, the teleology of communal life, and the superiority of the common good over the good of the individual. It is this extensive adaptation of Aristotle that set Aquinas and his circle apart from earlier theologians, and emancipated them from dependence on the canonists. Aquinas and his followers for the most part turned their backs to the decentralising tendencies of feudalism that were at the same time losing ground in practice, and focused their attention on the consolidated city-states and kingdoms that bulked ever larger in contemporary experience. The assertion of public authority against private right was granted a new theoretical benediction in Aquinas' Aristotelian outlook.

The thinkers discussed here include Aquinas, his teacher Albertus Magnus, his associates Vincent of Beauvais and Hannibald, and his direct students Peter of Auvergne, Ptolemy of Lucca, Remigio de' Girolami, and Giles of Rome. While most of these writers were Dominicans, institutional affiliations were now of less importance than adherence to the emerging Thomist outlook. For this reason these writers can be seen as a coherent group espousing the same general theories. Modern commentators have tended to confine their studies to Aquinas alone without closely examining the academic milieu in which he worked.[1] Here a tentative attempt is made to remedy this deficiency so as to understand more clearly both the traditional elements and the original contributions of Aquinas' thought.

THE MORAL PURPOSES OF WAR AND KILLING

Aquinas' most extensive treatment of war, found in the 'Pars Secunda Secundae' of his Summa Theologiae, indicated his over-riding concern to place warfare within the overall moral scheme of the Christian aim of salvation. It is in this attempt that he is both most traditional and also most innovative. The traditional Augustinian attitude was most fully expressed in the first article of quaestio 40, where Aquinas inquired whether war was licit under any circumstances. To the argument that those who live by the sword perish by the sword (Matt. 26: 52) he countered with Augustine's opinion that use of the sword was licit for those in public authority.[2] The second objection, the evangelical precepts to resist not evil and to give place to wrath, was answered with Augustine's interpretation of these precepts as pertaining to the inward disposition. Aquinas then imported the Aristotelian concept of the common good that on occasion must be defended. Furthermore, according to relevant

---

[1] General works on Thomas Aquinas and his circle include F. Copleston, *Aquinas* (Baltimore, 1955); E. Gilson, *The Christian Philosophy of St Thomas Aquinas* (New York, 1956); M. D. Chenu, *Introduction à l'étude de Saint Thomas d'Aquin* (3rd ed., Paris, 1954; trans. as *Toward Understanding Saint Thomas*, Chicago, 1964); M. Grabmann, *Thomas Aquinas: His Personality and Thought* (1928), (rep. New York, 1963); F. J. Roensch, *The Early Thomistic School* (Dubuque, Iowa, 1964); G. de Lagarde, *La naissance de l'esprit laique*, II: *Secteur social de la scholastique* (2nd ed., Louvain and Paris, 1956), esp. chs. 3, 5, 8, 11. On the writings themselves see M. Grabmann, *Die Werke des hl. Thomas von Aquino* (3rd ed., Muenster, 1949) and P. Mandonnet, *Des écrits authentiques de Saint Thomas d'Aquin* (2nd ed., Fribourg, 1910).

Among the many commentaries on the just war theories of the Thomists, the following may be cited here: Regout, *La guerre juste*, pp. 79–93; D. Beaufort, *La guerre comme instrument de secours ou de punition* (Hague, 1933); H. Gmür, *Thomas von Aquino und der Krieg* (Leipzig, 1933); B. de Solages, 'La genèse et l'orientation de la théologie de la guerre juste,' *Bulletin de littérature ecclésiastique*, II (1940), 61–80; O. Schilling, *Die Staats- und Soziallehre des hl. Thomas von Aquino* (Paderborn, 1923), pp. 177–83; Chenu, 'L'évolution de la théologie de la guerre juste,' in *La parole de Dieu* (2 vols., Paris, 1964), II. 571–91; J. Tooke, *The Just War in Aquinas and Grotius* (London, 1965); Walters, 'Five Classical Just War Theories,' esp. pp. 11–200.

[2] S.T. 2–2, q. 40, art. 1, obj. 1, ad 1. I have used the Ottawa ed. (5 vols., 1941), but refrain from giving page or folio references since there are so many editions of the Summa Theologiae in current use. For these eds. see I. T. Eschmann's catalogue in E. Gilson, *Christian Philosophy of St Thomas Aquinas*, p. 388.

passages from Augustine, the good of enemies must be supported even against their own wishes.[3] The third objection, that war contradicts the virtue of peace, Aquinas countered with the Augustinian observation that since just wars were waged in defense of peace, they were not evil unless the peace desired was itself evil.[4] The fourth objection, this time based on medieval conditions, held that warfare was sinful because the Church prohibited the warlike exercises of tournaments, to which Aquinas answered that tournaments were prohibited only when they resulted in injury, death and depredation.[5] As an opposing argument he cited the advice of John the Baptist to soldiers to be content with their wages (Luke 3 : 14), adding that this advice did not prohibit military service in general.[6] In this passage, then, Aquinas justified warfare in a Christian context by time-honored reference to Augustine's teleology.

Elsewhere in the Summa Theologiae Aquinas expanded his moral justification of war, holding that princes entrusted with public authority to care for the community could legitimately kill malefactors for the welfare of the whole community, just as a physician could amputate a putrid limb to save the whole body. Private persons of course lacked the authority to kill malefactors.[7] In a question about prayers for enemies Aquinas first justified fighting enemies to restrain them from further sinning, both for their own good and for that of others, and then approved prayers that asked God to inflict temporal ills on enemies for their correction. In this sense prayer and action (*oratio et operatio*) were complementary rather than contradictory.[8] In his commentary on the Sentences of Peter Lombard, Aquinas held that one can do harm to enemies to avoid greater evils or to support greater goods such as justice,[9] and in the *Summa contra*

---

[3] S.T. 2–2, q. 40, art. 1, obj. 2, ad. 2. Aristotle himself did not seem to use the term 'common good,' but in *Politics* 1.1.1252a, he certainly described the concept.

[4] S.T. 2–2, q. 40, art. 1, obj. 3, ad 3. That wars were waged in pursuit of peace was also part of Aristotle's teleology: *Nicomachean Ethics*, 10.

[5] S.T. 2–2, q. 40, art. 1, obj. 4, ad 4.   [6] S.T. 2–2, q. 40, art. 1, sed contra.

[7] S.T. 2–2, q. 64, art. 3, resp., ad 1, ad 3.

[8] S.T. 2–2, q. 83, art. 8, ad 3. The Dominican Hannibald paraphrased in somewhat turgid fashion Augustine's contention that love of enemies justified killing them. One should wish temporal ills to befall enemies when those ills were expedient to Church or kingdom, but also one should only wish spiritual benefits for enemies, not temporal ones: *Scriptum super Libris Magistri Sententiarum*, to 3,30, art. 1, resp., printed in the Parma edition of the *Opera Omnia* of Aquinas (25 vols., Parma, 1852–73; rep. New York, 1948–50), XXII, 299f.

[9] Aquinas, *Commentum in IV Libros Sententiarum*, to 3, 30, art. 2, *Opera Omnia*, VII, 328.

Gentiles he viewed punishment of wickedness as a divinely authorised means of restoring moral order and concord.[10]

Having justified punishment of enemies Aquinas turned to justify the agent of that punishment, the military profession, as ordained to defend the welfare of the republic, divine worship, and also the poor and oppressed.[11] He upheld the Augustinian notion that officials in authority could legitimately kill evil-doers when they were motivated by charity. Citing two homilies of Gregory the Great, he justified such killing on three grounds: correcting evil-doers; preventing the prosperity of evil men from injuring the multitude and the Church; and maintaining divine justice.[12] To Gregory VII's opinion, wrenched out of context to be sure, that knights could not exercise their office without sin Aquinas objected that they had the legitimate function to pursue the common utility of the Church and the community by defending territory. While he cautioned knights to be content with their wages and not to fight without cause, he conventionally interpreted Gregory's moral stricture to apply not to the military profession itself but to the sins that frequently resulted from it.[13] This representative sample of passages shows Aquinas as remaining unqualifiedly within the conventional Augustinian framework.

An innovative side of Aquinas' thought on war and killing emerged when he used Aristotelian political postulates to justify princely authority to wage war. First among these postulates was the assertion that man by nature was a social and political animal. Politics then became a practical art whose end was right action, defined as a virtuous community life in which the welfare of the community overrode individual claims. In this community law existed to pursue the common welfare whose chief feature was peace.[14] Fortified with these convictions, Aquinas wrote to the

[10] Aquinas, *Summa contra Gentiles*, 3, 140, 146, *Opera Omnia*, v, 279.

[11] S.T. 2–2, q. 188, art. 3, resp.

[12] Aquinas, *Quaestio Disputata de Caritate*, arts. 8, 10, in *Quaestiones Disputatae et Quaestiones XII Quodlibetales* (Turin and Rome, 1927), pp. 546f.

[13] Aquinas, *Commentum in IV Libros Sententiarum*, to 4, 16, q. 4 art. 2 quaestiunc. 3, *Opera Omnia*, VII², 767. Hannibald interpreted Gregory's statement to mean that knights need not desert their profession unless they wished to undergo penance: *Scriptum super IV Libros Sententiarum*, to 4, 16, Expositio textus, printed in the Vivès edition of Aquinas' *Opera Omnia* (34 vols., Paris, 1871–80), XXX, 680. Cf. above, ch. 1, n. 73.

[14] This summary is adapted from C. T. Davis, 'Remigio de' Girolami and Dante. A Com-

duchess of Brabant that since princes were instituted by God to further the common good, they therefore had the duty to defend it.[15] In his treatise on kingship written for the king of Cyprus, he favored a province over a city for it was more capable of mutual defense against enemies.[16] One of the greatest dangers to the maintenance of the public good was destruction of peace and the subsequent disintegration of the city or kingdom through enemy attack. The king's duty was to keep secure from external enemies the multitude committed to his care.[17] In the Summa Theologiae Aquinas held that wars had as their goal the conservation of temporal peace. He rejected unequivocally the opinion that peace was not a meritorious goal since it gave rise to many lascivious acts, reasoning that since the peace of the community was a good in itself, it could not be rendered evil when some men wrongly used it. Furthermore many other men benefited from peace because it inhibited the worse evils of homicide and sacrilege.[18] A man even became a martyr when he died in defense of the community against an enemy bent on corrupting the Christian faith.[19] In this passage Aquinas combined, somewhat clumsily perhaps, the traditional Christian glorification of martyrdom in defense of the faith with the potent convictions of Aristotelian political theory to form a solid justification of defensive wars. Defense of the common good became a licit prerogative of every community. Aquinas' conclusions were more conventional than novel, but his reasoning represented an unprecedented injection of Aristotelianism into the theology of the just war.

Since defense of the common good by a just war was a moral imperative, it was necessary for Aquinas to elaborate on virtues that supported the just war and to prohibit vices that impinged upon it. The two relevant virtues, fortitude and prudence, had been fre-

---

parison of Their Conceptions of Peace,' *Studi Danteschi*, XXXVI (1959), 110–14. For the problems of interpreting the Thomist circle's political views, see J. Dunbabin, 'Aristotle in the Schools,' *Trends in Medieval Political Thought*, pp. 65–85.

[15] Aquinas, *De Regimine Iudaeorum ad Ducissam Brabantiae*, 6, paras. 735–6, *Opuscula Philosophica*, ed. R. M. Spiazzi (Turin and Rome, 1954), p. 251.

[16] Aquinas, *De Regimine Principum*, I, 2, para. 749, *Opuscula Philosophica*, p. 259.

[17] Aquinas, *ibid.*, I, 16, paras. 826–7, p. 276.

[18] S.T. 2–2, q. 123, art. 5, obj. 3, ad 3. Cf. S.T. 2–2, q. 40, art. 1, obj. 3, ad 3; S.T. 2–2, q. 50, art. 4, resp., ad 1–3

[19] Aquinas, *Commentum in IV Libros Sententiarum*, to 4, 49, 5, 3, *Opera Omnia*, VII², 1241. Cf. Kantorowicz, 'Pro Patria Mori,' *King's Two Bodies*, pp. 240–3.

quently mentioned by earlier theologians, while Aristotle's *Ethics* and *Politics* were replete with discussions of military virtues. Aquinas evidently took upon himself the task of combining these two strands of thought. Thus a soldier who faced death in a just war to defend the common good had need of much fortitude,[20] but this was not a self-sufficient virtue since it was ordained to victory and peace. Aquinas here cited Aristotle's observation (*Ethics* 10, 7) that no one would be so foolish as to make war for its own sake, since he would thereby turn his friends into enemies to be killed.[21] In his commentary Aquinas departed from a strict literal exposition of the text and propounded his own, stronger conviction that the common good was in effect divine. While this Thomist apotheosis of the common good would eventually revolutionise medieval political thought, Aquinas himself employed it to encourage that highest form of fortitude operative in wars waged in its defense or in defense of the *patria*.[22] Although fortitude may well have been implicitly directed toward defense of the *patria* and the common good in Aristotle's own analysis, or may have seemed implicit to his thirteenth-century readers, the explicit relationship appears to be the contribution of Aquinas himself.

Thus endowed with fortitude, an army in pursuit of victory must follow the direction of the proper official who himself must be possessed of prudence sufficient to direct an effective defense and promote the ordered concord of peace.[23] Aquinas thus combined Aristotelian and patristic analyses of virtues proper to war into a novel synthesis, yet his description of the vices motivating wars was less extensive. He considered wars waged for reasons other than pursuit of the common good as dangerous both to the soul and to the community, for they were waged out of motives of greed and vainglory and often resulted in the surrender of liberty to the yoke of the enemy. Aquinas approved Torquatus' killing of his own son for the latter's disobedience in waging a war to enhance his own reputation.[24]

---

[20] S.T. 2–2, q. 123, art. 5, resp.; *Summa contra Gentiles*, 3, 34, *Opera Omnia*, v, 183.
[21] Aquinas, *Expositio in X Libros Ethicorum*, 10, lect. 11 (to *Ethics* 10.7.1177b), *Opera Omnia*, XXI, 350.
[22] Aquinas, *ibid.*, 3, lect. 14 (to *Ethics* 3.6.1115a), *Opera Omnia*, XXI, 97.
[23] Aquinas, *Summa contra Gentiles*, 3, 128, *Opera Omnia*, v, 263f.; S.T. 2–2, q. 50, art. 4, ad 3.
[24] Aquinas, *De Regimine Principum*, 1, 8, para. 777, *Opuscula Philosophica*, pp. 265f.

Aquinas in his thought on war and killing did not enunciate any completely new doctrines but rather expressed the traditional thought in new Aristotelian terms. Other theologians in his circle followed his lead in employing these terms when discussing the moral utility of war. Albertus Magnus, for example, justified the use of weapons in instituting or defending the polity,[25] and then agreed that while war was a minimal good, its goal was the great goal of peace.[26] Here Albertus underscored the teleological view of war that he and Aquinas had found not only in Augustine but also in clearer form in Aristotle. Around 1250 Vincent of Beauvais, a fellow Dominican and friend of Thomas Aquinas, assembled various theological opinions to show that war was sometimes necessary to preserve liberty and territory and to increase dignity.[27]

At his death, Aquinas left incomplete his commentary on Aristotle's *Politics*, a work that was continued by his student Peter of Auvergne. Peter, most concerned to explicate Aristotle's thought for contemporary readers, was eager to show that in the Philosopher's thought war was justified by its goals, civic peace, tranquillity and the exercise of practical virtues. Thus military force repelled invaders and maintained control over subjects, and the bellicose virtues were ordained for the common good.[28] Wars waged against innocent men were unjust, but in a just war to defend the peace, the killing of

---

[25] Albertus Magnus, *Commentarium Politicorum Libri VIII*, 7, 2 (to *Politics* 7.2.1325a), *Opera Omnia*, ed. A. Borgnet (38 vols., Paris, 1890–9), VIII, 636.

[26] *Ibid.*, 637; *Summa Theol*, I, q. 67, memb. 1, *Opera Omnia*, XXXI, 676f.

[27] Vincent of Beauvais, *Speculum Doctrinale*, 11, 36 (Douai, 1624), p. 1015. Cf. Isidore of Seville, *Etymologiarum*, XVIII, 1, 2.

[28] Peter of Auvergne, *Expositio in VIII Libros Politicorum*, 7, lect. 2 (to *Politics* 7.2.1325a); 7, lect. 11 (to *Politics* 7.14.1333a), *Opera Omnia*, XXI, 640, 677f. Idem, *Commentarium in Libros Politicorum*, II, B.N. Lat. 16089, fol. 290ra: 'Bellum autem iustum necessario quantum ad finem ordinatur, nec contrarius bellum propter bellum sed propter finem bonum ut propter pacem. x ethicorum. et tale bellum est exercicium ad multas et fere omnes virtutes... qui enim sic in illo bello secundum vitam militarem exercent. primo exercent se propter bonum commune et iterum quia in actibus fortitudinis se exercent mortem in periculis non timentes pro bono communi.' *Ibid.*, v, fol. 312vb: 'Qui de cura hominum sunt solliciti incole et civitatis in quantum huius vel nisi vendere et emere tanto quia ad actus bellicos iniungere exercitati opera fortitudinis consuescunt. habent enim se sic ad deffendendo gregem et repellendo alia nocencia sicut principes in custodiendo populum et ita egrediuntur in actibus fortitudinis et aliarum virtutum moralium.' *Ibid.*, VI, fol. 318va: 'Oportet optime politentes esse animosos ad repellendum insultus hostium ut pacem ducunt.' Further study of this work would shed light on the relationship between Aquinas and Peter. Cf. Gilson's comment (*History of Christian Philosophy*, p. 749, n. 127): 'What prevented him [= Peter] from being a complete Thomist was his Aristotelianism.' Cf. Roensch, *Early Thomistic School*, pp. 92–9.

adversaries, although sinful under most conditions, was a good act.[29] Peter criticised the Spartan constitution because it was ordained to the primary goal of dominating other cities through military force that was not a good end in itself but only a means to a good end.[30] Yet when men deserved to serve others their masters could make just war on them when they rebelled.[31] A city did not need defenders at its foundation but later it did need fighters when it had expanded its territory up to the territory of another city lest it lose its freedom to other cities.[32] While Peter's opinion hardly seems surprising, it is a firm and unequivocal statement within an Aristotelian framework of the natural right and duty of a city or kingdom to wage war in defense of its territory and citizens.

Another of Aquinas' direct students was Ptolemy of Lucca who completed the treatise *De Regimine Principum* that his master left incomplete. For Ptolemy, warriors were a necessary part of a good polity for they protected the *patria* from external aggressors and aided the prince in carrying out justice.[33] Giles of Rome, an Augustinian canon and student of Aquinas, about 1280 wrote his own treatise, for the young Philip the Fair. In view of Philip's later career it is ironic that Giles's main purpose was to prove the right of the papacy to control kings. Within his scheme, however, Giles took pains to allow princes a free hand in waging wars in defense of their principalities. Kings and princes should know the strengths of their people, and on the basis of this knowledge the rulers must determine how best to organise their wars with adversaries. They must display fortitude in abundance when they waged just wars for the good of

---

[29] Peter of Auvergne, *Commentarium*, II, B.N. Lat. 16089, fol. 290ra–rb: 'Aliud autem est bellum iniustum quod exercet contra innocentes et non iniuriantes...dicendum quod interficere vel mutilare adversarios licet secundum se sit malum, tamen secundum quid, scilicet in bello iusto bonum est utrumque propter pacem.'

[30] Peter of Auvergne, *Expositio in Politicorum*, 7, lect. 11 (to *Politics* 7.14.1333b–1334a), *Opera Omnia*, XXI, 678–80.

[31] *Ibid.*, 7, lect. 2 (to *Politics* 7.2.1325a), *Opera Omnia*, XXI, 640. *Commentarium*, II, B.N. Lat. 16089, fol. 290ra: 'Dicendum quod duplex est bellum, scilicet iustum et iniustum bellum. bellum iustum et naturale est quando aliqui naturaliter servi existentes vel propter regionem, ut barbari...vel propter consuetudinem in turpibus. alii autem sunt naturaliter illorum domini propter virtutis insignium, tunc illi servire isti autem dominari iuste debent, et ideo si rebelles sunt illi, ad serviendum iuste surgit bellum contra eos. faciunt enim illi contra iustitiam naturalem.'

[32] Peter of Auvergne, *Expositio in Politicorum*, 4, lect. 3 (to *Politics* 7.4.1291a), *Opera Omnia*, XXI, 513.

[33] Ptolemy of Lucca, *De Regimine Principum*, 4, 24, 26, paras. 1101, 1104, *Opuscula Philosophica*, pp. 353f.

the kingdom.[34] Giles's mention of just wars here seems almost an afterthought, for he assumed that such wars were just without need of rationalisation. Like Peter of Auvergne, Giles also repeated Aristotle's contention that barbarians and naturally servile men were subject to a just war of conquest waged by men possessed of wisdom, prudence, and subtlety. He cautioned however against an overly broad application of this notion to his own time when he added that no citizen and no prince should do injury to other citizens and princes. Princes should tolerate other licit ways of life and peoples, for no one could live the virtuous life when he usurped the property of others.[35] In disagreement with Aristotle, Giles prevented intellectual superiority from serving as a justification for conquest by contemporary princes. He may have had in mind the conquest of barbarian infidels living on the fringes of Christianity. In another passage he exhorted warriors to bravery in the face of death when fighting a just war for the defense of the *patria*. Just warriors should avoid the shame of flight from battle; in defense of justice and the common good they should not fear for their lives.[36] In the concluding chapter of his treatise, Giles turned to a more general justification of the instrumentality of warfare. Citing Aristotle again, he approved of wars waged for the sake of peace rather than for their own sake. While some wars were waged out of wickedness, greed, and anger, just wars were waged for peace and the common good of the kingdom as potions and phlebotomies were employed for the good of the individual person. In a healthy society wars were unnecessary, but when the kingdom was threatened by enemies, all means of war were permissible to the end that peace and the common good of the citizens be achieved. Kings and princes bent on preserving the common good and civil peace merited eternal peace.[37] Giles here in effect rendered defense of the common good and civil peace a divine virtue with a divine reward. This divinisation of the teleology of the just war is the most extreme justification of warfare.

[34] Giles of Rome, *De Regimine Principum*, I, II, 14 (Rome, 1607; rep. Aalen, 1967), p. 89.
[35] *Ibid.*, II, III, 7, p. 365.
[36] *Ibid.*, III, II, 4, pp. 565f.
[37] *Ibid.*, III, III, 23, pp. 623f. In the treatise *Quomodo Possint Reges Bona Regni Ecclesiis Elargiri*, attributed to Giles, the same conclusion that the king had the duty to defend the *patria* and its subjects was reached by the more traditional argument of Romans 13 that earthly powers served as ministers of God: B.N. Lat. 6786, fol. 24v. Cf. Post, *Studies*, p. 451.

The concomitant glorification of the warrior was perhaps most cogently expressed shortly before 1300 by the Franciscan Richard of Mediavilla, who seems to have been strongly influenced by Aquinas' assimilation of Aristotle. For him violent death, otherwise the most terrible of events, was not terrible when suffered for a good end, as was death in a just war of the community in defense of justice.[38] The common good of the honor of the prince and the defense of the republic was served by the martial fortitude of the soldier. In commenting on the Maccabees' fighting on the Sabbath Richard considered someone who defended himself or divine law to be performing a liberal rather than a servile act.[39] Under Aristotelian influence both warfare and warriors found inclusion in God's providential scheme and in human nature itself.

The direct followers of Thomas Aquinas bore witness to the triumph of Aristotle's moral utility of war, as is confirmed by the very repetitiveness of their opinions. While wars born of various vices continued to receive opprobrium, wars waged for the common good were assumed to be just and consonant with human nature. The statecraft of emerging territorial units had received full theological benediction by the end of the thirteenth century. Under Thomistic scrutiny any lingering theological suspicions on the moral status of killing were overcome by reference to the Aristotelian teleology of the common good. Military service and warfare were positive if limited goods that were embraced and assimilated by the moral goodness of the political community. No longer was warfare seen only as a consequence of sin, for it was now viewed as rooted in the nature of human communities.

THE FORMULA OF THE JUST WAR

The justification of certain types of warfare stimulated the development of formulae by which the justice of particular wars could be determined. Both theologians and canonists had tried with varying degrees of success to provide such a formula that could satisfy the twofold requirements of conciseness and comprehensiveness.

---

[38] Richard of Mediavilla, *Super IV Libros Sententiarum*, to 3, 33, art. 4, qq. 2, 3 (4 vols., Brescia, 1591; rep. Frankfurt, 1963), III, 395f. For Richard's acceptance of Thomism, unusual for a Franciscan, and information about his life and works, see Gilson, *History of Christian Philosophy*, pp. 347, 695f.

[39] Richard of Mediavilla, *ibid.*, to 3, 37, art. 2, q. 4, III, 451. Cf. I Maccabees 2.

Aquinas provided one of the best of these attempts when he proposed three requirements for a just war: authority; just cause; and
just intention.[40] The authoritative mandate of a prince to whom care
of the common good of a kingdom or province was committed not
surprisingly merited first place among Aquinas' criteria. He reasoned
that a private person could not wage war because he could pursue
his rights in a law court, and similarly, a private person had no
authority to convoke a host necessary to make war. Just as a prince
had the licit right to protect the commonwealth against internal
disturbances, so also he had the duty to protect the commonwealth
against external enemies. The second requirement, the just cause,
referred to the guilt of the enemy that rendered him deserving of
attack. Third, the warriors themselves must be motivated by the
righteous intentions to promote good or avoid evil. Aquinas further
required the fulfillment of all three criteria, such that if the first two
requirements were met, the war could still be rendered illicit by the
presence of wicked intentions among the warriors. Like his colleagues, Aquinas insisted that a war be not only justified but justly
waged.

In this formula Aquinas turned away from the more complex
formulae of Raymond of Peñafort and Alexander of Hales to the
simple sort of formula offered by such canonists as Rufinus.[41]
Though admirable in its conciseness, the formula neglected the
earlier requirement that the warrior must be a knight, perhaps

[40] S.T. 2-2, q. 40, art. 1, resp.: 'Dicendum quod ad hoc quod aliquod bellum sit iustum, tria
requiruntur. Primo quidem auctoritas principis cuius mandato bellum est gerendum. Non
autem pertinet ad personam privatam bellum movere, quia potest ius suum in iudicio
superioris prosequi. Similiter etiam convocare multitudinem, quod in bellis oportet fieri,
non pertinet ad privatam personam. Cum autem cura reipublicae commissa sit principibus,
ad eos pertinet rem publicam civitatis vel regni vel provinciae sibi subditae tueri. Et sicut
licite defendunt eam materiali gladio contra interiores quidem perturbatores, dum male-
factores puniunt [Romans 13: 4]. ita etiam gladio bellico ad eos pertinet rempublicam tueri
ab exterioribus hostibus. [Psalm 81: 4; Augustine, *Contra Faustum Manichaeum*, 22, 75.]
Secundo, requiritur causa iusta, ut scilicet illi qui impugnantur propter aliquam culpam
impugnationem mereantur. [Augustine, *Quaestiones in Heptateuchum*, 6, 10.] Tertio,
requiritur ut sit intentio bellantium recta, qua scilicet intenditur vel ut bonum promo-
veantur vel ut malum vitetur. [C. 23 q. 1 c. 6.] Potest autem contingere ut si sit legitima
auctoritas indicentis bellum et causa iusta, nihilominus propter pravam intentionem bellum
reddatur illicitum.' [Augustine, *Contra Faustum*, 22, 74; Cf. C. 23 q. 1 c. 4.] For similar
assertion of the need of public authority, cf. S.T. 2-2, q. 41 art. 1 ad 3; S.T. 2-2, q. 64,
art. 7, resp.
[41] For the formula of Rufinus, see above, ch. 4, n. 3; for that of Raymond of Peñafort, above,
ch. 5, n. 5; and for Alexander of Hales, above, ch. 6, n. 21.

because it was assumed by this time that only knights and soldiers could legitimately fight, a development occurring as part of the consolidation of territorial units under princes with public authority and the resulting professionalisation and specialisation of occupations. Both theory and practice had thus combined to eliminate one of the requirements earlier considered essential. By the same token, the formula did not explicitly prohibit prelates from actively participating in hostilities, although by this time clerics usually employed knights to fulfill their military duties.[42] Aquinas in his third requirement bore witness to the importance of the need of right motivation that theologians and canonists alike tenaciously attached to the concept of the just war. While Aquinas recognised that clerics thus had generally ceased to fight, he also recognised that knights were still prone to fight out of wicked and selfish motives. In a sense Aquinas did nothing but return the formula of the just war to the simple definition proposed by Augustine. Thus shorn of its medieval accretions, the formula could then apply to societies other than Christian and beyond his own time. Noteworthy in this connection is Aquinas' citation, in support of the just cause, of Augustine's doctrine that the prior guilt of an enemy justified resort to war.

The concept of war guilt, broached by Cicero and detailed at great length in Augustine's works, was reduced by Aquinas to a simple formula that served as a basis for both later medieval and early modern theories of *bellum iustum*. The just cause constituted some fault or sin committed by an adversary that needed to be punished, and the right intention was to suppress injustice, return the situation to order and assure peace.[43] Noteworthy also is the generality of Aquinas' second requirement, for he did not mention any more specific crime such as invasion or seizure of property. The general category of prior guilt seemed so sufficiently clear to him that defense of the common good or community against any wrongful act could be subsumed under the general criterion. Nowhere in the formula is there even a hint of the modern distinction between offensive and defensive wars. In devising his formula Aquinas expressed no new insights, neglecting even to mention Aristotle, but

---

[42] Cf. Baldwin, *Masters Princes and Merchants*, I, 215f. For Aquinas' views on clerical activity in warfare, see below, nn. 87–92.
[43] Hubrecht, 'La juste guerre dans la doctrine chrétienne,' 115f.

rather restated traditional elements in new and concise form. The formula had come full circle back to the patristic doctrines. It is perhaps the universality and traditional cast of the formula that accounts for its durability throughout the succeeding centuries.

Yet Aquinas' formula was not devoid of specific content, for it did at least implicitly restrict the just war to a certain type of military action. Many instances of violence did not receive the status of wars. For example, violent quarrels were not really wars but rather a sort of private war waged by men of discordant wills without the sanction of public authority. Such quarrels were sinful except when one defended himself with due moderation and without trying to kill his adversary out of hatred.[44] When an agent of public authority attacked someone, the victim was not considered an enemy but rather as one guilty of unworthy resistance to authority.[45] Likewise Aquinas considered sedition as a mortal sin opposed to common utility.[46] In this way Aquinas denied that many of the hostile encounters of his day were actual wars but rather considered them instances of rebellion against the common good. Implicitly at least, he restricted the status of war to full-fledged wars between sovereign princes such as the national monarchs, the Emperor and the pope.[47] Having established the formula as his point of departure, Aquinas then focused his attention on the specifically medieval facets of the just war.

While the subsequent history of the Thomist just war formula is too lengthy to be examined here, the *Speculum Maius* of Vincent of Beauvais attests to its ready acceptance. In his *Speculum Doctrinale* composed around 1244 Vincent quoted Raymond of Peñafort's criteria for a just war, but in the *Speculum Morale*, completed by an anonymous compiler after the appearance of Aquinas' Summa Theologiae, the Thomistic formula replaced that of Raymond.[48] Its

---

[44] S.T. 2–2, q. 41, art. 1, resp. Cf. the *Speculum Morale* (attributed to Vincent of Beauvais in the Middle Ages), III, 5, 11 (Douai, 1624), p. 1194.

[45] S.T. 2–2, q. 41, art. 1, ad 3.

[46] S.T. 2–2, q. 42, art. 1, resp.; art. 2, resp.

[47] S.T. 2–2, q. 188, art. 3, ad. 4. In similar but more legally precise fashion canonists such as Innocent IV and Hostiensis denied to most cases of violence the status of war: above, ch. 5, pp. 145f., 175ff. For the later medieval restriction of this authority to princes, see M. Wilks, *The Problem of Sovereignty in the Later Middle Ages* (Cambridge, 1963), pp. 445f.

[48] Vincent of Beauvais, *Speculum Doctrinale*, 7, 28, p. 576; *Speculum Morale*, III, 5, 12, pp. 1194f.

simplicity and comprehensiveness along with the esteem accorded to Aquinas by many of his contemporaries account for its speedy acceptance.

CONDUCT AND CONSEQUENCES

Once Aquinas had proposed the three criteria for the just war he turned to consider its legitimate conduct and consequences, forming his opinions within the framework of medieval practice and Christian morality. The need for public authority he took for granted, but unlike others he neglected to specify those authorities who were qualified. With the possible exception of non-combatant immunity the questions he raised and the solutions he proposed were well within the theological and canon law traditions. For example, the last two articles of quaestio 40 (Summa Theologiae 2: 2) dealt with the legitimacy of ambushes and of warfare waged on feast days. As Aquinas posed it, the question of ambushes turned on whether they constituted fraud and were therefore illicit. On one hand, fraud and breach of promise contradicted the virtues of justice and fidelity, but on the other, God Himself had ordered Joshua to lay ambushes. In his conclusion Aquinas saw ambushes as a deceptive device, but deception was of two sorts, by word and by deed. To lie or break a promise was always illicit according to the laws of war, hence faith once promised must be maintained even with enemies, yet in another sense word and deed could legitimately be employed to deceive an enemy. Aquinas used the novel reasoning that since in Christian doctrine many things were hidden, especially from infidels lest they scorn such things, preparations for attack could be hidden from enemies lest they learn of them and turn that knowledge to the detriment of the just warriors. In a just war such dissimulation pertained to the use of ambushes that were neither fraudulent, unjust, nor repugnant to the ordered will, for only an unordered will wished that nothing be hidden from others.[49] Noteworthy here is Aquinas' use of the first person plural in his reply to the opposing arguments: he argued the case from the side of those whose war was already just and who were now preparing their strategy. Like many other commentators he did not treat the legitimacy of ambushes in an unjust

[49] S.T. 2–2, q. 40, art. 3, resp. Cf. *Speculum Morale*, III, 5, 12, p. 1196; Giles of Rome, *De Regimine Principum*, III, III, 9, pp. 579f.

war for the obvious reason that in an unjust war any hostile acts were *ipso facto* unjust.

Warfare during feast days appeared illicit on the grounds that such days were set aside for rest contrary to the performance of hostile acts, that battles were illicit during these periods, and also that fighting on the Sabbath was inordinate, and nothing should be done inordinately to avoid mere temporal misfortunes. To these objections Aquinas answered, after citing the example of the Maccabees, that observance of feast days did not stand in the way of pursuit of temporal well-being, for if a physician was justified in practising his healing art on the Sabbath, much more should the well-being of the community be attended to even if this care required fighting. Aquinas' reasoning, tinged with Aristotelianisms, was that the safety of the community by inhibiting large-scale killing and innumerable other temporal and spiritual evils was superior to the health of a single individual. Just wars could be especially waged on feast days when it was necessary to protect the community of faithful Christians[50] Aquinas' solutions to the problems of ambushes and fighting on feast days, achieved by novel and perhaps curious reasoning, nevertheless coincided with common theological and canonistic opinion to the extent that Aquinas shared in the somewhat muddled thinking of other writers. When a war was just because it was necessary, then logically it should be fought by any means and at all times.

Theologians and canonists debated these issues at such length, even when the logical conclusion was self-evident, out of a natural desire to limit violence and also because Augustine had obliged the maintenance of faith with enemies and because the Truce of God was a canon law regulation. The explication of received texts continued to exert a strong influence over the development of the canon law and theological theories.

The necessity of waging war was justified by the right of self-defense that had received extensive treatment in Roman and canon law. While Aquinas did not exactly relate self-defense to war he did construct a doctrine of self-defense that could serve as a legitimating condition of war. In his treatment an act of self-defense could have two effects: defense and death of the attacker. The intention to

[50] S.T. 2-2, q. 40, art. 4, resp. Cf. *Speculum Morale, loc. cit.*

defend one's own life, although licit in natural law, could become illicit when it was disproportionate to its end, as, for example, when the intended victim used more violence than necessary to repel the attack. Actual killing of attackers required public authority directed toward the common good, and thus to intend to kill in self-defense was illicit unless the victim was a public official or a knight fighting against enemies. Aquinas assumed tacitly that the knight was involved in fighting a just war, but cautioned against the private lust and hatred that rendered the killing illicit and the knight guilty of homicide.[51] Similarly he considered as vicious the refusal to resist injuries done to one's fellows when such resistance was possible.[52] It would seem logical to extend Aquinas' notions of self-defense and resistance to injuries to support defense of the *patria* by a just war, even though in Aquinas' own writings war was justified rather by its protection of the common good. Aquinas himself did not explicitly champion defense of the *patria* as a just cause for war.

If killing in self-defense and in defense of the common good was licit for public officials, the problem remained of how to carry out such killing and punishment. Modern just war theorists have sought to incorporate non-combatant immunity within their theories, while medieval canonists sought to exempt non-combatants from hostilities through the Peace of God. Both of these attempts assumed that non-combatants were innocent of any wrongdoing, but this assumption raised the question of whether non-combatants or mere knights or soldiers acting on orders deserved to be killed. While no satisfactory solution has been found either in theory or in practice, Aquinas did at least obliquely raise the issue. In the Summa Theologiae he justified the killing of sinners by reference to the common good that was corrupted by their sin. By contrast just men conserved and promoted the common good because they were the 'more principal part' of the community, and thus innocent men should not be killed.[53] Continuing to pursue the problem, Aquinas reasoned that someone who killed a just man sinned grievously for four reasons: he harmed men he ought rather to love out of charity; he injured someone undeservedly by acting contrary to justice; he deprived the community of a greater good; and he showed contempt

---

[51] S.T. 2–2, q. 64, art. 7, resp.   [52] S.T. 2–2, q. 188, art. 3, ad 1.
[53] S.T. 2–2, q. 64, art. 6, resp.

for God. At the last moment however Aquinas retreated from this line of reasoning to the *deus ex machina* explanation that a just man unjustly killed would be led to glory by God.[54] In so saying Aquinas diminished the vigor of his prohibition on killing innocent men.

While the foregoing passage assumed implicitly that the killing was carried out by public authorities, in his next response Aquinas turned explicitly to the dilemma faced by a judge who knew a man convicted by false witness was innocent. As a first step toward overriding the conviction Aquinas counseled the judge to disprove the false testimony. Failing that, the judge should have recourse to a superior judge, and if this also failed, then the judge did not sin in condemning the man to death, although a better choice was to kill the false witnesses. He did advise a minister commanded to carry out an unjust sentence to disobey the command, for otherwise the executioners of martyrs could claim an excuse, but if the sentence was not manifestly unjust, it could be carried out without sin for the minister had no right to dispute the sentence. The judge rather than the minister was guilty of killing an innocent man.[55] Aquinas probably realised that his advice was unsatisfactory, but could find no other solutions that did not derogate judicial authority. The convoluted casuistry here recalls the practical dilemmas discussed by Peter the Chanter and his circle. It is also evident that Aquinas did not construct an unambiguous solution to the problem of killing innocent men, for earlier in the same question he cited the parable of the tares (Matt. 13) and an Augustinian passage counseling restraint in killing sinners when they were hidden among good men. His general opinion, prompted by Christ's example, advised officials to allow sinners to live and reserve punishment to the Last Judgment rather than run the risk of killing good men. When there was no danger to good men but rather concern for their protection and welfare, then evil-doers could be killed with impunity.[56] Likewise in the *Summa contra Gentiles* Aquinas forbade the execution of the wicked when it could not be effected without danger to the good.[57] While these passages could be used to construct a theory of noncombatant immunity, two observations stand in the way of ascribing

[54] S.T. 2–2, q. 64, art. 6, ad 2.
[55] S.T. 2–2, q. 64, art. 6, ad 3.
[56] S.T. 2–2, q. 64, art. 2, obj. 1–2, ad 1–2.
[57] Aquinas, *Summa contra Gentiles*, 3, 146; *Opera Omnia*, v, 279f.

such a theory to Aquinas himself. First, nowhere in these passages was warfare itself specifically mentioned; and second, Aquinas' own views straddle the issue, for while he clearly did not approve the killing of innocent men, neither did he unqualifiedly prohibit it.

The dilemma was complicated in another way when subjects obeyed their lord when he fought an unjust or wicked war. Did their obedience render them guilty and deserving of punishment by death? Earlier canonists and theologians had grappled with this problem without arriving at a clear consensus, although they tended to restrict full culpability to the lord and his knightly followers. Aquinas posed the question more generally by inquiring whether someone could be punished for the sin of another. Thus if a subject shared his lord's guilt, he could be punished for it, but if he did not share the guilt, he could still be punished for 'medicinal' reasons unless his participation was limited to accidental consent. The punishment in any case worked for the good of the subject's soul if he bore it patiently.[58] This opinion is neither fully clear nor satisfactory in view of Aquinas' overall moral teaching, for it is difficult to understand why punishment for the sins of one's lord, especially when the subject gave only tacit consent, could serve any medicinal purpose other than a persecution that in Job-like fashion tested one's patience in the face of adversity. Furthermore, Aquinas did not apply his opinion explicitly to war. It is thus difficult, if not impossible, to attribute to Aquinas a clear doctrine of non-combatant immunity; he seemed to remain safely within the confines of Augustine's theory of war guilt whereby innocent men might legitimately be punished even by an unjust war for sins they had committed in other connections. Vincent of Beauvais did seem to hint at a theory of non-combatant immunity when he obliged a knight who waged a just war to refrain from punishing those subjects of his enemy who had refused aid, counsel, or favor to their rulers.[59]

Aquinas did not raise the issue of the obligation to perform military service, for he undoubtedly assumed that the general obligation of subjects to obey their princes was sufficiently clear, but he did interject a curious exemption from military service. Thus men who had recently built houses or planted vines, as well as newlyweds, were

---

[58] S.T. 1–2, q. 87, art. 8, resp.
[59] Vincent of Beauvais, *Speculum Doctrinale*, 7, 28, p. 576.

exempt from military service for two reasons. First, such a person so loved his new possessions and so feared their loss that he feared death more than the ordinary man and was therefore less valorous in battle; and second, if such a man should be killed in battle his friends and relations would be demoralised by his death.[60] Likewise the timid should be sent home, not to spare them from the perils of battle but to prevent other fighters from being so demoralised by such cowards that they too be moved by fear to flee the field of battle.[61] It is evident that Aquinas' primary intention here was to explicate a passage from Deuteronomy (20: 5) rather than to articulate an opinion relevant to contemporary wars.

Once a prince had decided to wage a just war and possessed the requisite manpower, he needed to know how to support his war effort and train his knights. Aquinas, in standard fashion, allowed the Christian prince to levy tribute on his subjects to promote the common utility of his people.[62] Although he did not however consider the question in greater detail, other members of his circle did provide a fuller exposition of the prince's right to tribute. Albertus Magnus justified the exaction of extraordinary war taxes when it was necessary to defend territory, but those taxes must not exceed a fair estimate of the required expenses.[63] In completing Aquinas' *De Regimine Principum* Ptolemy of Lucca specifically related the exaction of tribute to defense of the realm and pursuit of its common good,[64] and Remigio de' Girolami justified almost unlimited royal expropriation of subjects' temporal goods to defend the peace.[65] The major proportion of these exactions were expended on wages for knights and mercenaries. Unlike earlier theologians Aquinas devoted little attention to the problem of wages, cautioning only that knights remain content with their wages.[66] Ptolemy of Lucca was again more

[60] S.T. 1–2, q. 105, art. 3, ad 5.

[61] S.T. 1–2, q. 105, art. 3, ad 6.

[62] Aquinas, *De Regimine Iudaeorum*, 6, *Opuscula Philosophica*, p. 251.

[63] Albertus Magnus, *Commentaria in IV Sententiarum Libros*, to 4, 16, art. 46, ad q. 2, *Opera Omnia*, XXIX, 638.

[64] Ptolemy of Lucca, *De Regimine Principum*, 3, 11, para. 991, *Opuscula Philosophica*, p. 311.

[65] Remigio de' Girolami, *De Bono Pacis*, in Davis, 'Remigio de' Girolami and Dante,' p. 135.

[66] E.g. S.T. 2–2, q. 40, art. 1, *sed contra*, where Aquinas merely cited the relevant New Testament passage. A treatise of uncertain authorship more explicitly justified the payment of wages for defense of the community: *De Eruditione Principum*, 6, 1, *Opera Omnia*, XVI, 467. This treatise, though printed with Aquinas' works (under the alternate title *De Informatione Principum* in the Vivès edition), has been variously attributed to Vincent of

explicit when he advised kings to expend their resources on knightly wages and fortifications.[67] Vincent of Beauvais observed that hope for reward made for better soldiers, and even lauded the noble cavalry.[68] Albertus Magnus considered military service and payment of wages as licit, although he condemned the usual abuses such as attacks on innocent men, exaction of exorbitant wages, and the ostentatious display of prowess in tournaments that resulted in harm to persons and property. Like Alexander of Hales he did not categorically prohibit all warlike exercises since they were useful in preparing men for battles, just as David had taught archery to the Israelites.[69] He condemned mercenaries, for as men so insensitive to higher values, they sought their living by exposing themselves to the perils of battle in return for money. Thinking themselves of greater worth than they actually were, these men offered their services to the highest bidder. Albertus considered it more useful for princes to employ soldiers who were willing to fight for low wages, and, because they were unable to sustain themselves without taking plunder, had to fight. By contrast Albertus observed that wages were not so efficacious in enlisting great and noble men in warfare, for these men did not put their lives in danger for mere wages but rather in pursuit of great and worthy goals.[70] On this issue Albertus did not add much to the theory of the just war, since he was primarily concerned to explicate Aristotle, but he did exemplify the continuing preference of the theologians for the noble cavalry and the lasting prejudice against mercenaries.

Theologians customarily condemned the pillaging and destruction of feudal wars and mercenary bands while exempting these acts from sin when they were performed in a just war. Aquinas and his circle subscribed to this approach without contributing much original thought to it. Thus, for Aquinas, a prince who rightfully used coercion

Beauvais, William Perrault and Humbert of Romains: Mandonnet, *Des écrits authentiques*, p. 152; Grabmann, *Die Werke*, pp. 403f.

[67] Ptolemy of Lucca, *De Regimine Principum*, 2, 7, para. 868, *Opuscula Philosophica*, p. 284.

[68] Vincent of Beauvais, *Speculum Doctrinale*, 11, 67, p. 1033; cf. Ptolemy of Lucca, *ibid.*, 2, 6, para. 856, p. 282.

[69] Albertus Magnus, *Commentaria in Sententiarum*, to 4, 16, solutio, *Opera Omnia*, XXIX, 637. Cf. W. Arendt, *Die Staats- und Gesellschaftslehre Alberts des Grossen* (Jena, 1929), p. 44; for other theological opinions on tournaments, see above, ch. 6, nn. 88–9.

[70] Albertus Magnus, *Commentarium Ethicorum*, 3, tract. 2, 11 (to *Ethics* 3.9.1117b), *Opera Omnia*, VII, 251.

and violence against his enemies was allowed to retain his plunder, which was not considered rapine, but when a public official unjustly confiscated property, the confiscation was illicit and the official was bound to restore it.[71] This view confirmed the logically valid position that the prime element in determining the status of expropriated property was the justice of the underlying cause for the act of expropriation rather than the act itself. In a more specific passage Aquinas supported the right of just warriors to retain their plunder without sin provided their pillaging was motivated by justice rather than cupidity, and on the other hand he considered plunder taken in an unjust war as rapine for which the unjust warriors were bound to make restitution.[72] Thus the just motive legitimated the expropriation, as a just war rendered licit the burning and destruction of immovable property that was otherwise sinful.[73] Vincent of Beauvais perhaps best summed up the consensus of theological opinion when he allowed a knight who had waged a just war to retain as his legitimate possessions the plunder he had taken from his enemy and the latter's knights and subjects, but Vincent also cautioned the knight conscientiously to limit his plunder to an amount that compensated him for his labor, expenses and the danger that he and his soldiers had faced. The damages the knight exacted were thus compensatory rather than punitive. If the enemy should offer to submit the dispute to legal arbitration or to make satisfaction for his misdeeds, the knight should seek no more plunder. Vincent proposed as a further limitation on legitimate spoils that subjects who had rendered no aid, counsel or favor to a lord waging an unjust war were not to be despoiled nor in any way punished.[74] Vincent's opinion was important because it supported two potentially conflicting situations, the solidarity of interests between lord and vassal and the territorial consolidation then taking place. A lord waging a war was a leader of organised violence, whether his followers were knights, subjects or mercenaries. Vincent rather neatly straddled the issue, for this passage could serve to justify both the traditional feudal ethos and also that of the emerging territorial states. He also indicated clearly, if laconically, that subjects were not obliged to participate in

[71] S.T. 2–2, q. 66, art. 8, resp.
[72] S.T. 2–2, q. 66, art. 8, ad 1, 3.
[73] *De Eruditione Principum*, 7, 10, *Opera Omnia*, XVI, 475.
[74] Vincent of Beauvais, *Speculum Doctrinale*, 7, 28, p. 576.

their ruler's unjust war and that when they remained neutral they merited neither punishment nor infringement of their rights.

The moral status of captives in war had occasioned much debate among the Romanists and canonists, because according to Roman law captives became the slaves of their captors, and according to feudal custom war prisoners could be held for ransom. Aristotle had likewise considered captives as the legitimate servants of their captors, but the Church had prohibited the enslavement of Christians.[75] The theologians of Aquinas' circle were thus faced with a formidable task of reconciliation of divergent prior opinions. In his commentary to Aristotle's *Politics* Aquinas discussed the problem at great length, first entertaining the notion that the enslavement of war prisoners was not abstractly just but only just according to human convention. He then attempted to explain what he took to be Aristotle's position, that since it was unjust for wise men to be ruled by fools, slavery of the vanquished to the victors was justified according to the convenience of human life. The lure of taking captives incited warriors to more strenuous fighting that in turn served to avoid the greater evil of putting captives to death. Once again the individual good had to give way to the common good, but in Aquinas' own view this did not render just the servitude of an undeserving captive. Aquinas' minor argument concerned a noble captive who was enslaved and then sold. Were children born to him after his capture also considered slaves? Aquinas answered rather lamely that enslavement of nobles was unbefitting of their rank and concluded that only barbarians could be enslaved after capture in war.[76] Thus Aquinas did not provide a clear answer to the problem of captives enslaved as the result of an unjust war, and his treatment must be considered as an interpretation of Aristotle rather than as his own opinion. In a passage of the Summa Theologiae Aquinas did observe that subjects were not bound to obey lords whose dominion was unjust or usurped except to avoid scandal or greater dangers.[77] This passage has been somewhat speculatively interpreted as referring to a war

---

[75] For Aristotle's opinion on enslavement of war prisoners, see above, Introduction, n. 10; for the Romanists, above, ch. 2, nn. 55–8 and for the canonistic opinions, above, ch. 4, nn. 121–3 and ch. 5, nn. 100–2.

[76] Aquinas, *Expositio in Politicorum*, 1, lect. 4 (to *Politics* 1.6.1255a), *Opera Omnia*, XXI, 379f.; *ibid.*, 1, lect. 6 (to *Politics* 1.9.1256b), *Opera Omnia*, XXI, 385f.

[77] S.T. 2–2, q. 104, art. 6, ad 3.

that both adversaries claimed was just on their side. The eventual victors decided the justice of the war by the victory itself, and then justly enslaved prisoners, whereas in an unjust war of conquest the captured soldiers were not bound to submit and could revolt, given the prospect of success and the lack of threats of greater dangers.[78] Since this interpretation is not based on Aquinas' own statement, it appears doubtful that Aquinas himself formulated a clear position regarding enslavement. He appeared to have difficulty in resolving this problem within the confines of his own just war theory. While another modern commentator has concluded that Aquinas misunderstood Aristotle on this point,[79] Aristotle's own position is not at issue here, and it seems safe to judge Aquinas' discussion as inconclusive. His intent may have been merely to explain Aristotle in contemporary terms rather than to provide a full reconciliation with Christian doctrine and medieval practice. Peter of Auvergne in his continuation of Aquinas' commentary on the *Politics* could resolve this dilemma in no better fashion, for he contented himself with a paraphrase of Aristotle's position.[80] That the issue remained unresolved at the end of the thirteenth century is indicated by Ptolemy of Lucca's continuation of Aquinas' *De Regimine Principum* in which he paraphrased Aristotle's position without any qualification or concession to contemporary practice or debate, and even justified the enslavement of captives by reference to Roman practice.[81] The debate on slavery had come full circle without achieving any new insights.

In his analysis of the conduct and consequences of the just war Aquinas buttressed theological opinion with forthright justifications often couched in Aristotelian terms and provided full and careful exposition of traditional positions. He also advanced new perspectives, although his solutions to the problems of defensive wars, spoils, conscientious objection, and non-combatant immunity were less than comprehensive. Yet under his influence the hesitations and restrictions of the earlier theology of the just war were overcome, such that for his immediate successors the moral justification of communal political life overrode earlier moral objections to war. In

---

[78] Schilling, *Thomas von Aquino*, p. 183.

[79] T. Gilby, *The Political Thought of Thomas Aquinas* (Chicago, 1958), p. 270.

[80] Peter of Auvergne, *Expositio in Politicorum*, 7, lect. 2 (to *Politics* 7.2.1325a), *Opera Omnia*, XXI, 640; *ibid.*, 7, lect. 11 (to *Politics*, 7.14.1334a), *Opera Omnia*, XXI, 679.

[81] Ptolemy of Lucca, *De Regimine Principum* 2, 10, para. 884, *Opuscula Philosophica*, p. 288.

viewing the just war as a natural function of political authority he returned the problems of war to the level of military organisation, strategy, and tactics analysed by Vegetius' *De Re Militari* during the late Roman Empire. Aquinas and his immediate successors thus provided contemporary princes with detailed advice on how to prepare for and win just wars. While a fuller discussion of this advice lies outside the sphere of the present study, it merits brief mention here.

Scattered throughout his Summa Theologiae are elements of a code of military conduct. Soldiers must not engage in trade; the proper instructions, discipline, and morale are described; desertion is stigmatised; wearing of insignia and knightly parades and marches received theological benediction.[82] The eleventh book of Vincent of Beauvais' *Speculum Doctrinale* is a veritable manual of military organisation drawn from classical sources. Peter of Auvergne ranked the bellicose virtues along with wealth and justice as characteristics of a well ordered community, and advised princes to seek wise counsel when deciding to go to war.[83] Giles of Rome disputed Socrates' notion, as reported by Aristotle, of the military organisation necessary to defend the community, and accorded to the prince the right to plan strategy.[84] Since in every battle one side was the invader and the other side was the defender, those who besieged fortifications were guilty of invasion, as were those who were obsessed with doing battle, while defense of fortifications was qualified as a licit defensive art.[85] Here Giles pointed toward a full and explicit approval of defensive wars whose justice was self-evident in the legal as well as the moral sphere. Ptolemy of Lucca likewise advised princes to construct strong fortifications to defend the community and choose able knights to prosecute wars waged for the utility of the whole realm.[86] This advice may seem hardly original or surprising, but it was exactly the sort of advice that was eagerly sought by contemporary princes, and helps to explain the influence of Aquinas' benediction of the just war.

[82] For the citations, see J. M. Aubert, *Le droit romain dans l'oeuvre de Saint Thomas* (Paris, 1955), p. 37, n. 3.
[83] Peter of Auvergne, *Expositio in Politicorum*, 3, lect. 11 (to *Politics* 3.12.1283a), *Opera Omnia*, XXI, 481; *ibid.*, 4, lect. 12 (to *Politics* 4.14.1298a), *Opera Omnia*, XXI, 540.
[84] Giles of Rome, *De Regimine Principum*, III, I, 14, pp. 435–7; III, III, 5, pp. 566–8; III,III, 9, pp. 578–80.
[85] *Ibid.*, III, III, 16, pp. 598f.
[86] Ptolemy of Lucca, *De Regimine Principum*, 2, 11, para. 889, p. 289; 3, 21, para. 1021, p. 323.

PARTICIPATION OF CLERICS AND THE CHURCH IN WAR

Prior to Aquinas theologians and canonists had focused a substantial part of their discussions on war on the role played by the Christian faith, the Church and clerics in contemporary wars. For the most part Aquinas himself restated their conclusions in expanded form, although he did supply further precision to the problem of wars with infidels. According to the consensus of opinion upon which Aquinas drew, clerics were unequivocally prohibited from personal participation in war. In supporting the prohibition Aquinas referred to the division of labor within Christian society by which different functions were fulfilled by men of different status. Thus lesser tasks were forbidden to those whose duty was to perform more important tasks, as soldiers were prohibited from carrying on a trade. Likewise clerics were prohibited from warfare because such an activity inhibited contemplation, praise of God and prayer, and also because the ministry of the altar was incompatible with killing.[87] Although clerics were dedicated to the pursuit of spiritual goods by their office, they were forbidden to take up arms, not because war was sinful but because it was unsuitable to their office.[88] Just as marriage was a meritorious state except for those who took the vows of chastity, so also warfare was honorable except for those who took clerical vows.[89] The New Testament prohibited for clerics the military service that had been licit in the Old Testament.[90] Prelates were rather to support just warriors with exhortations and absolutions, but actual participation in fighting was an abuse of their office.[91] Even prelates with temporal authority were not to participate personally in punishments involving bloodshed but should delegate the exercise of these duties to a subordinate official unencumbered by clerical status. Aquinas' traditional treatment of this issue occupied the middle ground to which all theologians could subscribe. He did not mention the more extreme position, held by such theologians as Alexander of Hales, that based the prohibition on the clerical duty to be perfect in imitation of Christ Himself.[92]

[87] S.T. 2–2, q. 40, art. 2, resp.   [88] S.T. 2–2, q. 40, art. 2, ad 3.
[89] S.T. 2–2, q. 40, art. 2, ad 4. Cf. *Speculum Morale*, 3, 5, 12, pp. 1195f.
[90] S.T. 2–2, q. 64, art. 4, resp., ad 1.
[91] S.T. 2–2, q. 40, art. 2, ad 2. Cf. *Speculum Morale*, 3, 5, 12, p. 1196.
[92] S.T. 2–2, q. 64, art. 4, ad 3.

A much larger issue was the spiritual purposes of temporal wars that legitimated ecclesiastical initiation and prosecution of wars against enemies of the faith and the Church. For Aquinas the military profession was ordained partly to defend divine worship, and fighting on feast days was licit when it was necessary to defend the community of the faithful.[93] More to the point, the Church of his time was inextricably involved in wars of all sorts and would so continue for a long time. With so many clerics in crusading orders it was not sufficient merely to prohibit all clerics from fighting, but was necessary to analyse ecclesiastical wars since they were justified by reference to the history of the Israelites and Christian doctrine, and paid for from the Church's coffers. For Aquinas the justification of ecclesiastical wars for spiritual purposes turned on the questions of authority and the purposes for which that authority was exercised. Someone could kill even an innocent man in obedience to the ultimate authority of a divine mandate.[94] Members of religious orders, presumably the crusading orders, could wage war on the authority of a prince or the Church, although they of course could not do so on their own authority.[95] To justify wars undertaken at the behest of the Church Aquinas like many others turned to the Old Testament for precedents, and then sought to interpret these precedents in view of Christ's command to love one's enemies. The basic justification for going to war in the more purely exegetical and doctrinal aspects of Aquinas' thought was punishment of sin, by which someone did evil to an enemy people only to inhibit a greater evil or promote a greater good such as justice.[96] Hence the Israelite persecution of enemy tribes was necessary to prevent the Israelites from being led into idolatry and also to execute a divine mandate.[97] Likewise in pursuit of justice the Church was permitted to wage war on evil men to avoid greater evils and to foster greater goods.[98] Hannibald, a Dominican and Parisian colleague of Aquinas, more specifically allowed the Church to wage war on tyrants, persecutors

[93] Above, nn. 9, 50.
[94] S.T. 2–2, q. 64, art. 6, ad 1. Cf. *De Eruditione Principum*, 7, 12, *Opera Omnia*, XVI, 476.
[95] S.T. 2–2, q. 188, art. 3, ad 4.
[96] Aquinas, *Commentum in Sententiarum*, to 3, 30, art. 2, resp., *Opera Omnia*, VII, 328; Cf. S.T. 1–2, q. 105, art. 3, ad 1.
[97] Aquinas, *Commentum in Sententiarum*, to 3, 30, art. 2, ad 7, *Opera Omnia*, VII, 328.
[98] *Ibid.*, to 3, 30, art. 2, ad 8, *Opera Omnia*, VII, 328.

and incorrigible enemies of the Church as a work of charity and beneficence for the spiritual welfare of the victims.[99]

In his exegesis of Old Testament wars Aquinas distinguished between two types of cities hostile to the Israelites, one which was remote from Israelite territory and had not been promised to them by God, and the other that bordered on Israelite territory and had been promised to the people of God. When the Israelites defeated the first type of city all its men were to be killed while the women and children should be spared, but when they conquered neighboring cities all their inhabitants were to be executed in punishment for the sins of their ancestors. In this case the Israelites were acting as executors of God's will. The conquered territory was subjected to the rule of the Israelites, who were advised to spare the fruit trees for their own use.[100] Aquinas then introduced as general laws of war applicable to the Israelites a close paraphrase of Deuteronomy 20: peace should first be offered to the enemy, then, lacking a favorable response, the Israelites should wage war vigorously with full confidence in God. When battle was imminent the priests should comfort the people with the promise of divine aid. Men of faint heart should be excused from battle and sent home lest they hinder the more valorous fighters. When victory was finally achieved it should be enjoyed moderately by sparing women, children and fruit trees.[101] The direct relevance of these passages to thirteenth-century wars is indeed problematical, but they serve to indicate Aquinas' approval of wars waged for spiritual purposes. In this connection he did not explicitly state that Christians were legitimate heirs of the Israelites as God's chosen people nor did his exegesis of Deuteronomy expressly refer to his more general requirements for a just war. More conclusive evidence for Aquinas' view of contemporary ecclesiastical wars must be sought in his less exegetical passages.

The proper relations of orthodox Christians with infidels and heretics served as the point of departure for Aquinas' discussion of contemporary Church wars. In the Summa Theologiae he prohibited infidels from being compelled to accept the Christian faith since

---

[99] Hannibald, *Super Sententiarum*, to 3, 30, art. 2, resp., *Opera Omnia*, XXII, 300.

[100] S.T. 1–2, q. 105, art. 3, ad 4.

[101] S.T. 1–2, q. 105, art. 3, resp. Albertus Magnus saw the wars of the Israelites against the Amorites as an incessant war of truth against the error of iniquity: *In Evangelium Lucae*, 12, 52–3, *Opera Omnia*, XXIII, 280.

belief must be voluntary, but approved of just wars waged against them when they had harmed faithful Christians by blasphemies, evil persuasions and outright persecutions. Heretics and apostates as those who had formerly promised to uphold the faith could be compelled to fulfill their promises even by physical coercion.[102] This brief opinion settled the basic issues in traditional fashion, but it did not specify the proper relationships between Christians and peaceful infidels. Aquinas observed that the Church did not prohibit communication with pagans and Jews, for it did not have spiritual jurisdiction over those who had never received the faith, although he felt it necessary to point out that nevertheless Christian rulers had temporal jurisdiction over infidels found in Christian territories.[103] If Christian princes legitimately exercised temporal dominion over infidels residing in or traveling through Christian territory, was the reverse situation also legitimate, that is, could infidels legitimately hold dominion over Christian subjects? In view of the number of Christians living under Arab dominion on the shores of the Mediterranean this was not a mere academic question for idle dialectic.

Aquinas provided a full and careful statement that introduced new perspectives to the theoretical justification of peaceful contacts with non-believers. This was, after all, the age of Innocent IV's Mongol mission and its theoretical preparation, and also of the first period of Franciscan missionary activity climaxed by the career of Ramon Lull. Aquinas' position prohibited any new institution of infidel

---

[102] S.T. 2–2, q. 10, art. 8, resp., ad 3.

[103] S.T. 2–2, q. 10, art. 9, resp.: 'Primo ergo modo non interdicit Ecclesia fidelibus communionem infidelium qui nullo modo fidem Christianam receperunt, scilicet paganorum vel Iudaeorum, quia non habent de eis iudicare spirituali iudicio, sed temporali in casu cum inter Christianos commorantes aliquam culpam committunt et per fideles temporaliter puniuntur. Sed isto modo, scilicet in poenam interdicit Ecclesia fidelibus communionem illorum infidelium qui a fide suscepta deviant, vel corrumpendo fidem, sicut haeretici, vel etiam totaliter a fide recendo, sicut apostatae. In utrosque enim horum excommunicationis sententiam profert Ecclesia... Si enim aliqui fuerint firmi in fide, ita quod ex communione eorum cum infidelibus conversio infidelium magis sperari possit quam fidelium a fide aversio, non sunt prohibendi infidelibus communicare qui fidem non susceperunt, scilicet paganis vel Iudaeis, et maxime si necessitas urgeat. Si autem simplices et infirmi in fide, de quorum subversione probabiliter timeri possit, prohibendi sunt ab infidelium communione; et praecipue ne magnam familiaritatem cum eis habeant, vel absque necessitate eis communicent.' S.T. 2–2, q. 10, art. 9, ad 2: 'Dicendum quod Ecclesia contra infideles non habet iudicium quoad poenam spiritualem eis infligendam. Habet tamen iudicium super aliquos infideles quoad temporalem poenam infligendam, ad quod pertinet quod Ecclesia aliquando propter aliquas speciales culpas subtrahit aliquibus infidelibus communionem fidelium.'

dominion over faithful Christians because of the scandal and danger to the faithful, for the weaker among them would probably lose their Christian faith under the pressure of an infidel ruler. Did not the Apostle Paul forbid the faithful from seeking judgment from an infidel judge? Therefore the Church must not permit any extension of infidel dominion over the faithful. Yet, as Aquinas realised, this ideal solution conflicted with existing and well-established infidel dominion, for he observed that just as the divine law of grace did not totally supplant the human law of natural reason, so also the recent distinction between faithful and infidel did not abolish pre-existing dominion of infidels over the faithful. At this point he stated flatly that the Church had the right to abolish such infidel dominion because infidels by the very fact of their infidelity deserved to lose their power over the faithful, who then were to receive Christian lords. As Aquinas observed, the Church actually exercised this right on occasion, but often it did not in order to avoid scandal.[104] While upholding the Church's God-granted right to wage wars against infidels as it pleased, Aquinas nevertheless tacitly advised it against heedless and bloody wars against infidels. Mere infidelity no longer served as sufficient justification for a Christian crusade of conquest. On this point Aquinas' opinion was consonant with his Aristotelian conviction that any human community had the natural right to an independent existence regardless of its standing in relation to Christian faith, doctrine and organisation, although he himself did not point out this consonance. Aquinas' position put a theological seal of approval on Innocent IV's earlier and more explicit provision for Christian toleration of infidel dominion legitimated by natural law and historical longevity.[105]

To assert the principle of occasional and prudent toleration was a first step that called for additional theological and teleological justification. Aquinas provided this justification, *mutatis mutandis*, in his discussion of the toleration of infidel rites. Whereas the right rule of human beings was derived from the divine regimen and should imitate it, God in His omnipotence and goodness permitted some evils that He could prohibit, lest greater goods be destroyed or worse evils follow, and human rulers likewise rightly tolerated such evil

---

[104] S.T. 2-2, q. 10, art. 10, resp.
[105] For Innocent IV's opinions on the toleration of infidels, see above, ch. 5, nn. 199–201.

practices as infidel rites. For example, Jewish rites were to be tolerated because these formerly had prefigured Christian truth, hence good came out of these rites such that the Christian faith received testimony even from its enemies. Those infidel rites that offered no truth or utility should only be tolerated to avoid the evil scandal or dissension that could result or to avoid jeopardising the salvation of those tolerated infidels who little by little came over to the Christian faith. For this reason the Church even tolerated heretical and infidel rites on occasion when there was a great multitude of infidels.[106] Aquinas thus performed a great service in constructing a principle of limited toleration on the firm foundation of a Christian evangelical teleology. While he did not explicitly mention wars in this context, his concept of toleration would prohibit most such wars.

The limited toleration which Aquinas accorded to infidels in general he predictably denied to heretics. He reasoned that since corruption of the faith was more serious than corruption of money through counterfeiting and falsification, and since counterfeiters were usually put to death by princes, heretics even more justly deserved not only excommunication but death when they remained tenacious in their error, for the Church must provide for the salvation of others.[107] Aquinas elaborated a doctrine that justified limited Christian persecution of infidels and heretics, but he did not link this doctrine explicitly to his theory of the just war or to the crusades. The Decretalists had gradually developed a reasonably coherent doctrine of Church wars that justified crusades and other ecclesiastical wars and provided advice on the proper leadership and authority.[108] Nowhere in his writings did Aquinas specifically cite this canonistic body of doctrine, nor did he articulate a comprehensive theory of his own, for he evidently felt this task belonged rightly to his Decretalist colleagues. His specific comments on such holy wars and crusades were occasional and unsystematic. He upheld the violent confiscation of infidel property on the authority of Christian princes without specifying the legitimating conditions, although, in

---

[106] S.T. 2–2, q. 10, art. 11, resp.

[107] S.T. 2–2, q. 11, art. 3, resp. Vincent of Beauvais added the commonplace opinion that the Church had the right to seek imperial aid in its own defense: *Speculum Doctrinale*, 7, 29, p. 577.

[108] For the opinions of the Decretalists on the crusades, see above, ch. 5, pp. 195ff.

line with his principle of toleration, he did not deny infidels all property rights.[109] The remainder of his expressed thoughts on crusades seem to be limited to crusader vows and indulgences. A man could take the crusader vow without the consent of his wife or his feudal overlord in order to render aid to the necessity of the whole Church.[110] Aquinas also allowed a man undergoing penance, normally prohibited from fighting, to fight in obedience to a divine command and to aid the Holy Land.[111]

Aquinas was obviously referring to the indulgence granted in return for a crusading vow, for elsewhere he approved the granting of indulgences for temporal activities ordained for spiritual purposes, such as repression of the Church's enemies. For purely spiritual affairs moreover, indulgences could be granted at any time, since an indulgence of ten days was given to those preaching the cross as well as to those receiving it.[112] Among the requirements for an efficacious indulgence there must first be a worthy cause pertaining to the honor of God, or the necessity or the utility of the Church, and there must be legitimate authority for granting the indulgence, that is, the pope or his delegated officials. In the case of a crusading indulgence, the cause was aid to the Holy Land, and the authority was that of Peter and Paul as well as the present pope himself. If the crusader died before going to the Holy Land, did he still benefit from a plenary indulgence? Aquinas referred the solution of this complex question, obviously important to the crusader, to the letters of indulgence. If the letter granted the indulgence immediately in consequence of the vow, then the crusader received the indulgence, but if an actual voyage to the Holy Land was specified in return for the indulgence, the dead crusader lacked the indulgence.[113] Aquinas' treatment of this question recalls the careful casuistry of his Decretalist colleagues, but it may be the only instance of this very specific treatment of the legal consequences of the crusades in Aquinas' writings. Elsewhere

---

109 S.T. 2–2, q. 66, art. 8, ad 2.
110 Aquinas, *Commentum in Sententiarum*, to 4, 32, q. 1, art. 4, ad 1, *Opera Omnia*, VII², 963; *Quaestiones Quodlibetales*, 4, 7, 11, p. 79. Cf. Brundage, *Canon Law and the Crusader*, pp. 111f.
111 S.T. 2–2, q. 188, art. 3, ad 2, 3.
112 Aquinas, *Commentum in Sententiarum*, 4, 20, q. 1, art 3, quaestiunc. 3, sol. 3, *Opera Omnia*, VII², 845.
113 Aquinas, *Quaestiones Quodlibetales*, 2, 8, 16, p. 38; *ibid.*, 5, 7, 14, p. 109. Cf. Brundage, *Canon Law and the Crusader*, pp. 151f.

Aquinas observed briefly that the pope alone had the right to commute crusaders' vows.[114]

Aquinas' treatment of the crusades, less a systematic exposition than a series of casual and occasional remarks that barely even mentioned the Holy Land, was noteworthy only for its conventionality. He was obviously more concerned to propound a position that could serve to support attempts at mutual toleration. Writing at a time when the crusades and crusading ideals had started their decline, his sketchy analysis did not inspire his continuators to improve on it, for Peter of Auvergne, Ptolemy of Lucca and Giles of Rome elaborated upon his Aristotelian analysis of the naturalness of the political community while passing over the crusades in silence.

The elaboration of a theology of the just war was primarily the work of the mid and late thirteenth century, with the exception of Peter the Chanter's circle.[115] The contribution of Thomas Aquinas climaxed a thousand years of Christian speculation on war. A major aspect of that contribution was his bold and thorough application of Aristotelian political convictions to the analysis of war, for in this regard as in many others medieval theology and statecraft were ready for the advantages offered by the Philosopher's thought. Aquinas' use of Aristotle prevented him from attempting to transform the Church's spiritual superiority into the legal supremacy advocated by canonists such as Hostiensis. In his own writings and in those of his immediate followers defense of the Christian faith and the Christian people by means of the crusades received less and less attention, for increasingly the theories shifted their focus to wars between Christian princes, kingdoms and city-states.

Yet there were certain difficulties and deficiencies in even the most complete expositions of the just war. Aquinas' treatment was seldom as explicit and detailed as it might have been, as, for example, in his justification of war based on defense of the community. He was more concerned with the grounding of such fundamental principles as the common good than with their specific consequences. His major efforts at systematisation occurred in other more purely theological matters such as the reconciliation of reason and revelation, and his

---

114 Aquinas, *Commentum in Sententiarum*, 4, 38, q. 1, art. 4, quaestiunc. 4, solutio 2, *Opera Omnia*, VII², 1012.

115 The similar development of the theology of the just price was primarily the work of the thirteenth century: Baldwin, 'Just Price,' p. 58.

opinions on war were scattered throughout his voluminous writings. Since he did not devote his full powers of systematisation to the problems of war, it is necessary for the modern commentator himself to attempt this systematisation while guarding against wrenching those opinions out of the Thomist context. Certain commentators have speculatively interpreted how Aquinas would have pronounced his opinions on questions posed by modern analyses of the just war.[116] However in importing more modern concepts this method often distorts the shape of the Thomist synthesis itself. For example, Aquinas like many other theologians did not devote a thoroughgoing analysis to the concepts of self-defense and *ultio* or punishment in relation to the just war, nor did he explicitly relate the crusades to the just war, although these concepts seem necessarily related. In another regard almost all the theologians did not adequately cover the problems of truces, mercenaries and crusading orders. Explanation of these inadequacies lies in the received texts the theologians commented upon. The significance of the lack of a theological locus classicus as a springboard for commentaries cannot be overemphasised. While their canonistic colleagues were enjoying a wealth of texts about all aspects of war, the theologians remained captives of the paucity of passages they felt called upon to discuss, such that when they did discuss such contemporary problems as truces they had the unfortunate choices of either borrowing from perhaps unfamiliar canon law texts or devising their opinions in the unwonted fashion of pure speculation without textual basis.

In effect Aquinas proposed two separate but complementary formulae for the just war. One was the standardised formula, reworked and simplified, that is found in the Summa Theologiae (2–2, q. 40), while the other formula, less concisely but more frequently expressed, saw the just war as a defense of the community and the common good. While this common good applied to all humanity, in Aquinas' treatment it pertained especially to the Church, the Christian faithful, or the individual *patria*. Here Aquinas did not depart from a Christianised Aristotelian framework but rather fulfilled it by relating the just war specifically to the pursuit of the common good. Yet for Aquinas wars remained a kind of punish-

---

[116] E.g. Regout, *La guerre juste*, p. 92 and perhaps the whole of Tooke, *The Just War in Aquinas and Grotius*.

ment for sin even if the relationship was not made fully explicit. Indeed most theologians wrote with the Church's holy war in the back of their minds, so for Aquinas war had a twofold purpose: to punish sin and to right a wrong that detracted from the common good. The Thomist analysis attempted with less than complete success to synthesise the older Augustinian notion of war as punishment for sin with the newer Aristotelian-inspired *raison d'état*. This synthesis as developed further by Aquinas' successors pointed toward rather than achieved a clearer and more modern distinction between offensive and defensive wars. While rooted in the disappearing world of the knightly warrior and betraying an aristocratic cast, the Thomist theory of the just war looked forward to the age of the standing army as a discrete functional class within a national kingdom.

Conclusion

THE JUST WAR IN HISTORY AND THEORY

Remota itaque justitia, quid sunt regna nisi magna latrocinia?
Augustine, *De Civitate Dei*, IV, 4

Warfare has been as difficult to justify satisfactorily in theory as it has been endemic in practice. Often considered as an extraordinary phenomenon, it more accurately occupies a major place in political, cultural and social life. Some observations about the medieval just war theories as intellectual exercises, commentaries on medieval political developments and as part of the broader attempts to justify war are offered here.

The essential outlines of the medieval just war theories were defined by the end of the thirteenth century on the broad foundations laid in the twelfth century. It would be difficult to overestimate the influence of the sources upon which the scholastics based their commentaries. In a sense the whole tradition of the just war from ancient Greece to the modern period forms a seamless if intricate web. First and foremost, the Augustinian imprint remained crucial for the theories of lawyers and theologians alike. Thus warfare was seen as a function of divine providence designed to punish sin and crime. More broadly, the two major sources were the Bible and Roman law. Like Christians of the post-Constantinian era, the scholastics did not consider the pacific counsels of the New Testament to constitute a prohibition of all wars. For them Christ had brought a sword against His enemies. At every juncture the thinkers were confronted by Old Testament examples of just wars waged by Israelites and of priests who sought the aid of kings in punishing enemies of the faith. Taking these examples as normative for their own time and borrowing patristic examples of religious persecution promoted by prelates, canonists and theologians elaborated a justification of war waged on ecclesiastical authority against enemies of the Church and the faith. The Investiture Contest of the eleventh century furnished more recent examples of ecclesiastical demands for secular aid in combating those secular powers who resisted the Church's assertion of its own rights over Christian society.

Roman law provided the canonists with a digest of legal conditions appropriate to a state of belligerency. Thus the waging of a just war was the prerogative of legitimate political authority, and only a just war could create legal consequences advantageous to the just belligerent. For their part, the theologians often conflated the spiritual war of virtue against vice with physical warfare. This and the lack of a proper locus classicus for their debates rendered the theology of the just war deficient until the theologians were emancipated from their dependence on canon law by the reception of Aristotle, whose definition of the just war as a means of promoting the common good of a society arrived at just the right moment to be applied to contemporary societies. The canonists' dependence on Roman law led them to concentrate on the criterion of authority for a just war, while the theological debate attached more importance to the abstract justice of war. Thus while canonistic analyses of the just war and the crusade became more specific the theology of the just war by contrast became increasingly abstract. Hence no theology of the just war was as comprehensive and detailed as were the canonistic doctrines of Innocent IV and Hostiensis. For Hostiensis the most truly just war was waged at the behest of the Church against those enemies, be they Christian or infidel, who were contemptuous of ecclesiastical, especially pontifical, authority. The juridical theory of the crusade is a prime example of the canonists' use of biblical and Roman law sources, both of which were necessary but neither of which alone constituted a sufficient foundation for a Christian theory of the just war. The sword imagery, which figured so prominently in the debates over the spiritual and secular powers, played little part in the high medieval just war theories, perhaps because it was an unmanageable and inappropriate tool for understanding the complexity of contemporary warfare.

Hostility toward the foreigner was a persistent theme running through the sources. The Hellenic Greeks considered all wars against non-Hellenes to be justified; internal conflicts did not qualify as wars. The Romans similarly exhibited an instinctive animosity toward barbarian tribes that was reinforced by patristic persecution of pagans and heretics. The Carolingian ecclesiastics developed the notion of a holy war for the conquest and conversion of infidel peoples. Excepting the Carolingians, earlier Christian thought on coercion exhibited an ambiguity as to whether mere lack of proper belief itself constituted a sufficient justification for a holy war or whether unbelievers should be tolerated unless they offended Christians. The scholastics finally required that infidels or heretics commit specific offenses against Christians or the Church before the crusade became imperative. Thus the war of conversion adumbrated by Gregory the Great and practised by the Carolingians was explicitly prohibited in the commentaries of Innocent IV, Hostiensis and Thomas Aquinas.

A more crucial question is that of the relevance, the adequacy and the applicability of the just war theories to the contemporary political scene. While certain facets have remained constant, that part of the just war theories dealing with the crusades was a specifically medieval development. The crusade as a juridical institution existed only in the Middle Ages, and was a *sui generis* synthesis of the pilgrimage, the vow, the holy war and the just war that has continued to defy attempts at neat analysis. Within the just war the crusade coexisted uneasily at best, partly because there was no clear precedent to serve as an unambiguous guide. There were, after all, no crusades before 1095, and the medieval Romanists were not about to incorporate the crusade into their debate. Yet the reason for the fragmentary treatment of the crusades goes much deeper. Throughout the Middle Ages ecclesiastical writers betrayed a hesitation to involve the Church legally in bloodshed. In spite of their endless repetition of the Augustinian justification of legal violence on evangelical grounds, they continued, at least unconsciously, to consider Christian pacifism seriously, as witnessed by the peace movements. The moral suspicions attached to warfare or at least killing in the early medieval penitential literature went underground but did not cease to exist in the high Middle Ages, where it re-emerged as the scholastic hesitation to assimilate the crusades wholly into the just war theories. There was no word exactly corresponding to 'crusade' in their debates, and no treatise exclusively devoted to the crusading movement. Even the systematic treatments of Innocent IV and Hostiensis were casuistic rather than comprehensive, and Aquinas barely mentioned the crusades except in a quodlibetal sermon. The crusades often were discussed in functionally euphemistic and oblique terms such as *iter* and *peregrinatio*; rarely were they explicitly considered as the wars that they were. The legal fiction of the pilgrimage is but one indication of the scholastic suspicion of too direct ecclesiastical involvement in warfare. From their informed vantage points ecclesiastical writers certainly were aware of the Church's directive role in the various crusades within and without Europe, but they were reluctant to consider the crusading movement explicitly in legal or theological commentaries.

There are, no doubt, other factors that helped to explain this relative neglect of the crusades and the crusaders, such as the conservatism of jurisprudence, concern with more general ethical problems and preoccupation with the conflicts between empire and papacy, and the development of kingship. Yet scholastics took the opportunity to discuss many other, less significant, occupational groups and problems, and so additional explanations are called for. Here it is suggested that the scholastic reticence to accord full treatment to the crusading movement stemmed from a nagging suspicion that the crusade was an unsuitable means to ecclesiastical and religious ends. True, the Decretists had considered the crusade to the Holy Land as an absolute moral necessity, but they seldom devoted much attention to the theoretical bases or practical consequences of such crusades. The thirteenth-century debates, while continuing to approve the crusade to the Holy Land, were sobered by the decline in crusading fervor, the reverses suffered in the Holy Land, and the diversion of the crusading movement to other purposes. As a consequence, the many papal crusading bulls from Calixtus II's *Eis qui Hierosolymam* through Eugenius III's *Quantum predecessores* to Innocent III's *Ad liberandam* all failed to be included in official decretal collections. Thus the extensive papal crusading activity was not offered as a topic of canonistic jurisprudence. The Dominican Raymond of Peñafort, compiler of the Gregorian decretals, betrayed a cautious restraint in treating Christian–Saracen relations, and, crossing the conventional intellectual lines between orders, the Franciscan theologians of the mid-thirteenth century echoed his caution. For his part Aquinas' treatment of the crusades was so abstract and generalised as to be of little practical guidance. It was only in justifying wars and crusades against heretics that the scholastics shed their reticence. Still the lack of comprehensiveness remained, for how could the crusader's canonical status as a pilgrim be maintained for papal crusades within Europe? The sources are of little help here.

If this hypothesis concerning the reluctance to involve the Church too directly in bloodshed is accepted, then explanations of other deficiencies in the scholastic analysis of warfare are possible. That the crusading orders were passed over in almost total silence would appear to confirm the hypothesis. Perhaps better attuned to moral nuances of episcopal activities than the canonists, the theologians refused to make clearly binding the exhortation of laymen by prelates to go to war. For their part, the Decretalists were able to 'eclipse' the regalian obligations of the episcopacy such that thirteenth-century prelates were no longer to be faced with the dilemmas of whether and how they should participate in the wars of their secular overlords.

This clerical attitude should not be seen as a full pacifism, but rather as the persistence of the attitude developed in the early Church that saw military service as improper to clerics but tolerated for the laity. As an alternate mode of conduct this attitude persisted even in the thirteenth century. Bernard of Clairvaux in lauding the new militia of the Templars created the image of the warrior-monk, but even his influence could not sway the scholastics away from the by-then traditional functional distinction between clergy and laity. Hence the military orders did not receive full treatment at the bar of canon law or in theological debates. The crusader of the scholastics was to remain a rough layman. The hesitation to give the crusader full benediction also explains why the more spiritual dimensions of the crusading ideology that were so popular in the half-century after the First Crusade did not find expression in scholarly debates. The spiritual battle against vices and demons was not the function of the crusader, whose task was seen solely as a physical battle against flesh and blood. The restrained justification of crusades and other ecclesiastical wars of course constituted no barrier to unrestrained prosecution of these wars, as the career of Innocent IV bears witness. The complex movement of the Reconquista received no direct attention, perhaps because it was a special case covered by the general justification of wars waged for religious purposes.

The period of the Investiture Contest that witnessed the use of secular militia for purposes of ecclesiastical control over Christian society called into existence the competing and often hostile practices and ideology of the secular state, and it is here that the just war reveals its fullest significance. Just war theorising has often appeared to be created out of time, especially in the abstract and theological treatment of the Thomist circle. Yet it has actually been time-bound throughout its history, never more clearly so than in the high Middle Ages when it served to buttress the claims and practices both of the papacy and then of the national monarchies and city-states. The just war theories mirror changes in jurisprudence and statecraft and in concepts of the *patria* and the realm. Defense of the Holy Land and the Church gave rise to defense of the *patria*. The crusading idea nourished the just wars of states now claiming sovereignty. The theocratic megalomania of Hostiensis and thirteenth-century popes provided secular officials with the example of high theory in the service of low cunning.

The most clearly articulated theories were those developed by the Decretalists, who in their attempts to relate jurisprudence to contemporary society showed a growing concern to remove the settlement of disputes between lords and princes from the battlefield to the contentious forum of a competent judge. No longer was the just war a form of battle by which one party with divine aid proved the justice of his claim, for it had become an extraordinary legal remedy that supplemented ordinary legal procedures in cases of necessity. Realising that the whole notion of justice in war ultimately turned on divine or human authority, the Decretalists turned their debates away from considerations of just cause and divine intervention to considerations of various authorities and jurisdictions. Employing specific Roman law procedures extensively, the Decretalists constructed a theory of the just war waged on superior authority, in which the legal rights and duties of both just and unjust parties received detailed elaboration. The notion of justice became assimilated to that of legality, and war was seen as an extraordinary form of a lawsuit. In an age in which violence was common and public authority was insufficient to protect private persons, the scriptural counsels of patience seemed impractical and therefore gave way to the Roman law notion of self-defense and to condemnations of the vices to which fighting gave rise. Hence the canonists accorded to everyone, even clerics, a limited right to defend themselves, but this right was restricted in such a way that it did not merit the legal status of a just war. Every hostile act except immediate self-defense required superior authority. Defense of the *patria* required a just war waged on the authority of its legitimate protector. The Roman law served the canonists not only as a basis for defense of the *patria*, but also for defense of the Church in all its senses. Church jurisdiction was directed first toward reducing violence through the Truce of God and the Peace of God, and later toward rendering all violent disputes justiciable in ecclesiastical courts that invoked borrowed Roman legal procedures. When recourse to war was justified, canonists sought to have it waged on ecclesiastical authority.

The extensive development of canonical just war theories in the high Middle Ages is due both to the evolving discipline of law and to broader political developments. Canonists assumed that no war would be undertaken without some cause, but as churchmen they were confronted with the necessity of finding a judge or court competent to adjudicate cases where a just cause was claimed. That they upheld the competence of church courts is not surprising, for their contention arose during the period of the lawyer-popes such as Innocent III, whose bulls extended ecclesiastical jurisdiction into all areas of secular life. They realised that the moral justice of a certain cause for war only came under canon law jurisdiction when it was brought into the external forum, and thus they shifted their focus to the development of the Church's judicial competence.

The practical explanations for the emphasis on authority become evident when they are seen in the context of major attempts by kings, the emperor and the pope to establish their authority. Canonists were far from unanimous in their comments on conflicts between emperor and pope, king and subjects, and lord and vassal. The superficial unanimity of their formulations of the just war camouflaged deep divergences that if carried through could result in openly contradictory positions. There were in effect three major positions on the requisite authority for a just war. The most restricted position, best explained by Hostiensis and seconded by Dante, limited the right to wage a full just war to the Emperor. In some special cases Hostiensis accorded the right to the pope. The second position, advanced by Innocent IV among others, limited the waging of a just war to those authorities having no superior over them. The third position, espoused by William of Rennes, granted the right to wage war to every feudal lord who had no superior within the feudal hierarchy. These three positions encompassed the major institutions of medieval governance, the empire, the papacy, feudal monarchies and autonomous city-states.

The comparative viability of these positions depended upon their compatibility with the rise of the national monarchies. The imperialist and papalist positions were destined to founder in the fourteenth-century conflicts for they depended upon vigorous prosecution of claims based on Roman law and the Holy (Roman) Empire. Universal papal jurisdiction was incapable of fulfillment, hence late medieval attempts to enforce it became increasingly sterile, inflexible and ineffective. The second position was more flexible in allowing the coexistence of independent secular monarchies in addition to the Empire, for it allowed each ruler to defend his *patria* and to punish those who resisted his jurisdiction or invaded his rights and territory. In this sense Innocent IV can be seen as a proponent of the rising secular monarchies. The third view, feudal in outlook, applied to situations in which a lord's right to wage war was limited not by a superior authority but by his own vassals, who were not obligated to fight a war under him unless the war was just and their rights were respected. As such it was most able to comprehend the balance of forces that existed within feudal monarchies. Both the second and third views set limits to the lord's right to wage war based on rights proper to the lord's vassals or subjects. While it is unlikely that the *actio mandati* would be used in a feudal court in the manner envisaged by Innocent IV, his view complemented William of Rennes' elaboration of the rights of vassals to share in the spoils of war and to secure compensation for damages. The appeal to self-interest as a reinforcement of moral suasion stands as one of the most original and imaginative scholastic proposals to limit warfare.

The theology of the just war developed along different though parallel lines. Like the canonists the theologians viewed the defense of the *patria* as the primary just cause, emphasised public authority and condemned the greed, lust and cruelty of war. Like Innocent IV, Peter the Chanter and Aquinas even attempted to limit participation of vassals in an unjust war by appeals to self-interest. While most theologians did not discuss the problems of dominion divided among popes, emperor, kings and princes, the Chanter, Gervais of Mount-Saint-Eloi and Aquinas in various ways accorded the right to wage just wars to kings alone. The most distinctive theological contribution was the naturalness of the just war based on the naturalness of human societies and the pursuit of the common good. Once this was accomplished within the Thomist circle, the tension between the New Testament and warfare disappeared. With these new premises, and since he was not looking at contemporary societies in the concrete, Aquinas could prohibit clerical participation in violence without qualification or nuance. For the first time since the patristic period, churchmen were theoretically emancipated from feudal duties. Aquinas' vantage point rendered his just war analysis much simpler than those of the canonists.

The various just war theories developed within broader intellectual and political trends. A careful comparison of the theories with other types of contemporary literature and a study of their effects on practice lie outside the present scope, but it is possible to demonstrate some close correlations between the theories and high medieval society. The thirteenth century witnessed the emerging concept of sovereign states as independent units competent to act as their own judges in deciding when and how wars in their own defense were justified. The king became 'emperor in his own kingdom.' Writing around 1284, the provincial French lawyer Philippe de Beaumanoir, otherwise so solicitous of the rights of the nobility, ascribed to the French king the extraordinary powers necessary to defend his realm.[1] Beaumanoir's position deserves close attention, for his defense of noble prerogatives led him to proclaim that each baron was sovereign in his own barony, and that the count of Clermont's special rights over the property of his subjects in time of war was justified by his concern for the common good.[2] From this it appears that Beaumanoir would support the right of the nobility to wage its own

---

[1] Philippe de Beaumanoir, *Coutumes de Beauvaisis*, ed. A. Salmon (2 vols., Paris, 1899–1900), c. 49, para. 1510, II, 261f. J. R. Strayer has noted the general trend that extraordinary royal encroachments on customary prerogatives and immunities of Church and nobility were justified by invocation of the necessity to defend the realm: 'Defense of the Realm and Royal Power in France,' *Studi in onore di Gino Luzzatto* (3 vols., Milan, 1949), I, 290, 293. Cf. Kantorowicz, *King's Two Bodies*, pp. 249–58.

[2] Beaumanoir, *ibid.*, c. 34, para. 1043, II, 23; c. 58, para. 1662, II, 351.

private wars, a position that was hardly new though it still had a long history ahead of it. Yet Beaumanoir was unwilling to champion this position without qualification, for even in a case of private war between nobles the competent judicial authority of the region should prosecute malefactors, because in offending their adversaries they had also offended the justice of their sovereign lord. While such nobles could undertake their own wars, they were prohibited from making war on their king or resisting his justice.[3] In effect Beaumanoir took a middle position that did not prohibit private war entirely, but nevertheless took into account the centralisation of royal justice. For all its theoretical inconsistencies, this position of incomplete royal territorial jurisdiction was an accurate description of the situation in northern France during Beaumanoir's time. It was just this shifting mosaic of conflicting jurisdictions upon which Innocent IV based his distinction between the just war and defense. Only later did royal jurisdiction develop into full sovereignty.

If monarchs wished to limit private war for the sake of their own jurisdiction, the Church also sought to limit private warfare for its own reasons, such as the protection of churches and clerics. The peace movement had given way to secular jurisdiction over violence, but since the later scholastics had a long memory, they gave these efforts their benediction. After all, internal peace freed chivalric bellicosity for use in the various crusades. The reduction of private warfare was a joint effort of Church and monarchies.

Yet the just war theories were double-edged. Not only could they support ecclesiastical programs, but once matured they could also be turned against the ecclesiastical hierarchy itself as they indeed were in the famous conflict between Philip the Fair and Boniface VIII around 1300. By that time the just war theories had evolved into a right to war theory within the elastic restrictions of Christian morality. Warfare of monarchs was assumed by an indulgent clergy to be just unless directed against its own interests. Thus when Philip made war on England and Flanders he invoked the claim of his necessity to defend the realm and its common good. Even the French clergy had to yield its privileges to this imperative and the pope had also to yield. Many clerics actively supported Philip's attack upon the Church and championed his just war. As the just

[3] *Ibid.*, c. 59, para. 1673, II, 357f. Cf. Keen, *Laws of War*, pp. 73f.

war nourished in clerical circles could be directed against feudal particularity, so it could also be wielded against the position of the clergy itself. Canonists and theologians had prepared both sides well for the clash between the French king and the pope. By 1300 the just war theory became lost in a flurry of statute law. What with Augustine had started out as a problem of morality and scriptural exegesis ended up as a tool of statecraft in the hands of secular monarchs. The just war of Cicero's Rome reappeared when similarly favorable conditions allowed it to do so. The just war had become the *bellum legale*, a war waged in defense of legality rather than morality.[4]

Thus armed with a potent instrument of rule, secular rulers were able to oppose the violence of justice to the violence of private warfare, for to control justice was to limit internal warfare. The development of the just war can be seen as an aspect of the transition from 'segmentary' states in which private warfare was necessarily tolerated to 'unitary' or sovereign states enjoying a monopoly of licit violence.[5] That this development also made possible ever larger wars between sovereigns is no surprise, for here the kings borrowed a technique from the papacy. Exercise of superior jurisdiction limited brigandage and piracy. The canonists searched for means to justify limited wars, Innocent IV considering these lesser wars as defense or exercise of jurisdiction. In the fourteenth century his position led to the concepts of marque and reprisal, and in this form his distinction between limited wars and just wars passed into early modern international law. Attention shifted to consideration of warfare as distinct from other forms of hostilities, all of which invoked specific legal conditions. The legists of the late Middle Ages took up the effort to secure for national monarchs and city-states the monopoly of violence within a territorial area that improved their maintenance of law and order and provided them with a competitive advantage in exerting their sovereign rights.[6] Although this development came to fruition much later, its program was formulated by the medieval scholastics. The seemingly endless repetition of the basic foundations of the just

---

[4] Cf. J. Kunz, '*Bellum Justum* and *Bellum Legale*,' *American Journal of International Law*, XLV (1951), 530–3.

[5] Cf. A. W. Southall, 'A Note on State Organization. Segmentary States in Africa and in Medieval Europe,' *Early Medieval Society*, ed. S. Thrupp (New York, 1967), pp. 147–55.

[6] Keen, *Laws of War*, pp. 218–38; F. Cheyette, 'The Sovereign and the Pirates, 1332.'

war within the jurisprudential and theological systems cast the die for all succeeding theories of the just war. The thirteenth-century *defensio regni* employed by the lawyers of the last Capetians was continued by Machiavelli's Prince, More's Utopians, Richelieu's *raison d'état* and the more recent 'reasons of national security' as tools of sovereignty and internal control. Similarly, the crusading ideology took root in states later to become imperial powers in the non-European world. For example, it provided the ideological foundation for the Spanish settlement of the New World. Ironically, the real victors of the medieval just war were the new monarchs of early modern Europe. In spite of themselves, the medieval theorists of the just war assisted at the birth of the Leviathan.

In at least implicit recognition of the inadequacies of the theories, the canonists and theologians detailed many imaginative proposals to limit participation in unjust wars. Recognising that the knight's dual position of land-holder and fighter was torn against itself, that vassals desired stringent limitations on their service, and that the problem of manpower was a crucial one, they shrewdly sought to deplete the army of an unjust war leader and to fill the armies of the crusaders. Yet implementation of the *actio mandati* and similar measures were sabotaged by the use of mercenaries and the defense of the *patria*. Given the structure of authority and the rapacious and pugnacious mores of medieval knights, a frontal attack on all warfare was impractical. The recent school of ethologists grouped around Konrad Lorenz have viewed man as a basically aggressive creature who will kill and die in defense of his territory. Whatever the merits of these theories, the medieval scholastics implicitly believed them. The just war theories were perhaps the best compromise between aggression and Christian pacifism that the Church could devise.

As with so many other systems of thought and action, the medieval just war theories contained within themselves the seeds of their own dissolution. Even allowing for the difficulties of justifying warfare, the medieval just war was too time-bound to survive the religiously orientated period intact. It was fine for Aquinas in the thirteenth century to exalt the common good of separate societies, rather than the common good of all humanity, when the pope was seen as a kind of benevolent guardian of the human race, but by the time

Grotius wrote, this papal role had disappeared while national states were fiercely locked in combat. More fundamentally, perhaps, the just war theories of all save the speculative philosophers were too closely linked to the feudal system that endowed them with practical reference. By 1300 this system had already been radically transformed. Once the monopoly of licit violence held by the knightly class eroded, the more comprehensive medieval theories could be only vestigial, partly because they failed to treat mercenaries adequately. Only the mercenary's wages and abuses were mentioned, not his office. In a scholarly society with an aristocratic bias he continued to be the target of lingering suspicions and opprobrium long after he had become a crucial part of royal and city-state armies. Likewise the citizen levies that had been and were to become significant were neglected by the clerical observers. The *milites* of the theories were no longer 'knights' with social, political and cultural roles but officials who functioned merely as soldiers in a just war. Laws of treason that stressed the duties of subjects rather than those of vassals would end earlier legal benediction of the give-and-take relations between a king and his vassals.[7] The response on the part of late medieval legists to these changed conditions was a kind of quotation-mongering that was fine as technical jurisprudence but deficient in practical viability. Mercenaries and standing armies of Renaissance Italy and the new monarchies dealt the death blow to just war theories based on feudal rights and duties.

Since the medieval theories were developed to meet the problems of specific historical situations, their relevance to an overall theory of the just war is limited. Yet some of their unique problems may contribute to broader discussions of the right to wage war, even if they only call attention to the weaknesses of the just war tradition. A Christian pacifist would find little comfort in the medieval theories, for Christian dogma was used as a rationalisation for legal killing, even of the most indiscriminate sort in that consecrated war and its bloody martyrdom, the crusade.

Perhaps the greatest weakness of all medieval just war theories was their dependence on an assessment of prior guilt legitimating a particular war. The Manicheanism whose pacifism Augustine

[7] F. C. Lane, 'The Economic Meaning of War and Protection,' *Venice and History* (Baltimore, 1966), p. 384; idem, 'The Economic Consequences of Organized Violence,' *ibid.*, p. 425.

banished reappeared in the very different form of the punishment of evil by warfare waged by the good. From Augustine to Aquinas the concepts of avenging injuries, punishment and defense are often explicitly conflated. In an actual situation it is psychologically very difficult for the aggrieved party to distinguish lust for vengeance from defense of his own rights or even defense of the vaguely-defined moral order, so as to pattern his response accordingly. The problem of intervention by an impartial third party was not considered. After all, if one party was guilty of acting unjustly it should not fight but rather surrender while the other side was automatically justified. Armed with claims to ecclesiastical authority over Christian society, the Church could call upon any other power to punish the guilty party. Thus the concept of intervention by an impartial third party as well as the concepts of neutrality and free passage of an army were irrelevant to the medieval theories. The right of intervention by a third party, such as by More's altruistic Utopians who avenged injuries done to their allies but not those done to themselves, only appeared in early modern times and with different assumptions about the international community.

These observations also highlight another deficiency of most just war theories: they do not really analyse an unjust war except as a mirror image of a just war. If one side is just, the other side is necessarily unjust. Within the theories, this consequence cannot be avoided. For the just war to be incorporated within international law, some injustice on both sides must be assumed and the rules of conduct must be enforced impartially on both sides. Either both sides must be at fault, or neither side. The concept of blame ensures that there will be many 'just' wars. In this sense the medieval crusade against heretics, considered as outlaws lacking in rights, was not an expression of a nascent international law but the very denial of an international law of warfare.[8]

Lacking a competent tribunal to pass judgment on the justice of a war and to enforce its decision, the authority who declares the war is both morally and legally compromised. There is an unavoidable circularity which argues both that an authority with no superior has the right to declare a just war and that the declaration of a just war is the prerogative of authority with no superior. The guilty state

[8] Pissard, *La guerre sainte*, pp. 83f.

thereby comes under the *de facto* jurisdiction of the aggrieved state, which then acts as judge, jury and executioner in its own cause. If justice is the will of the prince, then he will naturally consider his own cause to be just. To forestall that conclusion, Augustine and medieval scholars necessarily assumed that the ruler acted out of pure and impartial motives and without passion, a position that militates against what we know about rulers of any age. Consequently both princes could claim justice, so that the war would be fully justified on both sides, an absurdity in theory, practice and common sense. With this the whole structure tumbles down.

The just war is really an ethical and religious doctrine surfaced with an often thick veneer of legality. In perspective any war amounts to 'self-vindication without due process of law.'[9] That everyone agrees with the abstract definition of a just war is irrelevant; the just war theory is simply too successful to be effective. Its only ability to restrain unjust wars lies in its powers of moral suasion to influence the practical virtue of politics. Further, the claim that necessity justified warfare absolved the prince of all responsibility for his conduct of the war. At least from a distance clerical observers could content themselves with the stock assumption that divine Providence sometimes permitted even unjust wars to punish people for sins they had committed in another connection. With necessity and Providence as escape clauses, the concept of the just war is emptied of its meaning. Within the theory there is simply no way to prevent a successful war from being treated as a just war. In the Middle Ages no one waged war or was invaded unless he was a lord of some sort. Simple peasants were just despoiled. The chivalric cast of the medieval theories ensured that only those wars were fought that stood a good chance of being victorious. Partly because of the permissiveness of the theories, might made right.

Certain other facets of the medieval just war precluded its general applicability in modern times. There was too much attention placed on the petty wars and brigandage of the feudal nobility. Singular nouns, such as prince, knight and enemy, indicate that warfare was seen as a conflict of individuals. By contrast, modern observers view war as armed conflict between sovereign territorial states and peoples. The ecclesiastical as well as the feudal orientation of the

[9] Bainton, *Christian Attitudes*, p. 240.

medieval just war, that it was primarily a means to defend the Church, limited its ability to restrain the wars of the rising national kingdoms. As a theory became more systematically coherent, it also became more irrelevant as a guide to contemporary practice. For example, Aquinas did not discuss war taxes nor did he provide much advice to princes about the proper response to hostile threats from vassals, overlords and claimants to vacant thrones, just the threats that fueled so many wars. Conversely, the more a theological or canonical theory included practical advice, the more incoherent and problematical it became in theory. Thus the practical casuistry of Peter the Chanter, who neglected to discuss truces, or the technical treatment of Innocent IV obscured the broad outlines of the just war in a welter of detail that was difficult to apply even in a specific instance, since no casuistic framework could cover every specific problem without the backing of coercive authority. The scholastic just war in its balance of competing values imposed a perpetual intellectual gymnastic on human minds and acts. The very complexities of the theories had to be swept away by the notion of primary obligations to the state before the just war could be accommodated to the reality of the modern world. At this point the just war theory as a restraint on violence became a dead letter.

There have been few groups of men equipped with such penetrating logic as the medieval scholastics. To their credit they did not commit some of the follies of more recent apologists for the just war. Since the just war avenged injuries already committed, there was no room for a doctrine of preventive war. In the current revival of interest in the just war, the criterion of self-defense has been seen as a crucial motive for a just war, but modern discussions of the subject have been marked by many confusions. Attempts have been made to distinguish a just war of defense from an unjust war of aggression. The scholastic position by contrast justified all hostile acts in defense of justice. No hostile act was licit or illicit by itself, but according to the authority on which it was committed. Provided that the cause was deemed just and the authority was competent, all means of prosecuting the war, including 'aggressive' acts, were licit. Their approach was later to be termed the *ius ad bellum*, the right to war, whereas many modern commentators have concentrated, without notable success, on defining the limits on violence according to a *ius in bello*, the complex of rights and restrictions to be observed in wartime.[10] In the medieval theories aggressive war and non-combatant immunity received little attention. Fighting and dying in warfare was a function of the knightly class. When their cause was just, there were only vague moral limits on their conduct, such as condemnation of the lust for conquest. Rather than attempting to eliminate war altogether, the scholastics more realistically and modestly tried to reduce the incidence of violence, but even here their effectiveness was limited by their feudal bias.

Any assessments of just war theories are bound to be ambivalent, as were the theories themselves, for they were an unstable compound that was always in danger of splitting into its component parts and destroying the delicate balance. At the very least the just war placed the burden of proof on would-be just warriors to demonstrate or rationalise the grounds for their actions according to generally accepted principles. For the past 3000 years, just war theories have had the dual purpose of restraining and justifying violence, essentially a self-contradictory exercise. Either the just war was a moral and religious doctrine, in which it was deprived of coercive but not normative force, or it was a legal concept that served as a cloak for statism. It remains an open question whether just war theories have limited more wars than they have encouraged.

[10] Cf. R. Tucker, *The Just War: A Study in Contemporary American Doctrine* (Baltimore, 1960), esp. pp. 71, n. 65, 131, n. 19, and 151; R. Osgood and R. Tucker, *Force, Order, and Justice* (Baltimore, 1967), pp. 292–301; F. Struckmeyer, 'The "Just War" and the Right of Self-Defense,' *Ethics*, LXXXII (1971), 48–55; R. Kann, 'The Law of Nations and the Conduct of War in the Early Times of the Standing Army,' *Journal of Politics*, VI (1944), 77–105.

APPENDIX: A JUDGMENT OF A WAR
BETWEEN TWO PRINCES

Gervais du Mont-Saint-Eloi, *Quodlibetum* 1, 84, B.N. Lat. 15350, fols. 289vb–290rb.
Reprinted by permission of the Bibliothèque Nationale, Paris.

'Duo principes existentes sub dominio superioris bellant adinvicem, nec petita nec obtenta licencia superioris domini et dampnificat unus alium. querebatur utrum dampnificans alium qui eum dampnificaverat teneatur ei restituere illud in quo eum dampnificavit. arguebatur quod non. Nullus tenetur sustinere vel incurrere dampnum ubi potest se ab illo preservare, sed princeps ille nisi bellasset contra alium et in bellando dampnificasset cum multa dampna incurrisset ab alio principe. ergo in tali articulo potuit contra alium bellare et eum dampnificare, nec tamen tenetur ad restitutionem.

Contra. isti principes habent dominum superiorem a quo potuerunt petere ius suum, nec facere sibi ius. ergo malefecerunt. ergo dampnificans alium in hac casu tenetur ad restitutionem alioquin reportaret commodum de malicia sua. si habuit iustum bellum et in modo non excessit, vel si excessit ex necessitate excessit, quia non potuisset se defendisse et sua iura tueri nisi modum [290ra] excessisset propter maliciam adversarii et ex hoc in modo tali fuerit excusabilis ut notatur ibi. puto quod translatum est dominium illorum qui iuste debellati fiunt in debellantes lege iustice interveniente auctoritate eorum qui hoc potuerunt ordinare. Et sic non tenetur illa restituere an habuit iniustum bellum, quod fit v modis, ut notatur [C. 23 q. 2 c. 1] cum suis concordantiis [= *Glossa Ordinaria*]. unus est ratione persone, ut si sint ecclesiastice, quia eis non est licitum bellare. alius est ratione rei, quia non est pro repetendis rebus vel pro defensione patrie. tercius ratione cause, ut si non ex necessitate sed ex voluntate pugnetur. quartus ex animo, ut si fiat animo ulciscendo. quintus ratione defectus auctoritatis, quia non fit auctoritate superioris domini auctoritate cuius debet fieri, et tunc distinguo, quia aut talis accipit ab illis a quibus nescit se esse in aliquo dampnificatum et sic rapit alienum ut alienum est, et ideo raptor est et tenetur ad restitutionem, sicut raptor, quia nullus debet reportare commodum de sua malicia, ut habetur [X. 2.14.9]. reportaret autem commodum de malicia sua si non teneretur ad restitutionem talium ablatorum. aut non rapit nisi ab illis qui eum vel nunc vel alias dampnificaverint de quibus probabiliter presumit quod per iustum modum repetendi nullo modo rehaberet causa. et tunc dico quod peccat sic reaccipiendo sibi debitum et est ei penitencia iniungenda tamquam usurpanti sibi officium iudicis, cum non sit iudex in hac causa que est sua, et etiam ex hoc forte quod ex avaritia accipit. sed non accepit quod accepit ut ita alienum quin sciret sibi esse debitum vel in se vel in equivalenti, et tunc puto quod pro quanto scit sibi est debitum nec restitutum quod non est ei imponendum in foro penitencie quod restituat, dum tamen proponat firmiter in animo quod si postea sibi restitueretur, ipse non retineret sibi, quamvis in foro exteriori iniungi debeat ei restitutio, quia super omnia et ante omnia spoliati sunt restituendi, unde [X. 2.13.5]. predo etiam secundum rigorem iuris restituendus est, tamen in foro penitencie non oportet quod iniungatur, quia cum de iure non possederit quantum reaccepit, quia debuit eum posuisse in possessione eius. non debet dici proprie spoliatus ut notatur [x. 2.13.14], nec restitutio peti potest cum nulla possessio iuris hic fuerit, unde quamvis peccaverit in illum contra quem bellavit, ratione iniuriose accionis, et ideo quantum ad hoc teneatur ei ad emandam non tamen ratione rei, sicut si per campos et per sata eius irem ad sata campi nostri quem ille michi abstulit et possidet et colligerem de satis nostris. ego iniuriarem ei in modo accedendi ad campum meum et quantum ad hoc tenerer ei ad satisfactionem non quantum ad hoc quod accepi seminata in campo meo propter res acceptas. ad hoc potest valere quod dicit augustinus ad macedonium [*Epist. 153*, 23; C. 14 q. 5 c. 15], non sane quicquid ab invitis accipitur [290rb] iniuriose auffertur. nam plerique nec medico volunt reddere honorem suum, nec operario mercedem, nec tamen qui ab invitis accipiunt per iniuriam accipiunt que pocius per iniuriam non darentur. dico ergo quod quantum ad aliqua tenetur restituere et quantum ad aliqua non.

Ad primum argumentum nullus dampnum tenetur sustinere ubi potest vitare. dico quod verum est ubi bono modo potest. sed per bellum non potest nisi sicut dictum est.

Ad illud in oppositum habuit dominum suum superiorem etc. dico quod bene ostendit hoc argumentum quod male faciunt si bellant sine licencia eius. sed non oportet quod teneantur ad restitutionem omnium acceptorum in tali bello. alioquin oporteret quod quis restitueret capam [= rapinam?] suam illi qui forte rapuerat ei quam recuperavit in illo bello.'

BIBLIOGRAPHY

The bibliography includes only those works that have made a material and significant contribution to the preparation of this book. Basic bibliographical works, individual works within an author's *Opera Omnia* and various editions are usually omitted.

I. MANUSCRIPT SOURCES

The numbers of manuscripts, unless otherwise noted, refer to Paris, Bibliothèque Nationale, Fonds Latin.

Alanus Anglicus. *Apparatus: 'Ius Naturale.'* 15393; Paris, Bibliothèque Mazarine 1318.
  Apparatus to Compilatio I. 3932.
Anonymous. *Quodlibet.* Vatican, Lat. 782.
Bernard Botone. *Summa Titulorum.* 3972; 4053.
Damasus. *Apparatus to Compilatio I.* 3930.
  Summa Decretalium. 14320.
Gervais du Mont-Saint-Eloi. *Quodlibetum.* 15350.
Giles of Rome. *Quomodo Possint Reges Bona Regni Ecclesiis Elargiri.* 6786.
Gloss: *'Ecce vicit Leo.'* Paris, Bibliothèque Nationale, Nouvelles Acquisitions Latines 1576.
Godfrey of Fontaines. *Quodlibetum.* 14311.
Gui de l'Aumone. *Summa de Diversis Questionibus Theologiae.* 14891.
Hugh of St Cher. *In IV Libros Sententiarum.* 3073, 3406.
Huguccio. *Summa.* 3892, 15396 (first part), 15397 (second part).
Jean de la Rochelle. *Summa de Vitiis.* 16417.
Johannes de Deo. *Liber Poenitentiarius.* 14703.
  Summa super Certis Casibus Decretalium. 3971, 3972.
Johannes Faventinus. *Summa.* 14606.
Johannes Teutonicus. *Apparatus to Compilatio III.* 3930.
  Apparatus to Compilatio IV. 3931A, 3932, 12452, 14321.
  Glossa Ordinaria to Decretum. 14317; Vatican Lat. 1367.
Laurentius Hispanus. *Apparatus to Decretum.* 3903, 15393.
Peter of Auvergne. *Commentarium in Libros Politicorum.* 16089.
Peter of Salins. *Lectura in Decretum.* 3917.
Peter the Chanter. *Distinctiones Abel.* 455.
Placentinus. *Summa Codicis.* 4441, 4539.
  Summa Institutionum. 4441, 4539.
Radulphus Ardens. *Speculum Universale.* 3240; Paris, Bibliothèque Mazarine 709, 710.
Sicard of Cremona. *Summa.* 14996.
Simon of Bisignano. *Summa.* 3934A.
Stephen of Tournai. *Summa Decretorum.* 14609.
Summa: 'Cum in Tres Partes.' 16540.
Summa: 'Elegantius in Iure Divino.' 14997.
Summa: 'Et est Sciendum.' Rouen, Bibliothèque Municipale 710 (E. 29).
Summa: 'Inperatorie Maiestati.' Munich, Staatsbibliothek, C.L.M. 16084.

Bibliography

Summa: 'Omnis qui iuste iudicat.' Rouen, Bibliothèque Municipale 743 (E. 74); Luxembourg, Bibliothèque 144.
Summa: 'Quoniam Status Ecclesiarum.' 16538.
Summa: 'Tractaturus Magister.' 15994.
Tancredus. *Apparatus* to Compilatio I. 3931A, 14321, 15398.
Vincentius Hispanus. *Apparatus in Decretales Gregorii IX.* 3967, 3968.
William of Antona. *Postilla in Josue.* 526.

II. PRINTED SOURCES

Abbas Antiquus (Bernard of Montemirato). *Lectura in Decretales Gregorii IX.* In *Perillustrium tam Veterum quam Recentiorum in Libros Decretalium Aurea Commentaria.* Venice, 1588.
Abelard. *Sic et Non.* In P.L. 178.
Alain of Lille. *De Fide Catholica adversus Haereticos.* In P.L. 210.
  Liber Poenitentialis. 2 vols. Ed. J. Longère. Louvain and Lille, 1965.
Albertus Magnus. *Opera Omnia.* 38 vols. Ed. A. Borgnet. Paris, 1890–9.
Alexander of Hales. *Glossa in IV Libros Sententiarum.* 4 vols. Quaracchi, 1951–7.
  Summa Theologiae. 4 vols. Quaracchi, 1924–48.
Ambrose. *Opera Omnia.* In P.L. 14–17.
Anselm of Bec. *Opera Omnia.* 6 vols. Ed. F. S. Schmitt. Edinburgh, 1938–61.
Anselm of Lucca. *Liber contra Wibertum.* In M.G.H., *Libelli de Lite,* I.
Aquinas, Thomas. *Opera Omnia.* 25 vols. Parma, 1852–73; Rep. New York, 1948–50.
  Opera Omnia. 34 vols. Paris (Vivès), 1871–80.
  Opuscula Philosophica. Ed. R. M. Spiazzi. Turin and Rome, 1954.
  Quaestiones Disputatae et Quaestiones XII Quodlibetales. Turin and Rome, 1927.
Augustine. *Opera Omnia.* P.L. 32–45. Certain works are available in critical editions in C.S.E.L.
Azo. *Lectura in Codicem.* Paris, 1611.
  Summa Codicis. Lyon, 1564.
  Summa Institutionum. Lyon, 1564.
Bartholomew of Brescia. *Glossa Ordinaria in Decretum Gratiani.* In *Glossa Ordinaria in Corpus Juris Canonici.*
Bartholomew of Exeter. *Penitentiale.* In Morey, A. *Bartholomew of Exeter, Bishop and Canonist.* Cambridge, 1937.
Bernard Botone. *Glossa Ordinaria ad Decretales Gregorii IX.* In *Glossa Ordinaria in Corpus Juris Canonici.*
Bernard of Clairvaux. *Opera Omnia.* In P.L. 182–3.
  Opera Omnia. 4 vols. to date. Rome, 1957–.
Bonaventura. *Opera Omnia.* 11 vols. Quaracchi, 1882–1902.
  Opera Omnia. 15 vols. Paris (Vivès), 1864–71.
Burchard of Worms. *Liber Decretorum.* In P.L. 140.
Codex Theodosiani. Ed. T. Mommsen and P. Meyer. Berlin, 1905.
Collectio Sangallensis. In M.G.H., *Leges.,* v.
Corpus Juris Canonici. 2 vols. Ed. A. Friedberg. Leipzig, 1879, 1881.
Corpus Juris Civilis. Ed. T. Mommsen, P. Krueger, and W. Kroll. Berlin, 1872–7.
Corpus Juris Civilis. 5 vols. Lyon, 1612. (With Accursius, *Glossa Ordinaria.*)
Durantis, William. *Speculum Iudiciale.* 3 vols. Venice, 1585.
Einhard. *Vita Karoli Magni.* Ed. G. Waitz. In M. G. H. *Scriptores Rerum Germanicarum.* Hanover, 1905; transl. L. Halphen. Paris, 1923.

Bibliography

Frontinus. *Strategematicon*. Ed. A. Dederich. Leipzig, 1855.

Gaudenzi, A., ed. *Bibliotheca Iuridica Medii Aevi*. 3 vols. Bologna, 1892–1914.

Giles of Rome (Aegidius Romanus). *De Regimine Principum*. Rome, 1607; Rep. Aalen, 1967.

Glossa Ordinaria in Corpus Juris Canonici. Printed with *Corpus Juris Canonici*. 3 vols. Venice, 1592–1600. (Vol. I: Liber Sextus, 1592. Vol. II: *Decretales Gregorii IX*, 1595. Vol. III: *Decretum Gratiani*, 1600.)

Godfrey of Fontaines. *Les Quodlibets onze-quatorze de Godefroid de Fontaines*. Ed. J. Hoffmanns. Louvain, 1932.

Goffredus of Trani. *Summa in Titulos Decretalium*. Venice, 1570; Lyon, 1519.

Gratian. *Decretum*. In *Corpus Juris Canonici*, I.

Gregory I. *Liber Moralium, sive Expositio in librum B. Job*. In P.L. 76.

    Registrum Epistolarum. 2 vols. Ed. P. Ewald and M. Hartmann. (M.G.H., *Epistolae* I–II). Berlin, 1891–9.

Gregory VII. *Registrum*. M.G.H., *Epistolae Selectae*, II. Ed. E. Caspar. Berlin, 1920–3.

Gregory IX. *Decretales*. In *Corpus Juris Canonici*, II.

Gregory of Tours. *Historia Francorum*. Ed. W. Arndt. In M.G.H., *Scriptores Rerum Merovingicarum*, I. Hanover, 1885.

Halitgar of Cambrai. *Liber Poenitentialis*. In P.L. 105.

Hannibald. *Scriptum super Libris Magistri Sententiarum*. Printed with Aquinas, *Opera Omnia*, Parma edition, XXII; Vivès edition, XXX.

Henry of Ghent. *Aurea Quodlibeta*. 2 vols. Venice, 1613.

Hincmar of Rheims. *Opera Omnia*. In P.L. 125.

    Epistola Synodi Carisiacensis ad Hludowicum Regem Germaniae Directa. In M.G.H., *Leges*, sectio II, tomus 2.

Hostiensis, *Lectura in Decretales Gregorii IX*. Venice, 1581.

    Lectura in Decretales Innocentii IV. Venice 1581.

    Summa Aurea. Venice, 1574.

Hrabanus Maurus. *Opera Omnia*. In P.L. 107–12.

    Epistolae. In M.G.H., *Epistolae*, V.

Hugolinus. *Summa super Usibus Feudorum*. In Gaudenzi, *Bibliotheca*, II.

Innocent IV. *Commentaria. Apparatus in Quinque Libros Decretalium*. Frankfurt, 1570.

Isidore of Seville. *Etymologiarum sive Originum Libri XX*. 2 vols. Ed. W. M. Lindsay. Oxford, 1911.

Ivo of Chartres. *Decretum*. In P.L. 161.

    Panormia. In P.L. 161.

Jerome. *Commentariorum in Michaeum*. In P.L. 25.

John VIII. *Epistolae*. In M.G.H., *Epistolae*, VII.

Leo IV. *Epistolae*. In M.G.H., *Epistolae*, V.

Maximus of Turin. *Homilia CXIV*. In P.L. 57.

Monaldus. *Summa Perutilis*. Lyons, before 1516.

Monumenta Germaniae Historica. Epistolae. 8 vols. Berlin, 1891–1939.

    Leges. Hanover, 1835–.

    Libelli de Lite Imperatorum et Pontificum. 3 vols. Hanover, 1891–7.

    Scriptores. Hanover and Berlin, 1826–.

Nicholas I. *Epistolae*. In M.G.H., *Epistolae*, VI–VII.

    Responsa ad Consulta Bulgarorum. In M.G.H., *Epistolae*, VI.

Odofredus. *Lectura Codicis*. Lyon, 1552.

    Summa in Usus Feudorum. Alcalá, 1584.

Bibliography

Patrologia Latina. 221 vols. Ed. J. P. Migne. Paris, 1844–65.

Paucapalea. Die Summa des Paucapalea. Ed. J. F. von Schulte. Giessen, 1890.

Peter the Chanter. Summa de Sacramentis et Animae Consiliis. Vols. I, II, III (1), III (2a), III (2b). Louvain and Lille, 1954–66.

Verbum Abbreviatum. In P.L. 205.

Peter Damiani. Epistolae. In P.L. 144.

Peter the Lombard. Libri Sententiarum IV. 2 vols. Quaracchi, 1916.

Peter of Poitiers. Sententiarum Libri V. In P.L. 211.

Philippe de Beaumanoir. Coutumes de Beauvaisis. 2 vols. Ed. A. Salmon. Paris, 1899–1900.

Placentinus. Summa Codicis. Mainz, 1536.

Summa Institutionum. Lyon, 1536.

Pseudo-Augustine. Epistula XIII. In P.L. 33.

Pseudo-Cyprian. De XII Abusivis Saeculi. Ed. S. Hellmann. In Texte und Untersuchungen zur Geschichte der altchristlichen Literatur. 3. Reihe, 4. Band, (= XXXIV[1]). Leipzig, 1909.

Quinque Compilationes Antiquae. Ed. A. Friedberg. Leipzig, 1882.

Raymond of Peñafort. Summa de Casibus. Rome, 1603.

Summa Juris. Ed. J. Ruis Serra. Barcelona, 1945.

Remigio de' Girolami. De Bono Pacis. In C. T. Davis, 'Remigio de' Girolami and Dante,' 123–36.

Richard of Mediavilla. Super IV Libros Sententiarum. 4 vols. Brescia, 1591; Rep. Frankfurt, 1963.

Robert of Courson. 'Le traité "De Usura" de Robert de Courson.' Ed. G. Lefèvre. Travaux et Mémoires de l'Université de Lille, x, 30. Lille, 1902.

Robert of Flamborough. Liber Poenitentialis. Ed. J. J. F. Firth. Toronto, 1971.

Robert Pullen. Sententiarum Libri VIII. In P.L. 186.

Rogerius. Summa Codicis. In A. Gaudenzi, Bibliotheca, I.

Rolando Bandinelli. Die Summa Magistri Rolandi. Ed. F. Thaner. Innsbruck, 1874.

Roland of Cremona. Summae Liber Tercius. Ed. A. Cortesi. Bergamo, 1962.

Rufinus. Die Summa Decretorum des Magister Rufinus. Ed. H. Singer. Paderborn, 1902.

Schmitz, H. J. Die Bussbücher und die Bussdisciplin der Kirche. 2 vols. Mainz and Düsseldorf, 1883, 1898.

Sedulius Scotus. Liber de Rectoribus Christianis. Ed. S. Hellmann. In Quellen und Untersuchungen zur lateinischen Philologie des Mittelalters, I[1].

Summa Parisiensis. Ed. T. P. McLaughlin. Toronto, 1952.

Summa Trecensis. Ed. H. Fitting. Berlin, 1894.

Thegan. Vita Hludowici Imperatoris. In M.G.H., Scriptores, II.

Thomas of Chobham. Summa Confessorum. Ed. F. Broomfield. Louvain, 1968.

Vegetius. Epitoma Rei Militaris. Ed. C. Lang. Leipzig, 1869.

Vincent of Beauvais. Speculum Maius (including the Speculum Doctrinale and the Speculum Morale). Douai, 1624.

Wasserschleben, H. Die Bussordnungen der abendländischen Kirche. Halle, 1851.

William of Auvergne. Opera Omnia. 2 vols. Paris, 1624; rep. Frankfurt, 1963.

William of Rennes. Glossa. In Raymond of Peñafort, Summa de Casibus.

III. SECONDARY WORKS

Alphandéry, P. and Dupront, A. La chrétienté et l'idée de croisade. 2 vols. Paris, 1954–9.

Arendt, W. Die Staats- und Gesellschaftslehre Alberts des Grossen. Jena, 1929.

Bibliography

Arquillière, H. X. *L'augustinisme politique*. Paris, 1934.

Bainton, R. H. *Christian Attitudes toward War and Peace*. Nashville, Tennessee, 1960.

'The Early Church and War,' *Harvard Theological Review*, XXXIX (1946), 189–213.

Baldwin, J. W. *Masters, Princes and Merchants. The Social Views of Peter the Chanter and his Circle*. 2 vols. Princeton, 1970.

'The Medieval Theories of the Just Price,' *Transactions of the American Philosophical Society*, XLIX⁴ (1959).

Beaufort, D. *La guerre comme instrument de secours ou de punition*. The Hague, 1933.

Beeler, J. *Warfare in Feudal Europe, 730–1200*. Ithaca, 1971.

Benson, R. L. *The Bishop-Elect. A Study in Medieval Ecclesiastical Office*. Princeton, 1968.

'The Obligations of Bishops with "Regalia",' *Proceedings of the Second International Congress of Medieval Canon Law*. Ed. S. Kuttner and J. J. Ryan. Vatican City, 1965.

Berger, A. 'Encyclopedic Dictionary of Roman Law,' *Transactions of the American Philosophical Society*, XLIII² (1953), 333–809.

Black, H. *Black's Law Dictionary*. 4th ed. St Paul, Minn., 1951.

Blake, E. O. 'The Formation of the "Crusade Idea",' *Journ. Eccl. Hist.* XXI (1970), 11–31.

Bonnaud-Delamare, R. 'La paix en Aquitaine au xiᵉ siècle,' *Recueils Bodin*, XIV (1961), 415–87.

Bouthoul, G. *Traité de sociologie: les guerres. Eléments de polémologie*. Paris, 1951.

Boutruche, R. *Seigneurie et féodalité*. 2 vols. Paris, 1959–70.

Boyd, W. K. *The Ecclesiastical Edicts of the Theodosian Code*. New York, 1902.

Bridrey, E. *La condition juridique de croisés et le privilège de croix*. Paris, 1900.

Brown, P. R. L. *Augustine of Hippo*. London, Berkeley and Los Angeles, 1967.

'Saint Augustine,' in *Trends in Medieval Political Thought*, pp. 1–21.

'St Augustine's Attitude to Religious Coercion,' *Journ. of Roman Studies*, LIV (1964), 107–16.

Brundage, J. A. *Medieval Canon Law and the Crusader*. Madison and Milwaukee, 1969.

Calisse, C. *A History of Italian Law*. Trans. L. B. Register. Boston, 1928.

Chenu, M. D. 'L'évolution de la théologie de la guerre juste,' *La parole de Dieu*. 2 vols. Paris, 1964. II, 571–92.

Introduction à l'étude de Saint Thomas d'Aquin. 3rd ed. Paris, 1954. Trans.: *Toward Understanding Saint Thomas*. Chicago, 1964.

Cheyette, F. 'The Sovereign and the Pirates, 1332,' *Speculum*, XLV (1970), 40–68.

Chodorow, S. *Christian Political Theory and Church Politics in the Mid-Twelfth Century. The Ecclesiology of Gratian's Decretum*. Berkeley and Los Angeles, 1972.

Classen, P. *Gerhoch von Reichersberg. Eine Biographie*. Wiesbaden, 1960.

Cochrane, C. N. *Christianity and Classical Culture*. Oxford, 1940.

Cram, K. G. *Iudicium Belli. Zum Rechtscharakter des Krieges im deutschen Mittelalter*. Muenster and Cologne, 1955.

Deane, H. *The Political and Social Ideas of St Augustine*. New York, 1963.

Davis, C. T. 'Remigio de' Girolami and Dante. A Comparison of Their Conceptions of Peace,' *Studi Danteschi* XXXVI (1959), 105–36.

Delaruelle, D. 'Paix de Dieu et croisade dans la chrétienté du xiiᵉ siècle,' in *Paix de Dieu et Guerre Sainte*, pp. 51–71.

Dudden, F. H. *Gregory the Great*. 2 vols. London, 1905.

Life and Times of Saint Ambrose. 2 vols. Oxford, 1935.

Bibliography

Dunbabin, J. 'Aristotle in the Schools,' in *Trends in Medieval Political Thought,* pp. 65–85.

Dupront, A. *Le mythe de croisade. Etude de sociologie religieuse.* 6 vols. Thèse, Lettres, Université de Paris, 1956.

Duval, F. *De la paix de Dieu à la paix de fer.* Paris, 1923.

Engreen, F. E. 'Pope John the Eighth and the Arabs,' *Speculum,* xx (1945), 318–30.

Erdmann, C. *Die Entstehung des Kreuzzugsgedankens.* Stuttgart, 1935; Rep. 1955.

Fichtenau, H. *The Carolingian Empire.* Trans. P. Munz. Oxford, 1957.

Ganshof, F. 'La paix au très haut moyen âge,' *Recueils Bodin,* xiv (1961), 397–413.

Gaudemet, J. 'L'étranger au bas empire,' *Recueils Bodin,* ix (1958), 207–35.

Gilmore, M. *Argument from Roman Law in Political Thought, 1200–1600.* Cambridge, Mass., 1941.

Gilson, E. *History of Christian Philosophy in the Middle Ages.* New York, 1955.

Gleiman, L. 'Some Remarks on the Origin of the *Treuga Dei,*' *Etudes d'histoire littéraire et doctrinale.* Université de Montréal, Institut d'Etudes Médiévales, *Publications* xvii (1962), 117–37.

Glorieux, P. *La littérature quodlibétique de 1260 à 1320.* 2 vols. Paris, 1925–35.

Répertoire des maîtres en théologie de Paris au xiiie siècle. 2 vols. Paris, 1933–4.

Gmür, H. *Thomas von Aquino und der Krieg.* Leipzig, 1933.

Grabmann, M. *Die Werke des hl. Thomas von Aquino.* 3rd ed. Muenster, 1949.

Harnack, A. von. *Militia Christi.* Tübingen, 1905.

Hartigan, R. 'Saint Augustine on War and Killing,' *Journal of the History of Ideas,* xxvii (1966), 195–204.

Herde, P. 'Christians and Saracens at the Time of the Crusades. Comments of Contemporary Medieval Canonists,' *Studia Gratiana,* xii (1967), 361–76.

Heuss, A. 'Die völkerrechtlichen Grundlagen der römischen Aussenpolitik in republikanisher Zeit,' *Klio,* Beiheft xxxi (1933), 18–25.

Heydte, F. A. F. von der. *Die Geburtsstunde des souveränen Staates.* Regensburg, 1952.

Hoffmann, H. *Gottesfriede und Treuga Dei.* M.G.H., *Schriften,* xx (1964).

Horoy, C. *Droit international et droit de gens public d'après le Decretum de Gratien.* Paris, 1887.

Hubrecht, G. 'La "juste guerre" dans le Décret de Gratien,' *Studia Gratiana,* iii (1955), 161–77.

'La juste guerre dans la doctrine chrétienne des origines au milieu du xvie siècle, *Recueils Bodin,* xv (1961), 107–23.

Imbert, J. 'Pax Romana,' *Recueils Bodin,* xiv (1961), 303–19.

Kantorowicz, E. *The King's Two Bodies. A Study in Mediaeval Political Theology.* Princeton, 1957.

Kantorowicz, H. 'De pugna. La letteratura langobardistica sul duello giudiziano,' *Rechtshistorische Studien.* Ed. H. Coing and G. Immel. Karlsruhe, 1970. Pp. 255–71.

Studies in the Glossators of the Roman Law. Cambridge, 1938.

Keen, M. H. *The Laws of War in the Late Middle Ages.* London and Toronto, 1965.

Kunz, J. '*Bellum Justum* and *Bellum Legale,*' *American Journal of International Law,* xlv (1951), 528–34.

Kuttner, S. *Kanonistische Schuldlehre von Gratian bis auf die Dekretalen Gregors IX (Studi e Testi, 64).* Vatican City, 1935.

Repertorium der Kanonistik (Studi e Testi, 71). Vatican City, 1937.

Bibliography

LeBras, G., Lefebvre, C., and Rambaud, J. *L'âge classique, 1140–1378. Sources et théorie du droit* (*Histoire du droit et des institutions de l'église en Occident*, VII). Paris, 1965.

La Brière, Y. de. 'La conception de la paix et de la guerre chez Saint Augustine,' *Revue de Philosophie*, XXX (1930), 557–72.

Lane, F. C. *Venice and History. The Collected Papers of Frederic C. Lane.* Baltimore, 1966.

Legendre, P. *La pénétration du droit romain dans le droit canonique classique de Gratien à Innocent IV* (*1140–1254*). Paris, 1964.

Leyser, K. J. 'The Polemics of the Papal Revolution,' in *Trends in Medieval Political Thought*, pp. 42–64.

MacKinney, L. 'The People and Public Opinion in the Eleventh Century Peace Movement,' *Speculum*, V (1930), 181–206.

Mandonnet, P. *Des écrits authentiques de Saint Thomas d'Aquin.* 2nd ed. Fribourg, 1910.

Maritain, J. 'Considérations françaises sur les choses d'Espagne,' in Mendizibal, A., *Aux origines d'une tragédie: la politique espagnole de 1923 à 1936* (Paris, 1937), pp. 7–56.

Mausbach, J. *Die Ethik des heiligen Augustinus.* 2 vols. Freiburg im B., 1909.

Meijers, E. M. *Etudes d'histoire du droit.* III. Ed. R. Feenstra and H. F. W. D. Fischer. Leyden, 1959.

Mommsen, T. *Droit public romain.* 7 vols. Trans. P. Girard. Paris, 1889–96.

Muldoon, J. 'The Contribution of the Medieval Canon Lawyers to the Formation of International Law,' *Traditio*, XXVIII (1972), 483–97.

' "Extra Ecclesiam non est imperium." The Canonists and the Legitimacy of Secular Power,' *Studia Gratiana*, IX (1966), 553–80.

'A Fifteenth Century Application of the Canonistic Theory of the Just War' (to appear in *Monumenta Iuris Canonici*).

Nicholas, B. *An Introduction to Roman Law.* Oxford, 1962.

Nussbaum, A. *A Concise History of the Law of Nations.* Rev. ed. New York, 1954.

'Just War – A Legal Concept?', *Michigan Law Review*, XLII (1943), 453–79.

'The Significance of Roman Law in the History of International Law,' *University of Pennsylvania Law Review*, C (1952), 678–87.

Osgood, R. and Tucker, R. W. *Force, Order, and Justice.* Baltimore, 1967.

The Oxford Classical Dictionary. Ed. M. Cary *et al.* Oxford, 1961.

Paix de Dieu et Guerre Sainte en Languedoc au xiiie siècle. (*Cahiers de Fanjeaux*, IV). Toulouse, 1969.

Paradisi, B. 'La paix au ive et ve siècles,' *Receuils Bodin*, XIV (1961), 321–95.

Perrin, J. W. 'Azo, Roman Law and Sovereign European States,' *Studia Gratiana*, XV (1972), 89–101.

'*Legatus*, the Lawyers and the Terminology of Power in Roman Law,' *Studia Gratiana*, XI (1967), 461–89.

Peters, E. *The Shadow King. 'Rex Inutilis' in Medieval Law and Literature, 751–1327.* New Haven and London, 1970.

Philippson, C. *The International Law and Customs of Ancient Greece and Rome.* 2 vols. London, 1911.

Pissard, H. *La guerre sainte en pays chrétien.* Paris, 1912.

Post, G. *Studies in Medieval Legal Thought.* Princeton, 1964.

Powicke, M. *Military Obligation in Medieval England. A Study in Liberty and Duty.* Oxford, 1962.

Bibliography

Prinz, F. *Klerus und Krieg*. Stuttgart, 1971.

Purcell, Maureen. 'Changing Views of Crusade in the Thirteenth Century,' *Journal of Religious History*, VII (1972), 3–19.

Rad, G. von. *Der heilige Krieg im alten Israel*. Zurich, 1951.

Ramsey, P. *War and the Christian Conscience*. Durham, N.C., 1961.

Recueils de la Société Jean Bodin pour l'histoire comparative des institutions.

Regout, R. *La doctrine de la guerre juste de Saint Augustin à nos jours, d'après les théologiens et les canonistes catholiques*. Paris, 1935.

Seckel, E. *Über Krieg und Recht in Rom*. Berlin, 1915.

Sicard, G. 'Paix et guerre dans le droit canon du xiie siècle,' in *Paix de Dieu et guerre sainte* (Cahiers de Fanjeaux, IV, 1969), pp. 72–90.

Smalley, B. *The Study of the Bible in the Middle Ages*. 2nd ed. Oxford, 1952.

Solages, B. de. 'La genèse et l'orientation de la théologie de la guerre juste,' *Bulletin de littérature ecclésiastique*, II (1940), 61–80.

Southall, A. W. 'A Note on State Organization. Segmentary States in Africa and in Medieval Europe,' *Early Medieval Society*. Ed. S. Thrupp. New York, 1967, pp. 147–55.

Southern, R. W. *Western Society and the Church in the Middle Ages*. Baltimore, 1970.

Stegmüller, F. *Repertorium Biblicum Medii Aevi*. 7 vols. Madrid, 1950–61.

Stickler, A. 'Il potere coattivo materiale della Chiesa nella Riforma Gregoriana secondo Anselmo di Lucca,' *Studi Gregoriani*, II (1947), 235–85.

'Sacerdotium et Regnum nei Decretisti e Primi Decretalisti,' *Salesianum*, XV (1953), 575–612.

Strayer, J. R. 'Defense of the Realm and Royal Power in France,' *Studi in onore di Gino Luzzatto*. 3 vols. Milan, 1949, pp. 289–95.

Struckmeyer, F. 'The "Just War" and the Right of Self-Defense,' *Ethics*, LXXXII (1971), 48–55.

Tooke, J. *The Just War in Aquinas and Grotius*. London, 1965.

Trends in Medieval Political Thought. Ed. B. Smalley. Oxford, 1965.

Tucker, R. W. 'The Interpretation of War under Present International Law,' *The International Law Quarterly*, IV (1951), 11–38.

The Just War. A Study in Contemporary American Doctrine. Baltimore, 1960.

Ullmann, W. *The Carolingian Renaissance and the Idea of Kingship*. London, 1969.

The Growth of Papal Government in the Middle Ages. 3rd–4th ed. London, 1970.

A Short History of the Papacy in the Middle Ages. London, 1972.

Vanderpol, A. *La doctrine scolastique du droit de guerre*. Paris, 1919.

Villey, M. *La croisade: essai sur la formation d'une théorie juridique*. Caen, 1942.

'Le droit naturel chez Gratien,' *Studia Gratiana*, III (1955), 85–99.

'L'idée de croisade,' *Storia del Medioevo*, pp. 565–94. (*Relazione del X Congresso Internazionale di Scienze Storiche*, III).

Vinogradoff, P. *Roman Law in Medieval Europe*. 2nd ed. Oxford, 1929; rep. Cambridge, 1967.

Wallach, L. *Alcuin and Charlemagne*. Ithaca, N.Y., 1959.

Walters, L. B. Jr. 'Five Classic Just War Theories: A Study in the Thought of Thomas Aquinas, Vitoria, Suarez, Gentili and Grotius.' Dissertation, Yale University, 1971.

Walzer, M. 'Exodus 32 and the Theory of the Holy War: The History of a Citation,' *Harvard Theological Review*, LXI (1968), 1–14.

Bibliography

Watt, J. *The Theory of Papal Monarchy in the Thirteenth Century.* New York, 1965.

Wilks, M. *The Problem of Sovereignty in the Later Middle Ages.* Cambridge, 1963.

Windass, S. *Christianity versus Violence: A Social and Historical Study of War and Christianity.* London, 1964.

Paris, Bibliothèque Nationale, Fonds Latin: 455, 526, 782, 3073, 3240, 3406, 3892, 3903, 3917, 3930, 3931A, 3932, 3934A, 3967, 3968, 3971, 3972, 4053, 4441, 4539, 6786, 12452, 14311, 14317, 14320, 14321, 14606, 14609, 14703, 14891, 14996, 14997, 15350, 15393, 15396, 15397, 15398, 15994, 16089, 16417, 16538, 16540.

Paris, Bibliothèque Nationale, Nouvelles Acquisitions Latines: 1576.

Paris, Bibliothèque Mazarine: 709, 710, 1318.

Vatican, Latin: 782 (microfilm in Institut de Recherche et d'Histoire des Textes), 1367 (microfilm in Institute of Medieval Canon Law).

Rouen, Bibliothèque Municipale: 710 (E. 29), 743 (E. 74) (both mss. on microfilm in IRHT).

Luxembourg, Bibliothèque: 144 (microfilm in IRHT).

Munich, Staatsbibliothek: Codex Latinus Monacensis 16084 (microfilm in IMCL).

INDEX

Abbas Antiquus, canonist, 150n, 187
Abelard, theologian, 213, 217
Accursius, Romanist, 40, 42–3, 45–53
actio mandati, 150–5, 169–70, 177, 225n, 299, 303
Adrian I, pope, 78
agency, 100. *See also actio mandati*
Agobard of Lyons, 30–1, 39
Ai, Old Testament city, 9, 20, 23, 72, 90, 139, 235
Alain of Lille, theologian, 216, 217n, 241, 251–2, 256n
Alanus Anglicus, canonist
  on authority and obedience in war, 139–40, 143, 148, 177, 180, 189, 223
  on causes of a just war, 128, 131, 137–138, 180
  on the Church, role of in war, 180, 187, 189
  on conduct and consequences of war, 148, 156, 157n, 162–4, 171–2
  on crusades, 197–8
  formulation of the just war, 128
Albertus Magnus, theologian, 258, 264, 276–7
Albigensian Crusade, 202, 206–7, 209, 256
Alexander II, pope, 78n
Alexander III, pope, 116, 127, 189, 196n. *See also* Rolando Bandinelli
Alexander of Hales, theologian, 217, 220, 233–4, 243–4, 252–6, 268, 277, 282
Ambrose, bishop, 12–15, 65, 252
  spurious canon attributed to, 77–8
ambushes, 9, 23, 70, 90, 105, 156, 235, 271–2
Amorites, 21–2, 64, 72, 91, 100, 221–2, 225, 253
Andrew of Isernia, Romanist, 50

Anselm of Lucca, canonist, 37–8, 55–6
Aquinas, Thomas, theologian, 4, 258, 291, 297, 299–300, 303
  on authority for war, 224, 234, 258–261, 263, 268, 270–1, 281, 283, 300
  on causes of a just war, 268–9
  on the Church and clerics, participation in war, 269, 282–9, 291, 294–295, 300
  on conduct and consequences of war, 8n, 260, 264, 271–81, 283–4, 307
  formulation of the just war, 26, 87n, 220, 267–71, 290–1
  justification of war and killing, 236, 259–69, 272–3, 280–1, 283–4, 305
Aristotle, 3–4
  influence of, 214, 258–67, 272, 277, 279–81, 286, 289–91, 293
Augustine, 16–26, 111, 233, 252
  on authority and obedience in war, 18, 20–5, 72n, 140, 233, 306
  on causes of a just war, 18–19, 21, 96n, 115; influence of, 64, 115
  on conduct and consequences of war, 16–20, 22–4, 70; influence of, 160–1, 234–5, 272, 274
  formulation of the just war, 18–20, 63, 90, 139n; influence of, 63, 138, 139n, 269, 292
  on heretics, persecution of, 23–5, 74, 197
  influence of, general, 56, 64, 213–14, 258, 292
  justification of corporal punishment and war, 16–18, 57–8, 60, 74, 294, 302, 304–5; influence on Aquinas and his circle, 259–61, 264, 275, 291; influence on canonists, 57–8, 60, 76, 92

321

justification of war and killing—*contd.*
  by the Romanists, 45, 48–9, 51n
  by the theologians, 214–18, 227–8, 256, 293
Justinian, 40, 45, 51–3, 114

killing in war, attitudes toward, 294, 304
  of Aquinas and his circle, 260–1, 264–265, 273–5, 282
  of Augustine, 22–3
  of the Decretalists, 159–60, 175
  of the Decretists, 94, 107–8, 111
  in the early Middle Ages, 31–2, 37–8
  of Gratian, 59, 69, 73, 75, 82
  of the theologians, 215–18, 227, 250, 254, 256
  See also justification of war and killing
knights, *see* warriors

Lateran Council, Second, 70–1, 156
Lateran Council, Third, 8n, 183, 186, 189, 197n, 202n, 241, 244
Lateran Council, Fourth, 196–7, 204
latrocinium, 5, 165, 189
Laurentius Hispanus, canonist
  on authority for war, 137, 163
  on causes of a just war, 131n, 137–8
  on the Church and clerics, role of in war, 187n, 188n, 190
  on conduct and consequences of war, 163, 172, 184
  formulation of the just war, 128
  on infidels and heretics, 198n, 201–2n, 203
Leo IV, pope, 32, 75, 78–80, 116
Lex Aquilia, 41, 96–7
Lombards, 27–8, 78, 82
Lorenz, Konrad, 303
Lucius III, pope, 197n

Maccabees, 9
Machiavelli, 303
mandate, *see actio mandati*
Manicheanism, 17, 304–5
marque and reprisal, 168, 302
Master Martin, theologian, 231
Maximus of Turin, 27
mercenaries, 161, 174, 189, 241–3, 246, 277, 290, 303–4

militia Christi, 11, 18, 30, 35
Monaldus, canonist, 134n, 137, 144n, 167n, 170–1, 177, 204n, 225n
More, Thomas, 303, 305
Moses, 9, 17, 24, 228

Nebuchadnezzar, 89–90, 113, 222, 228
negligence, as cause for a just war, 138
New Testament, 10–12, 292
  in Aquinas, 259–60, 274, 282, 286, 300
  in Augustine, 17, 24
  in the Decretists, 113, 118
  in Gratian, 58, 61
  in the theologians, 215, 219
Nicholas I, pope, 33–4, 78–9, 217
non-combatants, treatment of, 2, 273, 306, 308
  according to Aquinas and his circle, 273–5, 277, 284
  according to Augustine, 19–20
  according to the Decretalists, 161, 179, 186
  according to Gratian, 70, 186
  according to the theologians, 256–7n
  also 7, 9. *See also* Peace of God

oaths, *see* feudal obligation
obedience in war, 299
  according to Aquinas and his circle, 274–5, 279–80
  according to Augustine, 22–3
  according to the Decretalists, 147–55, 170, 187, 191, 211
  according to the Decretists, 103–5, 123
  according to Gratian, 61, 69–70
  according to the Romanists, 46–8
  according to the theologians, 224–34, 239, 242, 248
obligation, 4–5, 140. *See also* feudal obligation
Odofredus, Romanist, 44, 46–9, 52–3
Old Testament, 8–10, 292–3
  in Aquinas and his circle, 271–2, 276–277, 282–4
  in Augustine, 17, 20–3
  in the Decretalists, 200
  in the Decretists, 89–91, 93–4, 100, 114, 118
  in the early Church, 11, 14